Writing the Love of Boys

# Writing
## the Love of Boys

*Origins of Bishōnen Culture in Modernist Japanese Literature*

Jeffrey Angles

UNIVERSITY OF MINNESOTA PRESS

MINNEAPOLIS

LONDON

The University of Minnesota Press gratefully acknowledges financial assistance provided for the publication of this book by the Japan Foundation.

JAPANFOUNDATION 🐦

Published by the University of Minnesota Press
111 Third Avenue South, Suite 290
Minneapolis, MN 55401-2520
http://www.upress.umn.edu


Library of Congress Cataloging-in-Publication Data

Angles, Jeffrey, 1971–
    Writing the love of boys : origins of Bishōnen culture in modernist Japanese literature / Jeffrey Angles.
        p. cm.
Includes bibliographical references and index.
    ISBN 978-0-8166-6969-1 (hc : alk. paper)
    ISBN 978-0-8166-6970-7 (pb : alk. paper)
1. Japanese literature—20th century—History and criticism. 2. Homosexuality in literature. 3. Modernism (Literature)—Japan.
I. Title
PL721.H59A85 2011
895.6'093526642–dc22

                                                            2010032182


Printed in the United States of America on acid-free paper

The University of Minnesota is an equal-opportunity educator and employer.

17  16  15  14  13  12  11        10  9  8  7  6  5  4  3  2  1

# Contents

# Note about Japanese Names

The Japanese names that appear in this book are in the traditional Japanese order, with the surname before the given name; however, when writing about Japanese writers and artists with pen names or distinctive given names, I follow the common Japanese convention of referring to them simply by their given name or pen name. For this reason, Murayama Kaita's name may appear simply as "Kaita" rather than Murayama, Edogawa Ranpo as "Ranpo" rather than Edogawa, and so on. Where the given name is not particularly unusual, as in the cases of Tanizaki Jun'ichirō or Hamao Shirō, I followed the Japanese custom and used only the surname. Sometimes the name Edogawa Ranpo appears in other English-language texts as "Rampo," with an *m*, but I kept these instances with an *n* to better approximate the way the word is written in Japanese.

Proper nouns and words that typically appear in English dictionaries are presented without italics and macrons; for example, the capital of Japan is represented "Tokyo" instead of Tōkyō. Other terms from Japanese are italicized and appear with macrons to mark the long vowels.

I have given English renditions of the titles of Japanese books and articles. When the English renditions of the titles appear in title case (with all major nouns capitalized), that means there is a published English translation of the work, and I reproduced the title as it appears in the published translation. Readers can consult the bibliography for citations of those English translations. When the English renditions of the titles appear in sentence case (with a capital letter only at the beginning), that means there is no translation available as of the time I wrote this book, and what I give is simply my own English gloss of the Japanese title.

# Introduction

When Western readers look at the manga (graphic novels) that have been so popular in Japan over the course of the last few decades, they are often struck by how often male–male affection and eroticism appears in their pages. In fact, male–male love has been one of the most important thematic elements in manga, especially manga for adolescent girls (*shōjo manga*), since the 1970s. One thinks, for instance, of the classics *Tōma no shinzō* (The heart of Thomas, 1974) by Hagio Moto and *Kaze to ki no uta* (The song of the wind and the trees, serialized 1976–84) by Takemiya Keiko, both of which present groundbreaking depictions of male–male friendship, jealousy, desire, and eroticism within the all-male world of European boarding schools.[1] By using flowery images, language ripe with florid overstatement, poetic expressions of desire, and bursts of passion throughout their work, these two manga artists presented same-sex desire and eroticism in a language that appealed immediately to their young, female readership. At the same time, they also explored society's tendency to shun same-sex eroticism through the reactions of the many schoolboys to the sexually active characters at the heart of their stories. The wild success of these manga were instrumental in forming the mold for many *shōjo manga* published in years to come.

Still, where do these modes of depicting love and erotic desire between men come from? Were the passionate, romanticized expressions of schoolboy desire found in Hagio's and Takemiya's work new in the 1970s? In some ways, they seem a product of their era. Certainly, the 1970s, an era in which Georges Bataille, Jean-Paul Sartre, and the Marquis de Sade were considered essential reading for any fashionable student in Japan, were revolutionary in their willingness to explore the cultural and existential ramifications of sexuality, especially in its nonheteronormative forms.[2] At the same time, however, the fascination with the cultural ramifications of sexuality is far older than just the 1970s. The particular combination of florid expressions of passionate, personal desire that one finds so often in manga about male–male desire has its roots in the early twentieth century, when a number of popular authors began to explore new modes of representing same-sex desire in literature. Needless to say, the Japanese, like all people, have always been interested in sexuality, and there is a long historical and literary record describing instances of nonheteronormative forms of eroticism. It is, however, one of the principal arguments of this book that it was during the early twentieth century that a core group of several key authors struggled to find a new language to write about the subject, and in the process developed modes of depiction that would prove influential for many years to come. Among the tropes that came to be associated with representations of male–male desire in the early twentieth century were schoolboy innocence, acute aestheticism, and almost "decadently" strong expressions of personal passion—tropes repeated in different variations within contemporary manga.

In exploring the Japanese preoccupation with homoeroticism in literature and popular culture, this study turns to the formative years of the Taishō period (1912–26) and the first decade of the Shōwa period (1926–89). These years witnessed tumultuous changes and tremendous cultural developments on virtually every front. The country experienced the thriving years of economic development and political involvement known as the "Taishō Democracy." This vibrant period of economic growth came to a halt, however, with the economic troubles surrounding the suspension of activities of the Bank of Taiwan in 1927, the rush on banks throughout Japan, and the series of economic "corrections" that cost many people their livelihoods. These economic problems were only exacerbated by the depression that spread across the world in 1929—a depression that, in turn, set the stage for the socioeconomic pressure and political turbulence that led up to the Manchurian Incident in 1931, the establishment of the puppet state of Manchukuo in 1932, and the full-fledged Japanese invasion of China in 1937. Meanwhile, changes in the ideological climate of the Japanese empire were equally dramatic. The interwar years saw the spread of psychoanalysis, modern social engineering, feminism, socialism, cosmopolitanism, nationalism, and many other ideologies and social movements. Directly or indirectly, these phenomena all presented the population with new ideas regarding the healthiest or most productive ways for men and women to behave, and they helped set the climate for the development of new and sometimes transgressive approaches to gender identity, including the *mobo* ("modern boy"), the *moga* ("modern girl"), or the androgyny that was such an object of fascination in this period. In tandem with these changes, these decades saw a tremendous amount of discussion about sex and gender roles in the rapidly expanding press. As newspaper and magazine circulations expanded and publishers found new, innovative ways to market material to the public, the publishing industry extended its reach to unprecedented lengths, thus making these new ideas increasingly accessible to citizens throughout the Japanese empire.

In the influential first volume of his famous history of sexuality, Michel Foucault dismisses the common perception that from the nineteenth century onward, Western European society had silenced discussion of sexual desire through censorship, taboo, and other mechanisms of repression. Instead, he points to a veritable explosion of writing about sex in the fields of law, sociology, medical sciences, psychology, physiology, evolutionary science, and so on. Ironically, at the same time that popular rules of sexual decorum were growing tighter among the lower and middle classes of Western Europe, institutions of law and science were inciting people to speak in greater detail about sex. Within the forums associated with these institutions, a vast body of literature about sex developed, although this literature was profoundly shaped by the interests of the powers sponsoring the discussion.[3]

Although Foucault's study deals with Western Europe, the situation was similar in Japan during the late nineteenth and early twentieth centuries. People often think about middle-class Japanese society as experiencing a series of increasingly tight strictures on the ways that people talked about sex in their personal lives or wrote about it in print; however, there was, in fact, a flood of writing that dealt with sexuality in all of its forms, including those forms of sexuality that turn-of-the-century Japan had relegated to the margins of morality. Discussion of sex was not so much suppressed as channeled into certain forums, which then discussed sex in their own terms. As in Europe and America, Japanese medical doctors, psychologists, educators, eugenicists, and sexologists wrote a great deal about sexual behavior and desire. Many of the fields that talked about sex were dominated by people with university degrees, medical credentials, or high social standing, and these qualifications allowed them to speak with authority about what they saw as the "truth" of sex. The general public reacted to this new discourse in a variety of ways, including writing articles for the columns of sexological magazines or producing erotica that borrowed the new modes of speaking for the purpose of titillation. Likewise, popular literature represented one important arena in which people could write about and react to the ideas regarding sex and gender circulating around them. In fact, this book argues that it is in the field of popular literature that one finds some of the most vital engagements with contemporary ideologies of sex and gender. In the midst of the complicated, multilateral exchanges and conflicting representations of erotic desire circulating in Japanese society, certain associations were repeated so often that they helped to shape ways that subsequent generations would think about eroticism and gender.

Male–male and female–female desire were two forms of desire discussed extensively in late nineteenth- and early twentieth-century Japan. The rhetoric used to discuss these forms of sexuality reveals that erotic desire between members of the same sex was treated as a key issue in the production of new ideas about gender and modern civilization. Social historian Gregory Pflugfelder's survey of the language employed to describe male–male desire from the Edo period (1600–1868) through World War II points to a large number of documents from the popular discourse of the Meiji period (1868–1912) that associate male–male sexuality with atavistic or uncivilized behavior.[4] He shows that as Japan fashioned itself into a modern, centralized nation-state, discussion of so-called "civilized" norms came to imbue discourse on sexuality "with an astonishing thoroughness and rapidity, disseminating not only through legal pronouncements but also through popular writings ranging from journalism to fiction and poetry." As the rhetoric of civilization came to bear on the discourse of sexuality, "male–male sexuality, which had enjoyed a prominent and respectable place in Edo-period popular texts, came during Meiji times to be routinely represented as 'barbarous,' 'immoral,' or simply 'unspeakable.'"[5] The thought of people engaging in erotic activity with members of their same sex provoked a growing anxiety, and newspapers, educators, sexologists, and other authority figures spilled much ink about the perils of same-sex eroticism. As Jim Reichert has pointed out in his survey of representations of male–male desire in Meiji literature, over the course of the fin-de-siècle period, Japanese writers tended to employ less affirming ways to handle same-sex desire, such as the trope of illness or even conspicuous silences regarding a particular character's amorous feelings. In fact, Reichert argues that one side effect of the creation of "modern literature" was the abandonment of open validations of male–male eroticism, which Japan, from the mid-Meiji period onward, increasingly treated as uncivilized.[6]

One finds confirmation of this in the essays of Edogawa Ranpo (1894–1965), one of the subjects of this study, who wrote in an essay from 1953 that the two major preoccupations of his life had been writing detective fiction and locating books having to do with amorous and erotic desire between men. During the 1920s and 1930s, his interest in male–male desire and its literary manifestations, he comments, was driven to new heights by his belief that almost no one, except for a few select friends, was interested in the subject.[7] For Ranpo's circle of associates, frank and positive discussion of male–male erotic desire had been relegated to the margins of acceptability. Ranpo's feelings of isolation notwithstanding, there were others in Japan who *did* think and write about the subject. As mentioned above, a good deal of this writing took place in fields such as psychology and medicine, which had become preoccupied with the meaning and implications of attraction between members of the same sex. Ranpo knew this to be the case, and in early 1933 he began attending the monthly meetings of the Seishin Bunseki Kenkyūkai (Group for Psychoanalytic Research) expressly because he knew psychology represented one arena in which he could talk about erotic desire between men.

To chart the ways the Japanese talked about male–male desire over the course of the last three centuries, Pflugfelder's study uses the central metaphor of "cartographies." He explains that people use key ideas or cognitive maps to negotiate and navigate the social realities confronting them in real life. Like political maps of the world, whose lines are redrawn whenever one country absorbs another or breaks apart, these conceptual maps change over time, and new boundaries are drawn to include different ideas within certain conceptual territories. For instance, it is instructive to consider briefly the differences between the conceptual baggage of *nanshoku* and "same-sex love," two key terms used at different points in Japanese history to chart manifestations of male–male desire.[8] During the Edo period, some of the key concepts used to describe male–male sexuality were *nanshoku* (also read *danshoku*, literally "male eros") and *shudō* or *wakashudō* (the way of the youth). When people wrote about eroticism between men during the Edo period, they usually described the partners as being of differing ages and playing different, well-defined roles within the relationship. Generally, the younger partner, the *wakashu*, had not yet undergone the *genbuku* ceremony that marked the coming of age, and he continued to wear youthful clothes and forelocks *(maegami)*. In fact, texts about male–male sexuality in the Edo period sometimes describe the fetishistic appeal of the *wakashu*'s forelocks, which serve as an outward signifier of youth and sexual availability. The *wakashu* was not necessarily expected to have sex with people of only one gender or the other. Many records from the Edo period describe relationships between *wakashu* and women; however, whenever the *wakashu* engaged in sex with a man, it was assumed he would let the older man take the lead sexually. The other partner in the world of *nanshoku* was the older *nenja*, who wore adult clothes, had his pate shaved in the fashion typical of adult men, and shouldered the mantle of adult responsibility in society. When engaging in anal sex with a *wakashu*, the *nenja* was typically described as playing the role of inserter. An invisible boundary of adulthood was seen as separating the *wakashu* from the *nenja*. Each played relatively inflexible roles, but humorous texts sometimes describe older men transgressing these given roles by, for instance, covering their shaved pate with a kerchief and pretending to be *wakashu*. Although certain people might declare their preference for *wakashu* by calling themselves *onna-girai* ("women haters"), a preference for the erotic pleasures of men was considered a matter of personal taste.[9] As the publishing industry expanded during the Edo period and presented the cosmopolitan public with an increasing number of texts on the pleasures of sexuality and the ways of the pleasure quarters, male–male eroticism also came to be frequently described within the rhetorical construct of *shudō* or *wakashudō*. Like the "way of tea" *(sadō)*, the "way of archery" *(kyūdō)*, and so forth, *shudō* was treated as a "way" *(dō)* that could bring great rewards if its intricacies were mastered by a connoisseur.

In the nineteenth century, the forms of male–male desire described as *nanshoku* and *shudō* came to be subsumed under the new notion of "same-sex love." As Japan turned to Germany to import the latest knowledge regarding medicine, forensics, and psychology, Japanese scholars encountered the notion of homosexuality, which had recently spread throughout Europe. As early as the 1880s, translators and authors of medical texts were fashioning various Japanese words to convey the concept of homosexuality. By the 1920s, the word *dōseiai* had become an especially common translation, although others continued to circulate for some time. Sociologist Furukawa Makoto surmises that the reason the word *dōseiai* eventually gained the widest currency was that during the 1910s and 1920s, the Japanese public and press were searching for a word to describe same-sex relationships between schoolgirls, which had recently become a subject of much concern. Many of the other words coined as translations of "homosexuality" incorporated overt references to intercourse or sexual desire. Furukawa argues that many people, however, tended to assume that male–male desire was largely physical and female–female desire was predominantly spiritual, so eventually the word *dōseiai*, which ends with the character *ai*, meaning affection or love of a spiritual nature, seemed the most appropriate to describe relationships between women.[10] Unlike other older discursive concepts, such as *nanshoku* or *shudō*, which referred specifically to relationships between men, the discourse of "same-sex love" incorporated both male–male and female–female attraction within a single conceptual territory. In other words, "same-sex love" referred both to male–male eroticism and to female–female eroticism, whereas *nanshoku* and *shudō* only described the age-graded eroticism between older men and younger boys. The reorganization of ideas surrounding eroticism was fundamentally grounded in the belief that sexuality should take place between a man and a woman, and therefore both male–male and female–female sexuality violated this fundamental rule in a similar way. In short, the concept of "same-sex love" led Japanese for the first time to see male–male sexuality and female–female sexuality as two manifestations of a single phenomenon.

Although the rubric of "same-sex love" emphasized the connections between these two forms of eroticism, it also downplayed the importance of other elements that had been important in structuring earlier formulations of desire. Since the sole issue in defining "same-sex love" was the sex of the partner, this meant that the age, roles, and sexual practices of the partners were no longer at issue as they had been in the *nanshoku* and *shudō* of the Edo period. Whereas *nanshoku* and *shudō* involved a difference in the age of the partners and assigned specific roles to each person both in and out of bed, relationships characterized as representing "same-sex love" did not necessarily involve such asymmetries.

Perhaps the most important aspect of the new concept of "same-sex love," however, was that medical practitioners, sexologists, and psychologists read a predilection for "same-sex love" into the interiority of its practitioners in ways one did not find during the Edo period with *shudō* and *nanshoku*. Eager to understand the reasons why certain people preferred the same sex, a number of important medical psychologists and sexologists divided instances of same-sex eroticism into those that were "acquired" *(kōtensei)* or "congenital" *(sentensei)*.[11] "Acquired" instances of same-sex desire were seen as developing later in life, perhaps due to environmental factors. "Congenital" cases, however, were generally seen as the product of mental or physical degeneracy that was relatively difficult, if not impossible, to cure. Regardless of this distinction, both "congenital" and "acquired" manifestations of "same-sex love" were seen as profoundly deleterious to one's health and threatening to the gender identity of its practitioners.

As medical psychologists warned of the dangers of eroticism between members of the same sex, numerous people throughout Japanese society, including many who were outside of the medical establishment, began to pick up on their assumptions, spreading them in educational journals, sexological writings, and numerous other forums. Educators and sexologists argued that like masturbation, profligate behavior with prostitutes, or such other "unproductive" sexual practices, sexual relationships between boys were unhealthy and adversely affected the bodies and minds of those involved.[12] As a result, warnings about the dangerous spiritual and intellectual effects of same-sex eroticism abound in early twentieth-century writings on sex and health; for instance, *Seiten* (The laws of sex, 1926) by Habuto Eiji, one of Japan's most prominent sexologists and a frequent commentator on the alleged evils of same-sex erotic practice, argued that it brings about "exhausted vitality, the rise of what is called 'neurasthenia' as well as other disorders, in due time the subsiding of one's developing strength and intellectual facilities, and subsequent low spirits."[13]

Some writers were even more alarmist, aligning same-sex desire with criminality. Because medical, psychological, and sexological discourse tended to align cross-sex desire with the family and the preservation of organized society, they associated same-sex desire with deviancy, poor health, and familial ruin. For instance, in *Hentai seiyoku ron* (On perverse sexuality), one of the most influential works of Japanese sexology, first published in 1915 and frequently reprinted thereafter, the writers Habuto Eiji and Sawada Junjirō give a number of examples of crimes arising from same-sex desire, including a Japanese student beaten to death in a violent come-on, a couple breaking into a building to conduct consensual sodomy, and a January 1892 murder in Tennessee in which one woman killed another.[14] Though Habuto and Sawada fail to question whether or not such crimes are, in per capita terms, more frequent among same-sex couples than cross-sex couples, the overriding message is that the passion of same-sex relationships, in conjunction with the weakness of the spirit and intellectual faculties it allegedly produced, gave rise to antisocial behavior that damages the fabric of society. *Nanshoku, shudō,* and "same-sex love" were not the only conceptual tools used to understand male–male desire in Japan from the early modern period onward, but the differences among these constructs illustrate the large gaps that could exist among the various conceptual and rhetorical structures used to describe love between men over the course of Japanese history. Indeed, even within a single time period, not all segments of Japanese society spoke about male–male desire in the same way. Representations of male–male desire generated for mass consumption tended to be quite different from those promulgated in official legal discourse. Both of these, in turn, differed significantly from images in medical and psychological discourse, which concerned itself with issues of health and pathology. Because these discursive realms remained somewhat independent of one another, the ways people throughout Japanese society talked about male–male desire remained rather uncoordinated.

To complicate matters, historical factors might cause one of these discursive realms, but not the others, to pick up the subject as a particularly salient issue. For instance, male–male desire became an important issue in the last few decades of the nineteenth century within the field of jurisprudence because of a series of changes in the legal code. In 1873 the centralized Japanese government promulgated the Kaitei Ritsurei, a law that prohibited anal intercourse *(keikan)* in its 266th article.[15] (Officially, violation of this statute could earn as many as ninety days of penal servitude, but evidence suggests only a handful of people were punished this severely under the statute.) The immediate reason for the promulgation of this statute was the concern of educators in Kyūshū who were unclear about how homoerotic acts should be treated under the rapidly changing laws of the early Meiji period.[16] Edo-period law in Kumamoto had a statute outlawing sexual violence perpetrated by men on other men, but early Meiji law, including the 1871 Shinritsu Kōryō, remained silent on the subject. Interestingly, the 1873 Kaitei Ritsurei remained on the books only until 1882, when a new penal code modeled after Napoleonic law, which had no statutes against same-sex eroticism, went into effect. Accompanying each of these changes was a round of discussions about the nature of same-sex desire and the relationship between personal behavior and the nation. After the sodomy statute disappeared from the books in 1882, it seems to have become less of a salient issue in legal circles. In subsequent decades, however, psychological medicine, sexology, and education all became increasingly concerned with "same-sex love" and discussed it at great length.

The uneven proliferation of these different strains of discourse about male–male desire means that at any given moment during the late nineteenth and twentieth centuries, there existed multiple ways of talking about it. Although certain conceptual models dominated at various times and in different forums, people living in the same age might well entertain different views about male–male desire. For this reason, authors living and working in the early twentieth century had a number of conceptual models they might draw on in exploring the subject of male–male desire. It is not surprising, therefore, that one finds reflections of many of these modes in the writing they produced.

## The Textually Specific Approach to
## Male–Male Desire in Literature

In her provocative introduction to *Epistemology of the Closet,* Eve Sedgwick points out the dangers inherent in social constructionist histories of sexuality that identify a specific time period or, even more specifically, a single date as a turning point in the history of understandings of same-sex desire. Sedgwick argues one effect of such studies is that they present an implied contrast between a falsely homogenizing understanding of a construct of same-sex desire as "we know it today" and an opaque past that loses its grainy historicity and internal contradictions. Such projects tend to renaturalize and reify notions of same-sex desire, while eliding the conceptual messiness and contradictions found within any given period, either past or present.[17] The greatest danger of such studies is that readers will begin to assume ideas used to understand same-sex desire represent "a coherent definitional field rather than a space of overlapping, contradictory, and conflictual definitional forces."[18] She argues that when various constructs relating to sexuality come into contact, they do not simply replace one another. Instead, earlier constructs rear up again and infiltrate later ones, producing instability and even contradiction with the latter. Only rarely, she hints, are categorical notions of same-sex desire unified or coherent. In analyzing several works of literature produced in late nineteenth-century Europe and America, Sedgwick shows the images of same-sex desire in them are not structured by one model superseding another and then dying away. Instead, the images are structured by "the relations enabled by the unrationalized coexistence of different models during the times they do coexist."[19]

Rather than mapping the larger, overarching, shifting contours of concepts related to same-sex desire, Sedgwick concentrates her attention on a handful of key texts. In doing so, she dissociates them from overarching historical narratives about the history of sexuality and shows that texts represent a performative space in which individual authors create and recreate ideas about desire between men. Her analyses reveal that each author toys with a complicated and interrelated set of concepts. (She discusses most of these concepts in terms of binary oppositions, for instance, knowledge/ignorance, natural/unnatural, urbane/provincial, innocence/initiation, man/boy, Greek/Christian, and so on.) By focusing on the picture presented by each text, she shows the terms used to represent male–male desire in literature are sufficiently complex that they are irreducible to one or another of the large, macroscopic schema described by historians. The inescapable conclusion is that images of male–male desire constructed by individual authors have as much—if not more—to do with other literary and thematic concerns shaping the texts as with the large, overarching concepts of male–male desire circulating in society. In short, Sedgwick problematizes the historical, macroscopic approach to sexuality by insisting on the individual specificity of texts and challenging readers not to gloss over the minute granulations of a text that produce its meaning.

When sketching the contours of the conceptual models used to represent male–male desire in modern Japan, Pflugfelder hints that discursive models were never completely uniform and homogeneous, even within a single realm. For instance, he points out that within medicine, there was disagreement among Japanese psychologists and sexologists about whether it was possible to use medical means, such as hypnosis or other forms of therapy, to "straighten out" people with a "congenital" preference for members of the same sex. The different responses to this issue reveal varying attitudes about how deeply lodged sexual preference was in the psychology of the patient and how malleable sexual orientation really is. Pflugfelder also demonstrates that the different modes of representing male–male desire were not entirely independent. Certain writers may move back and forth between discursive realms, drawing on various models found in each to develop their own strategies for depicting desire between men. These discrepancies sometimes manifest themselves at various points in a writer's career, or even within the same literary work. As Jim Reichert has noted, it is only by attending to the thematic, narratological, and semantic complexity of a body of literature that one truly begins to understand the depictions of desire presented within.[20]

Edogawa Ranpo's oeuvre provides a case in point. Ranpo was profoundly interested in finding out about male–male desire, and so he purchased a wide variety of texts touching on the subject—a selection ranging from the Greek classics to the works of Freud. As chapter 4 of this book shows, at different points Ranpo's work draws on a variety of disparate ideas presented in these different texts.

To complicate matters further, one sometimes finds discordant images of male–male desire even within a single text. *Kotō no oni* (The demon of the lonely isle), the only long novel Ranpo wrote that deals extensively with male–male love, is not much longer than two hundred pages, but it presents profoundly dissonant images of male male love. At times, the novel represents male–male love as deviant, whereas at others, it depicts it as closely akin to homosocial brotherhood. It is here that Sedgwick's argument has applicability to Japanese studies: when one tries to locate commonalities in representations of same-sex desire across various works, or when one tries to pigeonhole a particular author as presenting a specific formulation of desire, there is the danger of losing sight of the subtle disagreements and grainy inconsistencies present within the works in question. This is not to dismiss the grand contributions of macroscopic approaches to the history of erotic desire; both the macroscopic approach to the history of male–male desire and the microscopic approach to individual texts are two important means of exploring male–male desire in Japanese literature and cultural history. On the one hand, it is certainly important to think about themes repeated in various texts about male–male desire. Studies that lay out coherent narratives and trace the development of ideas across texts do the important work of uncovering the historicity of those ideas. On the other hand, it is equally important to examine key foundational texts that presented the public with influential images of male–male love and eroticism. It is this kind of close reading in which one finds the inconsistencies, dissonance, and conceptual mixing and matching which give rise to new modes of depicting and understanding desire.

In the works examined in this book, the hybrid representations of male–male desire are not reducible to the sum of their component parts. Quite the contrary. Each of the major authors examined in this study, Murayama Kaita (1896–1919), Edogawa Ranpo, and Inagaki Taruho (1900–1977), develop modes of describing male–male desire different from those of the authors and movements inspiring them. For instance, this book shows that all three were interested in Greek or pre-modern Japanese culture because both cultures placed a premium on the aesthetic appeal of *bishōnen* (beautiful adolescent men) and produced numerous texts about erotic or amorous desire involving attractive young men. Still, the expressions of male–male desire in the texts of these three authors are not mere passive reflections of kinds of expressions of desire one might find in classical texts. This study shows each author possessed distinct thematic interests and individual literary styles that also shaped his writing. While one might trace hints of the authors' interests in Greek or pre-Meiji Japanese texts in the writing of each author, these interests are just two of several elements fused into a new whole.

The three major figures examined in this study are the poet, painter, and short story author Murayama Kaita, the detective novelist Edogawa Ranpo, and the avant-garde prose writer Inagaki Taruho. These three authors produced works that dealt extensively with sexual desire, some of which became bestsellers in the Taishō and early Shōwa periods. Interestingly, contemporary publishing companies tended to emphasize the element of "unusual," even "perverse," erotic desire in the work of Kaita and Ranpo in particular, helping them earn a reputation as having treated the theme with unusual candor. For instance, the publisher Ars, which released *Kaita no utaeru* (Songs of Kaita, 1920), the first volume of Kaita's work to appear in print, ran a series of advertisements for the book in influential newspapers and literary magazines. In them, one finds the following description of Kaita's work:

> This book is a posthumous collection of the poetry, reflections, and other writing of Murayama Kaita, a member of the Nihon Bijutsuin [Japan Art Institute] who, while endowed with abundant natural talent, met a tragic death at the young age of twenty-two. He charged into the palace of art with extreme valor. He loved like a flame. He was constantly tortured by unusual sexual desires. He drank often, drew well, and composed poetry frequently. Leaving behind numerous superb works for the world to see, he rushed to his end, the curtain hurriedly falling on this short life of genius. Whoever reads this book will sense his strength and directness; readers will be enchanted by the magical, mysterious beauty of his passionate thought and will be unable to hold back their cries of wonder.[21]

This earliest of evaluations already identifies "unusual sexual desire" *(ijō na seiyoku)* as one of the salient characteristics of Kaita's life and work. Indeed, Kaita wrote so much and so often about his fellow schoolmate Inō Kiyoshi that his love is perhaps the best-documented incident of schoolboy passion in all Taishō-period literature. A review from August of 1920 by one of Kaita's earliest fans, the novelist and utopian writer Arishima Takeo (1878–1923), also notes the important role of sexual desire in Kaita's writing, calling Kaita a "centaur" whose "limbs were of dissipated Dionysian lust."[22] Partly as a result of such reviews, interest in Kaita and his writing grew to the point that the publisher Ars produced a second volume of his writing in 1921 and a book of photographic reproductions of his paintings in 1922. These three volumes quickly went through multiple printings and earned a lasting following for the deceased painter-poet. Personal accounts from the early Shōwa period suggest the influence that Kaita's work exerted over the popular imagination. Kusano Shinpei (1901–88), one of the best-known poets of the postwar period, wrote in his biography of Kaita that the shock of encountering Kaita's dramatic poetry was one of the major factors encouraging him to pursue a career as a writer.[23] Kaita's influence was not confined to the world of letters. A semiautobiographical story written in 1939 by Nakano Shigeharu (1902–79) mentions that Kaita's work inspired one of the main characters to try becoming a painter.[24] Although various people remained interested in Kaita for different reasons, Kaita's candor about his amorous feelings for other boys appears to have been one reason he remained alive within the popular imagination. In 1926 the writer Itō Ken (1895–1945) mentions Kaita's work in a list of Taishō-period works about "perverse psychology" *(hentai shinri)*, and in 1934 Ranpo wrote an important article about expressions of male–male desire in Kaita's work, which he admired greatly.[25]

Although Kaita's work reached a large audience, Ranpo's work circulated even more widely. After his literary debut in 1923, Ranpo quickly became one of the most popular and widely read detective writers of early twentieth-century Japan, and during the 1920s and 1930s his novels were serialized in virtually every important periodical of popular literature. In the late 1920s the Japanese publishing industry began publishing numerous multivolume sets of inexpensive books on various themes, and because of the vast popularity of Ranpo's work, any multivolume collection of detective fiction and popular literature almost inevitably included his stories. In 1931 and 1932 the publisher Heibonsha published the first edition of Ranpo's complete works of fiction in thirteen volumes. Within just three years, they released a second twelve-volume set of his work, and soon Shinchōsha, another of Japan's largest publishers, quickly followed suit with a ten-volume collection. One reason Ranpo's work appealed to such a broad audience was his willingness to treat various nonheteronormative aspects of sexual desire, including male–male eroticism, which medical practitioners and sexologists had started describing as "perverse" *(hentai)*. Publishers often emphasized the "astonishing" and even "perverse" content of Ranpo's writing to market his work. For example, advertisements for *Kotō no oni* often describe the content of the novel as "shocking" in order to entice readers. When the publisher Kaizōsha released *Kotō no oni* in book form, they ran a series of advertisements in the Tokyo edition of the daily newspaper *Asahi shinbun* that declared the work to be "the shocking masterpiece of Edogawa Ranpo, Japan's answer to Sir Arthur Conan Doyle." Specifically, it points to "the extreme perversion [*kyokudo no hentai*] and the brilliant spectacle of sick love [*byōteki na aijō*]" in the plot.[26] Other advertisements describe the presence of male–male love in less sensational terms, but still draw attention to it as a means of capturing the attention of curious readers. In the advertising blurb for *Kotō no oni,* written for the first edition of Ranpo's complete works published in 1931 and 1932, Ranpo's friend and fellow detective writer Yokomizo Seishi (1902–81) wrote, "the love for the same sex, which had been a long-standing desire of the author [*sakka no hisashiki ganbō de atta dōseiai*], had finally been incorporated into this novel."[27] An insert to another multivolume collection of Ranpo's works published in 1938 and 1939 emphasizes in boldface type that *Kotō no oni* is "a work in which the author dealt with the topic of same-sex love."[28]

The reputation Ranpo earned for his treatment of male–male desire in *Kotō no oni* grew in subsequent years as he published numerous essays about the subject in various magazines. Many originally appeared in smaller magazines, such as the newly formed literary journal *Buntai* (Literary style) or *Seishin bunseki* (Psychoanalysis), the journal of the Tokyo-based Seishin Bunseki Kenkyūkai, but a number appeared in important journals, such as the national monthly *Bungei shunjū* (Literary arts spring and autumn), the popular fiction monthly *Taishū bungei* (Popular arts and letters), and the youth-oriented monthly *Shin seinen* (New youth). Partly because of tightening censorship after the Japanese invasion of China in 1937, Ranpo did not reprint these essays during the late 1930s or early 1940s. They would have to wait until 1947, two years after the end of World War II, when Ranpo republished them in the widely reprinted collection *Gen'ei no jōshu* (Lord of the castle of illusion).

Contemporary literary historians remember Inagaki Taruho as one of the grand innovators of early Shōwa-period modernism. In fact, one of his admirers and friends, the novelist Mishima Yukio (1925–70) once wrote that in the literature of the Shōwa period, Taruho was a rare genius who held a place equivalent to the astronauts in history; one could divide literary history "into the world before Taruho and the world after Taruho."[29] Nonetheless, the overwhelming majority of Taruho's work from the 1920s and 1930s languished in relative obscurity until much later in the postwar period when Taruho won a literary prize and earned contracts to reprint his earlier work. One factor that caused him to earn attention only relatively late in his career was his tendency to publish extremely short fiction or essays—genres that, even when successful, are still less likely to produce the same impact on the literary imagination as the publication of a long novel, a substantial collection of novellas, or a hefty collection of essays.

This does not mean his work did not reach a broad public. His early work often appeared in widely circulated national journals such as *Shinchō* (New tide) or *Bungaku* (Literature), and in popular women's journals like *Josei* (Women) and *Fujin kurabu* (Housewives' club). Although some of these were republished in book-length collections during the prewar period, he seemed only minimally concerned with public opinion and the popular reception of his works. As a result, he experienced the emotional freedom to write about subjects that interested him, including some of his favorite subjects: love between boys and the aesthetic appeal of young men. Maybe because Taruho did not become a popular commodity in the literary market until the postwar period, one does not find publishers and reviewers describing his work in the same sort of sensationalizing rhetoric that helped sell Kaita's and Ranpo's literature. One reason for this might have been that much of his writing about boyish love appeared in magazines for women, which were less likely to frame their stories and literature with the kinds of sensationalizing rhetoric one finds so often in magazines for adolescent boys. Moreover, as this study will show, Taruho specifically chose a nonsensationalizing, flowery mode of writing about male–male desire that might appeal to female readers. In fact, one might argue he was a pioneer of the florid, romanticized depictions of male–male desire that resurface in the *shōjo manga* of the late twentieth century.

## SCHOOLBOY BISHŌNEN LOVE

One of the reasons for focusing on the writing of Kaita, Ranpo, and Taruho as a group is that they were some of the most outspoken and prolific authors to deal with male–male desire in Japan during the period between the two world wars. A second reason is that these three writers begin to forge representations of amorous and erotic desire between schoolboys that differ significantly from the representations of schoolboy desire in turn-of-the-century Japanese culture.

In order to understand the ways in which Kaita's, Ranpo's, and Taruho's representations of schoolboy love were different from what came before, it is worth briefly considering the novel *Wita sekusuarisu (Vita Sexualis)*, written by Mori Ōgai (1862–1922), one of the most important writers of the preceding decades. When Ōgai published his famous, semiparodic imitation of a naturalist novel at the turn of the twentieth century, he included a portrait of a school dormitory divided between boys who practiced two different types of masculinity: that of the "hard faction" (*kōha*) and that of the "softie faction" (*nanpa*).[30] These two forms of masculinity involved significantly different behavior, speech, manner, clothing, and sexual choices.[31] The novel describes the boys of the "hard faction" as gruff, coarsely dressed, dismissive of women, and professing a marked sexual preference for men, whereas the "softies" dress in a dandyesque fashion and prefer the opposite sex. (The two factions were not necessarily exclusive; in fact, the novel includes a character who makes a rapid transition from the company of the "hard faction" to the "softies.") Ōgai's novel describes adolescents of the "hard faction" using their status as upperclassmen to take advantage of attractive younger bishōnen and force them into a sexual relationship. Because a strictly hierarchical code of conduct governed virtually every aspect of dormitory life, young men confronted by upperclassmen often had difficulty protesting. Sometimes the sexual advances of "hard-faction" boys took on more aggressive forms. As historian Donald Roden notes, by the turn of the twentieth century, certain dormitories were the setting for "storms" (*sutōmu*), a "nightly ordeal of violence and sometimes homosexual predation" in which upperclassmen might well force themselves onto younger boys whose social position as inferiors meant a compromised ability to resist.[32]

During the late Meiji and Taishō periods, newspapers used increased media coverage of student affairs and violence among schoolboys to warn the public about the dangers of the brand of masculinity espoused by the "hard factions" within Japanese schools. Similar concerns were visible in reforms enacted by school administrators, such as the Christian, American-educated Nitobe Inazō (1862–1933), who worked to root out the aggressive and predatory culture of the "hard faction" in Tokyo First Higher School (Daiichi Kōtō Gakkō), the prestigious school that served as the gateway to

Tokyo Imperial University (Tōkyō Teikoku Daigaku). Still, the "hard-faction" masculinity that educators fought was not yet gone from schoolboy culture by the time Ranpo, Kaita, and Taruho entered their schools in 1907, 1909, and 1914, respectively. An essay by Ranpo indicates that the "hard-faction" aversion to weakness and femininity was alive and well in his school in Nagoya, and that anything smacking of feminine softness was treated with scorn.[33] In the midst of this culture of gruff masculinity, Ranpo was often teased because he was a bishōnen with unusually soft features. At the same time, however, he received a number of love letters from classmates who professed their affection for him and urged him to become their boyfriend. He eventually formed a bond of passionate friendship with another bishōnen. This relationship was relatively egalitarian and manifested none of the predatory sexuality described in other accounts of Meiji dormitories. Likewise, Kaita fell in love with another younger schoolmate, and much of his early poetry is dedicated to describing the boy's beauty. Taruho too appears to have been susceptible to the charms of young men, and many of his earliest stories (a number of which he set in Kwansei Gakuin, the same higher school in Kobe he attended) focus specifically on the amorous relationships that would sometimes develop among schoolboys.

The visions of amorous schoolboy desire described by Kaita, Ranpo, and Taruho stand in stark contrast to the codified, age-graded, "hard-faction" pursuit of male–male sexuality described in Ōgai's novel and in many Meiji treatments of schoolboy life. These three authors are among the earliest of a new generation of authors whose writing describes amorous schoolboy relationships based on an appreciation of bishōnen beauty and shared interests, not on the age-graded hierarchical relationships of "hard-faction" boys in the Meiji period or—going back even further—the *nenja/wakashu* pattern of male–male sexuality described so often in Edo texts. This new generation of authors also included Yamazaki Toshio, Kawabata Yasunari (1899–1972), Hori Tatsuo (1904–53), and Tachibana Sotō (1894–1959).[34]

In the writing of these authors, the sentimental depiction of egalitarian love between boys is due in part to the discursive shift in the early twentieth century that critic Isoda Kōichi has called the "revolution of emotion" (*kanjō kakumei*).[35] Isoda notes that throughout the first few decades of the century, one finds elaborate expressions of personal and intimate feeling in a wide variety of authors ranging from the naturalist writer Mushanokoji Saneatsu (1885–1976) to the symbolist, aesthetically inclined poet Kitahara Hakushū (1885–1942). These expressions of emotion, which often partake of the erotic, challenged the rigid Confucian notions of public morality seen in the official discourse of the late Meiji period and celebrated the individual spirit in ways sometimes considered shocking and self-indulgent at the time. This "revolution of emotion" was no doubt closely related to the rise of new, modern notions of love in the modern era, which came to see affection as an increasingly personal matter. As Saeki Junko has argued in her analysis of changing notions of love in the Meiji period, love *(ai)* came to be seen as purer and more spiritual than just eroticism and physical relationships, which were described by the word *koi*, referring to more physical manifestations of love. As a result, *ai* was seen as having a much greater bearing on the interiority of the individual and lending itself to a greater equality between the partners in a relationship.[36]

Kaita and Taruho, in particular, were part of this revolution. Borrowing the highly aestheticized and personal language of Kitahara Hakushū, Kaita celebrated the aesthetic appeal of bishōnen, especially that of the attractive younger classmate for whom he entertained amorous feelings. Kaita's and Taruho's writings emphasize that both thought of themselves as representing the vanguard of a new "aesthetic" breed of writer and artist who would celebrate intense personal emotion. As the discussion in subsequent chapters will show, questions of art and poetry were never far from an appreciation of boyish beauty for these two writers, and both saw their heightened sensitivity to male beauty as an important part of their artistic quest to develop a visionary seed of artistic genius. Both writers were part of a broader movement that used the celebration of love and eroticism between boys to further what William Tyler has called an "antinaturalist agenda" that "ushered in the more diverse and polymorphous age of the *modan* that followed Meiji-style modernity."[37]

Coincidentally, in 1921, the same year the second volume of Kaita's posthumous works appeared in print, the novelist Ozaki Shirō (1898–1964) published an article called "Bishōnen no kenkyū" (Research on bishōnen) in the monthly magazine *Kaihō* (Liberation). Ozaki notes that with the rise of the notion of "perverse sexual desire" *(hentai seiyoku)*, which described "same-sex love" as an inevitable consequence of deeply implanted instinct, ideas about male–male love and "way of the bishōnen" *(bishōnendō)* had undergone significant modification. Even though the brotherly bonds associated with Edo-period *shudō* had died out, he envisioned a new future in the artistic and literary world for the appreciation of bishōnen beauty: "I believe that as our artistic lives as Japanese gradually grow fuller and approach completion, a new practice of the worship of the bishōnen must arise in response to our deeply seated desires."[38] Kaita's poems and Taruho's short prose, with their disassociation from Edo- and Meiji-period codifications of desire, their idealizing worship of boyish beauty, and their seemingly innocent resistance to the tendency of sexologists to treat male–male love as pathological and deep-rooted, represent a development in the "worship of the bishōnen" *(bishōnen sūhai)* that Ozaki envisioned. Although many of Ranpo's stories feature dashing and attractive youths, Ranpo was less obvious in his "worship of the beautiful youth" than Kaita and Taruho. Still, when writing as an adult about his own boyhood crushes on other school-boys, he also did so in terms that emphasize the innocent, aesthetic side to these emotions, as if attempting to draw an implicit distinction between the crushes he felt and the erotic behavior sexologists condemned. In other words, his essayistic treatments of schoolboy love hint at the longing shared by Ozaki, who hoped for a new, nonpathologizing means for expressing the appreciation of bishōnen beauty.

## The Fad for Ero, Guro, Nansensu

A third important reason for examining Kaita, Ranpo, and Taruho side by side in this study is their important position vis-à-vis the social obsession in Japan with eroticism and the grotesque—a fad that resulted in a ready market for works dealing with marginalized forms of sexual desire, including male homoeroticism. After writing his schoolboy paeans to boyish beauty, Kaita tried his hand at writing mystery-adventure stories, in which he brought together his interests in male–male desire, crime, and decadence. In the process, he produced several stories that show the same particular combination of sexual desire and the uncanny that would recur frequently in the literature associated with the popular obsession with eroticism and the grotesque that swept Japan during the 1920s and 1930s.

In an article about Kaita, Ranpo recalls he was particularly taken with Kaita's creepy mystery stories when he read them as a student in the 1910s. Ranpo's interest is particularly evident in a number of his own works from the 1920s and 1930s that unabashedly borrow motifs and plot twists from his predecessor. Most importantly, the particular combination of eroticism and the grotesque that appears in Kaita's stories recurs frequently in Ranpo's stories of crime, murder, and erotic desire. Kaita's stories, in other words, represent a starting point for the interest in eroticism and the world of the bizarre that recurs in Ranpo's novels.

The terms *ero, guro* and *ero, guro, nansensu,* which are often used to describe this type of mystery novel and other titillating, sensational products of the culture of the 1920s and 1930s, are combinations of the roots of the English terms "erotic," "grotesque," and "nonsensical." In fact, Miriam Silverberg uses the phrase *ero, guro, nansensu* as an entry into her study of the culture of Japan during the 1920s and 1930s, showing that *ero, guro, nansensu* should not be merely seen as an aberration or the result of an escapist or reactionary movement within Japanese cultural history. Instead, she shows how integral eroticism, grotesquerie, and the nonsensical were in creating the new montage-like *modan* culture of the 1920s and 1930s, which shaped everything from the lives of working women to the ways ordinary Japanese citizens thought about their empire.[39] The phrase *ero, guro, nansensu* sometimes appeared in derogatory contexts to mean something like "the nonsense of the erotic and grotesque," but in the hands of many, the term was used in a sensationalizing fashion that suggested a particular interest in the phenomenon being described. In a newspaper interview conducted in 1930, Ranpo reacted to this second use of the terms by expressing his displeasure at being labeled an author of *ero, guro* fiction. He states that people started out using the words *ero* and *guro* in ways that reflected a sincere interest in sexual and unusual subject matter, but the recent, popular, sensationalizing use of the words "leaves an extremely bad feeling. The words are literally the same, but the meaning has become extremely superficial." *Ero,* in other words, had come to reflect a simple and shallow interest in the sensual, titillating, and erotically suggestive, and *guro* had come to signify something gruesome and shocking.[40]

What links the erotic, the grotesque, and the nonsensical is a sense that each represents the seamy and shadowy forces brewing in the undercurrents of society—forces not constrained by the ethical and civil codes of civilized society. In other words, the fad for *ero, guro, nansensu* represented a fascination with those primal, idian, irrational, erotic, and thanatotic urges ordinarily suppressed by the logical, civilizing superego of social ethics. As Pflugfelder explains,

> The celebration of the "erotic" [*ero*] in its myriad forms constituted a
> rejection of the Meiji dictum that sexuality was unsuited for public display
> or representation unless it conformed to the narrow standards of "civilized
> morality." The elevation of the "grotesque" [*guro*] betrayed a similar
> disregard for prevailing esthetic codes, with their focus on traditional canons

of beauty and concealment of the seamier sides of existence. Finally, the valorization of the "nonsensical" [*nansensu*] signaled a discontent with the constraining nature of received moral and epistemological certitudes.[41]

When applied to literature, the terms *ero, guro* and *ero, guro, nansensu* are used to describe a wide range of writing that depicts the sexual, bizarre, ridiculous, irrational, frivolous, or dandyesque. In its more erotic manifestations, *ero, guro, nansensu* writing frequently describes forms of sexual desire that Japanese society had in recent decades started to consider aberrant and perverse, such as sadomasochism, fetishism, male–male homoeroticism, female–female homoeroticism, and nymphomania. At the same time medical science and sexology identified and classified these forms of desire, it also imbued them with an element of danger or social unacceptability, thereby elevating their status as curiosities. By identifying and labeling these practices as depraved or deviant, medical psychology distanced them from its version of "normality" and "civilization." In this way, they ironically gave these forms of sexuality an electrical charge that would shock readers.[42] Pflugfelder notes that one element of the culture of *ero, guro, nansensu* was a "tacit alliance" between the medico-scientific understanding of sexual phenomena and consumer capitalism, which put certain forms of sexual desire "on display less for scientific reasons than because of their profit-generating possibilities."[43]

While it is true that the allegedly perverse forms of desire catalogued by doctors and sexologists feature prominently in *ero, guro, nansensu* literature, a close examination of the literature of the time, including that of Kaita and Ranpo, shows that the texts do not merely passively reflect the language and thinking of medical psychology. As this study shows, other generic, thematic, and personal factors were at work shaping the ways writers wrote about male– male desire. Moreover, even when sensationalizing authors such as Ranpo did borrow the language of sexology to describe "perverse sexual desire" *(hentai seiyoku)* in their novels, one finds this language deployed unevenly alongside other passages in which same-sex desire and other forms of eroticism are not marked with the pathologizing language. The result is that even these texts do not completely preclude the possibility of a curious fascination on the part of the reader or even a bond of identification with the characters described.

While Kaita and Ranpo contributed to the rise of the *ero, guro, nansensu* sensibility by drawing on the medical and psychological code of "perverse" sexual desire to create mystery fiction that might shock and perhaps even stimulate readers, Taruho contributed to the rise of the *ero, guro, nansensu* sensibility in a somewhat different fashion. Much of Taruho's earliest work featuring male–male desire is not plot-driven but written in a meandering, essayistic style that evokes a dandyesque world and that celebrates individual moments of aesthetic pleasure. In other words, Taruho's breezy and often unfocused style of writing presents a denationalized, depoliticized world of aesthetics that politically inclined authors would have considered *nansensu*. Perhaps for this reason, previous scholars commenting on Taruho's work have tended to focus far more on the visionary and sensual qualities of his writing than the ideological implications of his work. Nonetheless, as this study argues, Taruho's "nonsensical," apparently anti-ideological interest in the depoliticized, denationalized adolescent male body represents a refashioning of adolescent male subjectivity. As chapter 5 will show, Taruho, like Kaita and Ranpo, also draws on the code of "perverse sexuality" set up by medical and psychological researchers; however, when he does so, he is less interested in describing same-sex desire in negative, pathologized terms than using the language created by doctors, psychologists, and sexologists in ideologically subversive ways that refashion the terms of their own debate.

## Creating Queer Community and the Stakes of Identification

One final reason for treating Kaita's, Ranpo's, and Taruho's works within a single study has to do with the many intertextual and personal relationships among them. As mentioned above, Ranpo dedicated significant energy in the 1930s to searching for books and texts about love and eroticism between men, partly as a means of overcoming his sense that virtually no one in his circle of friends was interested in the subject. Like John Addington Symonds (1840–93) and Walter Pater (1839–94), who reacted against the sexual restrictions of Victorian England by turning to the classical world and the Renaissance to find images of men who loved other men, Ranpo reached out to explore the world of printed literature as a means of coping with his perceived isolation. The expressions of male–male love and erotic desire he found in novels, memoirs, and histories provided him some solace and encouraged him to believe he was not entirely alone, even though the writing he explored often came from countries and eras far away from his own. In *Feeling Backward,* Heather Love has remarked that the desire to forge a community through literary and historical exploration is "a crucial feature of queer historical experience, one produced by the historical isolation of individual queers as well as by the damaged quality of the historical archive."[44] Indeed, it was precisely because of isolation that some writers in twentieth-century Japan, such as Ranpo, turned to literature to find figures to whom they could relate.

Some of the first books Ranpo discovered were the works of Kaita, his fellow countryman, and he became obsessed with Kaita's writing, to the point that he wrote several short essays about Kaita's work and included references to Kaita's stories within his own works of fiction. (Although Kaita and Ranpo were born only a few years apart, Kaita had already died of tuberculosis by the time Ranpo first read his works about love between boys; therefore, Kaita represented to Ranpo an author from the near past, rather than a contemporary.) As chapter 4 will argue, Kaita represented a key figure for Ranpo in his project of forging an affective community of queer Japanese writers, and he comes to think of him as a champion of a new, modern Japanese aesthetic of love between boys.

At the same time, it is important to note that Ranpo's paeans to Kaita and the other explorations of queer literary history that followed also served another important function. By publishing his work in various journals and literary forums, Ranpo not only consoled himself but also helped further the work of a loose coterie of writers, including the detective novelist Hamao Shirō (1896–1935), the anthropologist Iwata Jun'ichi (1900–1945), and Inagaki Taruho, who although working in different genres all had a similar interest in exploring the history and literature of male–male love for the purposes of dealing with and, in some cases, even modifying the present condition and social status of queer men. One might say Ranpo became the focal point of a queer literary subculture—the first to emerge in twentieth-century Japanese literary history. The bonds between these authors were not necessarily predicated on a common class, especially when one considers that Hamao Shirō came from the aristocracy, and Ranpo, with a local, provincial official as a father, came from a somewhat more meager, middle-class background. Likewise, the affinities were not grounded in region, considering that all came from various parts of Japan and did not even maintain residences in Tokyo, the epicenter of the Japanese literary world. Instead, the connections among these authors were grounded in a shared interest in male–male sexuality that, in their eyes, transcended social background, place, and even time. In this regard, one might see this subculture as being particularly modern—a shared camaraderie grounded in an interest in a particular category of sexual behavior.

As chapter 4 will argue, one of the projects of this loose-knit group of writers was to draw on literary and historical examples of male–male eroticism to form conclusions about queer life and subjectivity in the present. Ranpo's own essays on the history of love and eroticism between men cite a variety of examples of male–male love culled from ancient Greece and early modern Japan, as well as nineteenth- and twentieth-century America, France, and England. He and his fellow writers strove to assert connections across the boundaries of nation and history, looking abroad and looking to the past under the assumption that a shared interest in a member of the same sex trumped other cultural, historical, and discursive differences. In doing so, they were perhaps inadvertently borrowing from the logic established by Japanese medical psychologists, who in their attempts to specify and categorize sexualities had suggested the "homosexual" represented a specific kind of desiring subject that had appeared around the world throughout history in different places and times.

From the vantage point of the early twenty-first century, it is clear that the sort of transhistorical eclecticism seen in the work of Ranpo and others is fraught with perils. Indeed, one of the major thrusts of queer scholarship since the 1980s has been to point out the dangers of overgeneralizing about the history and meaning of same-sex eroticism. Queer scholars have encouraged people to question any term that attempts to describe sexual acts, identities, preferences, and genders in terms that are allegedly universal and transhistorical. As many have argued, queer theory represents a post-structuralist reaction to the overly simplistic assumption on the part of gay liberationist and lesbian feminists that there was such a thing as a universal gay or lesbian identity and that there were necessarily continuities between people who engaged in same-sex eroticism, regardless of what nation, socio-economic class, ethnicity, or historical era they came from—exactly the same sort of assumption underlying the work of Ranpo and his compatriots.[45] Instead, contemporary queer scholarship has challenged scholars to think in increasingly subtle and evermore fine-tuned terms about the ways similar sexual acts have meant profoundly different things to different people at different times. As a result, a common theme has been to emphasize *differences* in implications of sexual acts and subcultures that might, to critically untrained eyes, look similar. For instance, the classicist David Halperin has written that one goal of his now classic study *One Hundred Years of Homosexuality* was to show the differences between the cultures of contemporary gay men, which grew out of a category created by nineteenth-century medical psychological discourse, and Greek pederasty, which was partially a product of a culture of misogyny, class hierarchy, and discrimination.[46] Similarly, Pflugfelder's studies into the seismic shifts in the conceptualization of male–male eroticism in early modern and modern Japan have showed us that when people in the seventeenth and eighteenth centuries spoke of *shudō*, especially in the context of a martial and roughneck culture of male samurai bravado, they were drawing on a profoundly different set of cultural assumptions than when twentieth-century Japanese spoke of "same-sex love" using words such as *dōseiai* that had originated in conjunction with sexological and medical discourse.

In short, queer theory has taught contemporary readers how to be sensitive to difference, and as a result, we have become increasingly skilled at examining the fine-tuned cultural concepts that have shaped the ways people have thought about sexuality within various, different temporal or ideological spheres. Nonetheless, queer studies have not finished the process of thinking through the ways the past lingers in the present, infiltrates our thoughts, shapes our existences, and interferes with our own neat attempts to create models to understand the present. As Halperin has noted, the study of influences, interferences, and consciously drawn continuities between past and present are just as crucial as historical ruptures, and "an adequate history of sexuality needs to make conceptual accommodation for both."[47]

Despite the welcome advances of queer theory and its emphasis on difference—or rather *because* of those advances—there is an acute need to continue to think about the ways the past is still with us and the ethics of identification in the deployment of historical paradigms of sexuality, even when in the service of positive goals. In the last several years, this has started to happen as queer theory has undergone what some have called "the affective turn." Instead of asking questions about how, when, and where queer people lived in the past, recent queer historians have shifted the terms of the debate, asking us why it is people in the present care so much about the past. Although historians are still interested in uncovering how people lived in the past, the questions garnering even more attention have become "Why care so much?" "In caring, what sorts of relationships is one trying to create with the past?" and most importantly, "What does this say about the person making the inquiry and their particular moment in time?"

In keeping with this "affective turn," this study does not seek to denounce Ranpo and his compatriots for their sometimes ahistorical deployments of older discursive modes of talking about male–male eroticism. Instead, it turns to what are far more important and productive questions about the purposes and effects of their acts of identification. What authors and texts do they turn to and how do they reference these texts? What are their purposes in drawing on those texts? What do they seem to be implying about queer life in the present? What aesthetic and ideological projects are at work in their deployments of the past? As subsequent chapters will show, the answers to these questions vary a great deal with the particular work under consideration; but to give one quick example, Kaita's often anthologized poem "Chi no koshō" (Pageboy of the Blood), discussed in chapter 1, deploys images of a deceased samurai's lover as part of his project to forge a new, decadent Japanese romanticism. Meanwhile, Ranpo's essay "Shudō mokuzuzuka" (Mokuzu mound commemorating the way of the youth), discussed in chapter 4, also presents a story of Edo-period samurai lovers who die together, yet this deployment of the figure of the samurai has a more overtly social agenda at work: to honor a past in which passionate love between men was not only in plain view but also earned the admiration of society—a past far different from Ranpo's own present.

Ranpo and his compatriots were not the first group of modern Japanese writers to deal with the issue of queer subjectivity; that distinction belongs to those medical psychologists and sexologists, such as Sawada Junjirō and Habuto Eiji, who in the first decades of the twentieth century followed their European counterparts and depicted "same-sex love" as a transhistorical, universal phenomenon—albeit one rooted in psychological pathology. What makes the work of Kaita, Ranpo, Taruho, and some of their compatriots so important is that for the first time in the modern era, these authors banded together in a concerted struggle to reexamine the subject of the "homosexual" that sexologists had created, drawing on a variety of images of male–male desire culled from the past and from the pages of other writers. While there were occasional authors who wrote about male–male desire during the 1910s and 1920s, it was not until the late 1920s that a loose fabric of literary writers began to pull together in a concerted effort to reexamine, probe, recontextualize, qualify, in some cases entirely reject the visions of male–male desire Japanese society had inherited from medical psychologists and sexologists.

## BIOGRAPHICAL CONSIDERATIONS

Although Kaita, Ranpo, and Taruho wrote extensively about amorous and erotic desire between men, the purpose of this study is not to assert they were necessarily "gay authors" in the sense that they expressed an exclusive interest in men. Kaita and Ranpo did have relationships with both men and women, and it seems likely Taruho did as well. While an adolescent school-boy in Kyoto, Kaita wrote a great deal about the attractive qualities of other boys, and as an art student in Tokyo, he developed feelings for his school-mate Yanase Masamu (1900–1945), who later became a key figure in the proletarian art movement; however, at about age seventeen, Kaita began ex-periencing passionate crushes on women, including a model at the art insti-tute where he studied. Much of his later writing describes his powerful desire for women, his failed attempts to have meaningful relationships with them, and his tendency to turn to alcohol and even prostitutes to soothe the erotic desire burning within him.[48]

Like Kaita, Ranpo developed a passionate friendship with another boy as a schoolboy adolescent, and in 1926 he wrote that his relationship with this schoolmate was his only experience with true love. In late 1919, however, Ranpo married a woman he had met while working in the Kansai region, and in 1921 they had their one and only child. Like many married couples at the time, Ranpo and his wife seem to have remained comfortable com-panions over the years, but they do not appear to have shared a great deal of romantic intimacy. In the late 1920s Ranpo devoted himself to finding books and other bibliographic sources having to do with male–male desire, and he began spending long evenings away from home wandering through the city, especially Asakusa Park, a spot known for cruising and male hus-tlers. Ranpo's own writings emphasize that his interest in male–male desire was not overtly sexual, and he asserts he did not act on his interest. Still, his fascination with the life and writings of the British essayist and poet John Addington Symonds—a married man who experienced erotic desire for men—hints Ranpo may have turned to Symonds's example to see how a married man might handle feelings for other men. Several friends have writ-ten that Ranpo was familiar with the gay bars in Shinjuku and other places in Tokyo during his later years, and he sometimes appeared at underground events held for gay people in private homes. For instance, the author Ono Kōji (1910–) has written an account of going with Ranpo to a gay bar in Shin-juku, where Ranpo was a frequent customer.[49] Even now, one hears rumors in the Japanese literary world about affairs Ranpo allegedly had with men.[50]

The frequency with which Taruho described same-sex desire in his liter-ature, usually in settings that closely match the places where Taruho himself lived and studied, makes it easy to jump to the conclusion that during his own schooldays, passionate schoolboy crushes were a daily fact of life for the young writer. Indeed, there seems to be little reason to disbelieve this assumption, although Taruho remains conspicuously silent about whether or not these crushes ever turned into physical encounters. His interest in the love of boys, at least as a concept, appears not to have waned in the post-war period, judging from his voluminous treatises *A-kankaku to V-kankaku* (The A-sensibility and the V-sensibility, 1954), *Prostata-rectum kikaigaku* (A study of prostata-rectum mechanics, 1966), and *Shōnen'ai no bigaku* (The aesthetics of the love of boys, 1968), which vociferously defend the love of young men. Still, in all of these works, he treats the love of boys as a primarily aesthetic experience and avoids any hint that he had personally engaged in erotic contact with other men. In fact, Taruho would sometimes chastise his friend, the poet Takahashi Mutsuo, for writing so explicitly about male–male homoerotic activity, stating that by focusing on physical acts Takahashi was soiling a pure and beautiful form of love.[51] After staying a brief time in Ranpo's home in 1949, Taruho married the aspiring writer Shinohara Chiyo in 1950 and moved to Kyoto, where he lived with his new wife and step-daughter, Miyako. Although Taruho shared a long life with his new family, his relationship with his wife appears to have been based on companionship, friendship, mutual interests, and convenience, rather than erotic passion.[52]

In any case, the primary focus of this study is not what Kaita, Ranpo, or Taruho may or may not have done in bed, but the ways in which they wrote about male–male desire in their works. Because each wrote autobiographical or semiautobiographical works about their schoolboy infatuations, biographical considerations are germane to a certain point. Many of Kaita's poems are dedicated specifically to the younger classmate with whom he was in love, and not surprisingly, a number of elements within his texts can be understood through knowing the nature of that relationship. Also, nonfictional writings, such as Kaita's diary and personal letters, form an important percentage of his relatively small oeuvre, and so any critic would be remiss in ignoring them. Moreover, Ranpo's impressive scrapbook and Taruho's body of essays give useful hints for the reasons why certain topics, themes, or modes of depiction appear in their work, so this study refers to the scrapbook and essays to gain a fuller understanding of their more overly literary texts. In short, the primary mode of analysis of this study is not biographical, although biographical considerations often shed a good deal of light on particular texts.

If anything, one of the principal arguments of this book is that biographical factors do *not* fully explain the ways any particular writer engages with erotic desire in his or her work. It argues that in looking at expressions of desire, one should also consider a host of other factors, including literary stylistics, genre-related considerations, and reader expectations. In his study of representations of male–male desire in Meiji fiction, Jim Reichert comments that multiple factors shape the ways in which authors might write about the subject. He notes that various types of language, characters, plot, and genres all had characteristic conventions that significantly shaped the means by which male–male desire might be described in a particular work.[53] Although biographical considerations might be relevant, especially in cases where works themselves make explicit reference to actual events in an author's life, other literary factors do as much, if not more, to determine the particular idioms in which the authors wrote.

In fact, one could go one step further and argue it is precisely through engaging, modifying, and reacting to older, preexisting texts and tropes that writers were able to create their own particular modes of depicting desire. Just as one finds modes of representation that do not perfectly match those circulating in the realms of medicine, jurisprudence, and so on, one frequently finds depictions of male–male desire that do not match what one might necessarily expect in a particular genre. Reichert has shown that writings on male–male desire in turn-of-the-century Japan often crossed generic borders and borrowed modes of representation one might typically expect to find in genres other than the one the author was using.[54] A similar situation holds true within the critical years of literary development during the first few years of the twentieth century. Kaita drew upon recent stylistic developments in poetry *(shi)* while writing his own tanka, short stories, and drama. Ranpo found inspiration for his fiction in various sources, including classical texts, the writing of other contemporary authors, as well as medical and psychological texts. Taruho turned to various sorts of texts, including ones by psychologists like Freud and Krafft-Ebing, then modified some of their ideas and language in his essays and fiction. The hybrid nature of these authors' language ultimately created new tropes and means of writing about desire between men.

## ADOLESCENCE AND THE FRACTURE IN THE SPECTRUM OF MALE–MALE DESIRE

In this study, I have generally chosen to use the words "male–male desire" or "desire between men" instead of "homosexuality" to refer to amorous and erotic desire between men. As many recent studies have shown, the notion of "homosexuality" in the West represents a specific formulation of male–male desire with its own historical roots and culturally bound implications. To talk about the works of Kaita, Ranpo, and Taruho as embodying "homosexual" feelings would set into play a number of modern assumptions associated with the word. (For instance, it is commonly assumed in contemporary America that a person who experiences "homosexual" feelings is most likely a "homosexual" or, at least, a "bisexual," and their preference for their particular choice of sexual partner is rooted in their own individual psychology.) Rather than applying culturally loaded terms such as "homosexuality," "heterosexuality," and "bisexuality" to describe the feelings, ideas, and characters described in Kaita's, Ranpo's, and Taruho's works, this study instead chooses to explore the language and terms the texts themselves use to depict amorous and erotic desire between men. The goal in doing so is to allow a better understanding of the ways these three writers thought about and represented male–male desire within the context of their own era. As Pflugfelder writes, "To impose such categories as 'homosexuality' and 'bisexuality' upon a society or conceptual universe, whether non-European or pre–nineteenth century, in which they would not have been understood in the same sense that they are currently understood, if indeed at all, and in which behavior often followed patterns quite different from those we associate with them in our own societies, is unwittingly to hide from view the experience of those very historical subjects whom we seek to comprehend."[55]

A second reason for using the words "male–male desire" over "homosexuality" is that the former term allows a more precise delineation between male–male desire and female–female desire. As mentioned previously, *shudō, nanshoku,* and other terms used during the Edo period did not apply to female–female desire. It was only with the development of the concept of "same-sex love" in the late nineteenth and early twentieth centuries that Japanese started to identify male–male desire and female–female desire as related phenomena. Still, Kaita, Ranpo, and Taruho rarely ever mention female–female desire; in the overwhelming majority of cases, when they speak of "same-sex love," they are specifically concerned with men. This suggests that either they were not especially interested in it or that when they were talking about "same-sex love," the first thing which came to their minds was simply desire between men. One gets a hint of this in one of the rare instances when Ranpo mentions desire between women, namely in the round-table discussion "Dōseiai no risō to genjitsu" (The ideals and reality of same-sex love), conducted in 1948 with Taruho. There, Ranpo talks at

great length about desire between boys, but his only mention of female–
female desire is a passing reference to the Greek poet Sappho, whom he calls
the "progenitor of female same-sex love [*josei dōseiai*]."[56] The fact he quali-
fies the word *dōseiai* with *josei* (women) in order to talk about erotic love
between women reveals that *dōseiai* by itself is not enough to pinpoint either
male–male or female–female desire specifically. For this, Ranpo had to employ a supplementary term. Although the word "same-sex love" incorporated
both male–male and female–female desire within the same conceptual territory, male–male love appears to have exercised a stronger pull over the
imagination of these particular authors.

Perhaps the most important reason for using the rubric "male–male desire"
over "homosexuality" is that many of the works examined in this study deal
relatively obliquely with depictions of sexuality. Some texts, such as Kaita's
poems and Taruho's essays, describe an intense admiration of boyish beauty
and feelings of spiritual love, while others, such as Ranpo's essays on his boyhood crushes, describe profoundly passionate friendships. While I argue
hints of erotic attraction are clearly manifested here and there in these texts,
genital sexuality is only one form of desire on a much broader spectrum
of male–male desire. As a growing body of scholarship has shown, the relationship between overt homoerotic and homosocial amorous desire provides a crucial key to understanding the spectrum of gender relations within
any given time period or society. In her groundbreaking work *Between Men*
on expressions of male–male desire in English literature, Eve Sedgwick describes a continuum of homosocial desire ranging from asexual "homosocial"
desire, which consists of same-sex friendship and bonding activities that
do not involve eroticism, to "homosexual" desire, which is overtly erotic.[57]
Sometimes, these forms of desire overlap. In other cases, the ends of the
continuum are split by a fracture arising from homophobic anxiety about
male–male sexual relations. Once the continuum is fractured, homoerotic
and homosocial relations appear profoundly different in character, and the
introduction of sexual desire into a relationship compels people to consider
the relationship in a different light. In other words, anxiety over same-sex
eroticism drives people to see friendships and erotic relationships as two
distinctly different phenomena.

In early twentieth-century Japan, a key factor governing the split between
homosocial and homoerotic desire was the notion of youth. During the early
part of the twentieth century, the ways the Japanese thought about youth
and adolescence underwent significant changes. Critic Karatani Kōjin has

argued that before the turn of the century, children were not viewed as qualitatively different from adults in any significant way, and the ontological notion of childhood was created only during the first few decades of the twentieth century. This notion was then made to seem "natural" through what Karatani calls an "inversion" *(tentō)*. He explains, "What we call 'the child' was itself discovered through such an inversion, and it was only after this that 'real children' or 'realistic children' could be seen. . . . [T]he 'child' that we see today was discovered and constituted only recently."[58] Karatani's provocative argument does not mention, however, one of the most important factors in establishing the notion of the child, namely a tendency to desexualize the young. Despite the advances of medicalized psychology, which read erotic desire into the behavior of children, Japanese society developed a tendency to deny children their status as erotic subjects and an increasing reluctance to treat them as sexual objects. In the ontological structure of childhood, the threshold of puberty separated childhood and sexual oblivion from adulthood. It is precisely because of this separation that works like Tanizaki Jun'ichirō's novella *Shōnen (The Children)*, which consciously violates the assumption of youthful sexual innocence by describing the homoerotic, power-laden games of children, appeared so shocking to contemporary audiences when published in 1911.[59]

Boys in premodern Japan were generally treated as full-fledged adults by their early teenage years, but during the first few decades of the twentieth century, increased levels of attendance in middle and higher schools meant an increase in the perceived length of time required for social maturation. Mori Arinori (1847–1889), the Minister of Education from 1885 to 1889, established a system requiring four years of compulsory education for all students; however, in 1907 the number of years of compulsory attendance was raised to six. School attendance remained poor through the last decade of the nineteenth century because students had to pay educational fees, and many families required them to work at a young age. In 1900, however, the system of fees for elementary school was abolished, and by 1907, 98 percent of children were receiving six years of education.[60] Meanwhile, the number of universities and higher schools multiplied as the number of students continuing on to secondary education rose. As the period of educational maturation grew, so did the perceived length of the period of emotional, social, and sexual maturation. Educators, psychologists, and sexologists, who considered the proper upbringing of Japanese youth to be one of their most important tasks, wrote with increasing frequency about the need to police the sexual practices of students and adolescents, whom they saw as being at a critical age in their sexual development. In conjunction with this task, they became increasingly anxious about student sexual activity, especially among members of the same sex. To give one typical example, *Bukyō sekai* (World of heroism)—the same youth-oriented journal to which Kaita submitted several mystery-adventure stories in 1915—published a special issue in 1919 about "correcting bad sexual desire" *(akuseiyoku kyōsei)*. This issue featured the advice of school administrators, religious figures, and numerous medical doctors about the importance of "proper" sexual behavior early on. It also included stories such as "Akuseiyoku ni ayamarareta shūsai no hisan naru matsuro" (The tragic end of a brilliant boy who took the wrong course of bad sexual desire), designed to scare students into behaving in ways psychologists and administrators would deem appropriate.

Nonetheless, these attempts to separate homoerotic activity from boyish camaraderie within the schools were not entirely successful, judging from the frequency with which the literature of the time describes schoolboy relationships. Late adolescence, however, was the time when the distinction between homosociality and homoeroticism was driven home. In the minds of many, graduation from school meant students should also leave behind the adolescent appreciation of boys and enter the "adult" realm of cross-sex desire and family. Late adolescence represented a transition when the male–male desire of youth was generally expected to give way to love between a man and a woman. The two forms of desire might spill over into one another during youth, but as youth gave way to adulthood, society typically expected the two to diverge.[61]

Much of the writing examined in this book reflects this social expectation in some form or another. When describing the youthful crushes of schoolboys, these authors all routinely treat male–male attraction as an innocent and especially poignant form of affection. When they deal with erotic desire among adult men, however, all treat the subject more circumspectly. Although Kaita seems to have retained sympathetic feelings toward male–male desire, he wrote two mystery-adventure stories in 1915 describing homoerotic desire as having little place within the adult world of modern civilization. Over the course of his early career, Ranpo seems to have struggled to find an appropriate idiom to describe eroticism between adult males. At times, he compromises with expectations imposed by the fad for *ero, guro, nansensu* and associates male–male erotic desire with strangeness, criminality, or even deviance. A careful reading of his works, however, reveals strong hints of his personal interest in male–male love, and even his most damning representations contain passages that contradict or even subvert these negative associations. Taruho was the most consistent of the three authors in terms of the ways in which he described same-sex desire, but one reason he is so consistent is that so much of his writing is specifically about the appreciation of young men, usually by boys who are around the same age or slightly older. Taruho's literary interests lie almost exclusively in describing *shōnen'ai,* the love of adolescent boys, rather than the sorts of amorous affections that might arise between males after graduating into adulthood. The clear implication of Taruho's works is that love between sexually mature adult men represents an almost entirely different experience from the love of younger men. In short, all three of the authors ascribed to the notion, common in early twentieth-century Japan, that the love of boys represented a different phenomenon than the adult love of men—an assumption that reflected and even contributed to a widening split within the spectrum of homosocial desire in early twentieth-century Japan.

# 1

# Blow the Bloodstained Bugle

*Murayama Kaita and the Language of Personal Sensation*

Eaarly in the morning of February 20, 1919, in Tokyo, a young artist named Murayama Kaita passed away from tubercular pneumonia, which had been exacerbated by the influenza epidemic that swept through Japan and much of the industrialized world in 1918 and 1919. A writer and art student, Kaita was only twenty-two years and five months old at the time of his death. Although his untimely demise brought an end to a promising career that had barely gotten underway, ironically, it set in motion the mythology of Kaita's life. Soon after his death, his friends published his work, which inspired the Japanese literary and artistic world to reexamine the life of this young artist and identify him as a passionate, inspired "genius." As this interpretation took hold, Kaita's name exploded into literary history.

Kaita is now best remembered as an aspiring student artist who, during his time at the Nihon Bijutsuin (Japan Art Institute), painted some of the most extraordinary, visionary, and iconoclastic paintings of the Taishō period. At the time, however, it was his *Kaita no utaeru* (Songs of Kaita) and its sequel—two posthumously published volumes containing Kaita's diary, poetry, and short stories—that really took Japan by storm.[1] With their bold, daring, and lushly worded expressions of personal desire, they struck an entire generation of readers as auguring a new era in personal expression, and many now canonical novelists and poets, including Arishima Takeo, Akutagawa Ryūnosuke (1892–1927), Yosano Akiko (1878–1942), Takamura Kōtarō (1883–1956), Murō Saisei (1889–1962), Kusano Shinpei

(1903–1988), and Edogawa Ranpo, expressed their unabashed admiration for his work.

Much of his earliest poetry dates from his days as a student in Kyoto; in fact, approximately half of his entire output dates from 1913 and 1914, when he was in love with a fellow schoolmate. Perhaps not surprisingly, his passion for this schoolmate features prominently in his youthful, exuberant,

Self-portrait of Murayama Kaita from 1916. Collection of the Mie Prefectural Art Museum. Photo copyright Fukushima Prefectural Art Museum and Mie Prefectural Art Museum 1997.

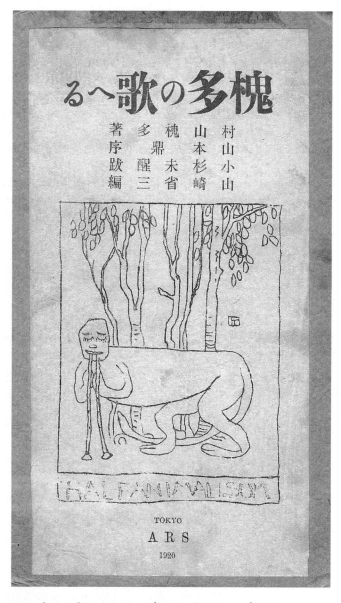

First edition of *Kaita no utaeru* (Songs of Kaita, 1920) with a cover illustration by Murayama Kaita. The words under the drawing are borrowed from the Naturalist writer Iwano Hōmei's treatise *Shinpiteki hanjūshugi* (Mysterious half-animalism, 1906). In Kaita's hands, these words serve as a sign of the brash, masculine, decadent vitality he thought should infuse modern art and literature. Collection of the author.

floridly worded work, which he circulated in the form of chapbooks. Some of the fanciful titles of these chapbooks—*Mara* (a Sanskrit-derived term for the male member) or *Aoiro haien* (The ruined garden in green)—hint at an interest in decadence, while others—such as *Sora no kan* (Feeling of the sky), *Kujakuseki* (Malachite), or *Arukaroido* (Alkaloid)—demonstrate a penchant for the rich, beaux-arts, exotic imagery just coming into vogue among Japanese poets. The poetry represents a convergence of romanticism and symbolism, both of which had played an important role in late Meiji letters, yet at the same time, their language is filled with a brevity, directness, and raw power that anticipate later modernist writing. It is because Kaita's poetry strains from a rich, indulgent, symbolist brand of romanticism toward modernism that his visionary works became bestsellers and influenced many other subsequent writers.

Many of the poems in these collections are in the first person, and because they, like the diaries and personal notes in Kaita's posthumous collections, describe personal feelings, including his passionate love for several young men, they give the impression of being unmediated records of Kaita's innermost thoughts. In fact, this strong sense of personal presence was a large part of what appealed to readers in the 1920s, judging from the frequency with which commentators wrote about his work in biographical terms. As this chapter argues, however, Kaita's writing, including even his diaries, strongly reflects current poetic and stylistic trends. Nowhere is this more prominent than in his writing on same-sex love. In describing his amorous and sexual feelings, he drew extensively on the motifs and stylistics of the newly burgeoning Japanese symbolist movement.

Kaita's writing indicates how keenly aware he was of standing at a turning point in the history of Japanese literature and art. Much like Arthur Rimbaud (1854–91), who shocked the French literary world of the nineteenth century with his bold, iconoclastic visions, Kaita saw himself as a leader of a vanguard that would revolutionize the ways Japanese artists and writers see the world. For this reason, he was quick to turn to new modes of expression such as symbolism and (in his prose works) a hallucinogenic brand of protomodernist writing. Also, like Rimbaud, Kaita saw his own propensity for male–male desire as allowing him to see the world through a different lens than others around him. In combining his interest in avant-garde aesthetics with the subject of male–male love, Kaita forged a new type of writing that celebrated male–male affection in highly aestheticized, conspicuously artistic language. Even when he drew on older styles of writing such as tanka, an ancient poetic form with over a millennium of history, he produced poetry that looked unlike what had come before. First, before examining the depictions of love in Kaita's own work, this chapter will begin by examining the introduction of symbolism, a movement that profoundly transformed Japanese cultural expression.

## Symbolism and Decadence in Japan

The late nineteenth century saw dramatic experiments with verse as Japanese writers, exposed to the various forms and traditions of the West, began forging new forms and types of poetic language. Just a few decades before, Japan began to open to external influences after a long period of relative isolation, and this led to an increased exchange in many areas, including literature. Japanese writers who came into contact with Western poetic forms were immediately intrigued by the possibilities of longer, freer forms of poetry not constrained by the restricted vocabulary choices and metric patterns of traditional Japanese verse. In order to describe the new forms that developed during this time, the Japanese revamped the word *shi*, a word that was used until that point to refer to longer poems in Chinese, to describe the category of longer poetry that became popular in the late nineteenth and early twentieth centuries. (Though some Anglophone critics render *shi* as "Western-style verse" or "poetry in the international style," *shi* quickly became so thoroughly naturalized as a poetic form that by around the 1920s, it is misleading to imply Japanese *shi* was always necessarily derivative of "Western" verse. It is also somewhat misleading to translate *shi* as "free-form verse" in order to contrast it with the fixed metrical forms of traditional Japanese verse forms such as tanka, renga, and haiku, because many early *shi* were in fixed metrical patterns inherited from traditional Japan.)

One of the most widely read experiments in rendering Western poetic language and ideas into Japanese was the collection *Omokage* (Vestiges, 1889), published by a group of poets headed by Mori Ōgai. Unlike other early translations, such as Toyama Masakazu and Inoue Tetsujirō's *Shintaishi shō* (Selection of poetry in the new style, 1882), which broke with the moraic patterns of traditional poetry, *Omokage* experimented with meter and style while retaining the diction and meter of classical verse.[2] Because of its ability to retain a strong sense of poeticity while incorporating new and fresh concepts and language, the collection went through numerous editions and was read by much of the Meiji and Taishō literary world, including Kaita. Although the seventeen poems in the first edition included

some Ming dynasty poetry and classical Japanese verse, most were translations of British and German writers, many of whom—most noticeably
Lord Byron, Goethe, and Heine—dated from the Romantic period. What
made *Omokage* and other early experiments with *shi* so important, in the
long run, was less the linguistic innovations than the powerfully direct expressions of subjective experience and personal sentiment characterizing
those collections.

This romantic interest in the subjective world of the emotions took a
new, dramatic turn when Japanese translations of French symbolist writers
began to appear in the first decade of the twentieth century. Donald Keene
has remarked that the current of symbolist-inspired poetry that swept early
twentieth-century Japan was so strong no author could remain in the mainstream short of adopting the symbolist style.[3] In the West, historians of symbolism have characterized the movement as an intermediate step between a
rationalist mode of representation and one that challenges the enlightenment
notion that all things are fully expressible through concrete description.[4]
When the symbolist writers rose to the literary vanguard in late nineteenth-
century France, they attempted to express ideas and sentiments in indirect,
elusive language they thought would appeal to the imagination rather than
hard logic. In order to convey the "mysterious essence" of things, they deemed
it necessary to develop a poetic language of obliqueness, subtlety, and allu-
siveness. By describing the familiar through oblique and sometimes even
illogical diction, language became symbolic, thereby broadening the range of
resonant associations a particular signifier might invoke. Paul Verlaine (1844–
96) played a key role in stimulating the development of symbolism in France
and later in Japan, where his work was the subject of influential articles and
translations. Although he wrote his most important verse well before the word
"symbolism" came into popular circulation in the mid-1880s, he helped sup-
ply the major symbols, the theme of personified nature, the tone of ennui and
world-weariness, and the search for mysterious profundity that became characteristic of much later symbolist writing both in France and in Japan.[5] Artfully illogical metaphors, loose webs of signification, and carefully constructed
discontinuities were included not to impede understanding but to capitalize
on the possibilities of the vague by making possible a new kind of highly subjective reading that compelled the reader to participate in the process of
interpretation. These "writerly texts" (as Roland Barthes might have later
called them) represented loosely organized strings of signifiers that invite
the reader to create meaning through an organizing act of interpretation.

One chief architect of this diffuse "writerly" style was Arthur Rimbaud, who also provided a model of the poet as a visionary of genius. In his way of thinking, "unremitting acts of violence against the tedium of common sense" could lead one to arrive at a semi-mystical understanding of things.[6] In a famous 1871 letter nicknamed "La lettre du voyant" (The Seer's Letter), he writes, "I'm lousing myself up as much as I can these days. Why? I want to be a poet, and I am working to make myself a *seer:* you won't understand this at all, and I hardly know how to explain it to you. The point is, to arrive at the unknown by the disordering of *all the senses.* The sufferings are enormous, but one has to be strong, to be born a poet, and I have discovered I *am* a poet."[7] By reordering the senses through hallucinogenic drugs and sexual experimentation, the adolescent Rimbaud hoped to develop his ability to see the world in new, radical ways, then use his visions as the inspiration for his own writing. The equation between the poet and visionary genius seen so often in the literature of the late romantic and symbolist periods, especially in the figure of young iconoclasts like Rimbaud, exerted a strong pull on the cultural imagination of Europe and, in turn, Japan, where young writers like Kaita read Rimbaud and yearned to experience the world in revolutionary new ways.

It was the poet, professor, and translator Ueda Bin (1874–1916) who played an essential role in introducing symbolism to Japan; in fact, he was the first in 1904 to translate "symbolist school" as *shōchōha,* the compound still in use today.[8] Around the turn of the century, he published a number of articles about the theoretical concepts behind symbolism, but the most influential of his works was *Kaichōon* (The sound of the tide), a 1905 collection of translations of European poetry.[9] Fellow poet Yosano Tekkan noted that *Kaichōon* gave "the same nourishment to Meiji and Taishō poetry that Po Chü-I's works had afforded Heian literature."[10] His renditions, which use florid, artfully worded language to capture a sense of musicality and gentle melancholy present in the original poems, are credited with revealing to the Japanese for the first time the distinctive nature of nineteenth-century French poetry, although these, like all early translation of poetry, involved a great deal of adaptation and negotiation to render the French into Japanese.[11] What is important for this discussion is that this collection inspired young poets such as Kanbara Ariake (1876–1952), the author of the first recognizably symbolist poems in Japanese, Kitahara Hakushū, and Miki Rofū, and in the early 1910s, it also became one of Kaita's favorite books.[12]

*Kaichōon* also helped introduce the notion of "decadence" to the Japanese public by incorporating poems plumbing the depths of the human spirit in all of its unseemliness, including a number of poems from the 1861 collection *Les Fleurs du Mal (The Flowers of Evil)* by Charles Baudelaire (1821–67). While symbolism and decadence originally represented two separate strains of European modernism, by the beginning of the twentieth century they had become inextricably tangled together, even within the minds of the European reading public. Indeed, as Peter Nicholls has noted, French culture had so frequently portrayed the writer as an embodiment of modern decadence that by the fin-de-siècle, it was impossible to separate the two ideas in the popular imagination.[13] It is little wonder then that in Japan, *Kaichōon* presented symbolist and decadent poetry side by side, reinforcing the impression that the two were intimately related.

One sees the connection between symbolism and decadence in one of the most important documents of the Japanese symbolist movement, namely the introduction to the landmark anthology *Jashūmon* (Heretical faith) published in 1909 by Kitahara Hakushū (1885–1942)—a poet who was profoundly influenced by Bin's translations and who later became one of the leaders of the Japanese poetic world. The following is a full translation of the introduction, which served as a manifesto for the burgeoning Japanese symbolist movement:

> The life force of a poem is found in intimation, not in simple
> explanations of phenomena. The poet addresses the faint, indistinct
> sobs of the spirit that arise amid the limitless trembling of emotion
> that cannot be fully expressed through writing or speech. He is enam-
> ored with the pleasure of barely audible music, and he takes pride in
> the grief of his own impressions. Isn't this the fundamental purpose
> of the symbol? We face the mysterious, we rejoice in visions, and
> yearn for the red of putrefying decadence. Alas! Even in our dreams,
> we, the disciples of a modern heretical faith, cannot forget the
> laments of marble sobbing in the pale white light of the moon. Nor
> can we forget the eyes of a sphinx tortured by a thick, Egyptian mist,
> sullied with crimson. Nor can we forget romantic music smiling in
> the sunset, nor the doleful screams of that state of mind surrounding
> the crucifixion of an infant. The ceaseless spasms of putrefying
> yellow wax, the olfactory sensation of a violin's A-string being
> stroked, the sharp nerves of whiskey smothering in frosted glass, a
> sigh deeply scented of poison, grass the color of a human brain, the
> melancholy of a nightingale exhaustedly singing while under the

anesthesia of the senses—all of these things too . . . At the same time,
how hard it is to cast away the touch of scarlet velvet escaping into
the faint sound of a distant horn![14]

For Hakushū, the symbol served as a tool leading the sensitive poet (who,
in Rimbaudesque fashion, becomes a seer) into a rich, mysterious world of
subtle sensory perception. Rather than using flat imagery to reproduce his
experiences for the reader, the poet should use fresh descriptions of sensation to encourage the reader along the path of imagination. Throughout
*Jashūmon,* one finds examples of items that do not belong to the classical
canon of Japanese poetry: images of sobbing violins, blood-red wine, and
twilight parks, as well as obscure Christian terms. Hakushū's use of images,
especially crepuscular ones, along with frequent evocations of ennui, sorrow, loneliness, and despair, are strongly reminiscent of the decadent school
of fin-de-siècle French writing and depart from established standards of
beauty, thus serving as a doorway into new, intense realms of perception.

Diary entries and accounts from Kaita's friends show he was fascinated
with the poetic experiments in both *Omokage* and *Kaichōon.* Much of Kaita's
poetry from the 1910s contains the strong statements of personal desire,
pseudo-symbolist metaphors, bold use of color, and synesthetic descriptions of sensation filling these collections. In fact, the similarities between
Kaita's style and those of the French poets in *Kaichōon* were readily apparent to contemporaries, judging from the writer Taketomo Sōfū's comment
in 1920 that Kaita's "impassioned, subtle, and profound emotions" seemed
"very close to those of Rimbaud and Baudelaire."[15]

One reason Kaita was initially drawn to *Omokage* and *Kaichōon* may have
had to do with personal connections between his family and the prominent
writers and translators Mori Ōgai and Ueda Bin. Before Kaita was born,
his father, Tanisuke, had been the teacher of Ōgai's younger brother, Mori
Junzaburō.[16] Tanisuke's ancestors had been the official doctors to the lords
of Tsuruoka Castle in Yamagata; meanwhile, Ōgai was one of the foremost
authorities on Western medicine in Japan at the time, so it seems likely
Tanisuke and Ōgai struck up a friendship while talking about medicine.
Meanwhile, Kaita's mother, Tama, was a maid in the Ōgai household. Eventually, Ōgai introduced Kaita's parents to each other, and the two became
engaged.[17] Tama left Ōgai's employ before giving birth to Kaita, her first son,
but she remained in close contact with her former employers, and in later
years, Kaita became friends with Ōgai's son Oto (1892–1967) and exchanged

occasional letters with him.[18] Although it is legend within the Murayama family that Ōgai was the person who bestowed Kaita with his unusual given name, Ōgai's diary only mentions the Murayama children once.[19] It recounts that during a trip to Kyoto in December 1909, Kaita's mother came to visit him with one of her sons—either the thirteen-year-old Kaita or his younger brother. Also visiting that day was Ueda Bin, who also shared a soft spot in his heart for Kaita's mother. After the Murayama family had moved to Kyoto, Tama met Bin, then a professor at Kyoto Imperial University, at the home of Mori Junzaburō. Bin was so taken with Tama's beautiful Edo dialect that he invited her to his house on a number of occasions to speak with her.[20] The fact that Kaita's family associated so closely with these prominent men of letters no doubt encouraged Kaita's interest in the arts and likely encouraged him to think of himself as a member of Japan's literary and artistic elite.

Kaita's family was also connected to the poet Kitahara Hakushū, the author of *Jashūmon,* through Yamamoto Kanae (1882–1946), a prominent artist who happened to be Kaita's cousin and played a critical role in fostering Kaita's interest in the arts. Kanae had been a close friend of Hakushū since at least the late Meiji period, when they served as founding members of the Pan no Kai (Pan Society), an organization that sought to promote interaction between visual artists and poets and to imitate the café discussions of art and literature common to France in the late nineteenth century. One attendee, the poet and playwright Kinoshita Mokutarō (1885–1945), later recalled, "we enthusiastically read the history of impressionism and the artistic debates about it. Ueda Bin was active, and influenced by his translations and so on, we dreamed of the lives of Parisian artists and poets and tried to imitate them."[21] Over the next few years, many of the most important writers and artistic figures of early twentieth-century Japan, including Ueda Bin, Nagai Kafū (1879–1959), and Tanizaki Jun'ichirō (1886–1965), attended the Pan no Kai meetings, which combined poetry, wine, and the company of women in almost equal amounts. Through these early interactions, Kanae forged a relationship with the Kitahara family, which he eventually cemented through marriage. In 1917 Kanae married Kitahara Ie (1893–1959), Hakushū's younger sister, thus becoming the famous poet's brother-in-law.

Once again, these early interactions no doubt inspired Kaita, who greatly admired the work of his older cousin Kanae, to pursue the work of the Pan no Kai writers. Although Kaita's diaries and jottings do not definitively prove that he read the groundbreaking collection *Jashūmon,* it seems highly likely, considering Kaita's cousin and mentor Yamamoto Kanae had contributed illustrations to the first edition. It is clear, however, that Kaita's poems picked up the highly aestheticized style, ripe with the lyricism and decadence seen in *Jashūmon*. His poems include many hallmarks of Japanese symbolist writing: intense descriptions of sensory perception, use of landscape and atmospheric conditions as indexes of emotional state, musical and rhythmic language, and repeated expressions of melancholia and love-haunted languor. Another important element Kaita emulated was the awareness of the idea of the poet as a sensitive, visionary genius. In "Shigatsu tanshō" (Short April verses), written only a few years after Hakushū's *Jashūmon* and less than a decade after Bin's *Kaichōon*, Kaita expresses his awareness that he was standing, along with his poetic compatriots, at the dawn of a new era in which poetry would evoke intensely personal worlds of sensation:

> Blow the bloodstained bugle!
> The wind of aestheticism
> Presses upon our breasts, first strong, then weak . . .
> The days of late May burn with red
> Then come round again, nostalgic and familiar
> Ah! So then
> Blow the bloodstained bugle
> If our armaments are complete![22] (18)

In this manifesto-like poem, Kaita asks his readers to transform their feelings, like the soft nostalgic familiarity one feels at sunsets of late May, into clarion calls to battle. He envisions the ranks of sensitive readers, potential poets, and artists as a militia armed with a new type of language. This poem might also be read as addressing not just a rising army of sensitive writers, but also Japan as a whole. During Japan's rapid modernization in the nineteenth century, the government had rushed to transform Japan from a feudal state into one with all of the accessories of modernity, including a modern military force. By the late Meiji and early Taishō periods, however, many intellectuals were arguing that in this process of external modernization, Japan had largely ignored the necessary concurrent changes to the inner world of the self. As the country moved from the late nineteenth-century emphasis on civilization to an emphasis on culture in the early twentieth century, more and more writers began to explore the experiences, perceptions, and

place of the individual within society. Without question, Hakushū's introduction to *Jashūmon* and Kaita's "Shigatsu tanshō" represent manifestations
of this introspective drive. The final lines, "blow the bloodstained bugle /
If our armaments are complete," then, in one sense, represent a clarion
call sounded to a nation that, having completed the process of building a
modern military state, now was seeking to establish an atmosphere of free
expression and emotional depth in which the citizenry of Japan might celebrate the self.

## KAITA AND THE PRINCE

This extended survey about the introduction of romanticism, symbolism,
and decadence in Japanese literature is essential not only because it helps set
the stage for the language Kaita would use in his literary evocations of boyish desire, but also because it illustrates how early twentieth-century poets
and writers participated in what Isoda Kōichi has called the "revolution of
emotion": a radical transformation in the sensibilities of late Meiji, Taishō,
and early Shōwa literary circles that encouraged writers to foreground their
own feelings, including even "decadent" or frivolous feelings that in earlier
moments might have been considered either too personal, frivolous, indulgent, or even scandalous to merit literary attention.[23] Indeed, the eagerness
with which contemporary authors such as Arishima Takeo extolled Kaita's
writing suggests that in the midst of this era of the transformation of sensibilities, there were segments of the reading public exceptionally eager to
see literature document personal desire as a manifestation of individualism.

Kaita wrote much of his verse about male–male desire around 1913 and
1914, when these transformations were taking place and Hakushū's influence over the literary world was at its height. The young boy to whom much
of this poetry is dedicated is a classmate named Inō Kiyoshi (1897–1989),
a younger schoolmate from the Kyōto Furitsu Daiichi Chūgakkō (Kyoto
Prefectural First Middle School).[24] Over the course of his short life, Kaita
experienced many fleeting attractions to both men and women, but the feelings he bore for Inō played a particularly large role in his emotional life.
Yamamoto Jirō, a close friend from grade school and the editor of one volume of Kaita's posthumous works, writes that Kaita's passion for Inō remained constant until the day of his death.[25] According to Yamamoto, just
hours before Kaita died in February 1919, Kaita stumbled outdoors in a
feverish fit and collapsed on the ground in the cold winter air. After his
friends returned him to his room, he deliriously murmured the names of

Inō Kiyoshi and a female art model Otama whom he had loved from afar. Some time later, after stammering to his friends that they should preserve his artwork and writing, he fell into a dreamlike state, muttered some cryptic phrases, and gave up the ghost. Because Yamamoto Jirō was not present at Kaita's death, this tale is most likely apocryphal. Still, even though one might call into question this anecdote's veracity, it is in keeping with the spirit of the diaries, poems, and letters, which frequently mention the names of people Kaita cared about; more importantly, it helps establish the mythology that grew up around Kaita after his death—the myth of Kaita as an impassioned young man who cared only for beauty.

When Kaita met Inō around 1912, the latter had been in Kyoto only a short time. Inō was a native of Fukui Prefecture, located along the Sea of Japan. He lived there until the age of fifteen when his father, Yasushi, the head of a local hospital, passed away. After that, Inō's mother brought him to Kyoto to enroll him in the same school Kaita attended, hoping Inō would eventually continue to his father's alma mater, Tokyo Imperial University.[26] Inō, who was a year younger than Kaita, was well known as a bishōnen at school, and he had unusually fine and delicate features that inspired passion in the hearts of many students, including Kaita.[27] This infatuation gave birth to a number of artworks, including a watercolor painted around 1913 that now ranks among Kaita's most famous paintings. Yamamoto Jirō has written that Inō had a "beautiful yet cool countenance that reminded one of da Vinci's *Mona Lisa.*" In a hyperbolic flourish, he states, "the visage of this young man would be lodged in all of Kaita's artwork, and his poetry would be exclusively given over to extolling his beauty."[28] Elsewhere, Yamamoto writes that Kaita was romantic, and "exactly like Keats, he released his dissatisfaction with reality in the mythological past, letting his fantasies run wild and becoming intoxicated to his heart's desire with dreams."[29] These fantasies worked their way into his artwork, providing Kaita with poetic and artistic inspiration.

As Yamamoto hints, Kaita's works do not typically represent Inō just as he was; instead, they present elaborate fantasies inspired by him. Even in Kaita's diary, which one might expect to be less overtly poetic than the poetry itself, the visions of Inō that appear are lyrical and cerebral in nature. For example, the entry from November 12, 1913, represents Inō less as an actual person than as a romanticized object of beauty. He describes an experiment in physics class in which students used a prism to bend light: "The beauty of the sunlight passing through the prism—purple, yellow, red—was

Watercolor portrait of Inō Kiyoshi painted around 1913 by Murayama Kaita. Inō was the inspiration for much of Kaita's amorous poetry written around this same time. Collection of the Shinano Drawing Museum. Photo copyright Fukushima Prefectural Art Museum and Mie Prefectural Art Museum 1997.

incredibly vivid, and I couldn't help feeling as if the sunlight, colorless and colored at the same time, was divine. 'Prism' would truly be a fitting name for you, Inō" (342).

The extent to which Kaita has romanticized his feelings is especially clear in the accounts of his nocturnal visits to Inō's home. The same day Kaita's teacher showed the prism, Kaita's diary reveals he wandered from his home on Teramachi Avenue to a hill near Inō's house just to gaze longingly at his home: "From the fields where the rice stalks were cut and piled up, I heard the distant, red sound of a flute. In front of your house, a friend called out to me 'Murayama,' and my heart trembled. / That exalted laugh of yours flooded from your home, together with the light burning inside" (342).[30] Another passage in Kaita's diary, from November 19, 1913, presents an account of a similar midnight trip to Inō's home:

On the river embankment, I saw the light in the eastern sky. Sensing the moon would probably appear, I told myself I would climb Mt. Yoshida and go to Kaguraoka. The moon was just rising over the lights decorating the surface of the city below. There was not a thing in sight that was not beautiful. I rested for a while at Munetada Shrine, intoxicated with the beauty of the landscape. Afterward, I looked down over your home, Inō, and was overcome with emotion.

Toward twelve o'clock, everything fell quiet. The stars were shining in the sky like specks of light reflecting on the sea. The moon was out, and my longing grew as hard as a jewel. A bell sounded in a temple or shrine. I lingered a few moments longer, looking down at the lake below your home and thinking of the song "Moonlight." Ah, how much I long for you! (343)

Yamamoto Jirō attributes the highly cerebral, imaginative element of Kaita's attraction to the fact that the two boys spent minimal time together in school and had little actual chance to get to know each other: "Kaita's contact with the young boy never consisted of more than two or three meaningless conversations of a few words. Nonetheless, the reason his love remained unchanged over the course of several years is that Kaita's romantic fantasies made him have dreams like those of Dante for Beatrice."[31] Yamamoto's desire to eulogize Kaita as an artistic and poetic visionary leads him to downplay the amount of physical contact between Kaita and Inō. It is true the two spoke little at school, but Kaita's friend Yamazaki Shōzō recalls that after Inō (whom he calls "Y") came to Tokyo in 1915, the two resumed contact.

> About that time, I heard from Y (who was living in Satakehara; Y was Kaita's *chigo-san* since their days in Kyoto) that when Kaita would commute back and forth between Tabata and the Nihon Bijutsuin, he would always stop by and pounce upon Y.
>
> I heard Y would ask, "What do you want?" and Kaita would respond, "Just let me hold you—just for a moment. That's all," then Kaita would give Y's cheek a lick.[32]

The word *chigo-san*, which Yamazaki uses to describe Inō's relationship vis-à-vis Kaita, comes from the word *chigo*, which historically refers to young pages serving Buddhist priests or older warriors—figures associated with male–male desire in the popular imagination of the pre-Restoration period. *Chigo* sometimes became the objects of their masters' affections, and numerous texts describe the passions felt for a particularly attractive acolyte or page. By the fifteenth century *chigo* were the subject of a growing body of texts known as *chigo monogatari* (tales of acolytes), which described male–male desire in religious settings and which consistently place the *chigo* in the position of the object of affection. In many cases, these tales describe an older priest's fascination for a lovely, adolescent *chigo*, who sometimes helps lead his admirer to enlightenment.[33] In the twentieth century, the word continued to appear in non-erotic contexts to identify adolescent boys associated with temples or shrines, but schoolboys often used it to refer to a younger boy loved by another older male. This word retained this connotation through at least the 1930s or early 1940s, when Iwata Jun'ichi noted in a guide to terms associated with male–male desire that the word *chigo* commonly referred to *"nanshoku shōnen,"* or youths involved in age-graded erotic relationships with other men.[34]

### THE AESTHETICS OF LONGING

Approximately half of Kaita's poetic output dates from 1913 and 1914, and a significant percentage of it addresses someone identified only as *kimi* ("you" or "thou") but who matches the description of Inō Kiyoshi. The poet Takahashi Mutsuo states a common opinion when he writes that among Kaita's poems "the ones that stand independently and sparkle as poetic creations are concentrated in the years 1913 and 1914 when Kaita's feelings of love for Inō were at their peak."³⁵ One reason for the appeal of these works is their use of lush, aesthetic language to express romantic feelings. Given the enormous influence of Hakushū in poetic circles, as well as Kaita's familial connections to Hakushū, it is perhaps no surprise much of Kaita's early writing borrows the stylistic touches seen in Hakushū's writing.³⁶ Instead of describing the bodily or facial appearance of the beloved himself, the poems employ less direct means to reveal the narrator's state of mind, such as providing elaborate descriptions of the surroundings or the feelings the beloved inspires. Also, Kaita's atmospheric descriptions often involve rich imagery such as one finds in the poetry of Hakushū's symbolist-inspired experiments: jewels, color-laden skies, fireworks, sunsets, and languorously sobbing instruments.

*Aoiro haien,* one of his handmade anthologies from about 1913, was dedicated to Inō, whom Kaita had nicknamed "the prince." Like many anthologies of poetry from the time, including Hakushū's *Jashūmon,* the collection begins with verse that gives a taste of what will follow:

## THE RUINED GARDEN IN GREEN

> *These poems are dedicated to my friend,*
> *the helpless and pretty youth whom I shall call "the prince"*

I long in earnest for extravagance—
For the extravagance of sipping alcohol in a garden
Where one is overcome by a feeling
Like the aroma of green plums (17)

The image of hard, unripe, green plums with an inviting fragrance suggests an undeveloped rawness not unlike that of an adolescent youth who has not quite reached the peak of maturity. With its intense yearning for sensual, indulgent pleasures beyond the narrator's reach, the poem sets a tone of longing appropriate to a collection of poems about unrequited love.

The image of the ruined or abandoned garden *(haien)* central to this introductory poem appears in a large number of other poems by Kaita. Numerous classical Japanese texts, such as *Ise monogatari (Tales of Ise),* which dates from around the twelfth century, use the image of ruined gardens, usually in descriptions of the domiciles of women living without male support, but Hakushū had used this image far more recently to express an emotional state in the famous forty-seventh poem in his series "Danshō" (Fragments):

> Down the light rain comes, down it comes
> Over the green of the abandoned garden
> Singing faintly as it falls
> Oh poppy flowers, poppy flowers,
> Softly shall you burn . . . [37]

Here, the abandoned garden, full of verdant overgrowth, is charged with romantic overtones. This poem forms the first of a sub-sequence about the narrator's feelings for the wife of another man, and the abandoned garden serves as a setting for this secret passion. Hakushū was not the first poet associated with symbolism to use the image of the ruined garden. Miki Rofū had helped to reintroduce it into the poetical lexicon with his anthology *Haien* (The ruined garden) of 1909. In a poem "Sariyuku gogatsu no shi" (A poem for departing May) included in this collection, Rofū used the image of an unkempt garden near his home in Zoshigaya, Tokyo, to express his melancholic feelings regarding the rapid passing of youth.[38]

Rofū's *Haien* represented a pioneering experiment in colloquial free verse and attracted significant attention at the time of its publication. In place of the metered lines found in Ōgai's poetic translations, Rofū incorporates extended tracts of language that closely resemble the unstructured rhythmic patterns and colloquial grammar of conversational speech, but he does not abandon literary language entirely. In 1914 Kaita followed in the footsteps of Rofū experimenting with the use of spoken language in his work by incorporating extended passages of Kyoto dialect in his poems. One such poem is "Nigiyaka na yūgure" (A lively evening), which is dedicated to Inō and describes one of the mile-long nocturnal voyages to Inō's house from Kaita's home along Teramachi Avenue to Kaguraoka, the hilly area where Inō lived on the far side of the Kamo River:

> "A lively evening, isn't it?
> Really full of life, don't you think?"
> On this pale blue, deep evening,
> What is so lively? What?
>
> The beautiful sky over the eastern mountains,
> The stars like a purple globe of rain
> In the drunken vernal sky over the hills
> Shine purple and light red like specks of hardened blood

"So lively, don't you think?"
A group of ladies arrive,
A wanton crowd, a line of jewels,
Their lovely white make-up shines in the dusk

Lights, lights, lights along the Kamo riverbanks
Shine in gold, the arc lamps cherry pink
"Really lively, isn't it?
A lovely night, don't you think?"

Drops of spirits fall steadily
From my thistle-shaped nerves
Alongside my footsteps as I spring along
The elegant lavender hem of Kaguraoka

"Lively, isn't it?"
Pleased at my response
The lovely ladies, so numerous, reply,
"Yes, indeed . . ."

"A lively evening, isn't it?
Really full of life, don't you think?
How lovely of late
Is the beautiful child for whom I yearn . . ."

As I descend Konoezaka Slope, I see the lavender
Plain of heaven reflected on the surface of the lake
The faint echoes of a silver flute
Trickle from the window of my beloved's home

"A lively evening, isn't it?
Really full of life, don't you think?"
With my unrequited love, I weep as I whisper,
"Yes, but how terribly lonely I am!" (42–43)

In the original, all the passages in quotes are in the dialect used by women of the Gion district pleasure quarters. The first two lines of the poem (*Nigiyaka na yūgure ya ohen ka / Honma ni nigiyaka ya ohen ka*), which give the poem its title and recurring refrain, represent the greeting of a group of courtesans or female entertainers whom the narrator encounters while strolling through the eastern part of the city. In the next to last stanza, the narrator imitates their feminine language to voice his own thoughts about the "beautiful one" for whom he yearns. In doing so, he adopts a stock role in the Japanese literary imagination, namely that of a desiring courtesan doomed to unrequited love by her station in life. Through this act of "narrative drag," the narrator assumes a role instantly recognizable to contemporary readers, and he gives voice to his own sad longings in a way that involves play across perceived boundaries of gender. Juxtaposed with these vernacular phrases is the aestheticized language that characterized Japanese poetry written under the influence of symbolism. The narrator paints an impressionistic picture of the city, relying heavily on descriptions of the evening sky and landscape to set the mood. At times, the sky is cool, dusky, beautiful, and quiet. At others, the light of the stars in the "drunken, vernal sky" *(sakebitari no haru no sora)* is compared to "hardened blood" *(chinori),* a simile that brings to mind a spattering of dark red stars across the heavens. The use of the images of reflected stars, silver flutes, and sobs of unrequited love reveal the degree to which Kaita romanticized these sentiments, transforming them into highly aestheticized poetry.[39]

In 1913 Kaita dedicated another highly romanticized poem, "Murasaki no mijin" (A fine purple dust), to "Inō no kimi" (You, my lord Inō). In this dedication, Kaita plays off the dual meanings of the word *kimi,* namely the second-person pronoun "you" and the original meaning of "lord" or "ruler":

A fine purple dust, my affection
Scatters over the blue heaven of autumn's end,
Dispelled in elegant fireworks
Over pale blue mountains and the vernal sky

A fine purple dust, my love
Seeks to catch you
Falling like a fountain or spray of pollen
Elegantly over your heart

As this fine purple dust entwines about you
You shine gaudily,
A jewel set in the heavens
With its faces veiled briefly in haze

A fine purple dust, my heart
Lies strewn over the heaven of autumn's end,
With a lament, it sobs with the skies
As you emerge in a burst of fireworks then hide away

A fine purple dust, my unrequited love
Disperses over you like a rain of crushed glass,
Somewhere, it may capture your love
Yet I ask no more that it be dust, to be beautiful

A fine purple dust, my yearning
Cannot withstand your scintillating form
And I weep, wandering into the lovely
Blue light of autumn's end (52)

This poem revolves around the comparison of the narrator's feelings to a cloud of dust that encircles his beloved but cannot hold him. This poem employs also several motifs popular in romantic poetry, such as the tears in the final stanza and the metaphor likening the narrator's beloved to a jewel. At the same time, there are also distinct touches of symbolist-inspired aestheticism. The use of atmospheric conditions and the extensive use of fanciful signifiers, such as jewels, dust, fireworks, fountains, and other images foreign to the traditional lexicon of Japanese poetry, combine to produce a work describing boyish desire in an idiom that could have been written only after Japan's encounter with symbolist poetry.

The use of landscape to set mood is a common motif in romantic and symbolist poetry. With these movements, landscape was usually presented not as an objective description of the external world but as a carefully crafted environment that served as a projection of the author's singular vision. Verlaine and Baudelaire, the progenitors of many of the motifs that came to dominate symbolist verse, often included shadowy landscapes in their work that seem to be pregnant with personal meaning. Perhaps it should therefore come as no surprise that Kaita, who eagerly read Verlaine's and Baudelaire's poems in *Kaichōon,* would also employ landscape in his earliest work for similarly subjective purposes. One of Kaita's most famous poems, an untitled work written in 1913, also uses atmospheric conditions and landscapes to suggest the effect produced by the beauty of his beloved. Here, however, landscape appears within the context of similes and metaphors instead of the less direct juxtaposition one would likely find in French symbolist poetry:

Ah, he who knows you
Knows spring one month in advance
Your eyes are the vernal sky
Your cheeks, flowering cherries, red as blood
Jewels cover your hands and feet,
Casting the sunlight in dazzling forms

And he who knows you
Knows summer two months in advance
With just a look, one's heart is set aflame,
Burning red as the sun setting over a land of fire
Simply stifled in the maddening heat,
One is driven to madness, wildly searching into eternity

Ah, he who knows you
Knows autumn three months in advance
Such a charming, sweet, and sad countenance
Your lips are hills and fields of cinnabar
Share with me just as they are
The dazzling autumn days in your exalted eyes

And he who knows you
Knows winter four months in advance
In your absence, all eyes fall to the ground,
All things lose light and color
Struck no longer by taste, scent, or sound
All merely waits in earnest for you, for spring to return. (15–16)

The text veers from realism toward high conceptualization or even ab-
stract description; the textual gaze also lingers on *kimi*'s flushed lips, eyes,
and cheeks as if particularly drawn to these erogenous zones. The poem,
in other words, is not completely desexualized. The body serves as the point
of departure for fantasy, and thus physical desire exerts an understated yet
powerful magnetic draw over the narrator. This poem introduces another
common motif in Kaita's work: the prominent use of the passionate color
red. The first stanza likens the addressee's cheeks to cherry blossoms, which
are not the traditional white or pink of the celebrated flower, but the intense hue of blood, thereby imbuing a traditional poetic subject with new,
vital intensity. Later, the sight of the addressee evokes the scarlet sun of a

land of flame, and toward the end, *kimi*'s lips evoke thoughts of an autumn landscape.

The collection of the Mie Kenritsu Bijutsukan (Mie Prefectural Art Museum) includes an early love letter Kaita wrote to an unnamed person, most likely Inō. Known in art historical circles as the "Pinku rabu retā" (Pink love letter), it shows Kaita used the motifs of landscape and the color red to describe his passions even in his personal writing. The letter is written in gray letters on brilliant pink paper and is decorated with disconnected, wavy lines and a small, faint sketch of a person seated by a fountain. Though the heavy watercolors obscure seven characters toward the middle of the letter, the majority of the text is legible:

Oh *kimi*!
Truly I cannot tell you
I am but one person yearning for you
My love is a beautiful electrical water fountain
In red [???????] in silver
Spewing, rising, then raining down
Over the garden of my heart. There in the shade
I suppress my cries of unreciprocated love
The red moon rises faintly
Oh *kimi*! At least try to feel pity
For this longing of mine
(Do not be alarmed at reading this letter
Others can forgive this bad habit of mine
Of writing this sort of thing . . . ) Oh generous *kimi*!
Hide this in the depths of your smile!

Farewell for now.          From the red demon[40]

As elsewhere in Kaita's work, landscape—here a park with an erupting fountain in the center—serves as a metaphor for the narrator's emotions. Halfway through the letter, Kaita begins to imagine himself, like the small figure he drew on the letter itself, within this garden of emotion, lamenting his unrequited love. The red moon, which appears at the edge of the letter, hangs in the sky over the fountain and adds an eerie but lovely touch to this metaphorical garden of passion, cloaked in the night of unreciprocated desire.

The letter is particularly relevant because it reveals how much pleasure Kaita took in his feelings of loneliness and unrequited yearning. Beneath the text, Kaita has written in pale roman letters, *"Chotto kirei deshō"* (Rather lovely, don't you think?), as if particularly pleased with his work. Kaita signs the letter "The Red Demon" *(akaoni)*, coining a sobriquet for himself combining the color red, which frequently appears in his descriptions of intense, passionate feeling, and the word "demon," a creature that in Japanese legend often pursues its own desires with single-minded, animalistic devotion. (This nickname also involves a play on his given name. *Kai* 槐, the first character of his given name, contains on its right side the character *oni* 鬼, meaning "demon.") The signature shows Kaita playfully adopting a decadent, desiring identity similar to that of the narrative persona of his early poetry. Both this letter, which was presumably written with a particular person in mind, and the early amorous poetry describe similar feelings in analogous literary styles. In other words, Kaita appears to have been cultivating the image of himself as a passionate, love-struck poet aching for a beloved who was, ironically, all the more important because of the distance between them.

Two motifs in the letter, namely the fountain and the red moon, also appear prominently in other pseudo-symbolist poetry. It was during the Meiji period that fountains became common fixtures in public parks. In 1877 the government constructed the first fountain in a public space in Tokyo's Ueno Park for the first Domestic Exposition for the Encouragement of Industry in imitation of the European expositions, which often placed large fountains in public squares. Within about two decades, a number of major parks throughout Japan had large fountains, but they still maintained an image of European modernity and sophistication that made them appropriate symbols for the poetry of authors like Kitahara Hakushū, who dreamed of places like the Tuileries in Paris.[41] "Fukiage no inshō" (Impressions of a fountain), written in July 1908 and included in *Jashūmon*, contains one such image of a fountain in a melancholy park. The first stanza suffices to give a taste of the languorous tone: "The fountain's slow dripping—/ The depths of a misty park, the light of the setting sun / The yellow murmur of the basin / All, now / The color of a sweet sigh."[42] Another poem, "Kōen no usugure" (Dusk in the park), the first in Hakushū's 1913 anthology *Tōkyō keibutsu shi oyobi sono ta* (Scenes of Tokyo and other poems), also describes a park with a fountain in an artfully melancholic tone much like the pink love letter. Finally, the motif of the red moon, which hangs with such bittersweet melancholy over the park in Kaita's letter, resembles the moon that appears in the fifty-first poem of "Danshō" in the anthology *Omoide:* "Red crescent moon, / Red crescent moon / Today again lying in bed / Your child blows his toy silver flute / How peaceful is his play!"[43] Kaita's use of these Hakushūesque motifs makes it clear he was borrowing new poetic trends to give voice to his own amorous longing.

## HINTS OF HISTORY, BATHS OF BLOOD

Although he often borrows the sorts of metaphors and language used in Japanese symbolism, Kaita's early work about love between men also often involves historical motifs, especially motifs having to do with ancient Japan, an era that fascinated Kaita. For instance, "Chi no koshō" (Pageboy of the blood), one of Kaita's best-known works, evokes the past in a poem describing a pageboy's love for his warrior-master who has recently been killed:

> Oh, beautiful pageboy
> Of the butchered noble!
> Oh, pageboy who stares with such intensity
> At the dripping blood of your master shining
> As it trickles and trails forth, red and gold, red and gold!
>
> Night has come
> Here on this deserted, merciless eve
> Someone begins to weep
> Yes, oh pageboy of the maddened blood,
> You too weep . . . You, beloved by the blood! (26)

In the Muromachi and Edo periods, *koshō* (pageboys) were young warriors who attended to the demands of their older masters and sometimes became the object of their affections and perhaps even their sexual partners. In the poem, the attendant stares at the trickling blood of his fallen master. In a macabre touch, the narrator interprets the shining scarlet blood flowing slowly from his master's corpse as a final expression of love for the pageboy beside him. This poem represents a departure from Kaita's tendency to describe amorous feelings, especially male–male attraction, in the first person. Here, the love draws on a specific historical paradigm of male–male desire, namely the bond of servitude and affection that might have existed between a warrior and his pageboy in the pre-Meiji past, and reverses the power dynamics implicit within it. The poet Takahashi Mutsuo has speculated, however, that although this poem is set in a time far removed from the Taishō period in which Kaita was living, it is probably not completely unrelated to

Kaita's own life. He speculates that Kaita, who suffered under a powerful love Inō did not reciprocate, may have imagined himself as the deceased lord and Inō as the page. The master's wounds, he argues, represent the "wounds" Inō has inflicted with his indifference, and the blood pouring forth symbolizes the passion Kaita poured into his letters and artwork, even though they evoked no response from Inō.[44] By insinuating a connection between himself and a fallen lord, Kaita presents himself as a hero slain for love.

The more clearly autobiographical poem "Chi ni shimite" (Stained in blood), which dates from about the same time, uses a similar image of streaming blood as a metaphor for passion and might provide evidence for Takahashi's interpretation. The poem, which appears as the fourth work after the introduction to *Aoiro haien,* was almost certainly one of the poems in the anthology dedicated to Inō:

> Stained in blood, I yearn for you
> On this May afternoon
> My red heart trembles
> Within my pathetic body
>
> In this abandoned garden which knows no end
> In this extravagant month of May
> When your shape stands before me
> Single-minded, I am no more
>
> My blood has run dry
> And I think I shall die
> I wish to dispose of you, so splendid and cruel of heart,
> And die stained in blood (19)

*Kimi,* to whom the poem is addressed, is described as beautiful yet cruelly indifferent, and the narrator yearns to escape his grip. The declaration of his wish to achieve this end through death is not a sincere expression of he intention to commit suicide but a fantasy demonstrating the extent of the author's melodramatic passion. The narrator's psychological suffering leads him to think of physical wounds, and the fantasy of a sanguine death serves as a metaphor for his distress.

As these poems show, in Kaita's eyes the beauty of bishōnen represented a magnificent and mysterious vision that led to the decadent and self-indulgent emotion he celebrated in his poems. The connection between youthful, male beauty and powerful emotion is particularly visible in an untitled poem from 1913 that floridly describes the poignant "music of decadence":

Oh, this is the sound of pleasure, still not fading,
In the dawn of a beautiful new world of poets . . . !
The deep, ceaselessly trembling emotion
In the windpipe of a male "him"

Oh beautiful, decadent sound
Of pleasure that shall never fade . . . !
It may dissipate if we drink the bloodstained wine
But it will come again, in the remnants of exhaustion

The sky lets fall raindrops that blanch
In the morning light of June
Oh, beautiful pale blue!
In it, I already see the passion of noon

Oh, beautiful, deep music
Which does not escape into eternity!
Oh, music of decadence which knows no day or night!
As you tremble so lightly, you invite unbearable pain (32)

Both in tone and choice of metaphor, this poem echoes Hakushū's statements in the introduction to *Jashūmon* that the truly sensitive poet is "enamored with the pleasure of barely audible music" and yearns "for the red of putrefying decadence" as he faces "the mysterious" and "rejoices in visions."[45] Like Hakushū, Kaita uses the metaphor of music to describe the subtle emotions that arise from suggestive images and symbols—emotions that only sensitive individuals can detect—and in his vocabulary "decadence" (*taihai*) refers to the indulgent celebration of one's emotions. The beautiful music of decadence, he announces, is audible in the work of the new generation of poets who passionately extol their feelings, and Kaita, who recognizes this music, implicitly positions himself as their spiritual kindred—one of a vanguard of artistic visionaries who would reshape modern poetry. In the final lines of the first stanza, he locates one source of this music in the trembling windpipe (*nodobue*, literally "throat flute") of a "him"—a slang word for a boyfriend. This comment shows Kaita saw amorous appreciation of men as one source of the intense, powerful emotion he valued so greatly.

## THE DESIRING PERSONA IN KAITA'S TANKA

Kaita was also the author of a large number of tanka, a short form of traditional Japanese poetry that has a history dating back over twelve hundred years. His complete works include 115 tanka from 1913 and 1914, the same years he composed his most often anthologized *shi*. (This is almost half of the total number of tanka he is known to have produced.) The fact Kaita became interested in tanka is entirely in keeping with his highly romantic tendencies and grandiose artistic inspirations. During the late Meiji period, the female poet Yosano Akiko had helped refashion this ancient form of poetry into a vehicle for powerful romantic expression with the intense evocations of amorous and erotic desire in her 1901 anthology *Midaregami (Tangled Hair)*, and a few years later Ishikawa Takuboku (1886–1912), the author of the influential collections *Suna no ichiaku (A Fistful of Sand, 1910)* and *Kanashiki gangu (Sad Toys, 1912)*, gave the form new life by breaking the tanka into multiple lines and using direct and unadorned imagery that frequently departs from the traditional poetic lexicon.[46] Many of Takuboku's poems describe heartache, disappointment, a sense of life's futility, and the intensity of momentary sensations. Although Akiko's and Takuboku's works elicited significant controversy, they were both quickly recognized as geniuses and helped contribute to a sense that tanka was the verse form of choice for artistic innovators and visionaries. For a young writer such as Kaita, who was preoccupied with cultivating his own sensitivity and developing his own abilities as an artist, the decision to write tanka seems a natural one. (No doubt Kaita would have been pleased to find that Yosano Akiko was quite taken with the posthumous collection of his work. Several newspaper advertisements for Kaita's work contain a blurb from her that extols, "Mr. Kaita's art is a tremendous marvel. I believe he is the first completely decadent poet to have been born in Japan."[47]) Although Kaita's poems are heavily colored with Akiko's almost obsessive romanticism and Takuboku's dejection, what makes Kaita's tanka unlike those of his contemporaries is their liberal use of symbolist motifs and strikingly imaginative metaphors. Critic Tamaki Tōru's study of early twentieth-century tanka argues Kaita's tanka were nothing short of groundbreaking. He comments they, along with the tanka of the writer Akutagawa Ryūnosuke, display a powerful, imaginative individualism that offered an alternative to the "realism of lonely Japanese people" that dominated mainstream Japanese tanka in subsequent decades.[48]

Most tanka from Kaita's schooldays describe feelings similar to those in his longer poetry: the yearning of a desiring, dejected lover whose ceaseless admiration for his beloved leads him to self-indulgent melancholia. Nonetheless, a handful of key poems show he took particular pleasure in playing this role. Judging from the dedications and theme headings, Inō provided the inspiration for a large number of tanka, but many describe him within highly romanticized terms, often as a "prince" or a "lord" who seems to have stepped right from the pages of classical literature. For instance, the following verse dates from 1913:

You, whom I call my
Lovely prince of flowering quince,
Watching you
All the daylong
Is more than I can bear

[*Utsukushii boke no ōji to imyō seru kimi wo hinemosu miru ga taesenu*]
(159)[49]

This poem, like a number of others, plays with the two possible meanings of *kimi:* the affectionate second-person pronoun meaning "you" and the root meaning of "lord," or one who bears princely or regal status. By calling the referent *kimi,* this poem evokes both senses of the word simultaneously, creating a poem that resembles what an amorous courtier might have sent to a beloved prince in the age of the classical court. The narrator has christened him the "prince" of *Chaenomeles lagenaria,* an ornamental quince *(boke)* that produces white or pinkish flowers in the spartan cold of early spring.

While it is clear the passionate, dejected but determined longing of the narrator of these poems corresponds in some degree to Kaita's own feelings, his poetry contains a certain amount of romantic role-playing, as does the verse of Yosano Akiko and other late Meiji poets who wrote on romantic love. For instance, a diary entry written November 19, 1913, soon after Kaita met Inō, describes the first time he passed a poem to the younger boy:

Today, out of mere caprice, I wrote the following poem and passed it to you in the side yard.

When I think
With all the world

Of you, Inō,
How my tears fall
With the rain!

*[Yo o komete Inō no kimi o omou toki namida wa ame to furinikeru ka na]*

As a result, when I met you watching a baseball game after class, you
blushed bright red, and I felt quite sorry for you. (343)

Kaita's statement that he wrote the poem just for fun *(tawamure ni)* suggests
he was adopting the role of a lovesick courtier merely on a whim. If so,
the poems should not be read as a transparent record of Kaita's feelings,
but as imaginative literature colored by fantasy. It is clear, however, the encounter in the schoolyard did spur Kaita's imagination. That night he made
one of his many nocturnal peregrinations to Kaguraoka to the home of the
young boy, and the next day, he gave eight more tanka to Inō, who quickly
put them in his pocket. In a hyperbolic flourish, Kaita's diary states that as
the boy took them, Kaita's eyes "overflowed with tears of gratitude" (343).
The diary does not tell us which eight poems he gave to Inō; it includes only
one poem, which was probably composed after their encounter:

I have started falling in love
With beautiful you
Who comes into existence
Congealing from the purple smoke
Of an incense burner

*[Murasaki no kōro no kebu no korite narishi utsukushiki kimi o
omoisomekeri]* (343)

Although the expression of budding love may accurately reflect Kaita's feelings of blossoming love, the genie-like image of his lover appearing out of
a waft of smoke is a fanciful product created by combining the love-struck
tone of late Meiji tanka and the exotic imagery of Japanese symbolism. The
result is a richly brocaded, aestheticized tanka poem narrated from the point
of a view of a young man whose feelings are almost decadently strong.

One recurring element of his amorous tanka is the decadent tendency
to treat the love object as a rich vision of beauty. The following poem from
1913 provides an example:

It is an opulent
Person whom I adore,
As opulent
As the color of
That Western wine

[*Yutaka naru hito o koso konome seiō no kano budōshu no iro no gotoku ni*] (159)

The phrase *yutaka naru* (meaning opulent, rich, ample, or abundant) could be describing either the physical or spiritual characteristics of the one whom the narrator loves. The narrator may be saying he prefers someone as abundantly full of life as wine is rich in color, or someone who is physically ample, with a body as splendid as wine. The simile in this poem recalls Hakushū's early poetry and Kaita's introductory poem to *Aoiro haien,* both of which use images of alcohol to evoke a fin-de-siècle air of decadent intensity. The desiring persona does not find himself unwittingly admiring such visions of beauty; instead, he embraces them. One poem from around 1913 describes the satisfaction the narrator experiences as he thinks about the person he has become under *kimi*'s influence:

Looking back upon
Myself as a child
Who bore this dissipation
All because of you
Has made me happy

[*Kimi yue ni kono hōratsu o seou ko to ware o mikaeri ureshiku narinu*] (160)

The narrator reflects that when he thinks about the "dissipated" or even "licentious" *(hōratsu)* person he has been, he experiences satisfaction, simply because *kimi* was the cause.

Another side to the desiring, "decadent" persona in Kaita's poetry is that of the lover who, like Goethe's Werther, is so consumed with longing that the slightest rejection sends him into utter despair. For instance, the following tanka from 1913 describes this misery:

In this world
Dispatching dull

Gray days every day
The misery I feel,
All alone . . .

[*Nibiiro no higoro o okuru sekai ni wa tada hitori no ware no awaresa*]
(161)

In his loneliness, the narrator experiences time as a never-ending string of
monotonous, gray days. Other poems comment self-reflexively on the narrator's position as the dejected lover:

Do not
Think of me with pity
Not I, the ruffian,
Who spends
Every day hated

[*Nikumarete higoro o okuru buraiko no ware o aware to omoitamau na*]
(161)

This poem probably addresses the same person as the poem that immediately follows, given the similarity in tone:

Oh, you, you . . .
Simply hate me in earnest
This way
All the more light
Will fall upon you

[*Kimi yo kimi tada hitasura ni ware o nikume kakute kimi ni wa hikari
mashinamu*] (161)

Both poems have a passive-aggressive tone that reveals the irritable side of
the infatuated lover. In rejecting the addressee's pity in the first poem, the
narrator insinuates he really wants something more. In the second, he tells
the addressee to go ahead and scorn him as that will amplify the distance
that separates them, making *kimi* look even better.

A number of the works Kaita wrote about this time contain clear hints
of erotic desire. Lips often appear as the focal point of this desire, as in the

poem that begins "Ah, he who knows you" quoted previously. The following example of a tanka on a similar motif was written in 1913:

Thinking of the touch
Of your lips my thoughts
Are thrown into disarray
How I long
For beautiful you!

*[Kuchitsuke o omoite omoi midarekeri utsukushiki kimi ika ni omou ya]* (161)

The erotic desire in this poem, which centers on the thought of a kiss between narrator and addressee, is all the more pronounced when read in the wake of the tanka immediately preceding it:

I think of luring you
In the coming spring
And seizing you
In the evening darkness
Of the Shogun's Mound

*[Komu haru wa kimi o izanai yoiyami no shōgun-zuka ni idakan to omou]* (160)

The "Shogun's Mound" *(shōgun-zuka)* was a hillock in the detached grounds of Seiren'in Temple in the hills of eastern Kyoto. This spot, named for a statue of a general said to have been erected there in the late eighth century, is higher than the surrounding land and provides a view of the city streets and Mount Hiei; however, it also offered enough privacy for erotic encounters. The mound was only a short walk from Inō's home in Kaguraoka, and so it makes sense Kaita imagined it as a possible place for a tryst.

### THE ARTISTIC EROTICA

The poems Kaita wrote after moving to Tokyo in mid-1914 to become an art student display less literary pretension than the earlier poetry written in Kyoto. Many of these new poems, which he probably never intended to circulate, describe the narrator's desire to become a great artist. Of the poems about art, the majority are concerned with the theme of confidence—either the narrator's utter lack or abundance thereof. With dizzying rapidity, the poems swing between the two extremes of despair and narcissistic self-congratulation. When one reads them without accounting for their flights of fancy or poetic hyperbole, the portrait that emerges is one of a manically depressed young artist, given to fits of frenzied production and outbursts of emotion—a view that does not always match friends' accounts that describe Kaita as pensive and reserved. Meanwhile, homoerotic desire takes a back seat as a theme.

One notable exception comes from 1915, when Kaita wrote three of his most homoerotic tanka, but unfortunately, these poems were marred when the editors at Ars attempted to protect the book from government censors. Well before the Taishō period, the Japanese government had in place a system of censorship designed to suppress material having to do with eroticism or political movements the government considered dangerous. As a general rule, government censors examined books, newspapers, and magazines *after* publication, and if they were found objectionable, the censors would require publishers to pull the offending work from circulation. As a result, a ban could have dire financial consequences for a publisher who had already put forth the money required to print the work in question. In order to avoid such losses, publishers resorted to a system of self-censorship in which editors anticipated potentially problematic words or passages, then used *fuseji*—blocked-out characters, usually an X, O, or a square—to hide them. Each of the following tanka contains *fuseji* concealing references to something erotic, almost certainly the male genitalia:

Staring long and hard
At ▪▪▪▪,
As my eyes glitter,
My heart
Is refreshed

[▪▪▪▪ *o jitto mitsumete waga medama kagayakeba kokoro sugasuga shikari*]

The male model's
Pointed
▪▪▪▪
Is so beautiful
I saw it in my dreams

*[Togaritaru otoko moderu no* ▪▪▪▪ *wa yume ni mishi hodo utsukushikariki]*

The hair of
▪▪▪▪ so resembles
▪▪▪▪▪▪
Of ▪▪—
How beautiful!

*[*▪▪▪▪ *no ke wa samo nitari* ▪▪ *no* ▪▪▪▪▪▪ *ni utsukushiki kana]* (167)[50]

These poems apparently drew their inspiration from the sight of a nude male model, whom he likely encountered at the Nihon Bijutsuin. (In 1917 and 1918, he did produce occasional sketches and paintings of nude men, making it clear he did encounter male models at school.) In the first two poems, Kaita treats homoerotic desire in relatively unadorned language, as if breaking from the highly romantic and effusive imagery of his earliest tanka. At the same time, however, the poems show an interest in parts of the body that, as the *fuseji* show, were not considered appropriate for polite conversation.

Another unusually straightforward poem about male–male desire is a long and relatively prosaic poem from 1915, "Densha no naka no gunjin ni" (To soldiers in a train). In it, the narrator describes how his feelings of self-doubt and dissatisfaction about his artwork are brought into high relief when he encounters a handful of powerful, attractive soldiers in a train. This poem was probably never meant for public consumption; instead, it appears to have been written as a private meditation helping the struggling artist work through his own feelings about his art:

My train moves forward
Outside are the magnificent fields and skies of May
The train flies through the outskirts of Tokyo
I am aboard one of the bogie cars I adore

The car is full of terrifyingly ugly people
Including five or six men kneaded out of the country mud
Who take unnatural, theatrical poses
Also there is a female foreigner speaking Japanese
Holding her albino-like child who screams and cries

A whole row of the color of shit, pimples, rancid fat
Foul breath, the ignorant imbeciles—Together they crowd this train
Together with the wrinkled face of a woman worn from wantonness

Suddenly, I bolt up—In the healthy menace of
Two officers by my side
What beauty!

Our warriors, strong men of the yellow race,
I sing my praises to you!
Your muscular countenances and attitudes
Elevate my rotten, degraded heart

Oh, soldiers, oh soldiers!
I have a memory of drawing a trifling picture
My dissatisfaction and regret over it make me weep
I am on edge, smeared with ash

Even though you do not speak, how your pride sparkles!
Oh khaki-clad officers of the infantry!
To you the study of art must mean nothing
With one shot, you could take my life in an instant

Ah! How I envy you! How jealous I am!
You have no dissatisfaction about paintings
Though I am silent, I do. I am neurotic, I am a fool
Whereas you glitter like a diamond with magnificent energy

I have become sad
But just look! I will shine like you!
Like your sword shining at your waist
My pride will be sure to shine forth

Oh, train! Go, go, go faster still!
I too will go
Not losing to these glorious soldiers,
I will go into the glorious heavens and show you all

Foolish idiots!
Oh, ▪ with dangling swords! Oh, auspicious defender of the empire!
What are you bragging about?
You, new conscript ▪▪s! (63–64)

The narrator's attraction to the soldiers clearly borders on the homoerotic. Unlike the attraction described in the poems about Inō, his attraction is not in response to physical beauty but the power they represent and their complete freedom from the kinds of concerns that dog him. The fourth to tenth stanzas describe the soldiers as an embodiment of a strong and vital force that stands in contrast to the weak, countrified, distracted people elsewhere. When the narrator sees the soldiers' beautiful, muscular faces and masculine demeanor, he reads in them the authority and strength he lacks. The narrator is quick to note that with their guns, the soldiers embody the institutionalized potential for violence keeping order throughout the Japanese empire, and alongside this power, his artistic difficulties seem insignificant. Interestingly, this admiration gives way to a volte-face, and the narrator begins deriding them, having recognized them as little more than ordinary men with flashy uniforms and big swords. The final paragraph contains three *fuseji*, which block out two words editors imagined censors might see as unpatriotic or even potentially seditious.[51] Ultimately, Kaita's poem should not be read as an expression of nationalist sentiment; if anything, it seems to say that in his eyes, while the military hero may be powerful, the power of the artistic genius is even greater.

## SHAPES OF DESIRE

Apart from the notable exception "Chi no koshō," with its depiction of an attractive youth alongside his dead lover, Kaita's poetry from the early 1910s tends to avoid terms that lock him into a particular codification of desire, such as the age-graded *shudō* of the Edo period. Likewise, it does not describe male–male desire within the framework of the predatory, tough, and misogynistic brand of "hard" masculinity that often appears in descriptions of schoolboy relations in the late nineteenth and early twentieth centuries. The avoidance of these particular codifications permits the expression of desire ungoverned by overt hierarchies in the social status. The result is some of the first descriptions in Japanese literature of schoolboy love that emphasize affection and attraction between schoolmates who are more or less equals on the social ladder. Moreover, Kaita portrays this relatively egalitarian attraction in highly aestheticized terms, as if to further emphasize the break between older age-graded relationships, which were so thoroughly governed by hierarchies of power. Love between young men, he seems to say, deserved a new language that would convey its directness and power— a language Kaita discovered in the styles, similes, and imagery of symbolism.

Though the narrators in the works do not ascend to the kinds of stock roles one sees in pre-twentieth-century representations of male–male desire, they do not break from tradition entirely; the consistent use of the bishōnen as aestheticized object of desire shows continuity with earlier formulations of desire. By fixing their gaze on the figure of the beloved, the texts adopt the characteristic stance of much Edo-period and Meiji-period popular discourse on male–male sexuality, which describes the youth more as an object to be appreciated and less as desiring subject in his own right. Never in these poems do we find more than a passing sign of the bishōnen's own desires; never is the narrative voice that of a bishōnen yearning for another male to seduce him.

If Kaita does adopt any role in his writing, it is a new image of the artist who wallows in emotion and experiences sensations to their fullest, savoring them in order to feed his own sensitive mind—an image closely tied to the sensitivity that Japanese symbolists saw as so crucial to their movement. As mentioned above, one relatively consistent theme throughout his earliest writing is the connection between aesthetic and erotic attraction and powerful, even "decadent" emotion—a theme that recurs in the writings of Taruho and even contemporary manga. Like Hakushū, who sought out unusual and exotic "visions" that would help stimulate his artistry, Kaita turned to the beauty of young boys to experience the kind of romantic emotion he associated with poetry and art. As the poems translated above suggest, he specifically cultivated his own feelings toward bishōnen, shaping them with the aesthetic language of symbolism in order to produce his writing. Although the resulting poetry is sometimes almost excessively dramatic, it reveals profoundly personal and sensitive moments. The relationship between the appreciation of male beauty, "decadent" emotion, and the quest for artistic vision apparent in these poems is particularly pronounced in "Bishōnen Saraino no kubi," a short, poetic prose work Kaita wrote in late 1913 or early 1914. It is therefore to this and other prose works that the next chapter turns.

# 2

## Treading the Edges of the Known World

*Homoerotic Fantasies in Murayama Kaita's Prose*

OVER THE COURSE OF HIS LIFE, Kaita wrote a number of works in prose. Just during his days as a schoolboy in Kyoto, he produced a half-dozen stories and plays. Although many are not polished or particularly refined, others display the visionary and even hallucinogenic qualities present in his poetry. Male–male desire features prominently in at least three works from his schoolboy days: the short story "Bishōnen Saraino no kubi" ("The Bust of the Beautiful Young Salaino"), the incomplete but sophisticated novella "Tetsu no dōji" (Children of iron), and the incomplete play "Shuten Dōji" (The saké-drinking youth). Although these works are in different genres, they share a number of characteristics. First, like Kaita's poems, they treat male beauty as a source of powerful emotions and intense vitality. Second, they are all extremely imaginative and, in some cases, overtly hallucinogenic. Third, they show a connection between powerful emotion and "decadent" images, such as frighteningly beautiful gorgons, murderous urges, and scenes of death, which anticipate the kinds of motifs that appear in Kaita's mystery-adventure stories. Fourth, they associate male–male desire and the intense emotions it brings with settings outside the ordered world of civilization.

The association between male–male desire and a position on the fringes of ordinary civilization is a theme Kaita picked up in the stories he wrote in 1914 and 1915. As mentioned in the previous chapter, most of Kaita's work was published posthumously, but the notable exceptions are a handful of stories he published in the adventure magazines *Bōken sekai* (World of adventure) and *Bukyō sekai* (World of heroism) to make some money to support himself. Although these works were written primarily for financial reasons, Edogawa Ranpo praised these works, so "full of madness, evil, and nightmares," as ranking alongside the crime fiction of Tanizaki Jun'ichirō and Satō Haruo (1892–1964) as some of the finest mysteries in Japan. Nakajima Kawatarō's history of Japanese mystery fiction is somewhat more muted in its praise. He notes that Kaita's stories, like many others in the same magazines, are somewhat unrefined, yet they pioneered a type of artistically inclined tale of the bizarre *(kaiki shōsetsu)* that uses first-person narration and detailed description to imbue fantastic accounts of mysterious and bizarre figures with realism.[1] In decades to come, popular authors like Ranpo, who wrote detailed narratives about crimes committed by reclusive and eccentric criminals, would further popularize such tales. Literary historian Suzuki Sadami has also commented that Kaita's stories exemplify a particular brand of Taishō mystery fiction *(tantei shōsetsu)* that associated mystery fiction with the search for thrills and curiosities.[2] As the following chapter will show, this brand of mystery fiction would expand significantly as writers during the 1920s and 1930s took advantage of new forums for publication to cater to audiences interested in the erotic and the grotesque.

This chapter begins by examining "Bishōnen Saraino no kubi," a tour de force full of hallucinatory qualities, proto-modernist language, and male homoerotic desire. The second half of this chapter examines "Satsujin gyōja" (The murdering ascetic), in which male–male erotic desire plays a large role, and "Akuma no shita" ("The Diabolical Tongue"), which has clear homoerotic overtones. Both stories portray desire within contexts that involve crime and even murderous behavior, yet the narration displays momentary sympathy or identification with the criminals. In these stories, Kaita suggests that civilization with its concern for regulations and order suppresses the vital élan that informs sexuality and renders life dangerous and exciting.

## KISSING THE SEVERED HEAD OF GENIUS

In late 1913 or early 1914, when Kaita was seventeen, he wrote "Bishōnen Saraino no kubi" ("The Bust of the Beautiful Young Salaino"). At this time, Kaita was getting ready to graduate from his school in Kyoto and was busy thinking about his future. Although he had his heart set on a career in art, his father, Murayama Tanisuke, was vehemently opposed to the idea and wanted him instead to go to an agricultural college. Partly to work out these issues, Kaita corresponded with his cousin and mentor, the artist Yamamoto

Kanae, who had been one of the first to recognize Kaita's gifts and who was studying art in Paris at the time. Although Kanae's letters to Kaita have been lost, Kanae's letter to his parents dated December 28, 1913, indicates his thoughts about his young cousin's future: "Has it been settled that Kaita will go to an agricultural school? Murayama [Tanisuke] won't listen to reason, and this is a real problem. I think it would be a shame to do anything to harm Kaita's natural gifts as an artist. . . . It seems that if he were to develop his talents, he might reach a point that people like me would be no match for him."[3] In fact, Kanae was so thoroughly convinced of Kaita's genius that in the same letter, he volunteered to pay Kaita's tuition to the Nihon Bijutsuin and offered to arrange for his close friend, the artist Kosugi Misei (1881– 1964), to take care of Kaita in Tokyo. In the end, Kaita prevailed and went to the capital to study art.

The surreal fantasy "Bishōnen Saraino no kubi," written soon before this decision was made, reflects Kaita's growing artistic aspirations and rising determination at a time when it was unclear whether or not he would be able to dedicate himself to the arts. On the surface, the hallucinogenic, homoerotic story features a competition between Leonardo da Vinci and a narrator named "Kaita" for the affections of an attractive youth, but if one probes deeper, one finds the story represents a fantasy of artistic transfer in which Kaita establishes himself as heir to the greatness of one of the major figures of European civilization and thus positions himself in the vanguard of the art world. Nowhere is the connection Kaita drew between male beauty, artistic vision, and the pursuit for genius more explicit than in this story.

On March 27, 1914, Kaita wrote in his diary that he had just learned "Bishōnen Saraino no kubi" was to appear in the April issue of *Tobano,* a coterie magazine published in Kyoto. He comments that the work made him "very embarrassed"; nonetheless, he hoped it would attract the attention of his teachers (344). In a letter to one of his teachers, he wrote, "In this month's issue of *Tobano,* a literary journal published in Kyoto, I have published a frightful piece of prose about stealing Leonardo da Vinci's lover. You might find it somewhat nauseating, but please take a look at it when you pass by the bookstore" (298). *Tobano,* however, ceased publication about the time the story was scheduled to appear. In a 1914 letter, he comments, "It is a good thing *Tobano* went under," as if the demise of the magazine had spared him discomfiture (402). Another undated letter asks, "Is that book [*sic*] *Tobano* still coming out?" (404). Yet another from late 1914 queries, "Hasn't *Tobano* started publishing again?" (409). Clearly, these letters carry mixed signals. On the one hand, Kaita wanted people to see his story, but on the other, he was also uncomfortable about it appearing in print. Perhaps his embarrassment stems from the work's unrestrained and seemingly personal expression of sexual desire, which climaxes in a kiss between a narrator identified with Kaita's own name and the disembodied head of the young man named in the title.

The prose has an experimental, modernist feel with short, almost telegraphic sentences that produce a feel of immediate intensity. Given the surrealistic description, brevity, and quick pace of the story, "Bishōnen Saraino no kubi" reads like a record of a dream. Like Natsume Sōseki's *Yume jūya (Ten Nights of Dream)* published in 1908, Kaita's surreal, dreamlike writing anticipates a strain of hallucinatory literature *(gensō bungaku)* within Japanese modernism that produced works like "Kasei no unga" ("The Martian Canals") by Edogawa Ranpo, *Issen ichi-byō monogatari (One Thousand and One Second Stories)* by Inagaki Taruho, and "Neko-machi" ("The Town of Cats") by Hagiwara Sakutarō (1886–1942).

The work begins with the narrator, a boy named "Murayama Kaita" like the author, gazing at the lights of Kyoto in the distance.[4] As he walks westward, he crosses a river. Although Kaita may have been imagining the Katsura River in western Kyoto as he wrote the story, the river also seems to represent the boundaries of the conscious mind with its social, civilizing order. When the narrator crosses it, he finds himself far removed from the order of the city, standing alone in a primordial no-man's land. His thoughts descend "into a deep, deep hole," as if turning inward to plumb the hidden, subterranean realm of the subconscious (202). Just then, the disembodied bust of a beautiful young man appears floating before him. As the title states, the head is that of Andreas Salaino *né* Gian Giacomo de Caprotti (c. 1480–1524), who at age ten joined the studio of Leonardo da Vinci.[5] History tells us Salaino was one of Leonardo's best-loved pupils and remained with him until the political turbulence that led to Leonardo's emigration to France. Leonardo is known to have been particularly partial to attractive boys, and in this Kaita no doubt saw a similarity between himself and the Renaissance master.

The disembodied head of Salaino that appears before the narrator is both a bishōnen and a gorgon simultaneously. His lips are "red as fire, red as flame" (202) then "feverish bronze," and his eyes are "as resplendent as the tail of a peacock" and shine "like a light, like a diamond" (202–3). These eyes, which look at the narrator "as if with a touch of embarrassment," serve as a silent index of Salaino's affection, and even though no words are exchanged, the narrator boldly asserts, "I knew he loved me" (202). In fact, the eyes even serve as the departure point for an ironic simile that suggests overt sexuality, even though Salaino's body is absent, robbing him of the ability to engage in corporeal sex: "His eyes were clad in layer after layer of emotion, like a kimono worn twelve layers thick. Underneath those layers of fabric would be his beautiful, opulent naked body" (202). Salaino's head is crowned with snakes like the Medusa, the gorgon of Greek mythology who possessed the power to turn anyone who looked at her into stone. At the end of the story, when Salaino's "long, sweetly scented hair" brushes against the narrator's cheek, however, it does so "softly, like a serpent's touch" (203). The hair no longer consists of medusan snakes but ordinary human hair, which moves lightly across the narrator's face.

As the flying head approaches the narrator, the ghostly figure of Leonardo da Vinci suddenly appears, and Salaino's head disappears into the darkness. The Renaissance artist challenges the narrator, asking him if he loves Salaino. When he responds with a yes, Leonardo asserts that Salaino belongs to him, and the narrator realizes Leonardo is his "rival in love" (203). With blood boiling, the narrator announces to Leonardo he will steal Salaino. With a combination of anger and amusement, Leonardo acquiesces. He states that if the narrator is sincere, he will cede Salaino to his "weak little opponent" who deserves his compassion (203). With this, Leonardo disappears, and Salaino returns. As the disembodied head approaches for a kiss, the impassioned narrator cries out, "Ah, my beautiful, my gentleman! You never belonged to Leonardo," and he announces that from that tonight onward, Salaino would rule the narrator's heart (204). The narrator has established himself as the rightful heir to the bishōnen Salaino and takes him from Leonardo.

Although at one level the story describes an erotic competition for the love of a youth, it also has a second allegorical meaning. As noted in the previous chapter, Inō inspired Kaita to produce numerous poems, drawings, and watercolors. Kaita saw bishōnen as embodiments of a beauty that naturally lent itself to the arts. This is particularly clear from a May 1915 diary entry in which Kaita compares Inō to a "Leonardo sketch" or a "Luini painting" (357). Pledging eternal allegiance to Salaino thus represents a fantasy in which the author symbolically professes his dedication to the muse of beauty and the pursuit of art.

Moreover, Salaino serves as a symbol of the artistic and ideological legacy of Leonardo da Vinci, the almost mythologically grand figure of the Italian

Renaissance. That Salaino comes disembodied to the narrator as only a head without any support suggests that when the inheritance of the high Renaissance reached Kaita in Japan, it was little more than a cerebral entity lacking grounding, support, or roots. In a sense, Leonardo's artistic legacy is disembodied, missing the historical context that would allow it to stand on its own. That this legacy of the Renaissance has come to him in a disembodied state, however, does not disturb the narrator of the story. He is eager to accept it, even without the support of ideology or tradition. The narrator "Kaita" has traveled for that purpose from the city of Kyoto, a city associated in the popular imagination with traditional Japanese culture since at least the nineteenth century, toward the west. As he stands in the mysterious, unpopulated world that is neither occident nor orient, he is left alone to confront Leonardo. There are no other people or artists surrounding him; he is alone to compete for the inspiration and heritage Salaino represents.

The biggest challenge to the narrator accepting this legacy comes from Leonardo himself. When he confronts the narrator, he emphasizes the difference in their ethnic backgrounds. The first time he addresses the narrator, he shouts, "You, the Asian! Murayama Kaita!" Moments later, Leonardo calls to the narrator using diminutive, even denigrating terms that emphasize difference in ethnic and cultural background: "a little yellow man from the East [*hingashi no kōshi*]" (203). The narrator, however, does not perceive cultural or racial differences as a barrier to artistic continuity. He ignores the perceived boundaries of race and national difference and insists on his right to Leonardo's inspiration and legacy. In short, the fantasy of taking Salaino from Leonardo represents a dream of transference in which Kaita, a young artist working far from the source of the techniques and ideas that shaped Western art, inherits the legacy of the artist so often considered a pinnacle of Western art and civilization.

One of the most likely sources for Kaita's information about the relationship between Salaino and the Renaissance master is the 1869 essay on Leonardo by the British art historian Walter Pater.[6] This famous essay appeared as part of the collection *The Renaissance,* which became an indispensable part of Western education soon after its publication.[7] Pater states, "of all the interests in living men and women which may have filled his life at Milan," the master's attachment for Salaino alone is recorded, and Pater uses this as evidence to argue the master possessed a special love for the attractive lad. As evidence, Pater describes a drawing of a handsome lad in the Uffizi Gallery in Florence, which "might well be the likeness of Andrea Salaino, beloved of Leonardo for his curled and waving hair—*belli capelli ricci e inanellati*—and afterward his favorite pupil and servant."[8] After describing the drawing, Pater shifts gears and provides a long, detailed description of a painting in the Uffizi that depicts the severed head of the Medusa, a painting many mistakenly attributed to Leonardo at the time Pater was writing.[9] He describes the Uffizi Medusa as a product of the master's interest in the "interfusion of the extremes of beauty and terror," which had manifested itself in the master's youth.[10] The description of the disembodied head of Salaino in the story, which also combines beautiful and frightful elements, echoes Pater's descriptions of the drawing of the handsome youth and the Medusa head that appear almost side by side in *The Renaissance*. Both Pater and Kaita mention the beauty of Salaino's hair several times, and both describe images of Salaino that show nothing more than his disembodied head.

The idea of kissing a severed head also bears an unmistakable likeness to the biblical tale of Salome. Legend has it that King Herodias granted his beautiful young daughter Salome a wish after a particularly fine dance, but as her trophy, she made the shocking choice of the severed head of John the Baptist. This tale enjoyed a revival in fin-de-siècle Europe, thanks to Oscar Wilde's (1854–1900) dramatic 1893 adaptation for the stage, which climaxes with a dramatic kiss between Salome and the severed head of the prophet who had scorned her sexual advances. This play, ripe with eroticism and decadence, stunned the artistic world, and Richard Strauss (1864–1949) adapted it into a 1905 opera that became the buzz of Europe. As music historian Alex Ross has noted, this "ultra-dissonant biblical spectacle, based on a play by a British degenerate whose name was not mentioned in polite company," was so "frightful in its depiction of adolescent lust" that imperial censors banned it from the Viennese Court Opera.[11] Mori Ōgai, who carefully kept abreast of the dramatic and artistic developments of Europe, produced the first translation of Wilde's *Salome* in the journal *Kabuki* in 1909, and a few years later, he included it in a best-selling collection of one-act plays, where Kaita, a fan of Ōgai's translations, might well have read it.[12] A letter dated 1914 indicates that if he had not read it, Kaita was at least familiar with the content of Wilde's play. In this letter, he records his aunt's humorous commentary on the play, replete with a clever pun: "What's up with that play *Salome* or *Zarame* or whatever? Granulated sugar [*zarame*] is too crunchy for me. No matter how much you love someone, what the heck are you going to do with someone's severed head? 'Gimme his head, gimme his head' and all that—It's crazy" (399–400).

Illustrator Aubrey Beardsley (1872–98), one of many European artists attracted to Wilde's electrifying play, produced a series of illustrations for an 1894 English edition of the play, and the series rapidly became some of his most famous work. Kaita's writings indicate he was tremendously fond of Beardsley, making it likely he knew of the Salome prints. Perhaps not coincidentally, one of his love letters to Inō praises the boy's beauty by comparing him to a Beardsley illustration. He writes, "I adore you and think you are the most beautiful person in the world, for you resemble so strongly one of the nervous beauties drawn by the artist Aubrey Beardsley. I truly adore the work of Beardsley."[13] Kaita does not explicitly mention the *Salome* prints, but the thought of Inō in conjunction with Beardsley may have represented a step toward the production of "Bishōnen Saraino no kubi," in which the protagonist kisses the severed head of his beloved.

Even if Kaita was familiar with Pater's *Renaissance* and Beardsley's prints for the English version of Wilde's *Salome,* this still leaves open the question of why Kaita might have chosen to include Leonardo as a character. Hagiographic descriptions of Leonardo from the early twentieth century show that in Japan, as well as in the West, Leonardo was often identified as a genius who represented the zenith of the Renaissance, which the Japanese recognized as one of the greatest eras of human achievement in history. For instance, *Sekai bijutsu shi* (History of the world's art), edited by Ogawa Ginjirō and published in 1905, holds up Leonardo as the pinnacle of the Italian Renaissance:

> Of all the artists we can count, even the ones who stand out the most and who show undeniable superiority in a certain field, there is none—regardless of who they are—who shows a genius that can compare to Leonardo da Vinci. Even if we do not find in him the fullest expression of the human spirit, we should identify him as the highest manifestation of it; in all situations, he is the most perfect representative of the Renaissance. His performance in each individual field showed the highest talent; he was a painter, sculptor, musician, poet, and architect as well as an engineer, mathematician, and naturalist.[14]

The image of Leonardo as the pinnacle of Renaissance achievement also appears in the writing of the art critic Iwamura Tōru (1870–1917): "He has been given a variety of titles. He has been evaluated as realist or idealist; he has been called daydreamer, magician, and scientist. One might say he is well suited to all of these titles; one might also say none of them truly fit. People

Illustration by Aubrey Beardsley for an 1894 English-language edition of Oscar Wilde's play *Salome*. Courtesy of Western Michigan University Libraries.

say he was a man of many talents, and he succeeded without exception at everything he put his hand to. Truly, he was an extraordinary genius."[15] The emphasis on Leonardo's many abilities is scarcely surprising, considering that even Giorgio Vasari (1511–74), one of Leonardo's earliest and most influential biographers, went to great pains to emphasize that Leonardo excelled not only in the visual arts but also in music, math, engineering, and many other fields.[16]

The May and June 1905 issues of *Nihon bijutsu* (Japanese art), published by the Nihon Bijutsuin, the same art institute where Kaita began studying in late 1914, carry a revealing lecture about Leonardo and his place in Renaissance culture by Ueda Bin, the same Kyoto-based translator who introduced symbolist poetry to Japan in *Kaichōon* and who had been so fond of Kaita's mother. After calling Leonardo a genius numerous times, Bin writes, "Speaking grandly, I believe he is the greatest person to have existed anytime between primitive times and the present day. Napoleon, Alexander the Great, Caesar—they all pale by comparison. Old, new, east, west—there is no one as great as he."[17] He continues by describing Leonardo as blessed with personal beauty as well as having talents in the visual arts, prose, poetry, mathematics, singing, musical performance, invention, engineering, military strategy, zoology, botany, mineralogy, and other fields of science. What is especially germane to Kaita and his world is the fact that this kind of hagiographic discourse provided fodder for Japanese critics who assumed Japan must produce similar figures of greatness before it could be seen as having "come of age" in the modern world. Bin writes,

> There are those in society who select the examples of the old masters of the West to stimulate, give incentive to, and spur on the contemporary Japanese art world. Why don't Japanese painters paint like Rafael? Why don't they think like Michelangelo? Or why don't they sense things like Leonardo, our subject today? There are many people who denounce the Japanese art world without good reason, asking them why they do not readily produce anyone on par with these geniuses.[18]

During the Meiji period, as Japanese society strove to refashion itself into a modern nation that could take its place among the fully independent, "civilized" nations of the world, the Japanese art world also underwent a seismic overhaul. Over the course of the Edo period, Japanese art had been incorporating Western knowledge, perspectives, and colors in woodblock prints and anatomical drawings, but the rapid increase of intercourse between nations just before the Meiji Restoration meant Japanese artists suddenly had unparalleled access to the artistic styles, techniques, and visual vocabulary of the West. As Meiji artists began mastering these elements, there was a sense among some Japanese critics that as long as Japan failed to produce artists on par with the great masters of European art history, the domestic art world still had not yet come of age.

In his article on Leonardo, however, Bin argues this line of reasoning is not productive. He notes that geniuses such as Leonardo are temporally and geographically remote from where Japan stood as a nation at the beginning of the twentieth century, and so for contemporary Japanese artists to paint in a style like the old masters is not necessarily useful. He writes, "Out of what necessity do the Japanese of today follow the works of these great geniuses and slavishly imitate their works? Instead, they should use creative thought and draw close to the beauty of their greatest creations."[19] What he felt Japan needed was not painters or sculptors who could work in a style mimicking that of the masters; Japan needed creative individuals who could learn from the masters while still moving in their own creative directions to produce something relevant to their own epoch. Bin suggests that Japanese artists, having inherited the technique of the European masters, should achieve greatness not through imitation, but through putting this inheritance to good use by forging new directions.

Kaita's writings reveal his wish to do exactly that. One of his earliest works to do so is the 1913 essay "Hito no sekai" (People's worlds), which mentions Leonardo in a discussion about what it means to be a genius. This essay employs the logic of evolutionary theory to describe the genius as a visionary who differs from the remainder of society and contributes the benefits of that difference to future generations. Kaita argues every individual inhabits a world that differs slightly from those of all other people, but the worlds inhabited by geniuses are significantly different from those of ordinary people. By sharing the visions reaped within their own individual worlds, geniuses help create a richer culture on which future generations can build, thus enriching life for all of humankind (291–92). The language and argument of this article strongly resembles that of a famous article on the meaning of genius by Takayama Chogyū (1871–1902), an important literary critic and novelist of the Meiji period. This article, first published in the magazine *Taiyō* (The sun) in 1896, argues that, before all else, the genius is creative and uses this creativity to create new worlds that did not exist before. Borrowing the language of German Idealism, Chogyū states that these worlds possess elements of the universal, unchanging truth, which then is introduced through the work of the genius to the rest of humanity.[20] Though Kaita does not explicitly evoke the notion of a universal "Idea" that represents the truest principles of the universe, he does place similar emphasis on the role of creativity and the concept of the genius as a creator. As examples of significant innovators, he mentions Newton, Plato, Darwin, Edgar Allan Poe, and Leonardo, each of whom, Kaita says, "created his own world." The essay concludes that the purpose of life is to "create worlds that are utterly different" from all that have gone before, "worlds that are close as possible to the worlds of geniuses" (291–92). "Hito no sekai" makes it clear that at the time he wrote "Bishōnen Saraino no kubi," Kaita was already concerned with the lofty goal of taking inspiration from figures of genius and using it to forge a new, artistic style.

Since, as Bin noted, Leonardo was one of the yardsticks used by the Japanese art world to measure its own developmental maturity, it is not particularly surprising that, as an aspiring artist, Kaita would long to be recognized as a genius on par with him. The fullest expression of these thoughts appears in a short manuscript in which Kaita addresses Leonardo directly. Written around the same time as "Bishōnen Saraino no kubi," this manuscript expresses Kaita's thoughts as he encourages himself in his artistic pursuits. He begins by describing feelings of inferiority vis-à-vis the Renaissance master: "When I think of your life, I always feel like bonds of strong leather constrain my body. That is because you are like me. It is because I am walking the same path as you. . . . I have many reasons to be ashamed about my own degree of ability as an artist. Ah, Leonardo, you are superior to me!" (296). Although Kaita feels paralyzed by Leonardo's grandeur, he vows to surpass him. He says, "I am here to tell you I now have many ideas superior to yours. In terms of aesthetics and ability, you have one up on me, but I believe I am not inferior to you" (296). The narrator vows his nineteenth year will represent a point of departure from which he will proceed down the master's path of excellence: "I will create like you; I will think like you" (296). In a rhetorical flourish, he ends with the following declaration:

You are smiling like the *Mona Lisa.*
　　Ah, how many times has your smile eaten into my life force!
　　That smile is your life; that smile is the high point of all humanity.

I too shall smile. Through that smile of mine, my life too will
smile.

Oh Leonardo! I will live like you. I will proceed like you.

Oh, how I, through my great incomplete self, shall smile like you!
(296–97)

The thought of Leonardo basking smugly in his position as a seminal figure of civilization is a thorn in Kaita's side, and it is no coincidence Leonardo smiles smugly at Kaita in the text of "Bishōnen Saraino no kubi."
Nonetheless, Kaita recognizes it is only through working like Leonardo
and giving everything to his own creative instincts that he will become
the legitimate heir to the master's legacy of greatness and perhaps even ex-
ceed him.

A diary entry from mid-May 1917 indicates that even three years later,
Kaita continued to think of Leonardo as a model of intellectual and artistic
clarity: "I want to put my head in order and clear it out. / I want to make
Leonardo my so-called 'mirror'" (360). The same year, the thought of
Leonardo makes an appearance in Kaita's famous oil painting *Kosui to onna*
(Lake and woman). Kaita had developed an amorous attachment for an
early middle-aged, distant relative named Sasa Misao (1885–?), who lived
near the home where he was staying in Tabata, Tokyo. Misao had treated
him kindly, and he responded with his affection. Kaita's friends, knowing of
his feelings for the older woman, started calling her his "Mona Lisa," perhaps
because the painting *Kosui to onna*, which used her for its model, bears an
unmistakable resemblance to Leonardo's famous portrait.[21] Both figures display an enigmatic smile, and both women occupy a similar position within
the entire space of the painting itself. Moreover, both sit in similar positions
with hands quietly clasped as if unaware of or even exempt from the flow
of time, while landscapes of mountains and flowing water unfold behind
them. Clearly, even three years after writing "Bishōnen Saraino no kubi,"
Kaita continued to think of Leonardo and his artwork. It is interesting to
note, however, that Kaita's "Japanese Mona Lisa" sits in a position that is a
mirror image of the figure in Leonardo's famous portrait. Quite literally,
Kaita is taking Leonardo's legacy and turning its leftward glance—a westward glance, if one follows the common mapmaker's practice of associating the left with the West—so it now faces to the right, toward the world of
the East.

*La Gioconda* (*Mona Lisa*, 1503–6), oil on wood by Leonardo da Vinci. Collection of the Musée du Louvre. Photo copyright Musée du Louvre/A. Dequier—M. Bard 2010. Courtesy of the Musée du Louvre.

*Kosui to onna* (Lake and woman, 1917), oil on canvas by Murayama Kaita. This painting reveals Kaita's engagement with the legacy of Leonardo da Vinci, one of the seminal figures of European art, in the creation of a new, modern Japanese artistic tradition. Collection of the Pola Museum of Art. Photo copyright Fukushima Prefectural Art Museum and Mie Prefectural Art Museum 1997.

## Kaita and Mystery-Adventure Fiction

The fusion of decadence and overblown expression present in "Bishōnen Saraino no kubi" recurs later in a handful of stories he wrote for the magazines *Bōken sekai* (World of adventure) and *Bukyō sekai* (World of heroism) in 1914 and 1915. *Bōken sekai* was first published in 1908 by Hakubunkan, a large publishing firm that made its fortune by publishing textbooks and popular magazines in the Meiji period. *Bōken sekai* was the second of three late Meiji- and Taishō-period journals specializing in adventure stories. The first was *Tanken sekai* (World of exploration), started in May 1906 by the publisher Seikōsha, which capitalized on the wave of patriotic sentiment accompanying the Russo-Japanese War to present tales of Japanese adventure and exploration abroad. In the wake of a conclusion to a war that many Japanese found disappointing, the stories in *Tanken sekai* presented new fantasies of imperialistic superiority and Japanese valor; in addition to fiction, it carried tales of exploration, record-breaking achievements, and scientific developments, mostly by Japanese explorers and adventurers. Nakajima Kawatarō has commented that Hakubunkan's journal *Bōken sekai* was clearly designed to take over part of the market share held by *Tanken sekai*.[22] One function of *Bōken sekai*, which was coedited by the popular author Oshikawa Shunrō (1876–1914), was to appeal to readers who had enjoyed tales of military adventure and heroism during the Russo-Japanese War.[23] *Bōken sekai* often contained allegedly true stories of adventure, exploration, military prowess, and accounts of "primitive" lands, all of which reflected Japanese nationalism and imperial ambitions. At the same time, however, it also included mysteries, including translations of Western detective stories, and ghost stories. Virtually every issue of the magazine contained a story or article by Oshikawa Shunrō; however, after a dispute with the publisher, Shunrō left Hakubunkan. In October 1911, he founded the periodical *Bukyō sekai* with the capital of an entrepreneur named Yanaginuma Kensuke. This monthly magazine, published from 1912 to about 1923, strongly resembled the magazine Shunrō had edited earlier, and it too carried tales of exploration, nonfiction adventure stories, editorials, sports-related tales, and translations of mysteries.

Kaita's introduction to these magazines came through the artist Kosugi Misei, a close friend of Kaita's cousin Yamamoto Kanae. As mentioned previously, when Kanae started writing letters from Paris in order to arrange for Kaita to go to Tokyo and study at the Nihon Bijutsuin in 1914, he had enlisted the help of Misei, with whom he had lived in Paris but who was at that time already back in Japan. Through letters sent from Europe, Kanae arranged for Kaita to enter the Nihon Bijutsuin, where Misei was currently a fellow, and to stay in a small, detached building on Misei's property.[24] Kaita lodged with Misei and his wife from July 1914 until the spring of 1916. Kaita became quite close to them; meanwhile, Misei encouraged not only Kaita's art, but also his writing. Misei had been a member of the staff of *Bōken sekai* since soon after Hakubunkan started publication in 1908. For several years, Misei produced the covers for almost every issue, took charge of illustrations for the magazine, and, in the process, illustrated many of Oshikawa Shunrō's stories. When Shunrō left Hakubunkan to start *Bukyō sekai*, Misei also began working on the illustrations for the new magazine. Through Misei, Kaita became involved with *Bukyō sekai*. This development was not out of character, considering he had adored fiction since grade school.

After publishing some sketches and a travelogue in the magazine, Kaita published his first piece of mystery-adventure fiction in the April 1915 issue. "Satsujin gyōja" (The murdering ascetic) contained a number of Kaita's original illustrations and occupied a significant percentage of the magazine's pages. Later, in August of the same year, the magazine published his "Akuma no shita" ("The Diabolical Tongue"), once again with his original illustrations. In late October, Kaita sent *Bukyō sekai* a third story, "Maenden" (Account of a magical monkey). Apparently encouraged by these early successes, Kaita also submitted the story "Madōjiden" (Biography of a magical boy) to the magazine *Bōken sekai*, which still had a larger circulation than its imitative offspring. *Bōken sekai* published this story in two issues, dated August and September 1916.

Although adventure stories *(bōken shōsetsu)*, tales of the bizarre *(kaiki shōsetsu)*, and detective or crime fiction *(tantei shōsetsu)* would evolve into increasingly separate genres in subsequent decades, authors in the early twentieth century typically incorporated elements of all three into a single work. The fiction Kaita published in *Bōken sekai* and *Bukyō sekai* was no exception. Each of these stories shares the spirit of adventure characteristic of these magazines, but they also incorporate elements of crime and ratiocination in their plots. "Satsujin gyōja" recounts the events that take place when the protagonist wanders into the wild mountains of Nagano Prefecture and encounters a gang of murderous bandits. "Akuma no shita" contains two parts, one which involves following a string of clues to discover a testament hidden in urban Tokyo, and another which describes the murderous ends one man goes to in order to fulfill his ravenous desire to eat human flesh. "Maenden," which probably drew inspiration from Edgar Allan Poe's famous story "The Murders in the Rue Morgue," is about a mysterious, magically endowed primate behind a series of grisly murders in Tokyo. (In fact, on May 20, 1915, a half year before sending "Maenden," Kaita wrote in his diary that he had tried his hand at translating Poe's "The Murders in the Rue Morgue," but nothing seems to have come of that attempt.) "Madō-jiden" is full of action and describes a series of battles between an ordinary mortal and a youth endowed with magical powers. While some of these battles take place on the ground, one of the action-packed confrontations takes place in an airplane hundreds of feet above the earth.

The immediate motivation for Kaita to write these mystery-adventure stories was financial need. By late 1914, Kaita was living on a shoestring budget. In order to purchase art supplies, books, and the growing quantities of alcohol he consumed, he scrimped on food. He grew thin, but even stinting on essentials did not provide enough money for all the supplies he needed or the trips he wanted to take, so writing for magazines represented a pleasant way to make a few extra yen. A 1915 letter comments, "They have used the story I wrote for the April issue of *Bukyō sekai,* and at the end of the month, I will be receiving ten yen" (419). Misei encouraged him to use this amount of money, a hefty sum for a poor student in early Taishō Japan, to take a trip to Nagano. In October of that year, he followed Misei's advice. On October 15, while staying at his uncle's home, Kaita wrote in his diary he would need about three and a half yen for art supplies (333). Again, he picked up his pen and wrote "Maenden" in order to get it. According to his diary, he wrote half of the story on October 20 and sent it to *Bukyō sekai* the following day, tossing it off with remarkable speed (335–36).

The fact that Kaita wrote these stories quickly for financial reasons does not mean they are undeserving of critical attention. As mentioned in the introduction, recent scholarship has identified Kaita as the founder of a specific strain of mystery fiction that anticipated the *ero, guro, nansensu* that would come to dominate popular literature in the late 1920s and 1930s. Indeed, as chapter 3 of this book will show, Edogawa Ranpo drew directly on Kaita's stories for inspiration. More importantly for the purposes of this book, two of these stories, "Satsujin gyōja" and "Akuma no shita," involve important homoerotic subplots. Both stories portray desire within contexts that involve crime and even murderous behavior, yet the narration displays momentary sympathy or identification with the criminals. Meanwhile, both stories relegate the main characters to a peripheral status within society, either by having them live as outlaws outside of the reach of the Japanese police or by simply describing their desires as having little place within the civilized world. It is significant Kaita should have chosen to describe male–male desire in conjunction with peripheral status, considering that both stories were written for the mystery-adventure magazine *Bukyō sekai*, which frequently published articles about alternative spaces outside of the Japanese state and the allegedly "uncivilized" behavior that takes place there. That Kaita wrote both stories during the year he developed his first major interests in the opposite sex, however, suggests other, psychological factors are also at work in shaping these stories. As the remainder of this chapter argues, both stories reflect the psychological dynamics involved in the process of accommodating an attraction to the same sex within an ideological regime that pathologizes such desires.

## The Return of the Repressed

Like many other pieces of crime fiction written about this time in Japan, "Satsujin gyōja" consists of a narrative within a narrative—a structure used by many Taishō- and early Shōwa-period mystery writers. This storytelling structure is particularly well suited for tales of crime and the bizarre, because the first narrative provides the reader clues about the demeanor, psychology, and credibility of the second narrator that can confirm or cast doubt over the veracity of the second, embedded tale. The first narrator does not have first-hand knowledge of the events of the second narrative, nor does he or she necessarily even believe in them. Skillful authors sometimes play with this structure, using the external narrative to hint at motives that might have shaped the embedded tale, or drawing unexpected connections between the embedded and the external narrative.

The first-person narrator who begins "Satsujin gyōja" is an artist never identified by name. As he is walking one night, he encounters a drunk; feeling a mixture of curiosity and pity for the man, the narrator invites him back to his apartment where they drink together. The drunken man turns out to be an archaeologist named Toda Genkichi, and it is he who tells the tale that forms the bulk of the work. Toda states he was once married to a girl named Toyoko whom he loved dearly. One year after their marriage, they went together to the mountains of Nagano despite news a band of roving murderers was hiding in the woods. Ignoring the reports, the two rented a villa deep in the wooded mountains.

As art historian Higashi Shunrō has noted, mountains in Kaita's work often serve as other worlds where "abnormal forces manifest themselves in forms that range from the bizarre [*kaiki*] to the mysterious [*shinpi*]."[25] In an early aborted play, "Shuten Dōji," written about a year before this story, mountains had appeared as a setting where, far away from the clutches of the law, natives engage in the murderous pursuit of hedonistic pleasure. Similarly, in "Satsujin gyōja" mountains serve as a lawless zone where ordinary concepts of virtue and evil do not apply and murder can be committed with almost zealous religiosity. There, law and morality lose the grip they exercise elsewhere, and forces suppressed by civilization spill forth. In other words, mountains represent a territory in which primordial, suppressed, and even antisocial drives manifest themselves, free from the civilizing force of law.

The primary agent of these forces is a reclusive bandit leader Toda encounters soon after his arrival. One day, he stumbles across a cave. Inside, Toda notices an ancient coffin, which contains within it a secret door—a threshold symbolically leading into a new realm of deadly power. When he crawls through, he discovers a secret lair of the bandit gang, which, by an incredible coincidence, is led by Nomiya Kōtarō, a boy with whom Toda shared an erotic relationship years ago.

Toda recalls that when he was a teenager, he had a reputation as a bishōnen. He says, "I was loved by numerous upperclassmen, but no one made as profound an impression on me as this Nomiya Kōtarō" (211). Nomiya was an upperclassman in his fifth and final year of higher school, where he was infamous as a delinquent. Although he was tough, skilled in judo, and got into lots of fights, Toda saw in him a "mysterious charm," and a relationship developed between them:

> He loved me, and in the end, he invited me back to his house. Every day afterward he would play only with me. He had no parents and was all alone, but he lived quite luxuriously, borrowing a room from a certain temple. In no way did he teach me anything bad. He did not influence me negatively in any way. Nonetheless, I was prohibited from playing with Nomiya in my own house. The stronger the prohibition was, the stronger my attachment to him became, and before I knew it, it had come to the point where I developed morbid, strong feelings of love for him. (211)

Here, as in many accounts of schoolboy relationships, the older partner is a strong, physically dominant boy and the object of his affection a particularly lovely bishōnen; however, unlike the relationships described in Mori Ōgai's

*Wita Sekusuarisu* (*Vita Sexualis*) from 1909 or the numerous newspaper articles describing the problems of "hard-faction" masculinity during the late
Meiji period, the older partner is not a predator feeding on the affections of
the innocent. If anything, he is a misunderstood and ultimately lonely youth
who craves affection, and Toda, the younger partner, eagerly reciprocates.

The choice of Kyushu as the home for the boys is a significant one. Popular and sexological writings of late nineteenth- and early twentieth-century
Japan often named Satsuma (the portion of southern Kyushu that is now
Kagoshima Prefecture) as the epicenter of a culture of male–male eroticism.
Various nineteenth-century sources describe local institutions in Kyushu,
such as the *hekogumi,* an organization formed by men banding together in
order to hone their skills at the martial arts, and *gojū,* organizations designed
to socialize young males, as creating all-male environments where eroticism
might blossom between virile young men. Although these institutions were
largely defunct by the late nineteenth and early twentieth centuries, Satsuma
had already become thoroughly associated with the practice of male–male
eroticism in the popular imagination. Pflugfelder has described the link between Satsuma and male–male eroticism in the popular imagination as the
result of new discourses relegating the practice of male–male desire to "certain peripheral areas of experience," namely the historical past, the south-
west of the country, and the world of adolescence, in order to help define
"more mainstream subjectivities—the new Japanese, the national citizen, and
the responsible adult."[26] One factor contributing to (or perhaps a symptom
of) the associations between male–male eroticism, martial masculinity, and
the island of Kyushu was the Meiji-era popularity of the novel *Shizu no
odamaki* (The humble bobbin), an Edo-period work by an unknown author
that describes an amorous relationship between two Satsuma warriors in
the sixteenth century.[27] In fact, the novels *Tōsei shosei katagi* (The characters
of modern students, 1885–86) by Tsubouchi Shōyō and *Wita Sekusuarisu*
by Mori Ōgai both mention *Shizu no odamaki* as a favorite work of the
tough groups of Meiji-period Kyushuites who routinely practiced male–
male eroticism. The popular association between the southern island, virile
masculinity, and male–male erotic practice lasted well into the twentieth
century, when in 1921 Ozaki Shirō wrote, "In the higher schools of particular regions, especially around Kyushu, the way of *nanshoku* [*nanshokudō*]
flourishes to a degree that has hardly changed from old times. The majority
of those are people who have dedicated themselves to martial arts such as
judo and kendo. From this, we can see the way of the warrior and the way

of the bishōnen [*bishōnendō*] should not be at all separated."[28] By identifying Kyushu as the home of the characters in his story, Kaita brings into play a series of cultural assumptions that associated men from the southern island with a brusque version of masculinity and a propensity for erotic passion between men.

Toda's own characterization of his feelings for Nomiya as *byōteki* (morbid, sick) hints that at least part of him buys into the notion that strong amorous feelings for the same sex are somehow unhealthy or even deviant. These reservations, however, seem to have arisen after Toda's marriage and were not present during his youth when he gave himself to Nomiya so enthusiastically. Nomiya had started dabbling in hypnosis, and this provided Toda with the perfect excuse to submit to the older boy: "Being put to sleep by Nomiya was always an extraordinary pleasure. I don't remember at all what sorts of things happened while I was asleep, but I felt an indescribable happiness when I gave myself to him so he could put me to sleep with his various powers. In the end, it got to the point where with one look from Nomiya, I would lose consciousness completely" (211). The willingness with which Toda turned himself over to the older classmate suggests he was not averse to what might happen while his defenses were down. Hypnosis did not induce the boy to engage in sexual behavior he found unappealing; rather, it provided Toda with a pretext for lowering his inhibitions and acting on desires already present. Before long, Nomiya left for higher education in Tokyo with tears in his eyes. As the schoolboys parted, Nomiya tells Toda their fates were linked, and they would certainly meet again. Even in Nomiya's absence, Toda's yearning for him remained intense: "Just thinking his name, I would feel longing so strong that tears would blur my eyes. No matter how much time passed, this feeling did not want to go away. This lasted until about the time I entered university. For some reason, I wanted to meet him so much that I went around looking for him, but I could not find him" (212). The longing continued as long as Toda remained single, but when he married Toyoko, the new relationship displaced his schoolboy love: "After getting a wife, however, I never thought about him. Not even once" (212). By turning his attentions to a woman, Toda succeeded in suppressing his feeling for the older boy—at least temporarily.

As he encounters his former love, Toda feels his old desires return. As Nomiya's hypnotic gaze penetrates Toda, it casts "the glitter of those eyes deep into my heart, and I became conscious that this person in the depths of this strange cave was the same person for whom I had long ago felt such a serious bond" (212). Toda realizes, however, there is a clash between his feelings for Nomiya and for his wife, who had only temporarily displaced Nomiya in his heart. He resolves to stay faithful to his wife and not to give in to the arousal he feels for his former companion. Meanwhile, Nomiya announces that despite their long separation, he had not forgotten Toda even for a moment. Nomiya admits he is the leader of the criminal gang, and he proclaims he will initiate Toda into his world by teaching him the joy of killing, the "greatest pleasure on earth" (213). These "musical words" draw Toda in despite his reservations: "Nomiya had a magic ten times more powerful than the mysterious magic which he had during our school days. I found myself drawn to him" (213). Nomiya tells him he burns with an undying desire for Toda, and he casts a hypnotic spell, providing the excuse Toda needs to drop his inhibitions. As Toda stands mesmerized, Nomiya says they will meet again at midnight, five days later, and he releases his captive.

In the following days, Toda finds a new joie de vivre, and his passion for Toyoko grows more intense, as if one part of him is cherishing the woman Nomiya has cursed. Each night, however, he is haunted by a dream in which he stands atop a mountain with valleys on either side. A city glitters on one side, and on the other is a foreboding lake of blood over which a single blood-red star twinkles like "a witch's eye" (215). Though not explained in the text, these dreams clearly depict Toda's feelings of being torn between the forces of law, civilization, and the ordered life of a modern citizen, represented by the city, and a more primitive, elemental, and intense life as a renegade, signified by the remote, sanguine lake. After these dreams, he finds himself in a discombobulated state, unable to focus on anything and acting as if afflicted with a "dual personality disorder" (215). Nomiya's hypnotic influence has drawn out two clashing aspects of his personality: one dominated by the rules of society in which heterosexual marriage plays a central role, and the other marked by a yearning for the exciting, "outlaw" world of male love his boyhood lover represents.

On the fifth day, Toda wanders outside into the garden, and his wife accompanies him. As Toda gazes at a neighboring mountain, he sees a red light like the one in his dream. Falling under Nomiya's hypnotic spell, he finds a knife in his pocket, which he uses to kill his wife in a single blow. As Nomiya used his hypnotic powers to resuscitate Toda's passion, he has also manipulated him to destroy the woman who had originally displaced it. Although Toda had relegated his schoolboy passions to the periphery by assuming the head of a household and the mantle of social respectability, his earlier passions did not die but were merely repressed and hidden from sight, ready to resurface when given the opportunity. As Nomiya leads Toda back to the mountains, Toda leaves behind his modern, family-oriented life and embraces the primitive, rough life of hedonistic excitement Nomiya represents. Back in the cave, Toda is "determined to do just as Nomiya said. He smiled with satisfaction when I responded I would never leave him again. Afterwards, we drank saké together and once again swore our brotherhood vows" (218). Toda remains in the mountains for five months, during which he kills dozens of people in his new "cold-blooded life of hedonistic pleasure" (218). In this community of male outlaws, Toda revels in the intoxicating pleasure of masculine, thanatotic power.

Toda's life outside the social grammar of the modern, civilized world comes to a rapid end when suddenly he regains his conscience. One snowy day as he wanders by the abandoned villa where he had killed his wife, he experiences a seizure, as if his memories of her and heterosexual life are struggling to break free of Nomiya's power. He falls, and this breaks Nomiya's hypnotic spell; Toda's conscience returns, and for the first time he realizes the horror of having killed his wife. In a rapid denouement to the story, he flees the mountains and tells his fantastic tale to the police, but they do not believe him. Since then, Toda says, he has recounted his story many times but has been unable to find anyone willing to believe him. By ignoring the antisocial, destructive forces lurking in the mountains, society relegates them to the relative safety of oblivion. Here, the story within a story comes to an end. The next morning, the artist who has recorded Toda's story awakens to find Toda gone. A couple of days later, he reads in a newspaper that Toda has been stabbed to death with a knife belonging to the bandit gang. The bandits have executed the sheep that left the flock—the sworn brother who abandoned his fraternal bonds.

This rapid denouement suggests the ultimate incompatibility between Nomiya's life of passion and the safe order of civilization. Meanwhile, Nomiya and his band of murderers remain hidden from society, much like the male–male erotic desire that had remained hidden within the depths of Toda's unconscious mind. When the bandits do reappear, however, they present a radical threat to the regime of "normality." Still, the flatness of the descriptions of Toda's feelings for his wife and the ease with which Toda recovers his long-buried desire suggests Kaita's interest lay more with the impassioned, renegade life Toda led with Nomiya than his typical, sedate home life with Toyoko. For this reason, one should see "Satsujin gyōja" as an exploration of the fantasy of an unrestrained space filled with masculine vigor, power, and male–male eroticism—a space the author, who was himself growing older and feeling the pressure to cede to the pressures and expectations of the heteronormative order of Taishō-period Japan, may have seen as increasingly difficult to access.

Still, one should not jump to the facile conclusion that, by pitting same-sex desire and criminality against the heterosexual family, the story is demonstrating an attitude that one might, in modern parlance, call homophobic. As discussed in the introduction of this book, sexologists and psychologists in Kaita's era typically drew a connection between crime and same-sex desire in order to point out the evils of the latter; however, Kaita's story focuses on the idea of same-sex desire and criminality as two *liberatory* activities that lead to a sense of personal fulfillment. As mentioned above, the text focuses far more on the fantastic, all-male space of the bandits than on the domestic sphere of Toda and his wife, revealing where the author's interest clearly lay. In fact, Nomiya almost certainly represents the daring, dangerous, insouciant figure that Kaita, with all of his infatuation with mysteries and adventure stories, imagined he might become if he threw off the shackles of ordinary civilization. (There are a number of unmistakable similarities between Kaita and his character Nomiya. Both were fascinated with the macabre. Both had the public persona of a strong, carefree fellow, but both were secretly lonely and yearned for the affections of particularly attractive, younger bishōnen from school. Both left their beloved bishōnen to pursue higher education, and both felt a profound, mysterious connection with the otherworldly mountains of Nagano.)

Meanwhile, Kaita is careful not to use any language that would ever condemn male–male desire. Even though Nomiya's criminal inclinations are indirectly linked to his inclination for male–male eroticism, the text treats him in a remarkably sympathetic light. Never does it denounce him as a monster; if anything, the inclusion of the stories of his roguish youth emphasize how lonely and misunderstood he was. Moreover, the story emphasizes the notion that male–male love manifests a kind of vital, primeval bravado that the transition from male–male to male–female love would simply suppress. Of course, the ending neutralizes any impression that Kaita might have been valorizing an antisocial existence of murder and misogyny. "Satsujin gyōja," in the end, represents no more than a fantasy. At the end of the story, the otherworldly, uncontrolled mountain society where men live, love, and murder remains separate from the remainder of the civilized world and virtually unknown by all but the artist who conveys Toda's account to the audience.

If anything, Kaita's story suggests the difficulty of crossing back and forth between the youthful, uninhibited, decadent "wildness" of male–male desire and the organized, "civilized" region of cross-sex desire and the family. At the same time, however, even though one might relegate male–male desire to the periphery of the unknown, it will continue to exercise its influence from the invisible reaches of that peripheral position. Even when suppressed to the social or individual unconscious, same-sex love does not lose its power entirely. Instead, just as Freudian psychology has suggested, suppressed feelings manifest themselves in unexpected ways at unexpected moments, thus thwarting attempts to rein them in.

It is interesting to note that just as Kaita turns the psychological connection between criminality and same-sex eroticism on its head, he also plays with the typical idea that hypnotism represents a means of dealing with same-sex desire. A number of the same Meiji and Taishō psychologists who condemned same-sex eroticism as deviant and pathological prescribed hypnotism as a means to modify sexual feelings and change the object of sexual attraction. Habuto Eiji and Sawada Junjirō, for instance, discuss hypnotism as one potential "cure" for same-sex desire in *Hentai seiyoku ron,* along with "recuperation therapy" (allegedly good for those experiencing same-sex desire in conjunction with neurasthenia) and "marriage therapy" (thus providing easy access to cross-sex eroticism). (Although this final form of "therapy" seems laughable to contemporary audiences, it did hold some currency in an era when many Japanese expected that, upon graduation, youthful schoolboy infatuations would naturally give way to more "mature" forms of desire.) Still, Habuto and Sawada are wary enough to note hypnosis is only "more or less effective" and is only highly recommended for those with "mild cases" *(keishō)* of erotic desire for the same sex, not "advanced ones" *(jūshō).*[29] As the number of sexological and psychological studies grew in the years after Kaita's death, various other writers continued to advocate hypnosis to straighten out practitioners of homoerotic desire. Ōtsuki Kenji (1891–1977), the psychologist and translator of Freud into Japanese, wrote in 1936 that parents and brothers should help guide adolescent relatives back to cross-sex love, but once adolescence is over and a sexual preference for the same sex has set in, the use of hypnotic suggestion therapy can provide particularly effective treatment. Ōtsuki says psychoanalysis is also effective, but since it takes much time, hypnotic therapy is the quickest remedy.[30]

The point here is that Kaita's story turns this medico-psychological dis-course about sexuality and hypnotism on its head, not by using hypnotism to cure male–male desire but to *evoke* it. Kaita is, in essence, countering the idea of hypnosis as a tool of healing with the idea hypnosis represented a sort of mind control. Hypnosis, Kaita suggests, might be used for the exact opposite purposes for which sexologists and psychologists had mobilized it—reactivating desires that heterosexist notions of family and adulthood relegate to the periphery of the social order.

## HUNGERING FOR FLESH

The relegation of male–male desire to an invisible but indomitable periph-ery is an appropriate ending for what would turn out to be the last important work in which Kaita would deal overtly with the subject of male–male erotic desire. After "Satsujin gyōja" appeared in *Bukyō sekai* in April 1915, the sub-ject of male–male erotic desire disappears almost entirely from his writing. Of the handful of other mystery-adventure stories Kaita published, only "Akuma no shita" ("The Diabolical Tongue") hints at male–male attraction, but in a less obvious fashion.

The main portion of "Akuma no shita" consists of a suicide note from an eccentric poet named Kaneko Eikichi who tells the story of his life.[31] He grew up with his parents and half-brother in the mountains of Hida in north-ern Gifu Prefecture, but when his mother dies, he develops a case of severe neurasthenia, which causes him to undergo a physical transformation. One day he finds his tongue has grown horrifically long and is covered by strange, wartlike bumps. Faint from the horror of this discovery, he hears a voice within his own head explaining, "Your tongue is the tongue of a devil. A diabolical tongue will be not be satisfied with anything less than diabolical fodder. Eat, eat everything! And seek out diabolical fare! If you do not, your tastes will never be satisfied!" (226–27) For months, he eats dirt, paper, mice, cattails, jellyfish, blowfish, rotten vegetables, lizards, leeches, newts, and other odd fare, but he begins to experience an irresistible desire to con-sume human flesh.

Even though Kaneko is reluctant to embrace his cannibalistic desires, they grow to the point he cannot help but leave propriety behind. One night, as he is passing through a graveyard, his hunger gets the best of him, and he frantically attempts to exhume a corpse to eat. Inside a coffin, he finds the decomposing corpse of a beautiful woman. Back at home, as he ecstatically consumes her flesh, he feels his "diabolical tongue dance about," and he feels

Murayama Kaita's own illustration for the first publication of "Akuma no shita" ("The Diabolical Tongue") in *Bukyō sekai* (1915). This illustration shows the character Kaneko Eikichi sticking out his tongue, which has become unusually large as the result of a mysterious illness. Collection of the author.

a great sense of satisfaction (228–29). Having left behind shame and fear, he begins planning to kill someone so he can consume a fresh corpse. One day, on a train, he spies a particularly attractive young man: "Although a little rustic in appearance, he was truly a graceful and beautiful young man. My mouth began to water. My saliva began to run" (229). Kaneko trails the young man through Ueno Park and knocks him out with chloroform. After taking his drugged victim home in a rickshaw, he gazes at the boy again. "Looking at him by the light of the electric lamp, I saw the young man was truly beautiful" (229).

Driven to new heights of excitement by the boy's beauty, Kaneko stabs him with a knife. "The eyes of the boy who had been out cold until just then, suddenly opened wide. In short measure, his black irises lost their light, and his face grew pale. I embraced the youth, who was as white as a sheet, and I lowered him into a holding chamber beneath the floor" (230). Over the course of several days, he slowly consumes the bishōnen's corpse, organ by organ. Only toward the end of this process does he notice a crescent-shaped birthmark on the right foot of the boy. Earlier on, Kaneko's testament had included in passing a mention of a birthmark on the foot of his half-brother, and with horror, Kaneko realizes he has just eaten his own flesh and blood. Horrified, he writes his last testament and commits suicide.

The text never overtly links Kaneko's cannibalistic desires with eroticism, but the story has undeniably strong erotic overtones. Kaneko's urges first appear when his tongue begins manifesting phallic qualities, becoming long, pointed, and dark in color. When Kaneko is about to taste human flesh for the first time, his tongue moves about on its own accord like a phallus suddenly grown erect. Finally, as he fulfills his secret desires for the first time, he experiences an orgasmic feeling of ecstasy. Although boys and girls whet his appetites equally, Kaneko chooses a particularly attractive bishōnen to fulfill his desires, and this gives the final scenes an unmistakable homoerotic ring. Significantly, the criteria he uses to select him are not girth or meatiness (qualities that might conceivably appeal to a cannibal) but general physical attractiveness. The final scene in which Kaneko plunges his knife into the body of his half-brother also has a clear sexual echo. (As Freud mentions in his famous study of the symbolism of dreams, "all elongated objects" as well as "all weapons and tools are used as symbols for the male organ: e.g. ploughs, hammers, rifles, revolvers, daggers, sabers, etc."[32]) After the boy dies, Kaneko gazes into his open eyes and lifts him to the secret chamber he has prepared. Apart from the murder, the scene is not unlike a cinematic

seduction with the male protagonist picking up and sweeping his lover into
the bedroom.

Hamada Yūsuke, a scholar of early Japanese detective fiction, has noted in
his discussion of the story that both hunger and the desire for sex involve
drives at the level of the id, and neither urge can be controlled through will-
power alone. Both involve a physical union between subject and object and
thus blur the boundaries between interior and exterior. Most importantly
however, Hamada notes both cannibalism and sex between men have been
treated as problematic in modern Japanese society.[33] Of course, the sever-
ity of the legal consequences of the two activities are profoundly different,
but Hamada rightly suggests Kaneko's cannibalistic desires, surrounded by
a cloud of secrecy, sound similar to the furtive erotic yearnings of a man suffering from a form of sexual desire he is afraid to act upon. As Kaneko strug-
gles with his developing appetites, a conflict develops between his desires
and society's expectations, and this conflict gives rise to confusion, shame,
and conversely, a heightened sense of elation when he finally does act on
those desires. The trope of secret desire, of course, is an especially powerfully charged one within ideological regimes that treat eroticism between
members of the same sex as problematic and dangerous, as did many of the
psychologists, sexologists, and educators of Kaita's era.

At the time he wrote the story, Kaita was eighteen years old, an age when
society increasingly expected individuals to satiate their sexual appetites
in marriages with members of the opposite sex—an expectation generally
(though not intrinsically) accompanied by a prohibition that excises eroticism from the acceptable spectrum of male–male relations. "Akuma no shita"
may be read as an exploration of the complicated feelings of one person suffering from some form of prohibited desire—desires relegated to the periphery of civilized society. Indeed, right about the time he published "Akuma
no shita" in 1915, Kaita's amorous feelings for attractive bishōnen disappear
almost entirely from his diary, poetry, and random jottings. Instead, they are
replaced by descriptions of the appeal of women like Otama, a model he first
encountered in late 1915 or 1916. Just as much of his early writing describes
pining from a distance for Inō Kiyoshi, his writing from Tokyo begins to
describe his unrequited longing for the beautiful women he meets.

Superficially, it seems Kaita had "graduated" from male–male desire to
cross-sex desire just as society expected; however, the fact Kaita wrote two
stories involving desire and secrecy about this same time seems no coincidence. Both stories involve men acting on desires the text aligns with the

uncivilized or bizarre. Although the connection between abnormal desire and peripheral status may seem a natural one for a magazine that routinely featured stories of exploration and faraway lands, Kaita's decision to include clear subtexts of homoerotic desire in these mystery-adventure stories may well have been triggered, at some level, by his own "graduation" to cross-sex desire and the relegation of his own adolescent desires for other boys to the periphery of his own experience.

As the fad for eroticism and the grotesque reached new heights in the 1920s and 1930s, an increasing number of authors would write tales with fantastic and bizarre plots reminiscent of Kaita's mystery-adventure stories. Like Kaita, many of these authors would reflect in their work, either consciously or unconsciously, major issues of the day, including the attitudes toward male–male desire. Of these, the most famous and popular was Edogawa Ranpo. As the following section shows, Ranpo was drawn powerfully to Kaita's writing because of its ripe and powerful expressions of homoeroticism, and several of his works, including those about homoerotic desire, can be read as a direct homage to his Taishō predecessor. For this reason, the next section of this study turns to him.

# 3

# The Appeal of the Strange

*Same-Sex Desire in Edogawa Ranpo's Mystery Fiction*

THE 1920S AND 1930S were a time of massive change in Japan. As the nation recovered from the devastating Kantō earthquake of 1923, the consumer market underwent a period of unprecedented expansion, as did the publishing industry and the related mechanisms of censorship. Meanwhile, the economy swelled then collapsed, driving the Japanese to increase colonial holdings on the Asian mainland. In conjunction with these developments, there emerged an increasingly complex, cosmopolitan, and hybrid modern culture that profoundly transformed Japanese life and expression.

In her study of the twenties and thirties in Japan, the scholar Miriam Silverberg argues the culture of the modern era consists of a mélange of different ideas, lifestyles, subcultures, social classes, and ethnicities that coexisted, sometimes forming jarring juxtapositions. In order to capture the sense of many things happening at once, photography, the graphic arts, cinematography, and even literature begin to use the montage as a common mode of production, since it highlights the plurality and multiplicity of any single given moment.[1] Silverberg notes that people became used to "code switching" to describe the increasingly complex culture of Japanese modern culture; people would employ a variety of different terms derived from various languages (Japanese, English, French, German, and the languages of the colonial empire) as well as various sociolects (languages of various social classes, segments of society, and regions) to describe to the cultural happenings around them. As more ideas flooded in from the West and the expanding empire, the number of codes to navigate only increased. Code switching was necessary, Silverberg argues, because as the culture grew increasingly complex there was no one ideological system defining modern Japanese language or culture; "there were many, including the rules of the ever-changing grammar of fashion, cooking, and other aspects of everyday life to which commentators on the moment were acutely attuned."[2] In other words, the code switching that took place constantly in the modern era was not just a simple matter of Japanese adopting ideas from the Western world; instead, it represented a means for individuals to navigate the different ideas, languages, and expectations of many different groups, classes, and subsets of society—none of whom had absolute authority over the ideology or culture of the era.

Indeed, literature, artwork, and expressions of popular culture show that individuals were constantly negotiating the ideas, language, and material culture of the twenties and thirties. In his study of Japanese crime literature, Mark Silver turns to the crime fiction Edogawa Ranpo wrote during this period not just because Ranpo represented a key figure in early Shōwa period culture, but also because Ranpo continually negotiated the complex code switching that took place as the Japanese nation entered the era of modernism, remaking itself in ways that would allow Japan to stand alongside the technologically advanced empires of the West.[3] He notes that as Japan moved into the Shōwa period, it found itself in a "double bind"; at the same as it drew on and adapted forms of knowledge and culture produced by the major international powers in the West, it also experienced a compulsion to create and identify its own cultural distinctiveness as a nation, while simultaneously coming to grips with its own increasingly plural, imperial culture. Silver notes impersonation, hybridity, and ambivalent relationships (primarily in relation to the West) dominate Ranpo's stories—relationships that reflect Ranpo's own awareness of his position as a Japanese citizen living in an era of change within a nation engaged in a cultural dialogue with the West at the same time as it strove to establish its own imperial dominance in Asia.

What is especially relevant to this book are the ways in which Ranpo engaged in "code switching" in his long, ongoing project to explore the world of sexuality, including the subject of amorous and erotic desire between men. Before turning to a more detailed discussion of his work, however, one should include a few words about Ranpo's career and the deployment of sexuality in his writing. Born with the name Hirai Tarō in the town of Nabari in Mie Prefecture, he spent most of his youth in Nagoya. As a student, he devoured adventure and mystery writing in translation, and later, while studying political science and economics at Waseda University, he began reading Sir Arthur Conan Doyle (1859–1930) and Edgar Allan Poe in English to quench his thirst for detective fiction and stories of the bizarre. With his debut work "Ni-sen dōka" ("The Two-Sen Copper Coin") published in *Shin seinen* (New youth) in 1923, Hirai adopted the pen name Edogawa Ranpo. Pronounced quickly, this humorous nom de plume sounds much like Edgar Allan Poe, revealing the extent of his admiration for the American pioneer of detective fiction; at the same time, however, it also follows the Japanese literary tradition of giving oneself an eccentric and therefore memorable pen name. While Edogawa (江戸川 "Edo river") is a perfectly good Japanese surname, it also is the name of a ward of Tokyo where the old merchant culture of pre-Meiji days continued to exist well into the twentieth century. "Ranpo," however, is a compound formed with two characters meaning "wild/disorderly" and "walking" (乱歩)—an amusing compound that, in combination with the surname, calls to mind a flâneur wandering restlessly, perhaps half drunk with wine or amazement, through the streets of the old *shitamachi* of Tokyo. This pen name suggests Ranpo's almost reckless willingness to traverse the complex terrain of new and old, premodern and modern, and as this chapter will suggest, Ranpo's works do exactly that. As Seth Jacobowitz, one of Ranpo's translators, has suggested, the image of Ranpo as a flâneur, which he emphasized in his own pen name, is an especially appropriate one for an author who dedicated much of his writing to describing the back streets of the metropolis, the hidden underside of modern life, and, by extension, the multilayered nature of Japanese modernity.[4]

Of course, Ranpo was not the first modern Japanese author to write mystery fiction.[5] Well before Ranpo entered the literary scene in 1923, not just Murayama Kaita but numerous authors, including Kuroiwa Ruikō (1862–1920), Oshikawa Shunrō, Okamoto Kidō (1872–1939), Kōda Rōhan (1867–1947), Tanizaki Jun'ichirō, and Satō Haruo, had incorporated elements of ratiocination, sleuthing, mystery, and crime within stories involving adventure, intrigue, the bizarre, and the grotesque. Some of these, such as the novella *Iki ningyō* (The living doll) written by Izumi Kyōka (1873–1939) in the 1890s, even feature the adventures of professional detectives. By the time Ranpo came on the scene, however, some critics were lamenting that Japanese writers seemed less interested in ratiocination and sleuthing than stories about bizarre and erotic crimes. Ranpo's debut story "Ni-sen dōka" focuses largely on the logical process of ratiocination used to solve a mystery; it includes an extensive description of an ingenious code (which involves both a popular Buddhist incantation as well as Japanese-language Braille), the means by which it is deciphered, and the unexpected reversal that occurs when a second message is found encrypted inside it.[6] This focus on the process of sleuthing delighted the doctor, criminologist, and future detective writer Kozakai Fuboku (1890–1929), who wrote in a review that the story had proved Japan finally had a detective writer as intelligent and capable as any in the Western world.[7] What was most significant, however, was that Ranpo applied the Western formula of mystery-solving to a distinctly Japanese context, carrying the reader into the back streets of the suburban slums of Tokyo and vividly depicting the world of two down-and-out students living on just a few *sen* per day.

The year after publishing this first story, Ranpo dedicated himself to writing full time and began churning out large numbers of stories for *Shin seinen* and other magazines. The success of his early work was so great that over the course of the 1920s and 1930s, the number of magazines soliciting stories and essays grew exponentially. Before long, he had published in virtually every important national forum of popular literature, and radio stations and private organizations routinely engaged him as a speaker. As a result, Ranpo quickly became one of the most visible and important popular authors of the era.

Much of his fiction from the 1920s and 1930s features heroes, sometimes flâneurs, detectives, or other urban explorers, who move from their own corners of society to mingle with various sorts of people both inside and outside mainstream society, but as early as the mid-1920s, Ranpo took up an interest in the world of "perverse sexuality." One of his early novellas, "D-zaka no satsujin jiken" (Murder on the sloping streets of D, 1925), involves a woman who was killed in the midst of sadomasochistic games with her husband. In this story, "perversity" makes its intrusion into the domestic space of the household, defamiliarizing the space of the home and suggesting there is more to the world of sexuality than normative sexual relations. The combination of mystery-solving and "perverse" sexuality first seen in this work figures prominently in many novels Ranpo wrote in years to come. As he rose to become a leading voice in the world of mystery fiction, this combination of eroticism and sleuthing set the stage for many other mystery authors, such as Oguri Mushitarō (1901–46) and Tachibana Sotō, who also depicted various forms of nonheteronormative sexuality in their work.

By publishing works containing elements of eroticism, authors like Ranpo and the editors of popular magazines such as *Shin seinen, Gurotesuku* (The grotesque), and *Hanzai kagaku* (Criminal science) contributed to the rise of the fad for what is sometimes known as *ero, guro, nansensu* (the erotic, the grotesque, and the nonsensical). Some postwar scholars have looked at this prewar fad as the result of attempts to seduce readers and sell copies of magazines to an eager public. Other scholars, however, have looked at the same literature as a means of withdrawing from the developments of on the international stage to create an alternative sphere of imaginative play that consciously resisted incorporation into the productive goals of the nation-state.[8] Both views are somewhat oversimplified in that they tend to overlook the important relationship between this literature and crucial social issues of the day. While it is true the literature of the fad for *ero, guro, nansensu* was born partly from market demands and the economic interests of the individual authors, it also served as a popular forum for exploring critical social issues. A growing body of studies has shown that such literature, although written for popular entertainment, involves key social and ideological issues that relate to the nation, the empire, science, medicine, sexuality, and the changing spectrum of gender relations.[9]

Popular authors like Ranpo found a perfect wedding of the erotic and the grotesque in the categories of "perverse sexual desire" *(hentai seiyoku)* described by sexologists and medical practitioners, and not surprisingly, these forms of sexuality begin appearing with increasing frequency in the literature of early Shōwa period. Beginning with "D-zaka no satsujin jiken," Ranpo's novels touch upon a host of issues related to sexuality, including gender transformation, sadomasochism, pygmalionism (doll-love), necrophilia, and so on. This chapter argues that although Ranpo did often employ sensationalizing rhetoric that might have helped him sell his stories, starting in the late 1920s, he also began an ongoing, concerted struggle to negotiate the meaning and significance of same-sex love. His early depictions of same-sex desire in fiction typically contain profoundly ambivalent messages. For instance, in several of the stories, characters encounter same-sex desire while traversing the landscape of contemporary Tokyo as flâneurs engaging in a "hunt for curiosities" *(ryōki)*. As a result, the descriptions of erotic desire in these stories are inevitably coded as curious and perplexing; however, they also display a clear fascination that sometimes seems at odds with the rhetoric used to describe it. One might argue this ambivalence is partly the result of attempting to apply the sensationalizing formulas of mystery fiction to a subject that, for Ranpo at least, held a degree of personal interest. In other words, the mixed messages are a result of switching between codes: a sensationalizing code that borrows the language of sexology to play up the "strangeness" of his subject matter and a more empathetic code in which his queer characters are able to voice their own desires.

This mixed rhetorical mode is most dramatically visible in the novel *Kotō no oni* (The demon of the lonely isle), which features a main character who has a sexual preference for other men. The story is narrated not by this character, however, but by a friend who repeatedly expresses his inability to understand his comrade's "mysterious love" (*fushigi na aijō*). Ranpo's decision to narrate the novel from the point of view of the friend gives him space to negotiate multiple code switches; the text vacillates between a critical and sensationalizing code, which describes manifestations of male–male eroticism as strange and even animalistic, and a more empathetic code when the character who prefers men has the opportunity to explain his own feelings. As a result, the text takes on a hybrid, almost pastiche-like quality. Ultimately, what makes this work especially worthy of study is not just its focus on same-sex desire, but its negotiation of codes as it explores the disconnect in the spectrum of homosocial relations haunting Japanese society in the early twentieth century.

## THE SEARCH FOR "STRANGE" SEXUAL DESIRE

Many of the representations of same-sex desire that appear in Ranpo's literature from the 1920s and 1930s appear within the context of what was called *ryōki* or "curiosity-hunting." This word, written with two characters meaning "hunting [for the] strange" (猟奇) exploded into popular circulation during the mid-1920s, and by the early 1930s it was regularly appearing in dictionaries of new, fashionable, and modern slang. As these dictionaries show, *ryōki* involved a scopophilic desire to uncover strange and bizarre "curiosities," especially ones having to do with the erotic, so the onlooker might experience a degree of precarious excitement and even titillation; for example, one dictionary from 1931 comments *ryōki* means the "search for the strange/unusual [*ki*]," but that "it is often used in cases having to do with sexual desire, such as chasing after the erotic [*ero*] and seeking out the grotesque [*guro*]."[10] Another dictionary published the same year concurs: "The word *ryōki*, which has become common in recent circulation, means, just as the characters suggest, searching for the strange [*ki*]. Within the word's nuances, however, one finds a strong tint of eroticism [*ero*] and the grotesque [*guro*]."[11] Because the act of hunting for the "strange" grew out of the same scopophilic drive that propelled people to explore the erotic, the grotesque, and the nonsensical, many publishers began to use the word *ryōki* in the titles of magazines and publications containing articles about these subjects. One sees this, for instance, in a 1929 newspaper advertisement for the inaugural issue of the magazine *Ryōki gahō* (Curiosity-hunting pictorial), which describes the magazine as full of photos of "the erotic and grotesque!!"[12] The 1931 photo collection *Gendai ryōki sentan zukan* (Pictorial of modernity, curiosity-hunting, and the trendsetting) includes a section subtitled *ryōki* alongside sections about *ero, guro,* and *nansensu,* suggesting that at the time, the word *ryōki* stood on equal par with the other terms as a popular obsession.[13]

People engaging in *ryōki* could conceivably satisfy their quest for "curiosities" in ways that were not erotic in nature, such as going to see the sideshows and public spectacles found in many of the large cities of Japan during this time; however, *ryōki* often involved seeking out manifestations of erotic desire Japanese society had started to label as "strange" in the Meiji and Taishō periods. In such contexts, *ryōki* was closely linked to the concept of "perverse sexual desire" that had gained currency due to the work of sexologists, medical practitioners, and moral reformers.[14] By designating certain sexual practices as perverse or deviant, the notion of perverse sexual desire excluded them from the realm of the normal and civilized. Ironically, by condemning these forms of desire, sexologists put in place boundaries of propriety that thrill-seeking curiosity-hunters might purposefully transgress. By labeling certain sexual acts and forms of sexual desire as strange, medical psychology and sexology helped turn them into precisely the kinds of "curiosities" curiosity-hunters might seek out. In this regard, the sexual dimension of *ryōki* is intimately related to the categorizing function of sexological discourse.

Not surprisingly, those who habitually engaged in *ryōki* were often looked upon with suspicion. One of the dictionaries quoted above includes an entry for *ryōkibyō kanja* (literally "patient with curiosity-hunting disease"). It states that a person who habitually engages in *ryōki* is a "perverse entity who seeks extraordinary stimulation and feels an interest in things that go beyond common sense. They are people for whom strolling in the Ginza, unemployment anxiety, the cinema, cafés, and such do not provide enough stimulation; therefore, they hunt about wildly in all directions."[15] Another source concurs that the *ryōkibyō kanja* is "a perverse modern youth who seeks out extraordinary types of stimulation" when the stimulation afforded by daily life "does not suffice."[16] Some sources discuss this phenomenon specifically as a product of modernity; for example, one dictionary asserts, "when the nerves of modern people no longer allow them to be content with the hackneyed and the commonplace, they begin to crave the stimulation afforded by the abnormal and the strange."[17] As examples, this source mentions the excitement afforded by staying in allegedly haunted inns or searching through secret, scary parts of town. It explains, "there is no problem as long as people are only interested in *ryōki*-like activities, but this can grow worse and people can have existences afflicted by *ryōki* [*hiryōkiteki sonzai*]. These people call themselves 'ultramodern' but their actions smack of insanity, for they gladly do unusual, terrifying things that violate common sense." As examples, the dictionary points to various "perverse groups" of men who go to live with lepers, dress in bright red girlish kimonos, grow their hair particularly long, or paint their faces with ink and rouge—all for the sake of increased levels of stimulation. The equation between modernity, a heightened need for stimuli, and perverse psychology is evident in a definition of *hentai shinri* (perverse psychology) found in another dictionary from 1931: "Perverse psychology is one special characteristic of modern man. As culture progresses and urban life becomes increasingly more complicated, people are not satisfied unless they have exceedingly strong stimulation. All of their interests and feelings lean increasingly toward the unhealthy."[18] In other words, early Shōwa commentators saw the rising interest in "strange" phenomena as intimately related to the advance of capitalism, and the tendency of the cities to heighten its inhabitants' need for stimulation.

*Ryōki* appears numerous times in Ranpo's oeuvre as a remedy for boredom. In the 1925 short story "Yaneura no sanposha" ("The Stalker in the Attic"), the protagonist Gōda Saburō is afflicted with a boredom so intense "it probably was a type of psychological illness. No matter what sort of entertainment he tried, no matter what sort of work he did, no matter what he would do, the world was not the least bit interesting to him" (1:249).[19] After trying various professions, experimenting with different pastimes, and moving multiple times, he finally develops an interest in crime fiction, which eases his boredom somewhat. Meanwhile, he takes to wandering in a *ryōki*-like fashion through the bustling district of Asakusa with its small shops, amusement areas, theaters, sideshows, and pleasure districts. The novel states, "Asakusa was like a toy box, which if suddenly emptied would rain down various gaudily colored paints. For a person with a taste for crime, the amusement areas of Asakusa were a superb setting" (1:251). As these outings grow more frequent, Gōda begins dressing up in a various costumes and pretending to be different types of people—laborers, beggars, students, and so on—while walking the streets. In fact, these *ryōki* searches begin to take on a homoerotic dimension. Gōda discovers cross-dressing gives him a considerable thrill, especially when he flirts with men:

> Of the costumes he tried, dressing as a woman pleased his morbid habit the most. Accordingly, he sold off his kimono, watch, and other things so he could earn some money to buy an expensive wig and used ladies' clothing. On those occasions when he would wear his beloved female outfits for an extended period of time, he would put an overcoat over his head and leave his lodgings under the dark cloak of night. He would then remove the overcoat at an appropriate place and set off. One time, he strolled around a lonely park; another, he entered a movie theater as it was closing. There, after purposely entering the seats reserved for male cinemagoers, he went as far as trying to play some risky practical jokes on the men there. He derived great pleasure from the illusion brought about by the clothing, and he imagined himself toying freely with various men as if he were a poison woman like Dakki no Ohyaku or Oyoshi the Python. (1:251–52)

Stories of seductive yet murderous women, often called "poison women" (*dokufu*), were popular in the late nineteenth century, and storytellers, storybooks, kabuki actors, and sensational journalists told their stories in various forms. In "Yaneura no sanposha," Gōda pretends to be these murderous seductresses and makes erotic overtures to the men in the movie theater while perhaps fantasizing about ushering them to an untimely death. Whether or not these "risky practical jokes" (*kiwadoi itazura*) involved actual physical contact is unclear, but the context makes it clear Gōda's play involves an explicit homoerotic dimension, and the fact that other men do not recognize him as a man only adds to the excitement. The inspiration for this passage almost certainly comes from the 1911 story "Himitsu" ("The Secret") by one of the Japanese authors Ranpo admired most, Tanizaki Jun'ichirō. In Tanizaki's story, the protagonist also tries wearing women's clothing in the streets in order to experience the thrill of seeing the world in a whole new way. He too relishes the looks other men give him, but although he also goes into a movie theater, his escapades do not go as far as erotic contact with other men.[20]

Ranpo's essays show that, like the main character in "Yaneura no san-posha," Ranpo himself sometimes wandered through the city in costume, try-ing to quell his boredom. According to the 1928 essay "Mudabanashi" ("Idle Chatter"), boredom drove him to spend whole afternoons and evenings sit-ting on benches in Asakusa Park and wandering about in disguise (16:29–34). He does not mention doing drag, but one of his most famous novels, *Inju (The Beast in the Shadows),* published in *Shin seinen* in 1933, suggests female clothing was one of his disguises. This complex novella describes the fear of a woman who claims she is being stalked by Ōe Shundei, a popular detective writer. Ranpo cleverly describes the character Shundei as resem-bling himself to an incredible degree, and even the names of Shundei's writ-ings sound strikingly familiar to readers who know Ranpo's fiction; from these hints, it is clear that in the comments about Ōe Shundei, Ranpo was indirectly making tongue-in-cheek comments about his own writing and lifestyle.[21] At one point, one of the principal characters makes the follow-ing speech in a denunciation of Shundei: "All detective novelists are mon-sters. Men try transforming themselves into women, and when they really get the taste for curiosity-hunting [*ryōki no shumi*], they go ahead and actu-ally try doing it. Why, a certain novelist dressed up like a woman one night and went parading around Asakusa Park. And then, he even tried imitating love with a man! [*otoko to koi no manegoto sae yatta*]" (3:257). The text does not identify Shundei—the character who conspicuously resembles Ranpo—as the writer in drag, but given the high degree of self-reference in the novella, it seems likely Ranpo was insinuating he had tried the guise in ques-tion. In any case, the text is unequivocal in stating that people interested in *ryōki* might turn to gender-bending dress and perhaps even homoerotic encounters to satisfy their yearning for adventure.

## The Appeal of Asakusa

The reason Asakusa appears so frequently in these and other contemporary *ryōki* narratives has to do with its sheer popularity as one of Tokyo's most bustling parks. During the Taishō and early Shōwa period, Asakusa Park was popular not just among *ryōki* seekers, but also among vast segments of the Tokyo population. Several decades before, in the years immediately after the Meiji Restoration, the government designated the area around Sensōji Tem-ple as one of Tokyo's first public parks, and a few years later two large ponds were created to the west of the temple's main hall. In 1885 a long row of brick shops called the Nakamise was created in front of the main hall of Sensōji, and an entertainment district known as Rokku developed nearby, complete with a large number of theaters, operetta houses, and, in later years, cinemas. Small shops, public performances, freak shows, caged animals, and gardens filled the areas of Hanayashiki and Okuyama. In 1890 private developers created the park's most famous structure, a tall brick tower with a wooden frame that dwarfed all other buildings in the Tokyo metropolis. Known officially as the Ryōunkaku, this building was popularly called the "Asakusa Twelve Stories" (Asakusa jū-ni-kai), and it stood at one end of the Rokku. Visible throughout the metropolis, this sixty-meter structure immediately became an important symbol of Japanese modernity, and the top of the tower became one of Tokyo's most important tourist attractions, offering an expansive view of the rapidly growing city until its destruction in 1923.[22] Most of Ranpo's visits to Asakusa Park were well after the colossal earthquake of 1923 had snapped the tower in two, leaving authorities with no choice but to demolish what little remained of the tower, but the memory of the tower and the bustling walkways of Asakusa Park before the earthquake held a strong appeal for him. In fact, one of Ranpo's most famous short stories, "Oshie to tabi suru otoko" ("The Man Traveling with the Brocade Portrait") published in *Shin seinen* in 1929, takes place in and around the twelve-storied tower, which had already become the object of nostalgia for Asakusa aficionados like him (6:9–24).[23]

The metropolitan parks offered space for people from different walks of life to interact, and as such, they served as a forum for flirtation, prostitution, or even full-fledged physical encounters. The dark corners of parks provided places where couples could avoid prying eyes, and from at least the late Meiji onward, they served as semiprivate sites of escape in a city where very few could afford a house or even an apartment by themselves. Two of the most popular places for amorous encounters were the parks in Asakusa and Hibiya. According to one article that appeared in *Chūō shinbun* (Central Newspaper) in 1916, even so-called "respectable" people such as doctors and schoolteachers went to Hibiya to meet on the park benches and fields to engage in "half-animalistic actions."[24] The scholar Inoue Shōichi has shown that sex in Tokyo's parks gave enough concern to police that they stepped up patrols in the parks for the specific purpose of inhibiting such behavior.[25]

Texts from the period show Tokyo's parks, including Asakusa, provided furtive meeting places for men. Inagaki Taruho's essay "Shōnen tokuhon" (Youth reader), a revised version of a text first published in the magazine *Gurotesuku* in 1930, lists an area on the far side of one of the Asakusa lakes

in a list of places where men might meet other men for sex.[26] In the short
story "Rōkō" (Squalid alleyways) published by the leftist writer Kataoka
Teppei (1894–1944) in 1934, two homeless workers meet on a park bench
in Asakusa and start an "unnatural relationship" *(fushizen na kankei)* that
continues for months.[27] Hamao Shirō's article "Dōseiai kō" (Thoughts on
same-sex love) from 1930 states it was common knowledge men could purchase the services of effeminate male prostitutes *(kagema)* after eight P.M.
in one corner of Asakusa Park; likewise, the art critic Andō Kōsei noted
that *kagema* were a common sight by the pond in Hibiya Park and behind
Sensōji in Asakusa.[28]

Ranpo's memoirs and essays, especially those written in the mid-1920s,
show he spent a great deal of time in Asakusa Park.[29] In fact, a newspaper
article from 1931 indicates he sometimes spent the night there. One day,
a reporter decided he would play detective and follow Ranpo, who was
already one of Japan's most famous detective novelists, from his house. After
trailing Ranpo to the park, he found him sitting alone on a bench near some
other men. When the reporter approached him, Ranpo was taken aback and
asked worriedly if the reporter intended to write about finding him there.
Ranpo then defended his presence in the park by saying he liked to talk with
the vagrants and the police. He also commented that he often spent whole
nights in the park, chatting with different men.[30] During these nocturnal visits, Ranpo apparently ran across people who had gone to the park to search for
erotic encounters. As early as 1926, Ranpo described in an article "Asakusa
shumi" (A taste for Asakusa) the kinds of people one might see at night in
the park. One of them is a "strange type of person" *(igyō no mono):* "Although
they are men, they are painted with white make-up. They say, '*Choi, Anata!*
Hey, you there!' to people passing by and beckon to them as they twist their
bodies seductively. These fellows are what are known as 'outdoor *kagema*'"
(16:23). The word *kagema* had first emerged during the Edo period to refer
to effeminate male entertainers who sold their bodies to men, usually in tea-
houses in the red-light districts of the cities.

Two novels written about that time contain scenes describing men flirting
in the park. These passages are worth examining in particular detail because
they reveal a great deal about the mechanisms Ranpo and other authors
of *ero, guro, nansensu* fiction employed in depicting "curiosities" like same-
sex desire. In both cases, the texts insist the protagonists are not personally
interested in such matters; however, both texts follow the actions of the men
with great attention as if fascinated with what might happen next.

Early in the novel *Issun-bōshi* (The dwarf), serialized from 1926 to 1927 in the *Asahi shinbun,* the text describes the promenades of the curiosity-hunting protagonist Kobayashi Monzō in Asakusa Park:

> Most of the people he saw were tramps looking for places to sleep, detectives, and uniformed police officers who made their rounds every thirty minutes rattling their sabers. There were also curiosity-seekers [*ryōkisha*] like Monzō. However, there was also a queer kind of person [*isshu iyō no jinshu*] that did not belong to any of these groups. As soon as you realized they had been sitting on a bench near you for a few moments, they would stand up, start walking along the same path as you, and wander back and forth aimlessly. When they met another person strolling on the dark path between the trees, they would look meaningfully into the other person's eyes or ask for a light, even if they already had their own matches. Their faces were shaved extremely neatly, and their faces were perfectly smooth. A lot of them wore navy-colored kimonos with sashes in the *kakuobi* style. (3:100–101)

Monzō wants to find out exactly what these people are doing, even though "it was not impossible to imagine from the way they walked" (3:101). One evening, he sees two men in the shadows:

> The couple was seated on a bench and was talking in low voices. One was a gentleman dressed in Western clothes and the other was a man who looked like a real playboy.
>
> As he stroked his mustache, the man in the suit stated in a muffled voice, "Unusually warm, isn't it?"
>
> "Yeah, real warm these last few days," answered the playboy quietly.
>
> The two seemed to be meeting for the first time, but there was something strange about the combination of the two. Both looked about forty. One of them was stiff and formal like a petty official, and the other was a pure Asakusa man through and through. The hour had grown so late they were in danger of missing the last train, but even so, there they were talking insouciantly about the weather. Very strange. The couple must have had some designs on one another. Kobayashi felt his curiosity grow.

"So, how's business?" asked the man in the suit as he stared up and down at the plump body of the other man. His tone indicated he was not particularly interested in the answer.

"Well . . . ," answered the plump man. He leaned forward and planted both elbows on his knees and hung his head as he spoke . . .

In due time, the man in the suit stretched with an "Aah" and stood up. No sooner had Monzō noticed this than the man cast a nervous glance in Monzō's direction. Strangely enough, he then sat down again on the same bench just a hair's breadth away from the plump playboy. Feeling this, the plump man cast a look in the direction of the suited man and immediately returned to his original posture. The balding forty-year-old gave a coquettish look as if embarrassed.

The man in the suit suddenly extended his arm as far as it would go—it looked like he had the arms of a monkey—and he took the hand of the plump fellow beside him.

The two whispered to each other in muffled tones for a moment and then stood up from the bench, having reached some sort of agreement. With their arms all but entwined, they walked down the hill together. (3:102–3)

Clearly, the two men are "cruising"—looking for potential sexual partners. Ranpo's attention to detail shows that Monzō, who is watching the scene, is fascinated by their behavior. In great detail, the narrative describes the intimacy of the couple's movements and gestures, which seem incongruous with the banality of their conversation. At the same time, the text contains conjunctions such as "strangely enough" (*fushigi na koto ni wa*) that portray the scene as rather odd. As a result, the passage sounds like it is narrated by someone curiously examining the customs of a group of people with whom he does not particularly identify, almost like an ethnographer observing a foreign culture. Following the passage is a statement that emphasizes that, despite his curiosity, Monzō cannot comprehend such expressions of homoerotic desire: "Monzō felt a chill run along his spine. It is a strange metaphor, but this chill was a lot like the one he experienced when he saw the wax dummies in a hygiene fair. It was not a feeling of unhappiness or fear or anything he could really describe" (3:103). The mention of wax statues in a "hygiene fair" (*eisei hakurankai*) brings to mind mannequins of dissected, deformed, or disease-ridden bodies, things that are disturbing only when one imagines oneself in a comparable state. Similarly, Monzō's frisson is an unconscious reaction to the thought of engaging in sexual intimacy with another man. With this passage, the narrative reassures the reader of the character's "normality," thus underlining the notion that the text is viewing these displays of "perverse" desire from a safe remove.

The 1930 novel *Ryōki no hate* (The fruits of curiosity-hunting) also describes an encounter that appears, at least at first, to have homoerotic overtones. The protagonist Aoki Ainosuke is standing near one of the lakes in Asakusa Park when he happens to see a group of apparently homeless adolescents wandering the street. Among them is a "fine-looking adolescent who stood out from the others" (4:217). He attracts Ainosuke's attention, and the two lock gazes. This flirting prompts Ainosuke to remember the "Asakusa street boys" who sell themselves to other men for money:

> The youth stared unflinchingly at Ainosuke. He was wearing spring clothes dominated by navy blue and, in the same color, a tweed cap that resembled one someone might wear with a school uniform. Floating up from the darkness beneath the visor, which was pulled down far over his face, was a pale face with soft contours. He was a beautiful youth.
>
> Ainosuke was by no means a pederast [*pederasuto*], so he wasn't especially happy about being stared at, but he didn't feel especially displeased either. (4:217)

Although the boy's advances do not flatter him, they do not bother him terribly as long as the boy does not try to carry them any further. For a few moments, Ainosuke becomes caught up in the sights and sounds of the bustling park, but the boy speaks to him and brings him back to reality:

> All of the sudden, Ainosuke heard someone say "Hey there!" The voice seemed to call out to him elegantly, almost as if whispering in his ear. He turned around and saw the beautiful youth from before standing there. He had slipped up alongside Ainosuke.
>
> Ainosuke was at a loss for words. That was because he had learned one time what would happen when an Asakusa *Urning* tried to seduce you. (4:218)

The boy begins whispering to him about money, and he tells Ainosuke there is a place nearby that can "make miracles." Ainosuke stares back at a loss. At this moment, the boy realizes Ainosuke has misunderstood his intensions, and he states, "Oh no, I'm not one of them. I'm not a woman." With this denial, the boy lumps together male hustlers with women, implying that men who sleep with other men are not completely male. The boy mumbles something about being a broker in miracles, and when the confused Ainosuke tries to clarify what he means, the boy suddenly departs. Much later in the novel, we learn the boy was not an "Asakusa *Urning*" (Ranpo uses the German term invented in 1864 by Karl-Heinrich Ulrichs [1825–95] to refer to men attracted to other men), but a member of a gang of criminals.

What is important for this discussion is the attitude of the protagonist when he mistakenly believes the bishōnen is coming on to him. Although Ainosuke does not seek an intimate encounter with the boy, he is curious about people like him. In fact, the text states a "curiosity-seeker like Ainosuke could not help but be aware of the existence of such boys" hustling in the park. Far from being an irritant, their presence recalls the bustling, cosmopolitan atmosphere of the park before the great Kantō earthquake of 1923:

> After the loss of the twelve-storied tower and the Egawa girls,
> Ainosuke was not especially excited by Asakusa, which seemed to
> just stretch on and on without interest. If pressed, one could still
> see traces of Asakusa's former strange appeal in the decadent
> Yanagi-bushi, Mokubakan, the strange things on the second floor of
> the aquarium, the groups of homeless in the park, and the street
> boys. It was the atmosphere these things evoked that made him set
> out for Asakusa at least once every two months or so. (4:217)

The Egawa girls, who performed in a theater beside one of the lakes, were one of the most popular shows in Rokku, startling audiences with their ability to balance on giant wooden balls while juggling and performing acrobatics. Yanagi-bushi was a form of music popular in Asakusa during the Taishō period, and it was performed in inexpensive music halls throughout the quarter. The Mokubakan was home to a popular merry-go-round that Ranpo visited frequently and described in his famous short story "Mokuba wa mawaru" (The merry-go-round goes round) from 1926 (3:191–99). Next to it was the aquarium, which hosted the Casino Follies (*kajino fōri*) on its second floor. Open for business in 1929, this intimate hall became well known for its titillating musical revues and performances, which were seen as epitomizing a new ethos of eroticism and decadent modernism. Ainosuke is, in other words, not interested in the hustlers of Asakusa Park for sexual reasons, but he enjoys seeing them because, like the other places he mentions, they recall the ethos of sexuality, innocent fun, and cosmopolitanism of Asakusa before the 1923 earthquake.

In short, the protagonists of both *Issun-bōshi* and *Ryōki no hate* are not looking for sexual encounters with other men, but both gaze upon manifestations of male–male erotic desire with interest, either curious to find out how it operates or eager to recall the cosmopolitanism of the past. Watching these manifestations of erotic desire proves interesting, even when the protagonists are reluctant to engage directly in the activities they are watching. In both cases, the text displays a certain "push-and-pull" dynamic. They evoke the scopophilic interest of the scene for readers while simultaneously preserving the boundaries between witnessing subject and viewed object. Such "push-and-pull" dynamics can be found in many texts from the heyday of *ero, guro, nansensu* that deal with those subjects that psychology and sexology had described as "perverse." Texts displaying these dynamics usually stir up reader interest by describing a certain phenomenon as frightening, strange, or outside the bounds of ordinary propriety. At the same time, they describe the phenomenon with careful attention to detail, giving the reader the impression he or she is catching a glimpse of a world ordinarily shut off from view. Ranpo's works are typical of this type of popular *ero, guro, nansensu* literature in that they appeal to the voyeuristic impulse while at the same time allowing the reader to maintain the comfort of moral and ethical superiority.

## "Strange" Islands, "Strange" Sex

In the late 1920s and 1930s, Japanese editors were seeking exciting, attention-grabbing stories to fill the vast numbers of popular magazines that were proliferating with unprecedented rapidity. In 1918, 3,123 magazines were registered with the state, but by 1932, the number had risen to 11,118. In the mid-1920s the magazine *Kingu* (King), published by Kōdansha, had made media history by selling more magazines per month than any other magazine in Japanese history. When first printed in 1925 the magazine sold 740,000 copies, and within a year it was selling a million copies per month.[31] Hakubunkan, the publisher of *Shin seinen* (the journal in which Ranpo had published his earliest stories), was eager to stake out its share of the rapidly expanding market for popular magazines, and it responded by creating the

magazine *Asahi* (Morning sun). Hasegawa Tenkei (1876–1940), the chief
editor of the new magazine, asked Morishita Uson (1890–1965), the editor
of *Shin seinen* at the time of Ranpo's debut, to approach Ranpo to encourage
him to write a novel for serialization beginning in their inaugural issue.
Although Ranpo had become one of Hakubunkan's brightest stars with the
resounding critical success of his novella *Inju,* Ranpo refused at first, claim-
ing he did not have the ability to create long, involved plots. Eventually,
however, his feeling of indebtedness to Uson prevailed, and he agreed.
The result was *Kotō no oni,* Ranpo's second book-length novel, serialized
in fourteen installments of *Asahi* between January 1929 and February 1930.
It is in this novel, perhaps more than any other part of Ranpo's oeuvre,
that one finds the distinctive combination of standoffishness and attraction
vis-à-vis "the strangeness" of adult homoeroticism that characterizes the
*ryōki* mentality.

The idea for the novel came to Ranpo while he was on vacation in the
Kii Peninsula in the southern portion of the Kansai region. His close friend
the writer and anthropologist Iwata Jun'ichi, who was originally from the
region, came to visit him, and together they spent a few days visiting the fish-
ing villages and islands at the southern tip of the peninsula. The time they
spent together provided inspiration for the novel in at least two ways. Iwata
had brought a volume of Mori Ōgai's writings, one of which included a reference to a Chinese story about men who purposefully crippled others. This
inspired Ranpo to continue thinking about the possibilities of maiming
human bodies through surgery, and at some point he came up with the idea
for a story about an evil hunchback who takes out his hatred on the world
by purposefully creating a race of mutilated people. More importantly for
the purposes of this study, the time Ranpo spent with Iwata inspired him
to write about male–male desire. As the next chapter will discuss in more
detail, Iwata was, like Ranpo, extremely interested in same-sex amorous and
erotic desire; in fact, in 1949 Ranpo wrote a short article that names Iwata
as one of his "great teachers" on the subject. During their trip together, the
two talked a good deal about the subject, and this inspired Ranpo to write
about it in a novel. In writing about *Kotō no oni* in his memoirs, Ranpo states,

> There is almost nobody in modern times who is interested in
> same-sex love other than when it appears in the context of writing
> about classical Greece, Rome, or the Genroku period. For that
> reason, I thought the idea of writing something about same-sex love

in modern times for a popular entertainment magazine might be misguided. However, in those days, I often talked with Iwata about the historical facts of same-sex love, both east and west. Perhaps I was influenced by our discussions. But because it was a detective novel I was to write, I was not able to write about this queer form of love as I liked. It was just a hindrance to the story. (20:201)

Nonetheless, Ranpo did include in *Kotō no oni* a character, Moroto Michio, who is drawn exclusively to other men. It is unclear what exactly Ranpo meant when he stated he was not able to write about this "queer form of love" (*iyō na ren'ai*) as he wished, but it seems he was disappointed that the generic expectations of mystery fiction, namely the need to explore the motivation and particulars of a crime, meant his character's feelings could not take center stage. While it is true Moroto's feelings are described here and there in *Kotō no oni,* the relationship between him and the man he loves is only one in a complicated tangle of subplots involving murder, adventure, and even the search for hidden treasure. Another reason Ranpo may have felt he could not write about same-sex desire as he wished may have been because he felt a need to cater to the popular obsession with the erotic and grotesque that was becoming increasingly common in mystery fiction of that period. Although the novel sometimes treats the character Moroto quite sympathetically, other parts of the novel "code switch" and describe male–male desire as strange and even deviant, especially in the beginning of individual installments, where the references to his "strange" sexual desires were particularly likely to catch the eyes of curious readers. In those parts of the novel, Moroto's preference for the same sex clearly appears as one element of the plot designed to startle and fascinate curious readers eager to encounter the "strange" and "grotesque." As Mark Silver has pointed out, Moroto's sexual advances to the heterosexual narrator are "meant to be the height of spine-tingling deviance and horror"—an element of the bizarre, grotesque, and "unnatural" that would shock and fascinate contemporary readers.[32]

Certainly, the novel does sometimes describe male homoeroticism in terms that are far from flattering, but to dwell exclusively on these is to gloss over the complicated code switching present in the text. As one strategy to catch the attention of readers, Ranpo at times has Minoura, the narrator of the story, describe Moroto's sexual proclivities as "strange," but elsewhere, Ranpo shifts the locus of narration and gives Moroto the opportunity to

describe his feelings in long quotations, thus breaking down the stereotypes established elsewhere in the text. The result is a complex "push-and-
pull" dynamic that consistently undermines expectations set up elsewhere
in the text.

In a carefully nuanced article about the novel, Jim Reichert has noted the
text "destabilizes such essential binaries as normal versus abnormal, fit versus unfit, hero versus villain, and respectable citizen versus deviant."[33] He
notes that by incorporating into his detective novel a number of "seemingly incompatible generic formulas, topics, and images," Ranpo creates a
web of mixed signals that complicates readings of the novel as expressing
either a clear endorsement or categorical disapproval of male–male erotic
desire. Reichert notes the terminology used to describe Moroto and his
sexual preference is constantly shifting, but he fails to notice the patterns
that govern the particular choices of terminology and the narrator's vacillat-
ing responses to Moroto.[34] As the following discussion will argue, there is a
pattern governing the descriptions of Moroto and his sexual desires, and
there are three factors at work within this pattern. First and most obviously,
the question of what is happening in the plot at any given moment has a
large bearing on the narrator Minoura's view of Moroto and therefore significantly shapes the language he uses to describe him. Second, the references to
Moroto's sexual preferences as strange or aberrant almost always appear at
the beginning of new installments of the novel, where they are likely to catch
the attention of readers eager to read about the erotic and grotesque. (Each
of the fourteen installments of the book consists of several chapters; therefore, when the novel is reproduced in book form, it is not possible to identify
where these individual installations began unless there are special annota-
tions.[35]) Third, *Kotō no oni,* like Ranpo's other novels and essays, treats homosocial desire as largely unproblematic and even desirable, yet homoerotic
desire is described with a tone that swings between revulsion and fascination;
therefore, the mode in which the text portrays male–male desire has much to
do with the degree of erotic tension involved at that particular moment.

Because the novel shifts tone so frequently in its discussion of male–male
desire, it is worth examining the relevant passages in the order they appear
in the text to understand the ways the text vacillates between codes. The
novel consists of a first-person narrative by a protagonist named Minoura.[36]
At the onset of his tale, he captures his audience's attention by stating he has
experienced things so frightening that they caused his hair to turn completely
white in the course of a single night. The long and bizarre tale in which he

explains this begins, "I think I must also withstand my embarrassment and also reveal a homosexual-like incident [*dōseiai-teki na jiken*] in which a certain person came between us" (4:10). As the story unfolds, the reader learns of a love triangle between Minoura, his male friend Moroto, and Minoura's lover, the beautiful and gentle young woman Hatsuyo. Minoura's first mention of the subject of male–male desire treats it as an embarrassing or shameful subject, but to interpret this passage as mere homophobia would be to miss the point of its inclusion. Ranpo often includes references to Moroto's sexual preference for men and his "strange" behavior in order to seduce his audience into reading further. Significantly, the "negative" references almost always appear near the beginning of installments where readers of *Asahi* were especially likely to encounter them. Minoura's passing references to male–male desire represent, in other words, a coy ploy designed to draw curious readers into the story. It is precisely these references, made all the more enticing by Minoura's reticence to indulge in any details, that would have whetted the appetite of readers intrigued by the early Shōwa-period fashion for "erotic, grotesque" displays of nonheteronormative forms of eroticism.

Minoura explains he and Hatsuyo were colleagues in a trading company and became engaged, but soon after their engagement, Hatsuyo began receiving offers of marriage from Moroto, a researcher in medical science. These offers are particularly surprising considering that Moroto "seems to have felt a rather serious homosexual love [*dōsei no ren'ai*]" for Minoura (4:13). Minoura explains that for several years Moroto "bore a certain incomprehensible love" for him. He did not respond in kind, but the two became good friends. He states, "Of course, I could not possibly understand that sort of love, but I did not find anything especially unpleasant in his profound academic learning, his speech and behavior, which suggested he might be a genius of sorts, or his features with their strange appeal. For that reason, as long as his behavior did not cross certain boundaries, I was not averse to receiving his goodwill as the simple love of a friend" (4:18). These feelings developed when Minoura was a seventeen-year-old student in his fourth year of technical school, and Moroto a twenty-three-year-old budding professional. Rumors begin to circulate the two friends are "queer" *(hen),* and Minoura noticed Moroto would sometimes flush when they would exchange glances. Minoura understood this as masked erotic attraction: "Such things went on at school as little more than play, so when I imagined Moroto's feelings, I would sometimes blush even when I was all alone. Still, it was not an especially unpleasant feeling" (4:18).

Minoura tacitly acknowledges Moroto's erotic affections, and although
he does not return them, he is not particularly disturbed by them either. If
anything, he seems to secretly enjoy them: "As far as I knew, Moroto was a
bishōnen with a most noble air, both in terms of body and spirit, and even
though I certainly did not feel a strange attachment to him, I gained a little
more confidence in my appearance when I considered he found me a suitable
match for his choosy tastes" (4:13). At some point, Moroto asks Minoura to
go to a public bath, and there, Moroto offers to scrub his back. Minoura comments, "At first, I interpreted this as simple kindness, but when I became aware
of his feelings, I still let him do it. My self-respect would not be wounded if
that's as far as it went" (4:18). The clear implication is that an asexual friendship would be permissible or even desirable, but a relationship that crosses
over into erotic behavior would be illicit and wrong. For this reason, Minoura
carefully polices the divide between homosocial and homoerotic desire, and
guards against sending any message that might invite a physical encounter.
For instance, he notes he and Moroto would frequently walk together, holding hands or putting their arms around one another's shoulders. Sometimes
he would sense a "strong passion" emanating from Moroto's fingers. This
would cause Minoura's heart to pound, and he would let Moroto hold his
hand "as he wished," but he would never grab Moroto's hand in return (4:19).

The issue of Moroto's unreciprocated feelings comes to the forefront
a half year into their friendship. One night after drinking, Moroto enters
Minoura's room. As Minoura reclines on his bed, Moroto stands over him
and abruptly says, "You are beautiful." For a moment, Minoura imagines
himself as a woman being courted by the handsome bishōnen standing over
him: "What he was saying seemed very strange. At that moment, the strange
thought flitted through my mind that I had been transformed into a woman,
and that the youth standing beside me with his beautiful face, which had
become all the more flushed and appealing because of his intoxication, was
my husband" (4:13). Moroto touches Minoura's hand and comments on its
desiring heat. At this point, there is a single line break in the text, as if there
is a skip in the narrator's consciousness of the events.[37] With this typograph-
ical interruption, which was not necessarily always reproduced in later reprintings of the text, the fantasy of cross-sex seduction is broken, and the
narrator recoils from Moroto's intimate touch. Moroto realizes he has gone
too far, and he apologizes.

Moroto puts his hands over his face. A moment later, he states, "Please
don't look upon me with contempt. You probably think I'm disgraceful. You

are a different race than I. You are a different race from me in every sense, but I cannot explain what that means. Sometimes I become so afraid I start trembling" (4:20). This passage hints that Moroto thinks of himself as profoundly unlike men who love women, and he begs Minoura not think of him as "disgraceful" or "contemptible" *(asamashii)*. Moroto's words suggest he has internalized the work of those Meiji- and Taishō-period psychologists and sexologists who argued that people who experience "perverse sexuality" had a distinct psychological constitution that distinguished them from so-called "normal" people.

Later in the novel, when readers learn about Moroto's past, however, one realizes a second meaning may be hiding behind this tearful outburst. One learns Moroto is the son of a cruel hunchback who lives on a small island separated from the rest of humanity with a small crew of deformed people.[38] Moroto's father has used a combination of torture and medical science to refashion ordinary people in unusual and sometimes surprising shapes, like the title character of the 1896 horror novel *The Island of Doctor Moreau* by H. G. Wells (1866–1946). (In one of several jokes embedded in the text, the name Moroto [諸戸] sounds like the near homonym *morōtō* [モロー島] or "The Island of Moreau." The reference to Wells's novel is made all the more explicit by Moroto's position as a medical doctor. Meanwhile, Moroto's given name, Michio [道雄], comprises two characters meaning "path [of the] masculine"—a subtle reference to his preferences for the same sex.) In a sense, the young Moroto, who has been sent to Tokyo by his father to research the newest developments in surgical science, is an unwilling heir to this merciless pursuit of a new "race" of freakish human beings.

The exchange in Minoura's room does not make Minoura feel hatred. He writes that as Moroto begged him to remain friends, "I kept silent out of strong emotion. However, as I watched Moroto begging with tears running down his face, I was helpless to prevent hot tears from welling up in my own eyes" (4:20). Although some part of Minoura appears to sympathize with Moroto, he is not willing to engage in a sexual relationship; nonetheless, Moroto's feelings only grow stronger as time passes:

> Not only did he not abandon his strange love. After that, it seemed to outdo itself, growing all the more intense and profound with the passing days and months. When we would run into each other, Moroto would usually spill out his heartrending thoughts for me in a kind of spoken love letter, which was without precedent. This kept

up until I entered my twenty-fifth year. Aren't such feelings almost impossible to comprehend? Even if I had retained the vestiges of youth in my smooth cheeks or I had not developed the musculature of ordinary adults and instead kept the sleekness of a woman, his feelings would still be equally hard to fathom. (4:20)

The ongoing nature of Moroto's passion seems to perplex Minoura as much as, if not more than, the very fact that it is directed toward him, a man. Given Moroto's passion, it comes as a great surprise he should begin courting Minoura's sweetheart, Hatsuyo. Minoura suspects Moroto is attempting to get back at him and steal his paramour, thus depriving him of the bliss of love Minoura had denied him earlier.

The second installment of the novel begins, "It was a terribly strange circumstance. One man's love for another was so great he tried to steal the other's lover. An ordinary person could not even imagine such a situation" (4:21).[39] While this explanatory statement recapitulates the plot, it also emphasizes the seemingly extraordinary nature of Moroto's actions in hopes of capturing the attention of new readers. As further enticement, the text incorporates a letter Moroto had written to explain his "strange feelings": "I am unable to feel any attraction for women. If anything, I feel hatred for them and feel like they are unclean. Can you possibly understand these feelings? What I feel is not just a simple feeling of embarrassment. It is something frightening. Sometimes I get so frightened that I cannot stand it" (4:21). Ranpo is clearly appealing to a common association in the popular imagination between male–male desire and a profound dislike for women that would make Moroto look abnormal, suspicious, and perhaps—according to the logic of sexology—even a potential criminal. Ranpo plays up these associations between male–male desire, misogyny, and even criminality by turning the reader's suspicions to Moroto when Hatsuyo is discovered murdered in her apartment a short time later. Minoura suspects Moroto is the murderer, even though he has no theory explaining how Moroto might have gained access to her room. A visit that Moroto pays to Hatsuyo's neighborhood soon after the murder gives him one bit of circumstantial evidence, but the primary reason for his suspicion is Moroto's "perverse" and "misogynistic" personality: "Perhaps these flights of fancy were all too ridiculous, but one cannot judge so-called 'people of perverse nature' [*henshitsusha*] like Moroto by the regular standards. Wasn't he incapable of love for the opposite sex? Didn't I suspect him of planning to steal my lover away from me because of his love for members of the same sex? And weren't his requests for Hatsuyo's hand in marriage just a little too ardent? Wasn't his pursuit of my love just a bit too crazed?" (4:41). Although the assumption that men who prefer men are psychological "perverts" willing to breach morality and ethics echoes the pathologizing statements of sexology, Ranpo overturns this assumption later in the novel when he does an about-face and transforms Moroto into one of the heroes of the novel.

Armed with only circumstantial evidence, Minoura goes to Moroto's house to confront him. The conversation that ensues entirely dispels the suspicion clouding Moroto's name. In fact, Moroto explains that his affection for the narrator was so great he started independently investigating Hatsuyo's murder on Minoura's behalf. Also, Moroto describes the loneliness and jealousy that drove him to begin courting Hatsuyo:

> I was so jealous of you and that woman I could hardly stand it.
> Before you met her, even if you were not able to understand my
> feelings, at least your heart did not belong to another. But your
> attitude completely changed when that woman Hatsuyo appeared
> before you. Do you remember that night—oh, it must have been the
> month before last—when we went to the Imperial Theater together?
> I could not stand the look in your eyes, which seemed to be chasing
> endlessly after some vision. What's more, didn't you tell me all about
> her? You were so cruel and cool about the whole thing; you were
> so happy. How do you think I was feeling then? This is all so
> embarrassing. As I always say to you, it is unreasonable for me to
> think I have any right to press you with these feelings. Still, I felt as if
> I had lost all hope in the world when I saw you like that. I was utterly
> dejected. I was sad about your love. Even more than that, I hated
> these unusual feelings of mine so much I could hardly stand it. (4:54)

In this scene, Moroto no longer seems a devious man with diabolical appetites, no longer the psychological degenerate earlier passages had made him out to be. If anything, he is lucid and articulate, and he has thought extensively about his situation as a sexual minority. When Minoura begins tearfully mourning the loss of Hatsuyo, Moroto responds, "I understand your feelings all too well. Still, your situation is a far happier than mine. Why? Because Hatsuyo's heart never wavered, even though I tried so hard to earn her hand in marriage. She never wavered, even though her mother, to whom she was bound in duty, recommended so fervently she accept my offers" (4:54–55). The comparison between the situations of Moroto, who suffers under the weight of unreciprocated desire, and Minoura, whose love was returned for at least a while, makes Moroto appear all the more unfortunate. This testimonial deflates Minoura's anger, and compels him and the reading audience to see Moroto in a more understanding light. Although his passion is for a man, his dejection and jealousy are presented so that even readers unfamiliar with male–male attraction might understand his motivations. The passages surrounding this quote avoid words such as "strange" or "perverse," thus opening a space for the reader to feel compassion or sympathy for him. By allowing Moroto to speak for himself and articulate his sorrows, his image undergoes a profound shift. Instead of presenting him as a degenerate with perverse sexual desires, he becomes a sensitive, suffering, even vulnerable man.

When Moroto provides valuable clues as to the identity of Hatsuyo's murderer, Moroto and Minoura become allies in the search for the killer, and Minoura realizes how little he knows of his friend. The beginning of the fifth installment of the novel reflects this reevaluation: "Through my long interactions with him, I knew he was a sexual invert [*seiyoku tōsakusha*], a researcher of the creepy field of anatomy and dissection, and a rather eccentric character, but I never imagined he had such outstanding abilities at detection" (4:58).[40] Minoura's suspicions about Moroto, based on flimsy suppositions about Moroto's sexual preferences, give way to a positive evaluation of his mental acuity. In the process, Moroto is transformed from suspect into one of Ranpo's eccentric detective heroes. Moroto and Minoura's shared mission gives the men a new sense of camaraderie and starts a form of homosocial bonding precluded before. When the narrative summarizes the nature of their relationship in the sixth installment, Moroto's desire for Minoura, though still described as "mysterious" (*fushigi*), is treated merely as an accent that makes their detective work a little more exciting:

Although the situation was quite serious, I developed a rather good humor about the whole affair. When I would look at Moroto, he also showed a light-hearted, childlike state of excitement. There is no question that in some corner of our young hearts, we took great pleasure in secrets and enjoyed adventure. Between him and me was something you could not exactly subsume under the simple word "friendship." Moroto felt a mysterious form of love for me. Of course,

I was not really able to comprehend his feelings, but I could understand them intellectually. What's more, unlike in ordinary situations, I did not find them extremely unpleasant. When we were together, there would be a whiff of sentimentality about our interaction like you might find if one of us were of the opposite sex. Perhaps that's what made our detective work together all the more pleasant. (4:75)

Elements of Moroto's homoerotic attraction for Minoura infiltrate the homosocial bonding, and as long as these feelings do not spill into overt eroticism, Minoura welcomes the spice they add to their common mission.

Here, Ranpo is clearly playing with one of the key conventions of English and American mystery fiction—the tendency to use an eccentric bachelor detective whose sexual interests are left conspicuously ambiguous. In the Sherlock Holmes stories of Sir Arthur Conan Doyle or the Philo Vance novels of S. S. Van Dyne (1887–1939), the detective heroes seem impervious to the charms of the opposite sex; however, their closest comrades are skirt-watching men who accompany them on their adventures. More than anything, such sidekicks highlight the protagonist's lack of interest in the opposite sex, thereby creating a structure in which the all-too-obvious absence of desire lends itself to a reading of the protagonist as somehow different than others. As Ranpo moves Moroto from the position of suspect to detective, he upsets the expectations established earlier in the novel, yet at the same time, he replaces the detective with classically ambiguous sexual interests with a new, different kind of hero who clearly prefers men. In other words, by openly addressing the issue of Moroto's sexual desires, Ranpo shatters the vagueness surrounding the homosocial relationship between detective and sidekick that plays such an important part in British and American mystery fiction. In fact, *Kotō no oni* is one of the first modern mystery novels to abandon that vagueness and to openly highlight the latent homoeroticism infiltrating the homosocial camaraderie between characters.

In their investigations, Moroto and Minoura realize Moroto's father, the hunchback Jōgorō, is the mastermind behind Hatsuyo's murder. When Moroto realizes his father is the culprit, he describes his own strange past on the island for Minoura. He had grown up in a strange home with hunchback parents. Although his tyrannical father would have preferred to keep him at home, he let Moroto go to Tokyo on the condition that he would study experimental medicine and eventually return to the island. Moroto's tale shows that the cruel personalities of his parents have shaped his fate in virtually every way imaginable, including his sexual preferences. As Moroto tells the tale of his strange past in the eighth installment of the novel, he reveals the reason for his aversion to the opposite sex:

> That is because the woman who calls herself my mother—that
> horrifically ugly hunchback woman—loved me not as a mother loves
> a child, but as a woman loves a man. It is almost too embarrassing to
> talk about. What happened is so awful that whenever I think about
> it, I feel a queasy churning in the pit of my stomach as if I am going
> to vomit. After I turned ten, I was reproached and tortured endlessly
> for the sake of my mother. Her face, which was as big as a ghost's,
> would come hovering over me and would start licking at me
> everywhere without regard to where she was touching. Even now,
> just remembering the feeling of those lips makes my hair stand on
> end. When I would rouse myself from that unpleasant, creepy-crawly
> feeling, I would find my mother had lain down in my bed. She would
> say, "You're such a good boy . . ." and request unspeakable things of
> me. She showed me every sort of ugly thing imaginable. My suffering,
> which was almost impossible to bear, lasted three years. To be
> honest, she was one of the reasons I wanted to leave home. I had seen
> all of the sordidness of that thing called woman. At the same time,
> I began to feel it was not just my mother who was unclean but all
> women, and I began to feel hatred for them. I suspect my inverted
> feelings of love [*tōsaku-teki na aijō*], which you know about so well,
> came from that. (4:103)

The result of this confession is that Moroto looks less like a "pervert" than a hapless victim of incestuous rape who, because of his dreadful experience, has turned from women forever. Once again, the text deconstructs the view of Moroto as a perverse misogynist and presents Moroto in a light that might be understandable to contemporary audiences. By giving the "invert" the right to speak for himself, the text allows him to present his "strange" sexual preference for men in terms intelligible to readers with little knowledge about same-sex eroticism. Of course, the explanation he provides promotes the popular misassumption that male–male desire is rooted in a dislike for women—a largely erroneous view that nonetheless gained wide circulation in the popular imagination and in the literature of sexology. At the same time, this explanation may also reflect Ranpo's familiarity with Freud's notion of the Oedipus complex. Freud had theorized that the web of attraction and repulsion infants feel for their parents contributes to the development of gender attributes and, under most circumstances, to a passion for members of the opposite sex. If something were to happen to upset the ordinary development of the male child, such as an overly close relationship with the mother that led to a sense of identification with her and her erotic feelings or, conversely, a trauma that stopped him from thinking about her as a sexual object, Freud theorized the child might instead displace his attraction toward members of the same sex. About the time he wrote this novel, Ranpo is known to have purchased two multivolume sets of Japanese translations of Freud. The first appeared in 1929, the year in which he serialized the majority of *Kotō no oni*. Ranpo is known to have read these works with great interest and, in the following years, even started attending a research group on psychoanalysis with one of Freud's translators in order to better understand the workings of the human mind as explicated by Freud and other psychologists.

The fact that the illustrator Takenaka Eitarō (1909–88), who illustrated many of Hakubunkan's publications, provided not one but two illustrations of this important scene shows how much editors played up the erotic and grotesque appeal of Moroto's seduction to capture reader attention. The first is strategically placed at the beginning of the eighth installment, where it would have been among the first things readers would have seen. As the mother's head turns, with her tongue exposed and eyes glowing with vampirish intensity, Moroto cowers beside her. For readers who have not yet read about the seduction, it is unclear what the massive lumps on the back of the mother are, and the question of what is actually happening hangs tantalizingly in the air. The second illustration appears in close proximity to the passage describing the seduction, and it shows Moroto as a boy recoiling from the ghostly figure of his mother hovering over him. Both illustrations contribute to a frightening atmosphere that highlights the grotesque and erotic elements of Ranpo's text.

When the two amateur detectives reach the mysterious island where Moroto spent his traumatic youth, Moroto is so disturbed by seeing his parents again that he begins to talk in his sleep: "During his nocturnal babblings, he would sometimes say my name. I felt alarmed and apprehensive when I realized how large a place I held in his subconscious. Even if he was a member of the same sex, wasn't it terrible of me to pretend to be oblivious while interacting with him, even as he continued to yearn for me? I gave serious

Illustration by Takenaka Eitarō for *Kotō no oni,* first published in *Asahi* in 1929. This is the second illustration Takenaka provided of the scene in which Moroto is seduced by his mother, thus explaining Moroto's horror of women and his sexual preference for men. Copyright Kaneko Yukari 1929. Courtesy of Kaneko Yukari and the Takenaka Eitarō Memorial Museum. This museum is located in Kōfu, Yamanashi Prefecture, and is dedicated to introducing the work of this representative illustrator from the early Shōwa period. See http://takenaka-kinenkan.jp.

consideration to the matter as I lay in bed unable to sleep" (4:140). While Minoura worries that compartmentalizing the homoerotic elements of the relationship is cruel to Moroto, he expresses reservations about the current state of their friendship. The fact that Minoura still experiences alarm at Moroto's erotic attraction shows he remains disturbed by the thought of Moroto crossing the line they have tacitly drawn in the sand.

When Moroto does cross this line in the penultimate installment of the novel, Minoura reacts with horror. The fateful scene comes soon after Moroto and Minoura discover an entrance to a vast complex of subterranean passageways that crisscross the length of the entire island. Armed with ropes, matches, and candles, they enter the caves in search of a treasure they believe lies there. In the meantime, Jōgorō or one of his henchmen cuts the ropes the two men have used to mark their way, and before long, the two find themselves hopelessly lost in a twisting labyrinth of pitch-black passages. After days of growing despair, Moroto says to Minoura, "Just like we have no light in this place, we are in a world without law, morality, customs, or anything. Even though I may only have a little time left to live, I want to forget all those things for at least a few moments. There is now no shame for us, no etiquette, no ostentation, no suspicion, nothing. We are like two infants born into a world of darkness" (4:157). Moroto pulls Minoura close to his side, and as they embrace in the darkness, their cheeks touch. Reminding Minoura they will never make it out of the caves alive, he begs Minoura to forget his new love and be with him: "Forget the customs of the terrestrial world, forget the shame they feel up there. Accept my request, and take my love" (4:161). In response, Minoura thinks,

> I had no idea how to respond to the loathsomeness of his request. Probably everyone feels like this, but whenever I think of anyone other than a young woman as an erotic object, I feel an indescribable disgust go through me like a cold chill, and my hair stands on end. It meant nothing for me to come into contact with the flesh of someone as a friend. In fact, it was a pleasant feeling. However, when it came to physical love, the flesh of a member of the same sex would make me feel sick to my stomach. Physical love was another facet of that thing called exclusive love. So was animosity.
>
> Moroto was trustworthy as a friend, and I was able to feel goodwill toward him. However, the more trustworthy he was, the more difficult it became for me to bear the thought of him as the object of sexual desire. Although I was desperate, and death was staring me in the face, I could not help feeling disgust. (4:161)

This passage, as well as the encounter that follows, is narrated from a relentlessly heterosexist viewpoint. Minoura assumes "probably everyone" is equally hesitant to entertain advances from members of the same sex, thus emphasizing what he sees as the fundamental strangeness of Moroto's desires. By appealing to the logic of heteronormativity, the text casts Moroto's erotic advances in a light that makes them look strange and perverse. Although Minoura admits the touch of a male friend can be quite pleasant, it takes on an entirely different character when motivated by the search for sexual fulfillment—a sure sign he conceives of homoeroticism and homosociality as two profoundly different forms of desire. Interestingly, this passage echoes the passages in Ranpo's memoirs about his relationship with Iwata Jun'ichi, the friend with whom he made the trip that inspired this novel. In his memoirs, Ranpo steadfastly denies the presence of any homoerotic relationship between him and Iwata. Ranpo's own memoirs recall that during the trip which inspired this novel, the couple's hands brushed each other in an erotically suggestive way, but this only filled Ranpo with a sense of "revulsion" when he thought of this touch as a prelude to eroticism (20:282).[41]

For a moment, Moroto withdraws into the darkness, weeping with disappointment. A moment later, however, he draws close to Minoura like a "snake approaching its prey":

> When I realized what has happening, the snake was already by my side. What on earth? Was he able to see my shape in the darkness or did he possess some sixth sense? I was so shocked that I tried to run away, but at some point, something caught my leg. A hand held me as fast as a trap holding a bird.
>
> Losing my momentum, I fell flat on the rocks. The snake came slithering up the length of my body. I wondered whether or not that mysterious beast could be Moroto. It was not so much human as a creepy sort of animal.
>
> I groaned in fear.
>
> This fear was completely different from the fear of death. It was a far more unpleasant fear that I cannot possibly describe.
>
> Like a goblin rising out of the sea, that hair-raisingly eerie thing that lives hidden deep in the heart of humanity had presented me with its bizarre and frightening form. I was in a living hell of darkness, death, and monstrous beasts.
>
> I had lost my power even to groan. I was too frightened even to raise my voice.
>
> Cheeks that burned like fire laid themselves over mine, which were sweaty with fear. Panting breath like that of a dog, a strange body odor. . . . Then sleek and slippery mucous membranes sought out my lips and came crawling over my face like a leech. (4:162)

Moroto's desires seem to have transformed him from his usual, attractive, dapper self into some inhuman, animalistic monstrosity whose form is barely intelligible.[42] Here, *Kotō no oni* returns to the codification of male–male desire implicit in earlier descriptions of Moroto's "strange" love—one that treats homoeroticism as strange, frightening, and hardly even representable through language. At this point, Minoura's narrative breaks away from the caves and states that Moroto is no longer of this world. (We later learn Moroto had died before Minoura began committing his story to paper.) Minoura professes that he is afraid of writing something that might embarrass the dead, and so he fast-forwards to a point when something moves in the darkness next to the couple. There, the eleventh installment comes to a suspenseful close. In the twelfth and final installment, one finds the unexpected movement had come from a boatman who had been washed into the caves when his boat capsized in the sea. The couple is once again thrust into the world of humanity with all of its concern for shame and heterosexual normality, and Moroto quickly calls off his advances.

Few previous commentators on *Kotō no oni* have noted that the scene in the cave draws clear inspiration from a similar scene in *Sokkyō shijin*, Mori Ōgai's famous translation of Hans Christian Andersen's novel *The Improvisatore*. There, a painter named Federigo takes Antonio, the young male narrator, into a catacomb-like series of caves to be alone with him. With florid, romantic detail, the boy describes the experience of walking through a series of seemingly never-ending passageways and unwinding a spool of string to keep their bearings. Still, they lose the string and become lost in the darkness. When Antonio becomes frightened and frantically searches for the lost string, Federigo tries to calm him, first by offering him presents then by threatening to beat him. At this point, Federigo suddenly forces himself on Antonio: "Then he bound his pocket-handkerchief round my arm, and held me fast, but bent himself down to me the next moment, kissed me vehemently, called me his dear little Antonio, and whispered, 'Do thou also pray to the Madonna!'"[43] A moment later, they begin searching again, but soon they fall into despair. Federigo attempts to quiet him with a second affectionate advance: "I then wept bitterly, for it seemed to me that I never more should reach my home. He clasped me so closely to him as he lay on the ground that my hand slid under him. I involuntarily grasped the sand, and found the string between my fingers."[44]

*Sokkyō shijin* was wildly popular with young readers of Ranpo's generation, and Ranpo, like many boys his age, was well acquainted with the story. In fact, when Minoura and Moroto first enter the caverns, *Kotō no oni* includes a series of extended quotations from Ōgai's translation to describe the experience of walking through a series of seemingly unending caves. For readers aware of the homoerotic encounter in Ōgai's bestseller, the inclusion of these passages no doubt foreshadowed the coming homoerotic encounter;

however, Ranpo's novel recasts the scene in Ōgai's translation by making the scene explicit and, in typical *ero, guro, nansensu* fashion, playing up the "strange" and "animalistic" aspects of Moroto's desire to shock and fascinate readers.

While the use of the caves as a setting for homoerotic desires was almost certainly inspired by Ōgai's famous translation, they also serve a more symbolic function. The caves represent a space antithetical to the terrestrial world and irrational in every way, from their unpredictable shape to the invisible dangers lurking around every corner. As Moroto notes, the civilizing forces of law, morality, and custom do not hold sway there, and it serves as a space where ordinarily suppressed forces might manifest themselves. When Moroto foists himself upon Minoura, Moroto states he has come in contact with "that hair-raisingly eerie thing living hidden deep in the heart of humanity"—a dramatic metaphor for those urges driven into the underground world of the unconscious by the civilizing forces of morality and order.

On one hand, the scene strongly reinforces the impression of male–male erotic desire as perverse, animalistic, and to be resisted even in places far from watching eyes. On the other hand, however, the tremendous detail in the first part of the scene and the carefully worded writing suggest Ranpo took vicarious pleasure in presenting this scene in all of its detail to his audience. The author draws out the scene by having Moroto move slowly up the narrator's body like a snake. Only when Moroto's mouth locks upon Minoura's does the narrative break away from the scene in the cave and jump forward to a later point in the story. The decision to break away at a critical moment leaves the question of how far the seduction went tantalizingly unclear while, at the same time, protecting the novel from possible bans by censors concerned with obscenity.

Even though Ranpo may have taken a subversive pleasure in evoking this scene of male homoeroticism, the novel ends with a return to the "safety" of heteronormativity. The story of Moroto's erotic attraction to Minoura is, as the summary above has hinted, one of several subplots that involve tropes of normality, deformation, and even perversion—tropes structured by the logic of medical science and eugenics; however, within the last few pages of the novel, all of these subplots are given a quick denouement. After a few more days of wandering, Moroto, Minoura, and the boatman who came across them in the darkness discover a rope that leads them to Jōgorō, who is madly dancing on a large pile of gold. His ecstasy at finding the treasure has plunged him into incapacitating madness that prevents him from carrying out his cruel vision of turning Japan into a "country of cripples." Back in the light of day, Minoura finds his hair had turned white because of the fear he had experienced underground, apparently during his encounter with Moroto. The servants and mutilated prisoners on the island are saved, and Moroto uses his surgical skills to repair the cripples created in Jōgorō's cruel misuse of science, including a woman whom Jōgorō had surgically attached to a man. Minoura marries her and thus puts the encounter in the cave behind him, apparently relegating it to the dark, subterranean caverns of memory.

Moroto is unable to bury the past, however. He locates his birth parents and goes to visit them, but within a month, he falls sick and dies. The novel ends on a sentimental, even romantic note with an excerpt from the death notice sent to Minoura: "Until the moment he drew his last breath, Moroto Michio did not call out his father's name nor his mother's. He just held your letter close to himself, saying nothing but your name over and over again" (4:173). This coda suggests Minoura's rejection was what caused him to pine away and die. Jim Reichert correctly states that the ending suggests "although a world where the regime of normalcy prevails is inevitable, there is always a segment of the population that is sacrificed to this conventional social order."[45] Reichert has also noted that the heavy-handed tone of the last words opens the possibility of an ironic reading highlighting the impossibility of this tidy ending, which clears away all hindrances to Minoura's marriage.

Other ironic readings are also equally plausible. In the final lines, Moroto adopts the role of the valiant, romantic lover, who would sooner die for love than abandon his feelings. This romantic role is in keeping with descriptions of Moroto early in the novel as a singularly attractive bishōnen who is almost perfect in appearance, intellectual faculties, and academic credentials—complimentary qualities that are strikingly at odds with the image of him as an immoral, psychological "degenerate" that Minoura's narrative presents elsewhere. By focusing on Moroto in the final lines of the novel, the text provides one final blow to the damning treatments of Moroto presented elsewhere. In the end, he is not the erotic, grotesque creature seen earlier in the cave; if anything he is an unfortunate, love-struck man who in many ways conforms to the image of the dashing, romantic lover. Like much early twentieth-century European and American fiction about same-sex desire, which dispatches the main character in death, suicide, or brutal victimization, *Kotō no oni* ends with Moroto's death; however, in this case, the ending may well elevate his stock as a character. He does not die as a miserable, self-hating man, but as a star-crossed, romantic, tragic hero unable and unwilling to fit into the restrictive world of cross-sex normality. As the conclusion of this book notes, subsequent readers in the postwar period have picked up and teased out this possibility in creative rewritings of the text.

As mentioned earlier in this chapter, Ranpo seems to have thought of *Kotō no oni* as a failure in that he was not able to explore the subject of male–male desire in the way he had hoped (20:201). After writing *Kotō no oni*, Ranpo turned completely away from writing about homoeroticism within the forum of mystery fiction. Instead, he made the decision to turn to the form of the essay, writing numerous essays about various manifestations of homoerotic desire in the literature of Europe, America, and Japan. Although these essays fall short of endorsing homoerotic behavior wholeheartedly, they depart radically from the graphic, heavy-handed language of grotes-querie seen in the climactic cave scene of *Kotō no oni*. The relatively free form of the essay allowed Ranpo to avoid sensationalizing rhetoric and the generic demands of mystery fiction, which treated male–male desire in largely sensational terms and as a "curiosity" that might shock and startle readers. These essays, to which the next chapter will turn, represent an im-portant attempt to move from the conflicting, constantly code-switching views of same-sex desire forged in stories like *Kotō no oni* toward a more his-torically informed view of male–male desire.

# 4

# (Re)Discovering Same-Sex Love

*Ranpo and the Creation of Queer History*

In *Getting Medieval*, Carolyn Dinshaw writes that one of the reasons people explore queer history is to make cross-temporal connections between "on the one hand, lives, texts, and other cultural phenomena left out of sexual categories back then and, on the other hand, those left out of current sexual categories now."[1] She notes such impulses are grounded in the attempt to extend "the resources for self- and community-building into even the distant past," and she describes her own wish for "partial affective connection, for community, for even a touch across time."[2] In *Feeling Backward*, Heather Love further explains this desire for connection when she remarks, "The longing for community across time is a crucial feature of queer historical experience, one produced by the historical isolation of individual queers as well as by the damaged quality of the historical archive."[3]

As mentioned in the introduction to this book, Ranpo, living in early Shōwa-period Japan, did not have access to an affective community to whom he could discuss the subject of male–male desire, and around the time he wrote *Kotō no oni*, he started an ambitious project of researching the history of queer desire using literature and historical texts. The results of this research he presented in numerous essays published in various journals during the 1930s. His decision to write about same-sex desire in nonfictional essays might be seen as a result of his disappointment in the mystery novel *Kotō no oni*, which, as the last chapter argued, vacillated between lurid, sensationalizing rhetoric designed to attract reader attention and a more empathetic mode that allowed the queer character Moroto to explain his own feelings.

Essays permitted Ranpo to write in a more even-keeled fashion, freeing him from the genre-related demands of the mystery novel that would force him into either a negative portrayal or at the very best a pattern of code switching. In these essays, Ranpo begins the ambitious project of tracing a network of affective connection through literary history, showing that love between men played in important part in cultural history, and trying to make sense of what that misunderstood form of desire might mean in the present.

In 1949, Ranpo published a small article entitled "Futari no shishō" (My two teachers), about the two close friends who, during the 1920s and 1930s, played the biggest role in encouraging his research into the history of male–male desire in literature and popular culture: the lawyer, politician, and mystery writer Hamao Shirō (1896–1935), and the anthropologist, writer, and artist Iwata Jun'ichi (22:51–52). These two friends approached the study of male–male desire from different angles, but both argued male–male desire had played a large role in history and needed to be better understood by modern society. Inspired by them, Ranpo began reading an ever-widening array of books and articles about male–male desire. He developed an interest in the literature of pre-Restoration Japan and ancient Greece, both of which offered numerous stories of love and sexuality between men; likewise, he read a number of works by modern European, American, and Japanese writers who treated the subject in their writing.

Through these works, Ranpo began to construct a history of same-sex desire that, despite the many differences in the ways "same-sex love" was understood in his day and in the past, led him to assert the importance of male love in understanding world literature and history. In 1936 Ranpo asserted that from the time of ancient Greece to the present day, there were many "great masters of art and letters whose works cannot be fully understood" while unaware of the "psychology of same-sex love" (*dōseiai seishin*) that contributed to them. As examples, he points to American poet Walt Whitman (1819–92), British poet and literary historian John Addington Symonds (1840–93), British explorer and translator Sir Richard Francis Burton (1821–90), British social theorist and activist Edward Carpenter (1844–1929), French writer André Gide (1869–1951), Walter Pater, and Oscar Wilde (17:66). In some ways, this genealogical work anticipates the work of later scholars who, influenced by the gay, lesbian, transgender, and queer movements of the late twentieth and twenty-first centuries, would rectify the silence of earlier scholars and show the centrality of various forms of non-heteronormative desire in different arenas of world culture.

Still, Ranpo's essays fall short of endorsing all forms of male–male desire, from asexual, boyish crushes to overtly erotic acts, in an equal fashion. Like Symonds and Whitman, two of the authors he treats at length, Ranpo is especially eager to discuss instances of male–male desire that emphasize emotional and asexual passion, but his essays treat eroticism between men somewhat more circumspectly. In the end, although his writing suggests he was eager to open up avenues of communication that might lead to more sympathetic interpretations of same-sex desire, this was a project that remained only partially accomplished, considering how hesitant he remained about writing about male homoeroticism. The result is that Ranpo thinks about crossing, but does not ultimately bridge, the split between homosociality and homoeroticism on the spectrum of male homosocial desire.

This chapter traces the relationships Ranpo forged in his search to better understand male–male desire. It focuses on both the flesh-and-blood relationships Ranpo forged with contemporary Japanese writers and the ways he helped to create a loosely knit queer coterie, the first to emerge in twentieth-century Japanese literary history. In his relationships with Hamao Shirō and Iwata Jun'ichi in particular, one sees relationships grounded in a shared interest in male–male sexuality that, in their eyes, transcended social background, class, and even time. Indeed, one might see this camaraderie as subcultural and modern in that it is grounded in a particular, identity-related category of sexual behavior that Ranpo and his friends apparently saw as transcending other types of difference. As the following sections will argue, Ranpo and his friends used their writing, each in their own way, to argue against the tendency to treat male–male love as pathological and deleterious to society.

This chapter will also trace the affective relationships Ranpo and his coterie of friends created with writers, authors, and historical figures who had lived around the world in earlier historical moments. As their writings demonstrate, these affective relationships, which stretched across the boundaries of nation and time, were intensely real in that they shaped the ways Ranpo and his friends understood and wrote about desire between men in the present. These affective relationships were profoundly important in spurring them on as they strove to construct new, modern, and even "scientifically" informed representations of desire between men.

## RANPO'S FIRST "TEACHER": HAMAO SHIRŌ

Although many today remember Hamao Shirō, the first of Ranpo's two mentors, primarily as a mystery novelist, Hamao came from a lofty, aristocratic background unlike that of any other popular writer in the 1930s. His grand-father was Katō Hiroyuki (1836–1916), a highly influential Meiji-period political thinker who served as an instructor to the Meiji emperor, as a member of the Meirokusha, and as a member of the House of Peers. Hamao's connection to the highest echelons of government was made all the richer in 1918 when he was adopted from the home of his biological father, the prominent pediatrician Katō Terumaro, who had served as a doctor to the Emperor Meiji during the emperor's youth, into the home of Hamao Arata (1849–1925), an administrator who served as president of Tokyo Imperial University and the head of a body of advisors to the emperor and government. Given the strong relationship between his family and the government, it is no surprise that Hamao decided to study law, completing a law degree at Tokyo Imperial University in 1923.[4] Soon afterward, Hamao was appointed deputy prosecutor to a local Tokyo court, and in no time, he was promoted to the prosecutorial bureau of the greater Tokyo court system. In 1925 he was given the rank of *shishaku,* the fourth in a system of five grades of peerage established by the Meiji constitution. A few years later, in 1928, he opened his own legal practice, and in 1933 he became a member of the House of Peers in the Diet, a position he occupied until his premature death from a cerebral hemorrhage two years later at the age of thirty-nine.

Hamao's interest in same-sex desire, and male–male desire in particular, was closely related to his interest in crime and jurisprudence. A number of his first essays display a strong interest in criminal psychology and examine "perverse" erotic desires that might give rise to crime; however, what makes him particularly important for the purposes of this study was that he was one of the earliest people in the early twentieth century to argue vocifer-ously for the rights of sexual minorities in Japan. The public stance he took in his writing is all the more remarkable considering that his social status as an aristocrat and public figure no doubt put pressure on him to follow the same rules of propriety and decorum that relegated nonheteronormative sexuality to the margins of respectability.

In "Hentaisei no hanzai ni tsuite" (On crimes of a perverse nature) published in *Shin seinen* in 1928, Hamao discusses a number of crimes in Tokyo that involved various forms of erotic desire: a sadomasochistic relationship that ended in murder, a fetishist who stole women's undergarments for mas-turbatory purposes, one man's attempt to kidnap and have sex with a pre-pubescent girl, and so on.[5] Hamao does not condemn the desires leading to these actions; instead, he condemns only the criminal actions themselves.

Probably because "same-sex love" was foremost on the list of many sexologists' lists of "perversions," Hamao mentions it, but he states only that same-sex eroticism was not problematic in and of itself. He points out that because the Japanese legal system does not condemn erotic practice between members of the same sex, such relations could not be seen as criminal. He states crimes involving same-sex love were relatively uncommon in Tokyo because Japan, unlike certain European nations, did not ban same-sex eroticism as "unnatural sexual misconduct" (*fushizen inkō*).[6] As a result, there was little need to act in a criminal fashion to fulfill same-sex erotic desire, and sexuality between members of the same sex rarely came to police attention.

In fact, anal sex, called *keikan* (sodomy) by the legal establishment, had been illegal for a brief period of Japanese history. Article 266 of the Kaitei Ritsurei, promulgated in 1873, criminalized anal sex between men; however, this law lasted only until 1882, when a new penal code, the Keihō, came into effect.[7] Because it was silent on the subject of *keikan*, the Keihō abandoned the laws of several years before and in essence made anal penetration legal. (An earlier version of the law promulgated in 1880 had criminalized "obscene acts" that did not involve minors or coercion, but the wording of the law left it unclear whether or not male–male and female–female sexual acts fell under this rubric.) The change in the 1882 law was made largely in response to the suggestions of the French jurist Gustave Boissonade, whom the Ministry of Justice had brought to Japan to administer the writing of a new penal code. Although he proclaimed himself to be no friend of "disgraceful sins" such as sodomy, Boissonade pointed out that Napoleonic law had determined sexual relations were a personal matter that should be left out of the public realm, provided they did not involve minors or coercion.[8]

Like many of his contemporaries who wrote about same-sex erotic desire, Hamao distinguished between lasting preferences for the same sex and situational homoeroticism that arose as a result of being denied access to members of the opposite sex. For instance, he mentions that when men are incarcerated, they engage in sexual relations with other men but such behavior "does not appear to be pure *Homosexualität*." Although he did not think highly of Japanese sexologists, he was, in this regard, not unlike contemporary sexologists Sawada Junjirō and Habuto Eiji who, in their book *Hentai seiyoku ron*, distinguish between "innate" erotic desire for the same sex and desire that develops later, usually as a consequence of environmental factors.[9] As his choice of the German word *Homosexualität* hints, Hamao was drawn to the works of Austrian and German writers, such as Richard von Krafft-Ebing

(1840–1902) and Albert Moll (1862–1939), who located the roots of same-sex attraction in the psychological make-up of the individual. Like them, he agreed a sustained erotic preference for the same sex was not just simply a choice but something that had deep roots within the constitution of the individual.

In two articles published in 1930 in the women's magazine *Fujin saron* (Housewife's salon), Hamao uses the assumption that sexual preference is often innate to argue against pathologizing notions about same-sex eroticism inherited from sexology. Although these articles are relatively little known, they deserve special attention because they contain some of the most articulate arguments for the rights of sexual minorities in early twentieth-century Japan. In September, *Fujin saron* carried the first of Hamao's two articles: "Dōseiai kō" (Thoughts on same-sex love). In it, Hamao borrows the German word *Urning (ūruningu)* to describe people who continue to feel erotic attraction for the same sex even after others of their age group have started falling for the opposite sex.[10] This noun, coined by the German journalist Karl-Heinrich Ulrichs (1825–95), refers to an intermediate sex, consisting of the biologically male *Urning* (*Urninge* in the plural) and the biologically female *Urningin*. Significantly, these words (usually rendered "Uranian" in English) became popular among early critics who, like Hamao, advocated liberating nonheteronormative forms of sexual desire from the stigma of pathology. Throughout the article, Hamao provides the katakana gloss *Urning* for the Japanese compound *dōseiaisha*—a combination of the characters *dōseiai,* meaning "same-sex love," and the character meaning "person"—or he uses the words *Urning* and *dōseiaisha* interchangeably. This conflation of the two terms suggests that in this article, Hamao was working to rethink "same-sex love," which, as explained in the introduction, represented a Japanese interpretation of the European medicalized notion of homosexuality, through another European concept, namely the concepts produced by the early homophile movement in Europe. The result was a shift in the terms of debate of *dōseaisha* subjectivity. Although Hamao accepts the sexological belief that congenital *dōseiaisha/Urninge* are naturally predisposed to homoerotic desire, he criticizes writers such as Krafft-Ebing and Albert Moll who are "unable to see the *dōseiaisha* as anything other than a sick person."[11] He says that if one defines same-sex love as sick, it will of course be seen as pathological; however, Hamao notes, many other people, such as Edward Carpenter, present a quite different picture of love between members of the same sex. In fact, the argument same-sex desire is only as "sick" as it is defined to be comes directly from Carpenter's study *The Intermediate Sex,* which states, "men and women of the exclusively Uranian type are by no means necessarily morbid in any way—unless, indeed, their peculiar temperament be pronounced in itself morbid."[12] Hamao argues, "the word *dōseiai* has recently been misunderstood and has come to be loathed and detested by society," but this antipathy on the part of society is profoundly misguided.[13] For much of the essay, he describes the historical and contemporary condition of *dōseiai* without referring to the rhetoric of illness, thus attempting to liberate *dōseiaisha* from the stigma of disease.

One technique Hamao uses to improve the image of *dōseiaisha* is to draw a link between same-sex desire and famous people throughout history. He provides a long list of important artistic and political figures recognized in Europe as *Urninge:* Michelangelo, Shakespeare, Whitman, Wilde, Pyotr Tchaikovsky, Michel de Montaigne, Franz Schubert, Francis Bacon, Alexander the Great, and Julius Caesar. To this list, he tentatively adds the name Confucius, pointing out that the *Lun yu (Analects)* describe Confucius's terrible sense of loss when a close male friend passes away. Hamao comments that although Japanese historiography did not distinguish between platonic love and eroticism between members of the same sex, premodern figures like Tokugawa Iemitsu (1604–51), Oda Nobunaga (1534–82), Ōta Dōkan (1432–86), and Matsuo Bashō (1644–94) were all known to have experienced desire for other men. Following a line of argument presented by the British sexologist Havelock Ellis (1859–1939), Hamao argues most great men have lived in the company of *Urninge,* if they were not *Urninge* themselves.[14] Elsewhere, he recapitulates, "one cannot overlook the fact that among people who have *Urning*-like tendencies, one finds an extremely high number of exceptionally smart men."[15] He gives a partial explanation, saying one finds a parity among members of the same sex that one does not find among male–female couples; as a result, partners in same-sex relationships tend to encourage one another more than couples in cross-sex relationships. For example, Hamao writes that male students in love can encourage one another in their academic or athletic activities because they are standing on "the same front," facing the same problems with similar physical and intellectual capacities.[16] Despite his admirable goal of liberating male–male desire from the stigma of disease, such arguments clearly reveal Hamao was writing in the context of a male-dominated, even chauvinistic society that assumed that there are profound differences between the intellectual and physical abilities of men and women.

Hamao laments that people who experience same-sex erotic desire often "give up on themselves as sexual perverts [*hentai seiyokuja*], treat their actions as something to be ashamed of, and carry them out as furtively as possible." As a result, "in big cities such as Tokyo, these people humbly walk through the darkness" out of the sight of others, even though their erotic practices are not illegal.[17] He states that some such people take refuge in Asakusa Park and other metropolitan parks where they meet for surreptitious encounters. As a result, such places are visited by prostitutes and their customers, who include foreigners (the population that "seems to welcome the sex workers the most") and those experimenters who come to sample eroticism with the same sex out of an "interest in curiosity-hunting" *(ryōki shumi)*. The article ends with a strong statement addressed to "all *dōseiaisha*": "You all must first find out what exactly same-sex love is, but you must not feel pointless shame or hide yourself away. To do so is foolish. You must clearly grasp the social significance of this thing we call *dōseiai*."[18] He also sends a clear message to those who write on the subject: "Commentators too should grasp the substance [of *dōseiai*] and recognize its value." His list of further reading includes works by the early homophiles Edward Carpenter, Havelock Ellis, and Magnus Hirschfeld (1868–1935), who all argued for society to accept people who prefer the same sex. At the end of his list, Hamao remarks, "The reason I did not list any resources in our language is not for pedantic reasons. It is just there are no sources in our language worth looking at."[19] In a single sweep, Hamao dismisses the work of all Japanese sexologists who had vociferously argued that "same-sex love" has pathological and deleterious effects.

In response to his essay, Hamao received such a large number of letters from self-avowed *dōseiaisha* that two months later he published a follow-up article in the same magazine. "Futatabi dōseiai ni tsuite" (More on same-sex love) contains an even stronger call for freeing *dōseiaisha* from the stigma of illness. Hamao states that the letters he received from all quarters of the country were full of confessions of many "courageous" and "determined" individuals who described their intense suffering. From the point of view of contemporary researchers, this article is especially valuable in that it conveys the arguments of sexual minorities in an era of history that did relatively little to preserve their voices for posterity. Hamao sums up six major themes of the letters. First, all the authors felt utterly alone and isolated from other people like them. Second, they generally believed themselves to be "deformed" or "invalids cursed by a life-long illness." Third, the majority were ashamed of themselves. Fourth, many had received medical attention because of their sexual preferences, but this did not change them in any significant way. Fifth, the authors expressed feelings toward the opposite sex ranging from "cold indifference" to "misogyny"; however, some had gone ahead, married, and had children because these feelings were not understood by society. Sixth, some were unhappy to the point of considering or even attempting suicide.[20] Because much of the early discourse that discussed same-sex desire as pathological came from recognized "experts" or figures with medical degrees, it was presented from a position of superior knowledge and presumed to talk about the *dōseiaisha* while leaving little room for him to speak his own situation.[21] Hamao recognized the letters he had received as representing the voices of *dōseiaisha* who had internalized this sexological discourse and who now spoke from the compromised position of a stigmatized minority. He comments that the letters represented only the voices of a tiny fraction of all the *dōseiaisha* in Japan, and one should multiply the anguish described in the letters by a factor of thousands to gain a fuller picture of the suffering the medical establishment had wrought. Convinced "a true understanding of the *Urning* is the most pressing problem for modern society," Hamao states he decided to write his second article on behalf of the masses of silent, suffering others.[22] He demands society treat *Urninge* with greater respect. Women in particular need to understand the issue, because social pressure often forces *Urninge* into marriage against their will. Although he cautions it is best if the "extreme *Urning*" avoids marriage altogether, Hamao warns it is possible the groom may not say anything; therefore, women should be aware of the issue in case their husbands are hiding their true sexual preferences.[23] (It is worth reiterating that the magazine that published both of Hamao's articles was a women's magazine, and such passages show he is cognizant of speaking to a primarily female audience.)

To the male *Urninge* themselves, Hamao emphatically asserts, *"dōseiai is not an illness. It is a part of one's personality."*[24] As a result, there is no way to "cure" an "innate" erotic interest in the same sex. He contradicts those who say psychological disease or neurasthenia gives rise to feelings of *dōseiai*. In fact, he argues, if anything, social oppression gives rise to nervous disorders because *dōseiai* is so little understood in modern society—an argument Hamao has once again borrowed from Carpenter's *The Intermediate Sex*.[25] Because it is not an illness, there is no reason to look for medical help, nor suppress one's feelings and marry. Hamao asks, "Isn't it better that each of you, with your individual personalities, courageously proceeds with your own lives?"[26] The major opposition to acceptance stems from the conflation of same-sex desire with sickness and shame. Like Carpenter, Hamao argues that because scientists and doctors were the first to take up the issue in dealing with their "sick" patients, it is natural that people fell under the illusion all *dōseiaisha* were sick, but this mistaken impression can only be countered by information from *dōseiaisha* themselves. Here again, Hamao echoes Carpenter, who states, "the medico-scientific enquirer is bound on the whole to meet with those cases that *are* of a morbid character, rather than with those that are healthy in their manifestation, since indeed it is the former that he lays himself out for. And since the field of his research is usually a great modern city, there is little wonder if disease colours his conclusions."[27] Hamao agrees that only through listening to such testimonials can society gain a "true understanding" of the problems *dōseiaisha* face; one could not rely on medical doctors nor on journalists drawn by the "recent interest in the erotic and grotesque" to produce a "true understanding" of the phenomenon. As Hamao notes, such people only treat same-sex eroticism as pathological, bizarre, or an object of curiosity.

About the same time he wrote these two impassioned articles for *Fujin saron,* Hamao was also busy writing fiction, some of which appeals to the very same fad for the erotic and grotesque he criticizes as producing skewed portrayals of same-sex desire. Within the four years between his debut in 1929 and his death in 1932, he published numerous short mysteries and three full-length detective novels. A number of these stories involve elements of "perverse" sexual desire, presumably to add spice to the plot and attract contemporary readers. For instance, in his debut novella *Kare ga koroshita ka?* (Did he kill?) published in *Shin seinen,* a young man is erroneously executed for two deaths that take place when a couple's sadomasochistic games get out of hand. The text states that the married couple who are found dead in the novel did not lead "a normal sexual life." To satisfy themselves, they required elaborate sexual performances featuring interrogation and persecution: "The husband would doubt his wife, and he would torture her to make her confess. In acting out this game, he would attain satisfaction, and the wife also enjoyed being tortured."[28] The June 1931 short story "Madamu no satsujin" (Murders for madam), which appeared in the journal *Asahi,* tells the tale of a young man who willingly becomes the slave of a sadistic mistress.[29] As he participates in various sexual activities with her—bondage, sadomasochism, and a ménage à trois with another male slave—his self-effacing devotion grows to the point where he willingly takes the fall for her when she murders the other slave and kills a servant who may have witnessed the crime. In both stories, sadomasochism appears merely as a motive leading to murder, and there is only minimal exploration of the psychology of the characters who experience these desires.

In 1929, Hamao published "Akuma no deshi" (The devil's apprentice), the only work in which Hamao deals extensively with male–male desire, in the journal *Shin seinen*, but this story does not promote the kind of sympathetic, "true understanding" of "same-sex love" he called for in the articles for *Fujin saron*.[30] The entire story is told as a single epistle written by a jailed criminal, Shimaura Eizō, who attempts to shift moral blame for his actions onto a friend with whom he had an affair many years before. The addressee of the letter is Tsuchida Hachirō, who is now a prosecutor in the Tokyo courts, not unlike Hamao himself. Shimaura has been accused of killing his mistress by forcing her to take an overdose of sleeping pills. He insists, however, he did not commit the crime, and her death was a tragic accident. He admits he was plotting to kill his wife, but he did not have a chance to carry it out before this other tragedy occurred.

Before divulging the details, Shimaura reminisces over his past relationship with Tsuchida. During their days as students together in a school dormitory, the two shared a close relationship. Shimaura, the younger of the two, writes that he had been overwhelmed by Tsuchida's commanding personality, and believing he had found someone who truly understood him, he felt love for the older boy. He writes, "I felt you alone were both my brother and my lover," and "I respected you, even believing everything you did was right."[31] For two years, their "burning friendship" continued with such intensity that Shimaura declares, "For us, the opposite sex was nothing." This all changed, however, when Tsuchida transferred his affections to a younger bishōnen, abandoning the love and friendship Shimaura had believed would last forever.

As he sits in jail, he accuses Tsuchida of implanting a "diabolical philosophy" in him. He states that originally he would not have hurt a fly, but Tsuchida infected him, partly through their relationship itself and partly through showing him books about crime and homosexuality:

At the time, there were not as many books about fear and crime available in translation as there are now. Therefore, if we wanted to know about those things, we had no recourse but to refer to the original works. You would bring books from someplace—books by authors such as Poe, Doyle, Freeman, and also Krafft-Ebing, all of whom I had never heard of. Under the pretext of studying language, you introduced them to me in large numbers, didn't you? At the same time, you also explained Carpenter, talked about Whitman, and introduced me to Montaigne.[32]

The first three writers, Poe, Doyle, and R. Austin Freeman (1862–1943), are famous for their mystery novels, but the other authors all discuss same-sex desire in contexts ranging from the pathologizing to the liberating. Clearly, Shimaura believes male–male desire is one important factor contributing to the criminal desires he believes Tsuchida to have implanted in him.

After leaving school, Shimaura tries to break with what he has learned from Tsuchida by throwing himself into a relationship with a woman, Ishi-hara Sueko, who became "a goddess of salvation" for him.[33] This affair is cut short by her father's insistence she marry someone else, and in resignation, Shimaura marries another woman, named Tsuyuko, whom he does not love. Because he did not love his wife, any sign of sexual or emotional desire on her part sent him into a rage, and he began to imagine killing her as the only way out of his torturous marriage. At this point, he complains the traces of Tsuchida's diabolical philosophy begin to make themselves felt, implying the relationship he had with Tsuchida, the "woman-hater [onna-girai]," left behind traces of misogyny that are just now manifesting themselves in his marital relationship. About this same time, Shimaura runs into his former lover, begins an affair with her, and decides to murder his wife. He decides to trick Tsuyuko into taking an overdose of sleeping pills, but the plan back-fires when not she, but his beloved mistress takes the fatal dose. In short, Shimaura's long letter attempts to prove his innocence, first by explaining his version of the events—Sueko took the pills, but he did not intend for her to do so—and, second, by trying to blame someone else for the homicidal de-sires that led him to consider murder in the first place. The "devil" Tsuchida becomes the site of phantastic projection onto which Shimaura transfers undesirable qualities and socially unacceptable impulses within himself, thus turning Tsuchida into an embodiment of all the urges that cannot be inte-grated into the social self. As Keith Vincent has correctly noted, Shimaura's account of his "attempted escape from Tsuchida's influence is a desperate attempt to differentiate himself from the prosecutor and to (re)claim his het-erosexuality-as-identity."[34] At the same time, since Tsuchida is never given a voice in the story, the story is entirely one-sided, and Tsuchida never is given the chance to become more than some devilishly evil specter haunting his schoolboy lover's past. In fact, even the illustrations made by Takenaka Eitarō for the first publication of the story in *Shin seinen* show Tsuchida as a shadowy, ghostly silhouette without a clear face.[35] Tsuchida, the embodiment of these allegedly "antisocial" desires, in short, remains a hazy presence who never comes into clear view.

In short, "Akuma no deshi" implies a connection between male–male desire, crime, and perhaps even mental aberration that, ironically, Hamao would criticize harshly in his essays of the following year. Indeed, as the case of Edogawa Ranpo and his novel *Kotō no oni* shows, such inconsistencies were not entirely atypical in authors writing to appeal to the fad for the erotic and grotesque from the late 1920s through the 1930s; still, the reader is left wondering how to reconcile the 1929 novella and the impassioned defenses of same-sex desire Hamao published the following year. It may be that in writing "Akuma no deshi," Hamao was actually *parodying* the tendency of the medical and criminal establishment—two organizations allegedly designed to produce "truth"—to locate blame for criminal tendencies in far-fetched places, such as the erotic encounters of one's youth. In fact, one wonders if Hamao intended readers to believe Shimaura's story at all. First, the idea that Tsuchida was a little demon, implanting and cultivating evil tendencies in his disciple, seems strikingly at odds with his present position as a prosecutor in the Tokyo court system. In fact, Hamao wrote another story in 1929 called "Shisha no kenri" (The rights of the dead) that also stars Tsuchida as a prosecutor, but there is no hint whatsoever he is untrustworthy or decadent in any way. Second, Shimaura is careful to note that even in his youth, Tsuchida did not himself engage in any indecent acts, though he allegedly encouraged others to do bad things. If Tsuchida was indeed a moral degenerate, then one would expect Shimaura to present concrete evidence in his letter. Considering such factors, it seems increasingly likely Hamao structured the text so the far-fetched connection between same-sex desire and criminality falls apart under scrutiny, thus hinting at the absurdity of the hysterical, homophobic tendency of sexology to link criminality to erotic desire. Hamao, in other words, is illustrating the motions of homophobia within his story, leaving it up to the reader to determine whether these processes of homophobia even make sense.

## RANPO AND CARPENTER'S GHOSTS OF THE PAST

Ranpo got to know Hamao through his early essays on crime and literature, but when Hamao began publishing in *Shin seinen*, the same magazine that carried many of Ranpo's earliest stories, the two became friends. Many years later, Ranpo remembered Hamao as a multitalented man with a thorough knowledge of *rakugo* and the theater as well as a passion for mah-jongg, *shōgi,* and social dance (20:334). The primary factor in their friendship, however, he notes, was a shared interest in same-sex desire. Ranpo's memoirs describe Hamao as a well-read "researcher of homosexuality who had been influenced by Edward Carpenter and others" (20:334). In fact, Hamao was the person who first lent him Carpenter's *The Intermediate Sex,* the same book Hamao had praised in *Fujin saron* as the best study of the social ramifications of male–male desire in modern society.[36] In his writings, Ranpo acknowledged that Carpenter's work greatly encouraged his own interest in the subject (22:51). Indeed, one sees traces of Carpenter's arguments in many of Ranpo's essays from the 1930s exploring love between men.

*The Intermediate Sex,* which was first published in book form in 1908, argues there are "distinctions and graduations of Soul-material in relation to Sex—that the inner psychical affection and affinities shade off and graduate, in a vast number of instances, most subtly from male to female, and not always in obvious correspondence with the outer bodily sex."[37] In Carpenter's view, biological sex and internal personality operate along two independent axes, which range from masculinity, which he stereotypes as fiery, brutish, tough, and powerful, to femininity, which he conceives of as sensitive, emotional, and appreciative of beauty. In many cases, biological gender and personality tend toward similar directions, but there are many cases where the two do not correspond. The result is what he calls a "mixed or intermediate type," including "Uranians" that are attracted to members of the same sex. Carpenter finds Uranians display an "immense capacity of emotional love," which benefits society in fields like nursing and education.[38] In fact, Carpenter claims the love of Uranians is less likely to be constrained by social class and can therefore lead to beneficial educational and philanthropic results. This kind of love, he argues, is necessary for the rise of a "true Democracy," which can only exist when love connects even the "most estranged ranks of society."[39]

For at least twenty years before writing this treatise, Carpenter had been involved with various British socialist groups, including the Social Democratic Federation and the Socialist League founded by William Morris (1834–96). Many of Carpenter's works dating from before the turn of the century argue that the move toward socialism must be predicated on new values that respect spiritual growth and foster the personal fulfillment of all people, regardless of socioeconomic class. In *The Intermediate Sex,* Carpenter ideal-istically saw Uranian love as auguring this new set of values: "[I]t is possible that the Uranian spirit may lead to something like a general enthusiasm of Humanity, and that the Uranian people may be destined to form the advance guard of that great movement which will one day transform the common life by substituting the bond of personal affection and compassion for the mon-etary, legal and other external ties which now control and confine society."[40] In order to share this social message with the Japanese public, the socialist activist Yamakawa Kikue (1890–1980) translated *The Intermediate Sex* into Japanese, publishing it first in the feminist literary journal *Safuran* (Saffron) in 1914—just a few years after the book had appeared in print in Britain.[41]

In an article published in 1936, Ranpo discusses the work of Carpenter, Gide, and J. A. Symonds, all of whom "published serious works defending the spirit of same-sex love [*dōseiai seishin*]—or praising it rather—each in their own way" (20:66). All three of these writers, Ranpo says, felt as if they had no choice but to combat a "general lack of understanding" on the sub-ject. In his opinion, Carpenter was the boldest of the three, since his equa-tion between the "spirit of same-sex love" and socialism flew so strongly in the face of mainstream British thought. In addition to *The Intermediate Sex,* Ranpo's article also mentions two other works by Carpenter. The first, *Ioläus: An Anthology of Friendship,* was first published in 1902 and consisted of an anthology of writings on same-sex desire, and male–male desire in par-ticular, culled from classical Greece, Rome, and Persia, nineteenth-century Europe, America, and other nations.[42] The other, *Intermediate Types among Primitive Folk,* consists of several essays from 1911 and 1914 and attempts a transhistorical survey of male–male desire across various cultures. The pur-pose of these essays is to show that across various cultures, "intermediate types" had not always been the subject of persecution and denunciation. In fact, Carpenter argues quite the contrary; their "special nature" had led them to occupy positions associated with divination, the arts, and the military—all positions that served a "positive and useful function."[43]

Ranpo was particularly fascinated with the final chapter of *Intermediate Types,* which was entitled "The Samurai of Japan and Their Ideal." There, Carpenter argues the chivalrous ideals of *bushidō* were rooted in the per-sonal, amorous relationships between warriors. He writes, "It was not so much the fair lady of his dreams, or even the wife and family at home, that formed the rallying point of the Samurai's heroism and loyalty, but the younger comrade whom he loved and who was his companion-at-arms."[44]

Ranpo was as interested in the literary evidence Carpenter produced to support this thesis as the thesis itself. Ranpo notes that Carpenter demonstrates the central role of male–male desire in Japanese military life by quoting the work of German ethnographer Ferdinand Karsch-Haack (1853–1936), who had published a study in 1906 that surveyed a number of Japanese works of fiction. Among them were *Nanshoku ōkagami* (*The Great Mirror of Male Love*) by Ihara Saikaku (1642–93) and *Shizu no odamaki* (The humble bobbin) by an unknown Edo-period author. Ranpo was familiar with both novels, but he notes that Carpenter also discusses another less familiar work, *Mozuku monogatari* (Tale of weeds in the sea), an allegedly true tale of two bishōnen who committed suicide together in the early seventeenth century.[45] Surprised to first learn about this story from an author from "far-away England," Ranpo decided to locate the original text. He found versions in two collections of texts compiled in the Edo period, and he learned that humorists Ōta Nanpo (1749–1823) and Kyokutei Bakin (1767–1848) both knew the text intimately and had written postscripts to different versions of it.[46] Moreover, Ranpo found the story had appeared with minor modifications in Saikaku's *Nanshoku ōkagami* and the anonymous *Nanshoku giri monogatari* (Tales of male love and obligation).[47] Several Edo-period essays, guides to the city, and histories also mention the story, implying it was relatively well known to late Edo-period audiences.

Ranpo presents the fruit of these bibliographic searches in "Shudō mokuzuzuka" (Mokuzu mound commemorating the way of the youth) published in *Bungei shunjū* in 1936.[48] (Mokuzu is a type of soft seaweed, sometimes eaten as a vegetable. It is used as a metaphor in the name of the mound to represent the impermanent, unrooted, transient nature of the relationship between the two young men.) In his memoirs, he recalls this essay represented the culmination of much research. He proudly states, "It is not the kind of essay one can write in a single night. Reports based on extensive readings of documents are seen as relatively worthless compared to creative fiction, but in my opinion, my essay is equal to ten fatuous pieces of literary hackwork" (21:17). After describing how he first learned about the tale, he summarizes the story and corrects a number of small textual errors in Carpenter's retelling.

The protagonist is the pageboy Itami Ukyō, who, in his early adolescence, is so attractive that when Funegawa Uneme, two years his senior, catches a mere glimpse of him, Uneme cannot help but fall madly in love. In fact, Uneme is so taken with Ukyō that he develops a mysterious ailment no doctor can cure. Uneme's lover at the time, Shiga Samanosuke, pressures him to identify what is troubling him. (In Carpenter's version, Samanosuke, whose name is misspelled, is only a close friend of Uneme.) Uneme confesses his new love but states that since a relationship is impossible, he has no choice but to die. Samanosuke takes pity on Uneme and contacts Ukyō on his behalf. Ukyō replies with a favorable response, which heals Uneme's illness instantly. Although they must dedicate themselves to their lords and therefore have few chances to see one another, they make a pledge of mutual love. This state of affairs continues until another warrior named Hosono Shuzen also falls for Ukyō. The latter rejects Shuzen's advances, and Shuzen is so humiliated that he vows to kill Ukyō. Meanwhile, Ukyō finds he is in danger and takes matters into his own hands by going to Shuzen's own quarters and killing him. Although the authorities exonerate Ukyō, Shuzen's father presses the case and has the boy condemned to death by ritual self-disembowelment. When Uneme hears his beloved is to die, he rushes to Keiyōji Temple in Asakusa, where they exchange tearful words and commit suicide together. At the end of the tale, the star-crossed lovers are buried together in a mound in the temple grounds (17:57–58).

In his essay, Ranpo writes he found himself "gradually becoming so taken with this story of Uneme and Ukyō's love" that he decided to locate the mound where the two were buried (17:60). After some research, he learned Keiyōji Temple had moved several times before finally settling in Imado. Armed with the address, he made his way to the desolate site:

> Guided by the priest who lived and worked there, I entered the vacant lot at the back where the main building of the temple had burned down, leaving only its stone base behind. When I asked about "Mokuzu Mound," he said it was right there. Alongside the stone platform of what was formerly the main building, a large number of unrelated gravestones had tumbled over. They looked like fallen corpses. Among them was a naturally shaped stone of about two and a half or three feet in width. It was dirty, covered with weeds, and lay pitifully on its side. The characters "Mokuzu Mound" had been carved deeply into its surface in angular characters about five inches high. (17:61)

Ranpo found himself so moved that he visited the temple grounds three or four more times. On his most recent visit, he found the stone surrounded by

blooming flowers. The essay ends with the following description of the dejected place:

> With the summer flowers as its offerings, the monument to the two
> boys lay forlornly on its side, looking as if it had forgotten something.
>     Someone had drawn some meaningless angular and curved lines
> on the stone with white ink. This was probably the naughty
> handiwork of the neighborhood children. For the children, this
> monument was no more than a hunk of stone worthy of their graffiti.
> For the adults too, this was no longer anything more than a single
> piece of stone. (17:61)

In standing before the grave, Ranpo appears to be haunted by the ghosts of
the past—the ghosts of Uneme and Ukyō, who speak to him of their erotic
and passionate love from beneath the stone which itself seems to have forgotten them. Ranpo's essay implies that like the stone itself, this kind of passionate homoerotic love lies almost completely out of view, relegated to a
peripheral position by the changes in cultural mores that had accompanied
Japan's entry into the modern world. Still, their story refuses to remain suppressed and returns like a ghost in unexpected ways, finding its way back
to the Japanese consciousness through an unexpectedly roundabout route
of transmission: Karsch-Haack to Carpenter to Ranpo, who then shares it
with the Japanese reading public.

Ranpo's goal in writing this essay appears to be to show that Japanese culture has not always relegated male–male desire to the margins of respectability, and in the writings of Carpenter as well as the quiet cemeteries of Tokyo,
he has located those sites of ghostly return where those forms of desire have
made themselves felt. Between the lines of his essay, one reads a thinly veiled
hope to honor and redeem their past in the hopes of creating a present in
which men could enjoy passionate relationships while still remaining a part of
society. Still, Ranpo does not go so far as to say this outright. He never turns
the story of the samurai lovers into the lynchpin of an argument for a reconsideration of the pathologization, feminization, and general lack of understanding that plagued queer men in interwar Japan. Instead, Ranpo allows his
specters to walk onto the stage of history without presenting any program-
matic vision of what their experiences might mean for contemporary politics.

In *Spectres du Marx (Specters of Marx)*, Derrida develops the metaphor of
spectrality to talk about the ways the past continues to exist in the present,

making its continued presence felt among the living. What is especially important to Derrida is not simply that ghosts represent the incomplete work of mourning; it is that ghosts serve as silent, barely visible presences that do not voice their own experience directly but continue to linger and haunt contemporary imaginations, sometimes provoking reconsideration of the present and perhaps even inspiring change.[49] In the book *Politics Out of History*, which presents an extended reading of Derridean spectrality, Wendy Brown notes that when people in the present confront the specters of the past, "We inherit not 'what really happened' to the dead but what lives on from that happening, what is conjured from it, how past generations and events occupy the force fields of the present, how they claim us, and how they haunt, plague, and inspire our imaginations and visions for the future."[50]

In *Queer/Early/Modern*, Carla Freccero uses Derrida's notion of spectrality to develop a model of engaging with the aspects of the sexual past she calls "queer spectrality." She follows Michel de Certeau in noting that one common function of engaging the "phantasms" of history is to bury them under meaning, "calming the dead who still haunt the present" and "offering them scriptural tombs" in histories that will hide their alterity by putting them in nice, neat coffins that fit our understandings of their experiences.[51] The challenge for "queer spectrality" is not to entomb the ghost of the other in the present but to allow the ghost to continue to exist on its own terms while attempting to understand our *own* reactions to those ghosts as we live with them. Freccero writes that doing "a queer kind of history means" allowing the past to exist in the present in the form of a haunting—being open "to the possibility of being haunted, even inhabited by ghosts."[52] To be more concrete, one should not attempt to suppress the spectral visions of the pasts of others by forcing them into straightjackets of meaning. One should not, for instance, attempt to understand the sexual experiences of the samurai through recourse to modern concepts such as the notion of "same-sex love," which as Pflugfelder has showed, has its own historicity. Freccero argues, in fact, that in order to allow the "object-other" of the past to emerge and to speak, "there must be identification, if not identity, between the subject and object. And yet, at the same time, for that object to demand, to become (a ghost), somehow to materialize, it must have a subjectivity of its own."[53] One must allow it, in other words, to be other, to be different.

There are moments in Ranpo's essay when he makes statements that come close to treading upon the difference of the "other," especially in the beginning when he is summing up the work of Carpenter. There, Ranpo writes, "Carpenter speaks about the similarities between Japanese *bushidō*, Japanese military strength, and the military strength of the Dorians of ancient Greece; he explains that the secret of both lies in a Greek-style love of men [*Girisha-teki danseiai*]. This may sound somewhat odd to us in the modern era, but a far-away, third-party observer can sometimes say things that strike close to the bull's-eye, can't they?" (17:55) Although Ranpo's rhetorical question is not a categorical statement of affinity between the two cultures of *shudō* and Greek pederasty, it does threaten to collapse the distance between the two cultures. Still, one should perhaps read this passage less as an attempt to force the early modern Japanese practices of *shudō* into alignment with Greek homoeroticism than as a statement imbued with three important "queer" functions.

First, the alignment of Japanese warrior sexuality with martial strength levels a charge against the pathologizing twentieth-century rhetoric of "perverse sexuality" that described same-sex eroticism as an illness of the spirit that led to weakness and neurasthenia. One sees such statements in Habuto Eiji and Sawada Junjirō's 1915 classic of Japanese sexology, *Hentai seiyoku ron*. Habuto and Sawada saw the historical example of boy-loving samurai as such a problem to their theory of same-sex desire leading to weakness that they spent several pages explaining away what they see as the "mistaken" connection between samurai valor and their culture of male–male bonding. Their explanations range from the absurdly patriotic (people who link warrior valor to same-sex desire are simply forgetting about the "Japanese spirit" or *Yamato-damashii* that was so strong among samurai) to the illogically circular (healthy spirits lead to healthy bodies, so there was no way the "sick" spirits of those warriors who loved men could be healthy enough to contribute to the martial spirit).[54] Nonetheless, the sorts of rhetoric they espoused had made significant inroads into the Japanese popular imagination by the 1930s when Ranpo wrote his essay. In that regard, Ranpo's essay should be seen as a challenge to the paradigm of homosexuality-as-pathology created by the institutions of medical psychology and sexology.

Second, Ranpo's essay presents a queer vision of the warrior class to his readers in the mid-1930s when popular visions of samurai bravado were more likely to involve epic duels of swordsmanship, honor, and revenge than fights over the love of another man. Ranpo is subtly suggesting to his audience how little they might know of the lives of the samurai, even though the image of the intrepidly brave and valiant samurai hero continued to play an important role in the Japanese imagination. Indeed, as Japan entered the era of rapid imperial expansion during the 1930s, the figure of the samurai became an increasingly important trope in the way Japan imagined itself and described its own actions in propaganda and popular culture. The fact Ranpo chose such a widely distributed and important forum as *Bungei shunjū* in which to publish his story meant the article no doubt reached the eyes of tens of thousands of readers almost immediately, thus rousing Ukyō and Uneme's ghosts from the abandoned grave at Keiyōji and showing Japanese readers how little they knew about samurai culture.

Finally, one additional function of this article is to show the Japanese public that the historical archive, which had struck Ranpo as so empty when he first began to look into the history of homoerotic desire in the 1920s, was not as empty as it might seem at first glance. By publishing "Shudō mokuzuzuka" in such a widely circulated journal, Ranpo was showing Japanese society of the 1930s that they could look across time and find examples of passion, love, and erotic devotion between men. In the end, Ranpo's evocation of the historical was as much, if not more about countering the silences of the present as any past he sought to uncover.

## Ranpo's Second "Teacher": Iwata Jun'ichi

In subsequent years, Ranpo continued to collect a vast number of Edo-period books on male–male desire. These included original *ukiyo-zōshi* (popular fiction of the seventeenth and eighteenth centuries), *hachimonjiya-bon* (popular fiction published in Kyoto in the early eighteenth century), and other rare volumes.[55] In fact, he joked in one essay, called "Watashi no shūshūheki" (My habit of collecting), that he had collected so many books on the subject that he had come to resemble Akechi Kogorō, the detective hero of many of his novels, who lived among massive piles of tomes.[56] Following the publication of "Shudō mokuzuzuka," Ranpo did occasionally write about manifestations of same-sex desire in Japanese literature and history; however, the majority of his writing on love between men deals with expressions of desire in ancient Greek, European, and American literature. The primary reason was his decision to turn over the study of male–male desire in Japanese history to his friend Iwata Jun'ichi. Like Ranpo, Iwata was fascinated with male–male desire and its expressions in history and literature, and the two encouraged each other in their pursuits of bibliographic sources. In fact, they framed their attempts to find books and articles on the subject as a lighthearted competition to find as many books as possible. While Iwata tried to find as many references as he could on male–male desire in Japanese literature and history, Ranpo focused his energy on European and American literature.[57]

While still a young man of fifteen in his hometown of Toba, located on the seashore of Mie Prefecture, Iwata started writing to Takehisa Yumeji (1884–1934), an illustrator and artist who had gained great popularity during the Taishō period with his pictures of long, slender, delicate women. The first encounter between Yumeji and Iwata took place in 1915, when the artist made a visit to Toba, and as their friendship grew, Iwata went to Kyoto to help Yumeji prepare for a private exhibition. Encouraged by his friendship with Yumeji, Iwata quit school and enrolled in the Bunka Gakuin (Institute of Culture), where he studied art. In the meantime, Iwata learned to paint the willowy figures typical of the work of his mentor.[58]

Back in his hometown of Toba, Iwata held a small solo exhibition of his paintings in a local elementary school. For nearly a year, Ranpo, who had not yet made his literary debut, had been working in the electrical division of a shipbuilding yard in the same town. Ranpo went to see Iwata's exhibition, and there, they met for the first time (22:45).[59] Iwata's diaries reveal that over the course of the remaining time Ranpo spent in Toba, the two met six or seven times at a local church that served as a meeting place for intellectual youth, but eventually, the two went their separate ways without becoming close friends. Their reunion came some years later in late 1925. At that time, Iwata was an art student in Tokyo, and Ranpo was living outside Osaka. Ranpo had by this time established himself as a writer and was visiting Tokyo to participate in a radio discussion about the detective novel. Iwata heard the broadcast, learned from a newspaper where Ranpo was staying, then stopped by his lodgings.[60] That evening, the two had a long discussion in Ranpo's room, during which Iwata mentioned one of his youthful literary experiments: a story about homoerotic desire he had serialized in a local newspaper in 1920. Ranpo expressed a strong desire to see the story, and the two exchanged addresses so Iwata could send it to him.

The discovery of a shared interest in male–male desire led to a strong friendship, and this, in turn, led to a number of literary developments. Iwata provided illustrations for a number of Ranpo's early works when they were reprinted in Heibonsha's *Gendai taishū bungaku zenshū* (Complete works of modern popular literature) in late 1927. These illustrations so pleased Ranpo that he wrote in a supplement to the volume, "their grotesque appeal matches my work exactly, and they bring out the flavor of my fiction in a way several levels more skilled, monstrous, and bloody than my words alone."[61] About the same time, Ranpo invited Iwata to serve as the secretary of Tankisha, a group of writers who met in Nagoya between late 1927 and autumn of 1929 to brainstorm for plots, look over one another's work, and write joint works *(gassaku shōsetsu)* for publication in *Shin seinen, Sandē mainichi* (Sunday Mainichi), and other journals.

The most important developments, however, have to do with Ranpo and Iwata's shared interest in male–male desire. After discovering their common interest, Iwata and Ranpo began trying to locate as many books as possible having to do with love and eroticism between men. This soon became a consuming passion. Ranpo wrote in 1953, "In my life up to this point, the things in which I have taken the greatest interest are detective novels and the collecting of bibliographic sources on male–male love."[62] A large part of Ranpo's passion came from the feeling this "secret interest" seemed "to interest no one else, only us."[63] Although Ranpo and Iwata lightheartedly framed the project as a race to see who could find the most sources, they also shared many sources they thought might interest one another. The two

Edogawa Ranpo and Iwata Jun'ichi outside of Tsu Station, Mie Prefecture, in September 1938. Ranpo identified Iwata Jun'ichi and Hamao Shirō as his two "great teachers" on the subject of same-sex desire. Courtesy of Iwata Junko.

became regular correspondents and exchanged at least eighty-seven known letters and postcards between 1932 and 1944. Of these, about 80 percent dated from 1939 to 1942, and at least half have to do with desire between men.[64] (This was not Iwata's only correspondence about male–male desire. Between 1931 and 1941, Iwata Jun'ichi also exchanged 120 letters with the anthropologist Minakata Kumagusu [1867–1941] about various aspects of the history and meaning of same-sex love and eroticism).[65]

Because Iwata was not preoccupied with the demands of the literary world, he devoted himself to writing about the sources they had uncovered, and he began producing a series of essays on the history of male–male desire in Japan that would eventually appear as *Honchō nanshoku kō* (Thoughts on *nanshoku* in our kingdom). Iwata tried to publish them in the widely read *Chūō kōron* (Central review), but this did not pan out, and instead he serialized the first half in *Hanzai kagaku* (Criminal science), a monthly magazine that, in typical *ero, guro, nansensu* fashion, combined light essays on sexuality and criminality with detective and crime fiction. After nine articles or so, Iwata took a break to examine the sources he continued to locate, and during this hiatus, the magazine went defunct. After Iwata's death from illness in 1945, Ranpo had the remaining essays serialized in *Ningen tankyū* (Human explorations), a titillating, postwar journal that published essays on various manifestations of sexual desire. It was not until 1974, after Ranpo had passed away as well, that the work finally appeared in book form.[66] Iwata's work examines descriptions of male–male desire throughout history, drawing on texts ranging from the Heian-period imperial collections of tanka poetry to medieval and early modern works. In particular, Iwata focuses on several historical phenomena having to do with male–male desire. These include the *chigo* cults that arose in temples during the medieval period, the brotherly bonds that developed among warriors during the Period of Warring States, the sexual culture of the *nō* and *kabuki* theater, the brothels and male prostitutes of the Genroku period, and so on. Although one might criticize Iwata for implying a historical continuity between these many expressions of desire, one should recognize Iwata was breaking new ground by attempting to shine light on a "taboo" subject many other contemporary writers treated as unworthy of serious consideration. Iwata's point was to argue that same-sex desire has existed in various, disparate forms throughout history and, rather than just dismissing it as a subject unworthy of attention, love and sexuality between men was a subject that in fact had its own historicity. In this regard, Iwata anticipates the work of contemporary queer historians who suggest historical manifestations of male–male desire are interesting not only in their own right, but also as windows that allow a glimpse into the cultural ethos of a particular historical moment.

While working on this series of essays, Iwata also compiled a large bibliography of works on male–male desire. Around 1943 Ranpo, who was depressed from having been virtually silenced by the system of censorship during the war, gave Iwata all of the cards containing the bibliographic information he had collected, and he encouraged Iwata to compile a list under his own name. During the height of the Pacific War, Iwata compiled a collection of about twelve hundred sources, which he titled *Nochi iwatsutsuji* (Later wild azaleas).[67] Iwata tried to publish it in a private edition, but due to the paper shortage, it was not published until after the war, by which time Iwata had already passed away.[68]

In his memoirs, Ranpo recalls that during the early Shōwa period, Iwata was his only good friend (20:282). Together, they wandered around Tokyo, especially Asakusa Park, filled as it was with a variety of interesting sights, ranging from open-air performers to male hustlers. Iwata and Ranpo also visited countless used-book stores in Tokyo and other cities. In Kyoto, they went together to Sanbōin in Daigoji Temple in order to see the *Chigo no sōshi* (Book of acolytes), a scroll several hundred years old that contains graphic images of erotic encounters between priests, nobles, and an acolyte (22:45). On another occasion, they visited the island-studded seashore of the Kii Peninsula, inspiring Ranpo to write *Kotō no oni*. Ranpo comments in his memoirs, however, that their closeness does not mean they had a "relationship of same-sex love" (20:282). Although they would often stay together in the same room while traveling, "even touching his hand would be enough to evoke a feeling of revulsion." According to Ranpo, their closeness stemmed from other reasons: Iwata had much to teach him with his fastidious attention to bibliographical sources; he was a personable and talkative person who would sometimes put on airs, and so he appealed to Ranpo, who humbly described himself as quiet and slow-witted by comparison. No doubt, Ranpo's firm denial of any physical relationship between them was designed to keep tongues from wagging and to emphasize that his interest in male–male desire was purely intellectual. Although it is tempting to read Ranpo's anxiety about people thinking him queer as a reflection of some sort of internalized homophobia, one should further qualify this. If anything, Ranpo's fear is that his friendship might be misunderstood as carnal. As noted before, Ranpo consistently describes male–male homosocial bonding

as a profoundly different mode of relating than male–male eroticism: a clear
sign he conceived of the possible range of homosocial relations as split into
acceptable, even desirable modes of asexual interaction and erotic bonding,
which he saw as problematic.

## RANPO AND KAITA

One additional Japanese writer who inspired Ranpo's interest in love between
men was Murayama Kaita. Kaita had died in 1919, so the two authors never
met in person, but Kaita seems to have played a large role in Ranpo's imagination, judging from the many times Ranpo referenced Kaita's work in his
own writing. Ranpo's memoirs state that during his youth he was, like many
other male elementary students of the period, an avid fan of the adventure
stories of Oshikawa Shunrō. In order to read them, he began to purchase
*Bōken sekai* regularly at a local bookstore (20:15). When Shunrō left *Bōken
sekai* and founded the magazine *Bukyō sekai,* Ranpo also turned to the new
magazine, which he continued to read even after Shunrō died in 1914. In
the pages of this magazine, he encountered Kaita's writing for the first time.
Ranpo wrote in 1934 that the short story "Akuma no shita" struck him as
"completely unlike anything that had preceded it." His admiration increased
when he read "Satsujin gyōja" and "Madenen," two unconventional stories
full of "madness, crime, and nightmares" (17:68).

In the 1935 essay "Kyōshū toshite no gurotesuku" (The grotesque as
nostalgic longing), Ranpo mentions Kaita as one of Japan's foremost voices
of the grotesque. He notes that elements of grotesquerie appear in the work
of a number of modern Japanese authors, including Hirotsu Ryūrō (1861–
1928), Izumi Kyōka, Tanizaki Jun'ichirō, and Akutagawa Ryūnosuke, but
not often enough to be considered true "authors of the grotesque" (*gurotesuku sakka):*

> Instead, I want to name someone in another field, the artist
> Murayama Kaita, as a representative of the Japanese Grotesque
> School [*Nihon gurotesuku-ha*]. . . . His posthumous collection *Kaita
> no utaeru* contains three works he called mysteries, but they are not
> really mysteries as much as stories of bizarre and frightening
> fantasies. The tale of a mysterious adolescent who had a scarlet,
> thorny tongue like that of a cat remains particularly imprinted in
> my memory. Even now, I cannot forget [the story "Akuma no shita"].
> (17:49)

In elevating Kaita to the position of a master of poetic grotesquerie, Ranpo positions Kaita as one of the early architects of the sensibility that by the 1930s had come to be known as *ero, guro, nansensu*. Indeed, many of Ranpo's own erotic and grotesque works of fiction unabashedly borrow motifs, ideas, and themes from Kaita's writing. (Ranpo would often work into his stories references to other stories he loved as a form of paying homage to their authors.) For instance, the ending of *Yami ni ugomeku* (Wriggling in the dark, 1926–27) involves a cannibal who, like the main character of "Akuma no shita," has a frighteningly long tongue and who, after feasting on the flesh of a corpse, commits suicide, realizing there is no place in the world for people with desires like his. Similarly, the novel *Ningen hyō* (The human leopard, 1934–35) once again features a monster with an oddly elongated, almost feline tongue covered with needles that serve as the signifier, if not the source, of the owner's cannibalistic desires. Ranpo's 1930 novel *Ryōki no hate* (The fruits of curiosity-hunting) references "Akuma no shita" more directly in an early scene in which the main character wanders down the streets of Kudanzaka and remembers the strange events that took place there in Kaita's story (4:179).[69]

More important for the purposes of this study, however, was the interest Ranpo took in Kaita's depictions of love between boys—an interest that culminated in the essay "Kaita *Ni shōnen zu*" (Kaita and his *Portrait of two boys*) published in 1934 in the journal *Buntai* (Literary style). In this essay, Ranpo begins by describing his admiration for Kaita's mystery-adventure stories, but its central focus is male–male desire in Kaita's artwork and writing, which Ranpo sees as extolling the beauty of young men and the "love of the Greeks" (17:69). As case-in-point, he points to the watercolor *Ni shōnen zu* (Portrait of two boys) Kaita had painted in 1914.

In April 1933 Ranpo had rented a home in Kuruma-machi in the Shiba Ward of Tokyo, which contained an old, earthen storehouse behind the main house. He converted the structure into a study by filling it with books, Western-style furniture, and assorted oddities. While decorating the room on the second story, he decided to see if he could purchase one of Kaita's paintings for the wall. Ranpo's writings indicate he had first encountered Kaita's paintings at an exhibition in Ueno nearly twenty years before, when he stood for a full hour before one of Kaita's paintings.[70] In hopes of obtaining one of Kaita's pictures, he enlisted the help of the *Shin seinen* illustrator Matsuno Kazuo (1895–1973), who put Ranpo in contact with Nagashima Shige (1893–?), a friend of Kaita and fellow student at the Nihon Bijutsuin.

Through Nagashima, Ranpo got hold of *Ni shōnen zu,* which he hung in his study.

In June 1934 the stage designer Yoshida Kenkichi (1897–1982) visited Ranpo's study and wrote the following description:

> In this room, which remains dark all day (and cool all summer
> because the ceiling is so high and the walls of the former storehouse
> so thick), Ranpo works by the light of a lamp even in midday. On one
> of the shadowy walls is a large, framed watercolor done by Murayama
> Kaita early in his career. (Kaita wrote around three mysteries, and
> that was the reason Ranpo liked this painting and had someone help
> him obtain it.) It is as if the weird air emitted by the glass over the
> painting makes the room even darker.[71]

Accompanying the description is a sketch showing that Ranpo had positioned the painting to give him a clear view of it from his desk as he worked. In July 1934 Ranpo moved to Ikebukuro in order to escape the noise of the railway tracks near his Kuruma-machi home. This house also had an earthen storehouse in the backyard, and once again, he converted it into a study. The painting hung there until after Ranpo's death from a cerebral hemorrhage in 1965.

Kaita had painted the watercolor soon after moving to the home of Kosugi Misei in Tabata, Tokyo. A recently discovered manuscript written by the artist Yanase Masamu in the early 1920s mentions that Kaita was in love with two youths who regularly visited Misei's home, and he invited them to become the models for a watercolor—almost certainly the same one Ranpo acquired.[72] Art historian Sasaki Teru has used this information, Kosugi's diary, interviews, and photographs to arrive at the conclusion the boys were relatives of Kosugi who frequented the house in the early Taishō period.[73] The plump boy on the right of the painting, who sports a student's close-cropped haircut, gazes outside the frame of the work as if looking at the painter or something beside him. There is no sign he is interacting with the boy at his side; instead, his attention is focused on a spot outside the painting. Meanwhile, the tall, thin boy beside him gazes silently at his friend. His face provides little indication as to what he might be thinking. As a result, the relationship between the boys is unclear from visual clues alone.

Ranpo became convinced, however, that "what the picture depicts is not just a simple image of two boys. Hidden deep within it, one finds the

Murayama Kaita's painting *Ni shōnen zu* (*Portrait of Two Boys*, 1914). Ranpo purchased this watercolor and hung it in his study, where it remained until well after his death. Collection of the Setagaya Literary Museum. Photo first published in the catalogue for the exhibition "Yokomizo Seishi to *Shin seinen* no Sakka-tachi." Copyright Setagaya Literary Museum 1995.

Ranpo sitting underneath Kaita's 1914 watercolor *Ni shōnen zu* in March 1939. Ranpo's inscription on the picture identifies the place the photo was taken as the interior of the earthen storehouse he used as his study in Ikebukuro. Courtesy of Hirai Kentarō.

beautiful Greek love that dominated Kaita's life" (17:70). This is perhaps true to a certain extent. Yanase's manuscript indicates Kaita painted the boys because he had a crush on them, but Ranpo's essay focuses on the relationship between the two figures in the painting, not the relationship between the artist and his subjects. There is no definitive clue the boys are "in love," but Ranpo asserts they must be. In fact, he goes one step further and interprets the figure on the right as Kaita himself. He notes the boy on the right with the round, plump face that seems "so unyielding and mischievous" vaguely resembles Kaita himself. The boy on the left of the painting, he guesses, is Kaita's "Mona Lisa," the bishōnen Inō Kiyoshi "for whom he yearned so much" (17:70). Although Sasaki Teru's research has undermined this theory, one can understand Ranpo's guess in light of Yamamoto Jirō's claim that Kaita loved Inō so much that the young boy's face appeared in all of his artwork.[74]

In the same essay in which Yamamoto makes this statement, he includes a passage of several paragraphs, supposedly written or narrated by Kaita himself, that describe an encounter between two adolescent boys, one of whom is in love with the other. Ranpo quotes them to support his interpretation of the relationship between the boys in the painting as one of passion.[75] The passage describes a young boy gazing longingly at a slender bishōnen. The first boy approaches him and hands him a single cherry blossom he had pressed between sheets of paper. The gift of this "silver link of spring" moves the recipient, who will cherish it as a remembrance of boy who gave it to him.[76] Ranpo's essay claims that "except for the part about the cherry blossom, this dream, this magnificent, lithographic vision has been transposed into the watercolor portrait of two boys now hanging in my room" (17:71). Nonetheless, there are a number of noteworthy discrepancies between the passage attributed to Kaita and the watercolor. The text places the encounter in April, but Ranpo notes the scene in the painting probably takes place in summer.[77] The text describes the boys standing at a distance from each other until one boy approaches the other and gives him a cherry blossom. In the watercolor, however, the boys are adjacent to each other, and there is no sign such an exchange has or will take place. The passage attributed to Kaita concludes, "The lithograph shows a vision of utter joy," yet neither boy in the painting appears particularly enraptured.

In 1961 Ranpo published an abbreviated version of the 1934 essay on this painting. There, the relationship between the painting and Kaita's fantasy of an exchange between boys is even more confused. In the condensed version,

Ranpo summarizes the passage about the exchange; however, Ranpo's summary sounds more like the painting than the passage he was allegedly describing.

> Two youths are standing by one another in a topaz-colored April garden. The youth on the right has a round face that reminds one of Kaita himself, and the youth on the left has a thin face with moist skin. He is a "bishōnen who calls to mind an extravagant flute, whose notes sound endlessly." Enveloped in delicate emotion, the two are in love.
>
> After going to some trouble, I found a picture by Kaita showing this same subject matter, and I was able to get it from one of Kaita's friends.[78]

In his summary of the passage, Ranpo makes it sound as though the boys stand to the left and right as in the painting, but the passage never indicates the position of the two boys in relation to one another. He also declares that one boy in the text resembles Kaita, but there is nothing in the passage to justify this statement. In sum, the belief the painting was a liberal reworking of Kaita's fantasy was based on a reading of the painting that overlooks certain details and interprets others in ways that privilege the theme of male–male desire, which is not necessarily explicit in the semiotics of the painting itself.

The eagerness to interpret the ambiguous relationship between the two boys in the watercolor as one of love says less about the painting itself than about Ranpo's own keenness to uncover instances of male–male desire in art and literature. A number of writers have commented as much; for instance, the author Sunaga Asahiko writes that Ranpo's "particular passionate way of speaking" about the painting reveals Ranpo's own interest in the subject.[79] Sociologist Furukawa Makoto sees the fact that Ranpo placed the painting in a prominent position in his private study as showing a positive, affirming outlook on male–male love, which remained for him a largely "hidden passion."[80]

What these writers do not mention is that Ranpo's essays about the painting represent an attempt to disassociate the kind of boyish expression of same-sex love he finds in Kaita's work from the pathologizing rhetoric of sexology. By the time Ranpo was writing, enough people in the medical and educational establishments had written about the deleterious effects of male–male love that the amorous inclinations and erotic habits of adolescents had become the subject of grave concern. Educators, psychologists, and sexologists wrote about the need to police the sexual practices of students so that any indulgence in a "perverse" desire for the same sex could be stopped before it poisoned their young minds and bodies. For instance, the sexologists Sawada Junjirō and Habuto Eiji point out that even manifestations of "platonic love" could be perilous. They argue that great men like Socrates and Plato may have been able to satisfy themselves with a form of love that sublimated erotic desire into an idealizing "platonic love"; however, ordinary people are less able to control themselves, and so asexual love between members of the same sex often represents the entrance to a slippery slope that would place the adolescent in grave peril.[81]

Ranpo, however, paints a quite different picture of boyish adolescent love, emphasizing its youthful and platonic qualities. He portrays the encounter in the painting as dreamy and chaste, characterized more by a simple aesthetic appreciation of beauty than carnal desire. By commenting that the face on the left appears to be that of Kaita's "ideal lover" and "Mona Lisa" Inō, he reads into the painting a highly aestheticized form of desire that does not cross into eroticism. By foregrounding the aesthetic and qualities of the painting while deemphasizing any erotic subtext that might be there, he implicitly distinguishes between the kind of youthful love of boys he finds in the watercolor and more overtly homoerotic displays of desire. If anything, he seems to suggest the youthful relationship between the boys belongs to a special, cherubic category of male–male desire free of injurious effects.

Critic Matsunaga Goichi has surmised the painting spoke particularly strongly to Ranpo because it revitalized memories of passionate crushes he had experienced during his own youth.[82] Indeed, Ranpo's treatment of the visions of boyish love he finds in the painting echo the stories of schoolboy desire described in his own autobiographical essays about his youth in Nagoya. Published in the September 1926 issue of *Taishū bungei* (Arts and letters for the masses), "Ranpo uchiakebanashi" (Confessions of Ranpo) describes a relationship of boyish infatuation rather like the one he locates in Kaita's painting.[83]

In the essay, Ranpo writes he was a shy, gentle, and attractive adolescent. As a result, others teased him by calling him an "*ee ko*" (literally "good boy"), a diminutive term used to refer to effeminate boys, including bishōnen. This nickname caused him much embarrassment—so much so that even seventeen years later, just the memory of it was enough to send a chill up his spine.

Since his school was infused with an ethos of ultra-masculinity that treated anything weak and effeminate as "strictly off limits," the word *nanjaku,* meaning "weak" or "soft," represented the ultimate insult. Meanwhile, there were many boys at school who played the role of *chigo* and enjoyed serving as a junior partner in an amorous relationship. Students would gossip about who was seeing whom, but few of these relationships ever developed to the point of becoming "unclean" *(kegarawashii):* "We would sometimes go to a point that bordered on indecency [*kiwadoi tokoro made*], but we never experienced *that* sort of thing. For the most part, our relationships were platonic" (16:15–16).

As evidence of the asexual nature of their relationships, Ranpo describes a crush he had on an artsy, smart, athletic boy with whom he exchanged a number of love letters. (Love letters were common at school, he writes, and he received his fair share from other boys.) Ranpo and the other schoolboy spent little time together until the summer holidays, when they went on an outing to the sea with some other students and a teacher. Quite by chance, they happened to end up sharing a mosquito net, and each night, Ranpo and his admirer would lie next to each other. Ranpo secretly hoped something might happen between them, and as he waited, he experienced a "vague but oppressive pleasure." Nonetheless, "each evening would pass without anything happening," leaving him feeling "dissatisfied" (16:16). This forthright confession provides proof the feelings he bore the other boy contained some hint of nascent sexuality. Despite Ranpo's protests that the relationships between him and other schoolboys were "platonic," physical longing was present in the shadows, even if the boys did not act on it. The relationship took a surprising turn one night when the boy showed Ranpo a knife. When rumors circulated about this, a teacher interrogated Ranpo, asking if the boy had been threatening him. The teacher separated them, and for a long time afterward, teachers and classmates looked askance at the other boy. Meanwhile, Ranpo felt a "humiliation worse than death" (16:17).

The essay also tells of a happier, yet equally asexual relationship that Ranpo calls his "first love." Before launching into the tale, however, Ranpo prepares his readers with the following statement: "I'm not going to get all sentimental about a woman. I say this because my partner was not a woman. In any case, I suppose the result was the same. What I'm saying is that we were playing at same-sex love. One often finds that sort of relationship. It was truly platonic and passionate. In fact, it seems I used up all the love in my life for just that one person of the same sex" (16:15). From the outset,

Ranpo emphasizes that their relationship was one of two adolescents "playing at same-sex love" *(dōseiai no manegoto)* without ever engaging in a "real"
physical relationship. In this way, he draws a fine line between relationships
like his and the more explicitly sexual ones teachers and sexologists warned
against. Like Ranpo, the boy for whom he developed these feelings was
a bishōnen, and troublemakers at school often gave him a hard time too.
When Ranpo was about fourteen, the two became close and exchanged
many love letters full of "very wanton things" like the statement "I want to
gobble you right up" (16:17). Like a "shy young girl in love," Ranpo thought
about the other boy day and night, and when classmates teased him about
it, he blushed yet simultaneously felt an "unparalleled ecstasy" inside. Since
neither of the partners was in the junior *chigo* position, Ranpo and his friend
treated each other like equals and "loved each other like man and woman." As
Furukawa Makoto has noted, this description implicitly draws a line between
Ranpo's experiences and the *nanshoku* relations of the late Edo period, which
typically involved inequality of the sexual partners and often led to sexual
consummation.[84] Even more importantly, these descriptions distinguish
Ranpo's love from the "hard-faction" predatory relationships described in
Mori Ōgai's *Wita sekusuarisu* and journalistic accounts of schoolboy desire
from the turn-of-the-century relationships that predated Ranpo's schooldays by only a decade or two.

Ranpo's youthful passion was so strong that even the simplest touch
inspired great emotion. A single stroke of the other boy's hand would excite
him, and when they held hands, he "would become feverish" and his "body
would tremble":

> I still remember the happiness of secretly touching one another's
> hands at the house of a mutual friend where we had met. We did it
> right as our friend was watching us. There was a knothole in his desk,
> and when I stuck my finger in it from above, the other boy secretly
> put his hand inside and clasped my finger from below. I have never
> experienced that feeling ever again, not with anyone, not even a
> woman. (16:18)

Holding hands, however, was as far as their physical relationship went, and
the two never exchanged even a simple kiss. "Sadly," Ranpo concludes, "love
between members of the opposite sex is short, yet love between members of
the same sex is even more fleeting." The two grew apart, and before the other

boy finished his studies, he fell ill and died. Thus it was, Ranpo says, he expended all of his love during his youth when he still did not "understand matters having to do with sex."

One might well read Ranpo's treatment of Kaita's painting as an indirect attempt to defend the boyish attractions he had felt in his own childhood—powerful attractions that flirted with eroticism but that remained unconsummated and therefore, in his view, unsullied. His eagerness to idealize youthful, asexual desire, in effect, disassociates youthful male–male desire from other, more explicit forms of male–male eroticism and thus resists the growing wave of social anxiety regarding sexual desire among boys. To put it another way, Ranpo is asserting the innocence and harmlessness of a form of desire the sexological and psychological establishments had treated increasingly as problematic since at least the late Meiji period. Although Ranpo does not directly challenge these establishments, the essays about his own youth make it clear he believes that youthful, nonsexual manifestations of desire are not equivalent to adult erotic love. Throughout the essay, Ranpo repeatedly insists his relationships were platonic, revealing he saw asexual love to be different in character from love of an erotic nature.

The final few pages of the essay make it clear, however, that he considers not only male–male intercourse but also male–female intercourse to be "unclean." He writes he has experienced attraction to the opposite sex and even acted upon it a few times, but "it just did not feel like the real thing. Perhaps because it was accompanied by sexual relationships, it seemed there was something impure about it, and therefore, it did not feel like love." The essay assures readers his experiences with women were not entirely unpleasant, but the introduction of carnal sexuality rendered those experiences vaguely "animalistic" (16:18). The essay does not identify whom he is talking about, but his statements are sweeping enough to include even sexual relations with his wife, Murayama Ryū, whom he had married in 1918. (Even in that relationship, Ryū had initially been the one to express interest in Ranpo, who had been relatively aloof and seemingly little interested in women.)

Later essays express similar feelings; for instance, in the 1952 essay "Waga seishun ki" (Record of my youth), he states that during his teenage years, he found the opposite sex to be "abhorrent" and so did not try sleeping with women until he was in his twenties. He comments, however, that even after his abhorrence for the opposite sex dissipated, he was never able to think of a woman as a "sublime being," no matter how beautiful she was (22:30). In "Boku wa ren'ai funōsha" (I am a man impotent in love) published in 1949, he describes his aversion to sexuality—both same-sex and cross-sex—in language suggestive of medical psychology.[85] The essay begins with the declaration he is a *ren'ai funōsha,* literally, a "person incapable of love." He states he was unable to experience the passion of sexual love and blames his failure on society, which teaches that sexuality is ugly:

> From our youths, society drums it into us that our genitals and sexual activity are ugly, horrible things. Although the liquids expelled by the human body are in no way ugly, for millennia, our customs have treated them as so ugly we even find the smell of them to be horrible. The view that the genitals and sexual activity are ugly is closely related to this. Were that not the case, wouldn't we consider art, sculpture, plays, performances, and poetry that depict sexual activity to be the highest kind of art? (22:30–31)

Although this passage exaggerates greatly—the genitalia were never condemned categorically by all of Japanese society, and in fact, Japanese history has many examples of art and literature celebrating sexuality—Ranpo is right in noting the genitalia and sexuality had become the subject of considerable anxiety during the Meiji and Taishō periods, as "respectable" society eschewed expressions of nonheteronormative sexuality and censors began to crack down on explicit representations of the body and its sexual functions. He argues that as one tries to reconcile the "sublime beauty" of love with the "supreme ugliness" of the acts performed by those parts of the body, one only experiences confusion and shame (22:31). The idea that certain parts of the body were unseemly and best excluded from view and polite conversation clearly reflects the notions of bodily hygiene and propriety that had taken root among the Japanese middle class.[86]

In a round-table discussion with the comedian and raconteur Tokugawa Musei (1894–1971) published in *Shūkan asahi* (Asahi weekly) in 1954, Ranpo again repeats he finds sexual encounters with women unappealing. At one point, Musei says that he heard Ranpo never found the "ideal woman."[87] To this, Ranpo replies, "When I was a boy, I experienced something like love [*ren'ai*], but it was not love accompanied by sexual desire" (22:161). He suggests multiple reasons, but foremost is his belief that "sexual desire is something truly unclean." Half-jokingly, he explains, "People are born from the dirtiest part of the body. I just can't respect love that tries to get there as its goal. *[Laughs]* It's no good to teach people that. We've got to teach what is beautiful and what is sacred." When Musei asks him if he is perhaps more interested in "same-sex love" *(dōseiai),* Ranpo responds,

ER: That was in my youth. Before I felt sexual desire.
TM: So that was also before all those unclean things, eh? *[Laughs]*
ER: Platonic love for the same sex is not bad. I am quite interested in same-sex love, and in fact, I am researching it in books and other sources. I don't put it into practice that often though.
TM: "Don't often"? By that, do you mean sometimes you do? *[Laughs]*
ER: It means I am not totally disinterested in such things.
TM: Quite a literary way of putting it. *[Laughs]*
ER: I am interested in both women and in men, but it isn't good to put that interest into practice. (22:162)

Although it is impossible to know Ranpo's innermost thoughts about sexual desire between men—he might have been playing coy in this interview to avoid scandal—it seems clear that, at least in the ways he presented himself to the reading public, he espoused ambivalent feelings toward male homoeroticism. On one hand, he did possess a special curiosity about amorous and sexual practices between men that led him to collect books on the subject, but on the other, his writings express great anxiety over manifestations of male–male love involving overt expressions of sexuality. As if to rationalize these feelings, he theorizes that society teaches all people to feel horror of the genitalia. In this way, he accounts for his apparent disinterest in intercourse with women as well as any other socially induced anxieties he may have had about male–male eroticism.

After publishing his "confession" in 1926, Ranpo appears to have become increasingly hesitant to write about his own youthful sexual feelings. After reading a Japanese translation of the autobiographical work *Si le grain ne meurt ... (If It Die ... )* by the French novelist André Gide, Ranpo decided he would try his hand at writing a comparable work for *Purofiru* (Profile), a Kyoto-based mystery magazine. The result was the 1937 work *Kare* (He), which although narrated in the third person, describes the author's own life. Ranpo published four installments, in which he describes the circumstances of his birth and the first decade of his life, but the narrative breaks off soon before the protagonist enters puberty. Ranpo's memoirs state that when he reached the point where he was ready to talk about "a certain incident in my youth having to do with sexual desire" he became completely stuck. He explains, "I was too embarrassed to write about it. Perhaps if I was one of those authors of pure literature who wrote as if it was a matter of life and death, I would have been able to do it, but the reason I wrote detective fiction is that it is not about such life-and-death matters. I began writing for fun" (21:17).

Reading the first installments of the aborted work, one finds Ranpo frequently hinting at how fundamentally different he is from the other boys around him. In fact, the work begins with an epigraph from *If It Die . . .*, in which the eleven-year-old Gide burst into tears before his mother, repeating, "I'm not like other people . . . not like other people!" (17:10).[88] The text itself emphasizes how close he was to his grandmother, how little he liked his father as a youth, and how passionately he loved art and literature—all things that Ranpo, who had become interested in Freudian psychology and knew of the Oedipus complex, likely saw as symptomatic of an "inverted" personality. As luck would have it, *Purofiru* discontinued publication right at the time Ranpo became stuck, and he was spared the quandary of how to write about his first sexual desires. Although the magazine *Shupio* (named from the Russian word meaning "spy" or "detective") offered to carry the continuation of the work, Ranpo declined, and the world never learned what sexual event had caused Ranpo so much consternation.[89]

## "Secret Passions" and Psychoanalysis

In early 1933, around the time he purchased Kaita's painting, Ranpo began attending the meetings of the Seishin Bunseki Kenkyūkai (Group for Psychoanalytic Research) held each month in Tokyo. In his memoirs, Ranpo explains he became interested in psychoanalysis primarily because it dealt so often with same-sex desire (20:282). Other members of the group shared his interest, creating an atmosphere in which attendees could discuss the subject. The leader was Ōtsuki Kenji, a Marxist critic-turned-psychologist who had completed some of the earliest translations of Freud. (As mentioned above, it was around this time that Ranpo purchased two collections of Freud, including the one containing Ōtsuki's translations [20:282].)[90] Other members of the group included Yabe Yaekichi, another translator of Freud and the author of an introduction to psychoanalysis; the doctor and painter Koyama Ryōshū (1898–1991); and the psychologist and translator Iwakura Tomohide (1904–78). The group also contained literary figures, such as the critic and Naturalist theorist Hasegawa Tenkei; the translator of mystery fiction Tauchi Chōtarō; the anthropologist Nakayama Tarō (1876–1947); and the translators Katō Asatori (1886–1938) and Miyajima Shinzaburō (1892–1934). Also involved was Takahashi Tetsu (1907–71), who at the time aspired to become a fantasy writer but later in the postwar era became one of Japan's foremost sexologists, with large numbers of writings on "perverse sexuality" (20:282).[91] Because so many in the group were involved with literature and the arts, the meetings often involved discussions of these subjects. When the group created the journal *Seishin bunseki* (Psychoanalysis) in May 1933, they included not just academic studies of psychology but also discussions of art, literature, mythology, and even occasional literary works.

In the inaugural issue of *Seishin bunseki*, Ranpo began serializing an article called "J. A. Shimonzu no hisoka naru jōnetsu" (The secret passion of J. A. Symonds) about male–male desire in the life and work of John Addington Symonds, a Victorian writer known for his monumental studies of classical Greek poetry, literary biographies, and translations of Italian Renaissance autobiographies.[92] Ranpo had encountered Symonds's work in the course of his readings about male–male desire and developed a strong interest in his life and work. Ranpo states that his purpose in writing about Symonds is not to examine his scholarship but to use his texts and biography to speculate about his sexual preferences and how they manifested themselves in his writing (17:74). In the process, Ranpo uses the psychological language available to him to paint a relatively sympathetic psychological portrait of a man living with the psychic wounds inflicted by a society that does not understand his sexual orientation. How much Ranpo personally identified with Symonds and his plight is unclear; however, what is clear is that in writing this article, Ranpo is making an impassioned plea for society to understand those individuals who hide their homoerotic attractions for fear of being discovered by heteronormative society.

One of the main sources of Ranpo's information was an 1895 biography compiled from Symonds's memoirs, diaries, and letters by his former pupil Horatio F. Brown (1854–1926).[93] From reading Brown's biography, Ranpo could not have known that when Symonds started writing his memoirs in 1889, a major purpose was to describe his strong attraction to men, his personal struggle against Victorian morality, and his clandestine sexual life in order to provide a case study for psychologists and show others with similar feelings they were not alone.[94] The memoirs openly describe his youthful sexual feelings, initial sexual experiences with men, frequent encounters with male hustlers, journeys abroad to seek sexual gratification, and even some of his most passionate trysts. Although Symonds wanted to publish his memoirs to console men with similar feelings, he ultimately refrained from doing so. Instead, he willed the manuscript of his memoirs to Brown with the instructions they be preserved, and if possible, made public in the future when they might not cause trouble for Symonds's wife and four children. Brown, however, was eager to publish a biography of his friend, so he selected innocuous passages and combined them with excerpts from letters and diary entries to produce the biography Ranpo read. In doing so, Brown excised the arguments against Victorian society, but Ranpo's reading proves that even with Brown's heavily expurgated biography, an astute reader could catch a glimpse of Symonds's true erotic feelings and use them in his own argument for tolerance.

Ranpo begins by pointing to dreams that suggest Symonds experienced a homoerotic attraction to men; for instance, he draws attention to a recurrent dream in which "the beautiful face of a young man, with large blue eyes and waving yellow hair" visited Symonds, drew close, and kissed him before disappearing in the darkness (17:76).[95] Based on his reading of Brown's biography, Ranpo notes Symonds did not experience an Oedipal interest in his mother and a subsequent conflict with his father—the conflict that would, in Freudian thought, propel a young man toward an interest in the opposite sex. Ranpo notes Symonds experienced a "mysterious coldness toward his mother and a loving attachment to his father," and probably "in his case, his feelings of erotic feelings for the same sex [*dōsei renjō*] had to do with putting himself in the position of a woman" (17:80). Symonds's memoirs, which were in turn quoted by Brown, denied he was in any way "effeminate," but Ranpo reads this defensiveness as evidence he must not have been especially masculine. Ranpo states "it probably would not be wrong to think of him, in the words of Ulrichs, as one type of a female spirit in a male body *(anima muliebrio in corpore virili inclusa)*" (17:81), and he notes Symonds's dreams feature himself as the erotic object of other men, a passivity he guessed probably played out in bed.

In these passages, Ranpo reproduces a number of stereotypes prevalent in early twentieth-century discourse on male–male desire. First of all, he employs the trope of "inversion" seen in the writing of Ulrichs and many of his contemporaries. Ranpo makes Symonds's sexual orientation intelligible by assuming there was something "feminine" about Symonds, although the biography expressly denies this. Second, Ranpo reads this femininity into the very structure of Symonds's psyche. Ranpo attributes Symonds's alleged femininity to a disruption of the processes of the Oedipus complex; his subsequent attraction to men was not just a matter of actions, but an indication of a far more profound psychological constitution. Ranpo associates this attraction with "passivity," suggesting Symonds did not identify with the sexual aggressiveness of other men but wanted instead to be "loved"—a euphemism implying that Ranpo suspected Symonds of preferring a passive role in bed. (In fact, Symonds's unexpurgated memoirs are purposefully vague about what he did in bed.)

To Ranpo, Symonds represents a case study of an *"Urning"* who, despite his sexual desires, tried to live a life that would appear "normal" to most outsiders.

> Just now, I have said one could classify Symonds's personality as that of an *Urning*. Readers who do not know how serious Ulrichs, the man who created this word, actually was, this noun tends to evoke thoughts of dens of male hustlers in and around Berlin. Ulrichs did not use the word only to refer to such things. He also used it to refer to the unhappy people who go about hiding desires difficult to control—people who carry on living lives that are not the slightest bit different from those of regular people. Symonds was one of those unhappy people. According to his memoirs at least, his external life did not diverge from the ordinary path in any way. (17:81)

Although he had suggested earlier that Symonds was probably not an "ordinary" man, he states Symonds tried to live an "ordinary" life with a marriage and children. This, Ranpo guesses, was probably not enough to make him content.

> So what happened to the love he felt during his youth, his longing for Greek-style love? Did his unusual passion merely disappear along with his marriage? No, surely one cannot think it did. He probably struggled with it. Then, he probably overcame the feelings in his heart. He had too much refinement to put into concrete practice the desires in his heart just as they were. He was not courageous or shameless enough to rebel against the manners and customs of society. The legal code and social customs of England at the time were stricter than we today can possibly imagine. (17:82)

Of course, Ranpo did not have access to Symonds's complete memoirs, which show Symonds had hundreds of encounters and several significant relationships with men. The key point is that Ranpo builds an image of Symonds as an abstinent *"Urning"* who, confined by the strictures of Victorian culture, channeled his interest in men into spiritual love and bibliographic research. Ranpo uses this image to first, evoke reader sympathy, and second, suggest the "unhappiness" of the lives of seemingly "normal-acting *Urningen"* who feel as if they must restrain their sexual feelings.

In describing the intense pressure placed on such men in Victorian England, especially around the time of the highly publicized arrest of Oscar Wilde in 1895, Ranpo laments that such men did not have access to more "scientific" theories of same-sex desire. He writes, "We can imagine what it must have been like in Symonds's era, which was earlier even than Oscar Wilde. Symonds ended his life without ever seeing the spread of a scientific understanding of this kind of abnormal psychology" (17:82). Like Hamao Shirō, Ranpo optimistically assumes that if social stigmas were set aside, medical psychology could provide a potential source of liberation for men such as Symonds by explicating the nature of their desires and raising consciousness about them. In short, Ranpo sees medical psychology as a potential agent of deliverance, rather than a guilty party that had helped categorize and stigmatize same-sex desire in the first place.

Although Ranpo incorrectly guesses Symonds was "probably too cowardly and fastidious" to have sex with men, he does correctly detect that Symonds created a high-minded admiration of spiritual love as an attempt to negotiate a compromise between his sense of morality and his erotic desires (17:83). Ranpo provides a long excerpt to this effect from the 1893 essay "The Dantesque and Platonic Ideals of Love" in which Symonds argues that both the love of the Greeks and of the chivalrous knights for fellow men differ profoundly from carnal desire. Ranpo quotes Symonds as saying that in theory, "both Greek and mediaeval types of chivalrous emotion were pure and spiritual enthusiasms, purging the lover's soul of all base thoughts, lifting him above the bondage of the flesh, and filling him with a continual rapture" (17:83).[96] To Ranpo, this statement was evidence Symonds drew a sharp line between sexual relationships and the kind of aestheticized love seen in the idealistic camaraderie of the Greeks, Whitman, and other writers.

Much of the remainder of Ranpo's long article consists of a catalogue of passages in Symonds's works that deal with male–male desire and which Ranpo sees as indicating Symonds's own homoerotic interests. For instance, he surmises Symonds chose to write a biography about Michelangelo "because this great artistic master was unparalleled in extolling the virtues of Hellenism—that is, both in general and in the sense of same-sex love [dōsei ren'ai]."[97] Ranpo surmises Michelangelo possessed "effeminate feelings of the same sort as Symonds" and was probably "a sort of Urning," and this led Symonds to feel some sort of kinship with him (17:96). Ranpo provides a similar explanation for Symonds's interest in the artist Benvenuto Cellini (1500–1571), whose autobiography Symonds translated for publication in 1888.

Apart from the possible exception of Cellini, who seems to have reveled in the physicality of the boys he loved, Symonds discusses manifestations of male–male desire in terms of spiritual admiration, the appreciation of beauty, democratic philios, chivalrous honor, and other "noble" virtues (17:98). Symonds was, effectively, attempting to lend ideological respectability to the concept of male–male love by associating it with virtues contemporary readers would admire. One example of a passage in which Symonds links male–male love with traits that would have appealed to Victorian (as well as Japanese) audiences is the following excerpt from the 1873 Studies of the Greek Poets:

> Greek mythology and history are full of tales of friendship, which can only be paralleled by the story of David and Jonathan in our Bible. The legend of Herakles and Hylas, of Theseus and Peirithous, of Apollo and Hyacinth, of Orestes and Pylades, occur immediately to the mind. Among the noblest patriots, tyrannicides, lawgivers, and self-devoted heroes in the early times of Greece, we always find the names of friends and comrades recorded with peculiar honor. . . . In a word, the chivalry of Hellas found its motive force in friendship rather than in the love of women; and the motive force of all chivalry is a generous, soul-exalting, unselfish passion. The fruit which friendship bore among the Greeks was courage in the face of danger, indifference to life when honour was at stake, patriotic ardour, the love of liberty, and lion-hearted rivalry in battle. "Tyrants," said Plato, "stand in awe of friends."[98]

In his translation of this passage, Ranpo often renders Symonds's word "friendship" as danseiai (love of men)—a conspicuously vague choice of words that can be used for both brotherly and sexual love. Although Ranpo's principal argument has to do with the sexual interests of Symonds and not the nature of male–male desire in general, he does not challenge Symonds's arguments, giving the impression he largely agrees with them. In the case above, he does not comment on the content of the passage; instead, he leaves intact Symonds's central thesis that love between men is not necessarily pathological but linked to upstanding virtues. As a result, this essay that starts off as an exploration of one man's psychosexual development ends up covertly presenting Symonds's argument that love between men is not only *not* pathological but also desirable and beneficial to society.

In the essay "Hoittoman no hanashi" (On Whitman) published in *Shin seinen* in 1935, two years after his long essay on Symonds for *Seishin bunseki*, Ranpo discusses Walt Whitman as a modern writer who deals with the virtuous qualities of male–male love. Interestingly, Ranpo's article seems more concerned with Symonds's reaction to Whitman's work than Whitman's poetry itself. Drawing on Horace Traubel's memoirs of Whitman, Ranpo writes that from about 1872 to 1890, Whitman and Symonds exchanged a large number of letters. In one letter from 1888, which Ranpo translates into Japanese, Symonds presses Whitman to speak more about the nature of the "manly love" that appears in his famous collection *Leaves of Grass.*

> What the love of man for man has been in the Past I think I know. What it is here now, I know also—alas! What you say it can and shall be I dimly discern in your Poems. But this hardly satisfies me—so desirous am I of learning what you teach.
>
> Some day, perhaps—in some form, I know not what, but in your own chosen form—you will tell me more about the Love of Friends. Till then I wait.[99]

Whitman responded evasively, apparently knowing full well Symonds hoped for an explication of his views on male–male love. Symonds continued to send more letters approaching the subject more circumspectly and apologizing for his questions.[100] As if to play up the sensational qualities of this story for the popular, young audience who would be reading the article about this exchange in *Shin seinen*, Ranpo writes, "The tenacity of the introverted Symonds that burned like a blue flame. . . . The silence from Whitman each time. . . . Isn't this story so mysterious it's somehow frightening?" (17:64).

The result of this was a famous response Whitman sent in a letter dated August 19, 1890, which Ranpo had read reprinted in Symonds's *A Problem* in Modern Ethics: "That the Calamus part [of Leaves of Grass] has ever allowed the possibility of such construction as mentioned is terrible. I am fain to hope the pages themselves are not to be ever mentioned for such gratuitous and quite at the same time undreamed and unwished possibility of morbid inferences—which are disavowed by me and seem damnable."[101] Ranpo theorizes that Whitman's apparent irritation was due to a mistaken impression that in asking about the poems, Symonds was insinuating Whitman used male camaraderie to mask the "sick, criminal parts" of physical, erotic desire (17:64). Ironically, Whitman was ultimately agreeing with the idea put forth by Symonds in A Problem of Greek Ethics that male–male desire could have positive manifestations with beneficial attributes and effects, such as greater fraternity between men, but these qualities were somehow lacking in displays of outright male–male eroticism.[102] Both Whitman's letter and Symonds's study A Problem of Greek Ethics present the common assumption homoeroticism and homosociality are quite different forms of desire with different effects.

The interest of these two writers in forms of male–male love that excluded eroticism is quite similar to the interest Ranpo professed in his own essays. No doubt for Ranpo, as well as Whitman and Symonds, the distinction between camaraderie and carnal desire allowed him to render his own interest in "good" (in other words, platonic and brotherly) manifestations of male–male desire ideologically respectable. In Ranpo's eyes, the writings of Symonds and Whitman no doubt reinforced the notion homosociality and homoeroticism represented two neighboring but significantly different ways for men to interact with one another. Through translating snippets of their writing into Japanese and providing his own commentary, Ranpo was helping to reinforce for Japanese readers in the early twentieth century that there was a split in the homosocial spectrum that separated the ways men might relate to one another.

## RANPO'S "GRECOMANIA"

For Ranpo, Symonds's writings served as an introduction to the culture and writings of ancient Greece, which continued to fascinate him for years to come; in fact, Ranpo sometimes attributed his "Grecomania" to the discovery of Hellenistic civilization through Symonds (17:53; 22:90). The 1940 essay "Shosai no tabi" (Travels in my study) describes elaborate visions of daily life in the ancient Peloponnesus, thus demonstrating that Ranpo's interest extended to many areas of Greek culture, but Ranpo comments he was especially impressed by Symonds's 1883 *A Problem in Greek Ethics*—the treatise in which Symonds concluded male–male love had powerful social benefits (17:53). Clearly, the discovery that desire between men occupied an important position in classical culture accounts for a large part of Ranpo's interest in Greece. Ranpo perused Japanese translations of the Greek classics and also turned to the dual English and Greek editions of the Loeb Classical Library for works not yet available in Japanese. Among the titles he read were *The Lives of Eminent Philosophers* by Diogenes Laertius, which often mentions the affections certain thinkers bore for their teachers and followers, and *The Deipnosophists* by Athenaeus of Naucratis, which describes everything from the glories of food and the personalities of the cooks who made it to the philosophy, lifestyles, customs, and amorous proclivities of the people who consumed it.[103]

One additional work that particularly interested him was *Musa Puerilis* (sometimes also called *Musa Paedika* or *The Adolescent Muse*), an anthology of poetic epigrams believed to have been compiled by Strato of Sardeis, a poet from the early second century c.e.[104] Ranpo first discusses the collection in "J. A. Shimonzu no hisoka naru jōnetsu," where he provides a translation of Symonds's paraphrase of Strato's famous epigram of the garland weaver (17:92). This epigram, ripe with romantic longing, describes the narrator's passion upon encountering a particularly lovely youth in a garland weaver's stall. In the original, the narrator approaches the youth and speaks to him, but the boy blushes and hurriedly sends him away. The narrator then buys some flowers as a pretense to be near him and prays to the gods they might be together.[105] In Symonds's expanded, Victorian reinterpretation, the boy does not send his admirer away but suggestively kisses a bud and hands it to him. The narrator pretends to be hosting a bridal feast, and he asks the boy to come deck his room with flowers so they might be together for a moment.[106] In a later note appended to "J. A. Shimonzu no hisoka naru jōnetsu," Ranpo writes he realized how creative Symonds's version was only when he read other translations of the same poem after publishing his article; he concludes that Symonds's interpretation was undoubtedly colored by his own "passion" for male–male desire (17:92).

At some point in the 1930s or 1940s, Ranpo also translated a number of other epigrams from *Musa Puerilis*. In 1947 he unearthed drafts of two short translations and published them in the article "Shudō kasen" (Linked

verses on the way of the youth) in the magazine *Kindai kidan* (Strange tales
of modernity).[107] While some of the short poetic works in *Musa Puerilis* are
quaint and tender, a number, including the two in "Shudō kasen," are in a
comic vein. The first by Strato provides a clear expression of erotic interest
in a man's derrière: "If a plank pinched Graphicus' behind in the bath, what
will become of me, a man? Even wood feels." The second, which Ranpo mistakenly attributes to Strato but is actually by Statyllius Flaccus, is also comic:
"Just as he is getting his beard, Lado, the fair youth, cruel to lovers, is in love
with a boy. Nemesis [the goddess of retribution] is swift."[108] The work
implies that Lado, who was once cold to those who wanted him, is now filled
with frustrated sexual passion because the boy he desires is unresponsive
to his overtures. In his translation, Ranpo has rendered the Greek *erastes* as
*nenja*, the term used in the period of the Warring States and the Edo period
to refer to the older partner in a sexual relationship, thus equating the division of roles within the Greek system of erotics to the division of roles in
pre-Meiji *nanshoku*. In doing so, he assumes a rough equivalency between
the Greek system of *paiderastia* and the pre-Meiji system of *nanshoku*, which
typically featured the pattern of a one-way progression from younger, desired
*wakashu* to older, desiring *nenja*.

It is clear that here and in many of his other essays, Ranpo was following Carpenter and other early Western homophiles by drawing lines of com-
monality between various historical manifestations of same-sex eroticism,
thus establishing the sense that same-sex desire represented a transhistorical, even timeless experience. Although contemporary historians are quick
to note the differences between the cultures of ancient Greece and pre-
Restoration Japan, especially the issues of social class that determined where
and how male–male eroticism was practiced, it is important to note that
drawing such connections between historical manifestations of male–male
eroticism, past and present, East and West, help establish lines of identification that shaped the ways people in early twentieth-century Japan, such
as Ranpo, viewed expressions of eroticism. The text seems to be suggesting that if same-sex eroticism was practiced in both Greece (the country
often seen in Europe and Japan as the origin of modern civilization) and pre-
Restoration Japan, then how problematic could it possibly be? As David
Halperin has noted in his own writing about the uses of historical prece-
dent in studies of same-sex desire, it is easy to problematize the tendency for
people to collapse representations of same-sex desire from different moments

in time; however, to do so is to overlook the fact that those bonds of historical identification address powerful needs in the present, nurturing and giving strength to those forces within contemporary society at odds with the forces of homophobia.[109] It seems clear Ranpo turned to Greece for anti-homophobic nourishment in an era antagonistic to expressions of eroticism between men. To him, Greece represented an imaginary respite from the boundaries of forced heteronormativity—an imagined space in which heterosexual institutions and expectations did not govern the play of bodies, desire, love, and eroticism.

It is significant that this space of imaginary play came to take a position within Ranpo's imagination during the late 1930s and 1940s, right as the nation was sliding into all-out war. After the outbreak of full-fledged war between China and Japan in 1937, the rising sense of national emergency meant there were fewer places where authors such as Ranpo and his circle of friends could publish work about eroticism and its nonheteronormative manifestations. As the war grew increasingly intense, Ranpo's novels were targeted by censors. In 1939 censors stopped Ranpo from reprinting his 1929 story "Imomushi" ("The Caterpillar") in a collection of stories, apparently under the assumption the story's depiction of a horribly mutilated veteran and his unhappy fate might harm the war effort.[110] This decision came as a blow to Ranpo and threatened his financial livelihood, which by this point relied on the royalties from reprints. He responded by taking a lower profile, sometimes writing under a separate pen name, as if to disassociate the wartime works from his later legacy. What is important for the purposes of this study is that the national emergency meant that any writing he might do about same-sex desire would remain unpublished. All that remains from this era is his unpublished correspondence with Iwata Jun'ichi and the undated translations from *Musa Puerilis*. Denied an outlet for his own essays on same-sex desire as well as the ability to further the work of the friends who shared this interest, Ranpo turned instead to the realm of the imagination, dreaming about Greece as an alternative to the surrounding world.

When the war ended in 1945 and Japan entered the postwar period, Ranpo did not immediately return to writing fiction. Instead, he wrote a large number of articles and essays about various subjects, mostly the history of the detective novel in Japan. One exception was a 1948 round-table discussion for the small magazine *Kuiin* (Queen), which describes manifestations of same-sex desire in Japanese, classical Greek, and modern European and American literature.[111] His partner in this discussion was Inagaki Taruho, an avant-garde writer and a friend who shared Ranpo's interest in manifestations of schoolboy love and who, like Ranpo, had written works about boyish love that questioned the common notion that same-sex desire is deleterious to the health of the individual and nation. Because Taruho was one of the most creative and playful of the prewar writers on same-sex desire, it is to Taruho's works that the next chapter turns.

# 5

# Uninscribing the Adolescent Body

*Aesthetic Resistance in Taruho's Writing*

O NE DAY AROUND 1930, the prominent poet Hagiwara Sakutarō
came to Ranpo's apartment, which at that time was near Waseda University in Tokyo, to ask him about "secret clubs for massage" *(massāji no himitsu kurabu).*[1] He had also brought the young, aspiring writer Inagaki Taruho with him, sparking a friendship that would continue off and on for years. In his essays, Ranpo recalls going a few times to visit Taruho's "mysterious" home, which struck him as being "like a haunted house." Their conversations ranged across many subjects, from "the tin- and silver-plated devices of astronomy" to the appeal of the Port Arthur Naval Battle Hall, a show in Nagoya they had both visited and that displayed large illuminated panoramas of the famous naval battle of the Russo-Japanese War. Perhaps most important of all, at least for the current discussion, were the conversations they had about the beauty of "Greek bishōnen" and other manifestations of love between men.[2]

Over the years, this was a subject the two would return to multiple times. In 1948, a few years after the war ended and the publishing industry had started to recover, Ranpo received an invitation to do a round-table discussion in a small magazine called *Kuiin* (Queen), financed by a whiskey company. Ranpo responded he would do it only if Taruho could be his partner. The publisher treated them to a meal in a restaurant recently constructed in what used to be a burned-out field, and for a few hours, the two avoided the realities of occupied Japan by engaging in a long conversation about love and eroticism between men.[3] In this conversation, Ranpo talks mainly about the large number of titles he had uncovered during his bibliographic searches during the 1930s—especially Greek, European, and American works—and describes the highlights of a number of texts.[4] The magazine was printed on the poor quality paper common in the immediate aftermath of the war; therefore, it was hard to read; shortly afterward, the magazine went out of print, and the essay fell into oblivion. Both Ranpo and Taruho felt this to be a shame, and so in 1951, Taruho summarized the conversation for the Nagoya-based literary journal *Sakka* (Authors) and published it under the title "E-shi to no isseki: Dōseiai no risō to genjitsu o megutte" (One night with Mr. E: On the ideals and reality of same-sex love). Taruho planned to write a follow-up essay, drawing on Ranpo's prewar essays about love between men, but this plan never materialized.[5] As mentioned in the previous chapter, Taruho also planned to create an anthology of world writings about love and eroticism between men and asked Ranpo for some Japanese renditions of Greek poems. Taruho intended to call the anthology *Momoiro no hankachi* (Peach-colored handkerchief) in reference to his own 1924 story about a boy who falls in love with a schoolmate with a lacy handkerchief of this color, but when the anthology finally did materialize many years later, it included only Taruho's own writing from the 1920s onward, and Ranpo's contributions were not included.

In 1921, a few years before starting to write about boyish love, Taruho had come to Tokyo from his home near Kobe at the encouragement of the novelist Satō Haruo, who had read drafts of several of Taruho's earliest stories and recognized in Taruho an astoundingly original voice. Once in Tokyo, Taruho not only wrote but tried his hand in the art world as well, submitting some of his own work to the Dai-ni-kai Mirai-ha Bijutsu Kyōkai-ten (Second Futurist Art Exhibition) held in Ueno Park in late 1921. Of the two paintings he entered, one entitled *Tsuki no sanbun-shi* (Prose poem about the moon) was selected to appear alongside the works of other artists ranging from the prominent Russian futurist David Burliuk (1882–1967) to the young, rising artists Ogata Kamenosuke (1900–1942) and Hirato Renkichi (1893–1922).[6]

Just a couple of years later, in 1923, Taruho published his first and perhaps most famous work, the collection of contes *Issen ichi-byō monogatari* (One Thousand and One-Second Stories).[7] Borrowing inspiration for its name from the *One Thousand and One Arabian Nights,* Taruho's stories are tales for a fast-paced age—little snippets of prose rarely requiring more than a few seconds to read. The principal character is a mischievous but dapper "Tsuki-sama" (Mr. Moon), a personified, top-hatted version of the moon in the sky

TARUPHO

Inagaki Taruho's drawing *Tsuki no sanbun-shi* (Prose poem about the moon). This drawing bears the same title as the one Taruho submitted to the Second Futurist Art Exhibition held in Ueno Park in late 1921, and its style attests to Taruho's interest in the avant-garde. Courtesy of Inagaki Miyako.

Inagaki Taruho in his
twenties. Courtesy of
Inagaki Miyako.

who, along with several other astronomical entities, descends to earth, drinks
too much, fights in bars, and gets into all sorts of trouble. Full of surprising
plot twists and illogical connections like those seen in the work of the cine-
matographer Georges Méliès (1861–1938), *Issen ichi-byō monogatari* depicts
a strange, surreal and often funny world where all sorts of odd things tran-
spire. These stories may seem at first glance to represent little more than
amusing and witty snippets, but Miryam Sas has argued *Issen ichi-byō monogatari* represents Taruho's evocation of a particular vision of modernity:
a futuristic world dominated by "a poetry of rhythms and displacements,
flickers and exchanges." The brief, fragmentary stories are "free of totaliz-
ing knowledges and monolithic perspectives," and they depict "a universe
of accretions, where narrative proceeds by metonymy and leaps rather than
by the proceedings of causal logic."[8]

Commentators on Taruho's life and work sometimes draw attention to the
fact Taruho was born in 1900, a year that with its two round zeros seemed

to mark the advent of a new age of modern life and technology, and so perhaps it is only appropriate that as a young boy Taruho dreamed of things like science, aviation, and the heavens. For instance, the literary critic Takahashi Yasuo has noted many cultural and scientific advances that same year: Max Planck introduced the world to his constant $h$, thus entering a new era of quantum mechanics; the Wright Brothers made their first unsuccessful attempt at flying a glider at Kitty Hawk; Count Ferdinand von Zeppelin took his airship on its first flight in Germany; and Yokota Naganosuke from Kyoto took the cinématographe he had seen at the World's Fair in France back to Japan and conducted a tour through the country, amazing the Japanese population with the new art of motion pictures.[9] During his youth, Taruho was fascinated with technology and aviation in particular. In 1912, the American aviator William B. Atwater took a hydroplane from San Diego to Japan, and on the seashore of Suma, near Kobe, he gave a demonstration that Taruho watched with fascination.[10] The following year, when Taruho was twelve, the American-trained aviator Takeishi Kōha (1884–1913) made Japanese aviation history by attempting to fly an airplane between Kyoto and Osaka, but he crashed, thus becoming the first Japanese casualty of an aeronautical accident. Afterward, the wreckage of his plane was displayed as part of a memorial to him in Ten'ōji Park, Osaka. Taruho visited the plane, and although one wing was crushed and other smashed to pieces, the sight of the plane had a profound and lasting effect on him.[11] For many years, he dreamt of flying through the skies, moving away from earthbound reality and toward the astronomical entities that had captured his interest in science classes. In grade school at Kwansei Gakuin in Kobe, he and his friends started a coterie magazine they called *Hikō gahō* (Aviation pictorial), to which Taruho submitted some of his first essays about the importance of aviation and its potential contribution to civilization.[12] It is because of this passion for the skies that aviation and astronomy appear as major recurring motifs in his oeuvre.

Still, about the same time Taruho was starting to explore these themes, he also began to write about another major theme that would recur throughout his oeuvre, namely the love of adolescent boys *(shōnen'ai)*. The first and most frequently anthologized of these stories is the sentimental and nostalgic story "Hana-megane" ("Pince-Nez Glasses," 1924), which describes the affections of an unnamed narrator toward a lower-classman at his school, but this story was followed by a wave of others about schoolboys and adolescent males expressing their first romantic and sexual feelings. As time went by, Taruho's interest in same-sex love expanded to include other, more adult and more overtly sexual manifestations of love between men; in fact, during the postwar period, Taruho was sometimes known to quip his literature was guided by his interest in the "three A's": astronomy, airplanes, and anal eroticism.

This chapter examines the depiction of *shōnen'ai* (the love of young boys) in Taruho's early writing from the 1920s and its relation to his aesthetic vision. An important part of his modernist project involved the aestheticization of the male adolescent body, partly through placing it in a depoliticized environment free of overt markers of political and nationalistic ideology. At the same time, however, he describes bishōnen adolescent beauty in terms of a particular form of fashionable, European- and American-style cosmopolitanism he associated with modernity. In almost fetishistic fashion, he celebrates the adolescent male body as an aestheticized surface: a signifier that does not necessarily point to some greater interiority but nonetheless titillates through its own aesthetic pleasures. Taruho does occasionally allude to the pseudoscientific discourse of sexuality created by psychologists and sexologists, but what makes Taruho especially interesting is that when he does refer to sexological discourse, he does so not to classify and control homoerotic desire, but to celebrate it. Unlike Ranpo, who in his essays from the 1930s more or less accepted the analytical terms laid out by psychologists and then used them to make historical manifestations of same-sex desire comprehensible to modern audiences, Taruho modified the cultural baggage connected to psychological terms and used them in subversive new ways, helping to forge new images of love and affection between adolescent men.

## TARUHO'S EARLY AESTHETICISM

Two years after his literary debut, Taruho published the essay "Watashi no tanbishugi" (My aestheticism) in a 1924 issue of *Shinchō*, a national journal that played an important role in fostering modernist experimentation during the 1920s and 1930s.[13] In order to explain the aesthetic vision behind his early works and point out one possible direction for the burgeoning Japanese modernist movement, Taruho argues against the idea, common in the early Shōwa period, that the increasing speed of modern life and the rise of capitalism had led to a general sense of ennui that dulled people's aesthetic acuity. In this essay, Taruho suggests precisely the opposite: modern society provides plenty of opportunities for poignant aesthetic experiences.

To illustrate his point, he describes several such moments: students marveling at blue images of the moon projected onto the silver screen, lovers whose hearts are stirred by the "nostalgic" smell of gasoline, an audience marveling at an airplane releasing yellow fireworks then doubling back through the sky, and a person turning a city corner and catching sight of sparks falling from a lamppost. In each instance, something distinctly modern—cinema, airplanes, electricity, and even gasoline—sparks a transient moment of beauty that momentarily liberates the viewer from the constraints of mundane reality. Far from being a force dulling people's senses, Taruho suggests modern material culture offers new possibilities for fresh sensations.

Much of Taruho's early work celebrates this kind of small, fleeting, chance happening that somehow opens a window into new aesthetic realms. Of course, such sudden moments of poignant revelation and aesthetic awareness are not found only in literature like Taruho's. Many forms of premodern writing, including tanka, haiku, and other forms of traditional Japanese verse, are dedicated to capturing similar moments of individual revelation; however, in "Watashi no tanbishugi," Taruho insists the quiet moments of wonder invoked by new, modern, and chic things are more poignant than those embodied in older, canonical works of literature. He declares, "for he who is conscious of it, there is more value in a single cigarette than in [Goethe's] *Faust*" (1:62). In his view, the goal of the "new arts" *(shin geijitsu)* is to break with the kinds of things that have inspired the artists of yesteryear and to depict momentary encounters with things that give observers "a taste of the momentary and of fairy-tale-like transcendence, but also provide a hint of emptiness. This is because it is the moment in time that is most genuinely likely to enter the human heart; the fairy tale represents the highest form of aesthetic literature, and nothingness represents the one path to the liberation that serves as the eye for all arts" (1:63). As mentioned above, Taruho tends most frequently to find such moments in fleeting, momentary encounters with "modern" things, especially things he sees as *"haikara."* (This word, which Taruho uses with special frequency, translates roughly as "chic," but because it comes from a Japanese transliteration of the words "high collar"—a reference to the tall, starched collars on the Western clothing that represented the height of fashion among men in the late Meiji period—it came to apply principally to things that hinted of occidental, dandyesque fashions.) Still, Taruho's essay indicates that fashionable consumer products, clothes, and other commercial goods were not the only thing he thought of as *haikara;* he expands the traditional understanding of this word by using it to describe things related to science: physics-related themes like light and time, plus astronomical entities such as the moon, stars, and on occasion even the notion of outer space itself.

Taruho's attempt to capture lasting moments of aesthetic poignancy through depicting brief, fleeting moments may appear somewhat contradictory, but this contradiction is one that has recurred throughout modernist writing since its early inception. In fact, this seeming contradiction appears in one of the earliest attempts to define a distinctly modernist aesthetic, Charles Baudelaire's famous essay about the artist Constantin Guys, "Le peintre de la vie moderne" ("The Painter of Modern Life"). There, Baudelaire comments beauty was not unique and absolute, but comprises two elements: first, an "eternal, invariable element," and second, "a relative, circumstantial element which, as one wishes, could involve the time period, fashion, morality, or passion independently or all at once."[14] Baudelaire's essay champions the transitory, ephemeral, and conditional as a means of experiencing modern realities, and in a sense, sets the stage for writers like Taruho, who consciously embrace sudden encounters within a river of flux as a means to feel some moment of poignant beauty that might transcend the momentary. For this reason, many of Taruho's earliest, most experimental pieces of writing represent collections of episodic anecdotes that do not always unfold in a predictable fashion or lead to a concrete resolution. In fact, one corollary of his celebration of the momentary was that more teleological, plot-driven works would fail to capture the fleeting beauty that should be the raison d'être of the "new arts." Not coincidentally, many of Taruho's early works, including a number of his earliest writings on same-sex adolescent desire, feel like a series of short, episodic prose-poems, each of which brings the reader to a climactic scene that lingers almost like a cinematic still in the memory. As William Tyler has noted, by "avoiding plot-driven narrative and highlighting the episodic and cinematic," Taruho "put his early character sketches or *contes* in service of an agenda that prioritized heightened emotional and artistic receptivity as a key tenet of *modanizumu*," the Japanese approach to modernist literature.[15]

Because of his penchant for modern ideas and his avant-garde interest in the momentary, Taruho found himself most at home among the growing crowd of experimental writers and poets that would coalesce in the mid-1920s as the Shinkankaku-ha (Neo-perceptionists). Influenced by the radical experiments that had swept through the European art and literary scene in the wake of World War I, Shinkankaku-ha authors like Yokomitsu Riichi

(1898–1947), Kawabata Yasunari, and Kataoka Teppei valorized new avant-garde modes of writing as a means to describe individual subjectivity and sensation. In 1925, the year after he published "Watashi no tanbishugi," Taruho created the first of several pieces he would write for *Bungei jidai* (Era of arts and letters), the journal that served as the mouthpiece for the Shinkankaku-ha, and in March of 1926 he officially joined the ranks of the coterie. By the end of the decade, however, the group had drifted apart, but a handful of its members regrouped to form the Shinkō geijutsu-ha (New rising school). Perhaps because one of its central members, Naka-mura Murao (1886–1949), was involved with *Shinchō*, the journal in which Taruho had published "Watashi no tanbishugi" and many other early works, Taruho developed friendships with a number of the members of this group, although the death of his grandparents in 1931 and his 1932 move back to his childhood home of Akashi in Kansai prevented him from remaining a cen-tral part of their activities. Taruho stayed in western Japan until 1936, attempt-ing to support himself by running a used-clothing business out of his home, and during this time his literary output decreased significantly.

Despite the relatively short lifespan of the Shinkankaku-ha and Shinkō geijutsu-ha, these groups played an important role in Japanese literary history because of the vocal stand they took against the rising tide of prole-tarian literature in the late 1920s and 1930s. Like some of his fellow mod-ernist experimenters who advocated art for art's sake and refused to think of art simply as a means to raise political consciousness, Taruho was pro-foundly opposed to the proletarian art movement, which he saw as anchor-ing literature too closely to the ugly side of reality. Taruho's preferred method appears to have been the relatively innocuous forum that "light" modes of literary production afforded. Because Taruho avoids direct discus-sion of politics in his own writing, scholars have tended to examine his work solely in terms of aesthetic concerns and experimentation; however, these scholars are remiss in failing to note that his works reveal the stamp of ide-ology at almost every turn. The repeated celebration of the chic and mod-ern, the polyglot insertions of English, French, and Kansai dialect into his writing, the frequent appearance of people of ambiguous ethnic origins, and the influence of international modernist movements are all direct reflections of the cosmopolitan cultural ethos of Japan in the years before the rise of Japanese militarism.

One of the ways Taruho challenges the dominant ideology of his time is by openly valorizing the love of young boys. Taruho sees bishōnen as playing a special role in avant-garde aesthetics. In "Watashi no tanbishugi" he writes, "that thing known as the taste for adolescent boys *(pedophilia erotica)* is an essential quality of the extreme development of aestheticism" (1:65). In his view, the sexual admiration of women can be poetic, but the appreciation of adolescent male beauty involves an almost fairy-tale-like, otherworldly quality elevating it to the kind of experience Taruho finds so deserving of praise. In a long list of the sorts of things the "new arts" should value, he remarks they should celebrate "pointy things over round things." He follows this with the rhetorical question, "isn't the bulge poking out of a young man's pants far more sensual than the silk stocking of some dancing girl?" (1:65). With this humorous query, he aligns the sexual appreciation of adolescent boys with the kinds of *haikara* experiences he sees as stirring the aesthetic sensibilities. In doing so, he portrays the youthful male body as an invitation to a fresh, innocent world of awakened sensibilities, separate from what he sees as the more banal world of heterosexual desire.

In a lighthearted tone, Taruho concludes "Watashi no tanbishugi" with the assertion that in order to escape the prosaic constraints of everyday life, humanity requires the help of fairies—those carefree playful beings that exist between humanity and the divine. He sees the fairy as the hero of the new artistic age, and the role of the new arts is "to fairify" *(fearī-ka suru)* the new age of modernity by revealing a frivolous yet transcendent dimension to mundane reality (1:66). Here, Taruho is toying with the idea that queer men, especially ones who do not conform to models of strong, brutish masculinity, are sometimes pejoratively called "fairies" in English. If anything, he seems to be suggesting the playful, dandyesque qualities often associated in the popular imagination with the "gay sensibility" represents a driving force in the modernist aesthetic. This conclusion closely follows Taruho's assertion earlier in the same essay that throughout history, there has been a high degree of "inverted tendencies" *(tōsaku-teki keikō)* among artistic, philosophical, and religious innovators, especially in Japan. Taruho regrets this is not quite as true in today's world as in the past, but he believes "inverted tendencies" should be celebrated since they are evidence of an "awakening of the instincts" that can serve as a guide toward the future (1:65).

It is important to trouble this oversimplified equation between a "gay sensibility" (whatever that might be) and aesthetic vision, since such stereotypes only limit the ways in which people tend to think about same-sex desire. At the same time, however, what is intriguing about Taruho's work is that he places male homoeroticism on center stage at a time in history when

many authors of *ero, guro, nansensu* fiction, including his future friend Edogawa Ranpo, were writing about it in ways that were far more circumspect.
As mentioned in previous chapters, sexologists and educators of the 1910s
and 1920s had spilled a great deal of ink warning of the dangers of same-
sex eroticism for young boys. Just to give one example, *Bukyō sekai* (World
of heroism), the popular boy's magazine that specialized in stories of adventure, travel, and colonial exploration, had run a special issue in May 1919
about the dangers of "bad sexual desire" *(akuseiyoku)*, clearly designed to
scare its readership into keeping their hands (and other appendages) to
themselves. Yet, at the same time such magazines were busy casting a cloud
of anxiety over the adolescent male body, Taruho was relishing it in a way
that emphasized and even celebrated its homoerotic appeal. If anything,
Taruho's seemingly innocent pleasure in the adolescent male body represents an act of resistance against the homophobic anxiety promoted in the
early twentieth century by many in the psychological, medical, and educational communities.

## School without Scandal

Taruho's own contributions to the "fairification" of the "new arts" are most
visible in the stories he wrote about *shōnen'ai* in the mid-1920s. The first
of these, published when he was twenty-three, was the short story "Hana-
megane" ("Pince-Nez Glasses") released in the journal *Shinchō* in 1924. This
brief work recounts a passionate crush on a schoolboy classmate, a theme he
would explore again the same year in "R-chan to S no hanashi" ("The Story
of R-chan and S"), another short piece that appeared in the August issue of
*Josei* (Women). Both stories, especially the latter, describe settings that bear
an unmistakable resemblance to Taruho's own alma mater, Kwansei Gakuin,
which he attended from 1914 to 1919, leading one to suspect the stories
contain at least some autobiographical elements. In fact, the artist and critic
Takahashi Nobuyuki has attempted to match up the characters in Taruho's
work with people known to have attended school with him; for instance, he
has suggested that the bishōnen who is identified only as "KY" but serves as
the principal love interest in the story "Hana-megane" matches the description of a boy named Yamanaka Kahei who was two years behind Taruho
in school.[16] What is more important to note for this discussion is that both
stories, which rank among Taruho's most intimate treatments of adolescent
male desire, use the worldly setting of the international school as one of
many details highlighting what he saw as the fashionable, aesthetic nature of

the love of boys. The school, located in the cosmopolitan port city of Kobe, serves as a backdrop that positions the characters within a distinctly modern world, where Japanese and Western cultures come together to form a new, modern hybrid.

The narrator of "Hana-megane" has already graduated by the time the story begins, and much of his tale consists of his nostalgic reminiscences of a younger schoolmate KY.[17] The narrator tells us he first noticed the boy about seven years previously in a train on the way to school, when KY began singing several lines of a wistful tune. The words, quoted directly in English in Taruho's text, come from the chorus of the song "Old Black Joe" by the popular American composer Stephen Foster (1826–64). This tranquil and nostalgic song, written in 1860 to imitate the mournful style of southern slaves, became one of Foster's best-known songs and, in the eyes of many, an important piece of Americana. Apparently, it is not only the "gentle" quality of the boy's voice but also the fact he is singing in English that attracts the narrator's attention. In the text itself, the lyrics appear in English, a foreign orthographic insertion into the world of the Japanese text, which immediately signals the boy's cosmopolitanism. Moments later, when the narrator is describing the boy's physical appearance, he comments on "his face with its fair skin and tapering chin. He was so fair he reminded me of the foreign students who studied at the Canadian mission school which stood behind our school, surrounded by poplar trees" (1:170). Highlighting this seemingly Caucasian fairness are rosy cheeks and long lashes, which would have struck contemporary readers, especially those who had little exposure to the melting pots of Kobe and other major centers of international exchange, as exotic and charmingly foreign. Soon afterward, the narrator describes him as looking "like he might be of mixed blood" (1:170).

In short, several features of the young boy, from the language of his song to his appearance itself, align the boy with a form of beauty more international than that of the regular Japanese adolescent in the interwar period. Taruho is privileging an ethnically ambiguous form of beauty—one that seems an equal combination of Japanese and European and which echoes the visions of beauty seen in commercial advertisements marketing "modernity" to the masses during the Taishō and early Shōwa periods. Moreover, the description of KY is the first of many bishōnen in Taruho's works that matches the figures that had appeared so often in the work of Takabatake Kashō (1888–1966), an illustrator whose idealizing and sensual images of attractive bishōnen and *bishōjo* (beautiful young girls) had frequently appeared in popular magazines for adolescents in the Taishō and the early Shōwa periods. Takabatake's images feature youths with a combination of Western and Japanese features: pale complexions, ruddy cheeks, prominently ridged noses, and dark eyes.[18] In an article published in 1925, just one year after "Hana-megane," Taruho credited Kashō with giving form to a new type of cosmopolitan, seemingly biracial beauty compatible with the modern age—an assertion he supports by saying there was hardly an adolescent boy or girl who did not know Kashō's work (1:274–75).[19] Although it seems unlikely Kashō provided the direct inspiration for the bishōnen who appear in Taruho's work, both Taruho and Kashō were voices advocating a similar type of worldly beauty that appealed to the youth of Japan during the cosmopolitan period of the Taishō and early Shōwa periods.

Throughout the work, the text replicates the pattern visible in many Edo-period and early Meiji texts about same-sex desire, with an attractive, younger, slightly effeminate bishōnen serving as the object of desire for an older male. Of course, part of this has to do with the fact the narrator is recalling his own impressions of the boy, and not necessarily attempting to give voice to the boy's own feelings. Still, a big part of the attraction of the boy is his mystery—his feelings, intentions, and interiority remain hidden. He remains aloof, and this makes him all the more cryptic in the narrator's eyes. In fact, many of the episodes recounted in the story are about KY's secretive behavior and the ways this excites the narrator's attention. In an early scene before the narrator even knows KY's name, he witnesses KY trying furtively to convey a secret to an older student, but the older boy acts as if he cannot hear or understand. Finally, the young man leans down and KY whispers something self-consciously in his ear. The narrator does not explain why this scene strikes him as so fascinating, but it clearly has to do with the unspeakability of KY's secret and the desire to share it and form an intimacy impenetrable to outsiders. The boy remains opaque, giving little idea of what might be inside, but this only makes him all the more alluring. In other words, the secret does not give any insight into KY's feelings but merely titillates by suggestion. This scene is all the more curious because KY and the older boy are of different ages (one in higher school, the other in college) and therefore not necessarily an obvious combination of conversational partners in a world where even minute interactions among schoolboys were governed by age and class ranking.

Most of the dramatic, erotically charged scenes take place some years later, when the narrator is in his fifth and final year of higher school. KY, who has undergone an "awakening of spring," begins to flash big smiles at the narrator as if flirting. Taruho includes the words "awakening of spring" in English, as a reference to one of his favorite plays, Frank Wedekind's 1891 *Frühlings Erwachen (Spring Awakening)*, about the ways a group of adolescents deal with their budding aesthetic and sexual knowledge (1:172). (Around the age of thirteen, Taruho had read this play in a Japanese translation by Nogami Toyoichirō. His decision to include the reference to Wedekind's play in Roman letters was clearly a reflection of his tendency to associate aesthetic and erotic arousal with an international, cosmopolitan sensibility, but because Taruho did not read German, he used English—the first foreign language taught at Kwansei Gakuin, the international school he attended.) It is at this point KY begins to direct a special amount of attention to the narrator. When the narrator returns his attention, KY "got a look like he wanted to say something," yet remained silent and merely returned more "coquettish" looks (1:173). When the narrator finally makes a move and tries to talk, KY flees in embarrassment. Not long afterward, while they are in a train together, KY seats himself back-to-back with the narrator, and in a way no one can see, he slides his hand down around the seat division and along the narrator's side. He surmises KY is trying to pick his pockets, and he is thrilled the boy seems to be "such a splendid aesthete" who combines beauty and danger all at once (1:174). His reaction changes as KY's hands move not to his pockets but toward the top of his pants, perhaps trying to get inside—a move that cannot be interpreted as anything but an erotic suggestion. Startled, the narrator changes positions, and the boy's hand retreats. Although the implications of the movement are fairly clear, the narrator asks himself, "what could his strange movements possibly mean? I wasn't sure. I thought the best course of action was to look him straight in his smiling face and just ask. In the end, I never got up the gumption to do so" (1:175). The boy's desire, although glimpsed clearly through his actions, is never transformed into words, and the distance of observer and observed remains suspended between them.

Still, this distance never becomes corrosive; if anything, it allows the relationship, never consummated through open expressions of affection or erotic attraction, to move into a purely aestheticized realm. One sees this most dramatically in the beautifully narrated scene in which the boys exchange parting glances on their last day at school together:

He turned his fair countenance in my direction and smiled. I smiled back, and it occurred to me this would be the last time I would see him under these circumstances. It was as though he knew what I was thinking, for he gazed at me much longer than usual. We continued exchanging smiles across the distance as he crossed the exercise yard. The granite gravel strewn over the yard sparkled so brilliantly in the sun that it almost hurt my eyes. We kept smiling until he finally disappeared into the grove of trees nearby. (1:175)

The nostalgic and sentimental tone of the passage clearly indicates that the narrator recognizes the poignancy of the moment and realizes, despite his lack of access to KY's feelings, that there is some spark of attraction between them.

Because the narrator (as well as the reader of the text) has little more than general hints at what is going on inside of KY's mind, KY is in effect reduced to an animated surface. Indeed, the specific mode of narration Taruho employs in this and many of his other early works focuses on the boy as a surface—as if he were a mysterious cipher moving through the world. Rather than speculating about what might be going on in KY's mind, the text focuses on tiny details adorning the surface of his body: the songbook with a purple ribbon resting on his chest at their first meeting, his immaculate and neatly pressed clothing, but most of all, the furrows between his eyebrows. The lines that form between his eyebrows remind the narrator of a pair of pince-nez glasses—a form of eyewear that in the modernist years of the Taishō and early Shōwa periods reflected an especially dandyesque, *haikara,* Western flair. (In fact, Taruho had a special penchant for such glasses. The writer Uno Kōji states that when he and Taruho first met, Taruho always sported a pair of dapper pince-nez glasses that suited him so well he looked as if he were born with them.)[20] The narrator tells the reader that at first, his desire was apparently little more than curiosity, but his fixation on the creases in KY's brow suggests some other deeper attraction: "wasn't that proof I bore some special feelings for him? Didn't my feelings hide something that went beyond casual interest?" (1:70).

Toward the end of the story, when he describes an encounter with KY that took place five years after their graduation, the narrator explains his attraction in largely aesthetic terms. He is at the Imperial Theater in Tokyo preparing to see a production of Giuseppe Verdi's opera *Rigoletto* when he happens across KY wearing "thin pince-nez glasses with white tortoise-shell frames that sat over the creases between his eyes—the same creases that had reminded me of pince-nez glasses all those years before" (1:176). KY had not lost the beautiful flower of adolescence as the narrator had feared; he had maintained his charm, only with an added layer of "elegance and refinement," and this fills him with a paternal satisfaction as he realizes the boy he once cared about has grown up (1:176). The text never explicitly spells out the nature of the narrator's attraction, yet there is no question the narrator's feelings bridge both homosocial and homoerotic desire and most likely partake of both.

For Taruho, the spectrum of homosocial relations appears to be less fractured than for his contemporary Ranpo, who wrote about homosocial bonding, aesthetic appreciation, and homoeroticism as quite different modes of relating to one another. Taruho shows this especially clearly in a story published shortly after "Hana-megane," namely "R-chan to S no hanashi," included in the August 1924 issue of journal *Josei*, a magazine for women established just two years before in 1922.[21] This story, which ranks as one of Taruho's most important explorations of same-sex desire among schoolboys, was published not in a magazine for adolescent boys—the same sites in which sexologists and educators spread much of their anxiety about male–male attraction—but in a woman's magazine. As mentioned in chapter 3 of this book, the numbers of journals published in the interwar years exploded in the 1920s, and one of the areas of most dramatic growth was in the field of publishing for women. Although there were certain magazines among them that were written primarily by women for the sake of women, some of the new magazines, such as *Josei*, drew upon the creativity of a new, young generation of male writers who, like Taruho, were eager to take advantage of the possibilities of the new journals to publish their own work. Interestingly, journals like *Josei* were relatively quick to open their pages to writers associated with various aspects of modernism, such as Kawabata Yasunari, Kataoka Teppei, and Taruho. Just a few years previously, in 1922, Taruho's debut publication, the fairy tale-like story "Chokorēto" (Chocolate), had appeared in another magazine for women, namely *Fujin kōron* (Ladies' forum).

It is unclear why exactly Taruho brought the manuscript to *Josei*, but the prevalence of amorous and erotic relationships between schoolgirls in the culture of early twentieth-century Japan may have led editors of the journal to be especially receptive toward the story. As in the all-male schools for boys, the all-female schools established the mid- and late-Meiji periods became a site where women might form intense bonds ranging from friendship to passionate eroticism. By the early Shōwa period, schoolgirls had developed their own rich vocabulary to describe various aspects of love between women, including the term "S" (pronounced *esu*), which came from the initial of the English word "sister" and described both the object of one's affections or a passionate relationship in general.[22] The world of these relationships formed the backdrop of *Hana monogatari* (Flower tales), a collection of highly sentimental, aestheticized stories about love between schoolgirls, their female teachers, and other women that Yoshiya Nobuko started serializing in 1916. This widely read work helped establish the tone of the works that would appear in popular girl's magazines *(shōjo zasshi)* for years to come and laid the groundwork for writers such as Taruho to begin the process of aestheticizing male–male love for a female audience.[23]

The flowery tone of Taruho's "R-chan to S no hanashi" appeals to an aesthetic not unlike that of Yoshiya Nobuko's popular work, and the editors may well have chosen it because they hoped Taruho's stylized and romantic expressions of "same-sex love" would also appeal to readers. Like Nobuko's work, Taruho's story is characterized by a number of highly romanticized elements—relatively gentle characters, awkward conversations rich with amorous overtones, an aesthetic appreciation of tender moments and stereotypically nonmasculine things, expressions of passionate pining, and almost overflowing statements of desire. The scholar of Japanese cultural history Tsurumi Shunsuke has suggested Yoshiya Nobuko represents the pioneer of the sort of florid and extremely sentimental aesthetic that shapes the *shōjo manga* (girl's manga) and *tanbi shōsetsu* (aestheticized novels) about love between men that have been so popular among Japanese schoolgirls from the 1970s onward.[24] Nobuko's early work, however, focuses on relationships between schoolgirls and the women they admire, not on relations between young men. Although the success of Nobuko's stories may have likely influenced editorial tastes at *Josei*, it is important to note that Taruho was breaking new ground in writing for a female audience about aestheticized, romantic relationships between boys. "R-chan and S no hanashi" served as a historically important cross-over story that transported the aestheticized and sentimental treatment of love between boys seen in Kaita's more florid, symbolist moments to a wide, popular forum where it would appeal to a female readership. Although this story has so far attracted little attention from literary historians, it represents a landmark piece of fiction in the aestheticization of boy-love for a female readership.

It is crucial to note that this act of "crossing-over" and writing stories about male–male desire for an audience aware of a culture of female–female desire is something that probably could not have happened much before the 1920s. As mentioned in the introduction of this book, it was only a short couple of decades before Taruho wrote this story that Japan had embraced the assumption that amorous feelings and erotic practices between members of the same sex constituted a distinct typology of sexual behavior, namely that of "same-sex love."[25] Unlike other, older discursive concepts, such as *nanshoku* or *shudō*, which referred specifically to age-graded relationships between men, the discourse of "same-sex love" incorporated both male–male and female–female attraction within a single conceptual territory for the first time. It took some time for this concept to filter outward from the medical, psychological establishments and spread through the cultural imagination; in fact, it was only around the time Taruho wrote this story that the many variant phrases initially coined by psychologists and medical specialists had congealed into the standardized term *dōseiai,* the word still most frequently used today. These developments established the conceptual framework for Japanese audiences to see a parallel between male–male love and female–female love, which began to look to them like two related manifestations of a single phenomenon. What this meant for Taruho when he submitted his story of schoolboy affection to *Josei* in 1924 was that the editors were increasingly likely to see the descriptions of affection and erotic desire between two schoolboys as not dissimilar to the affectionate and erotic relationships that were so much a part of schoolgirl culture at the time—correspondences that would have been unlikely, if not impossible, only decades before, when descriptions of male homoeroticism tended to feature hierarchies of age and power, and remarkably little was being said of erotic love between women.

In many ways, the text is written in a way that might allow a female readership to identify with "S," the slightly older male lead in the story, and "R-chan" the bishōnen who is the main subject of S's interest. The boys who appear in this story are not brutish, stereotypically masculine, "women-haters" of the "hard-faction" roughneck type who populated the pages of Mori Ōgai's turn-of-the-century novel *Wita sekusuarisu;* most likely, such characters would have seemed unappealing or perhaps even offensive to a female readership, thus cutting off the possibilities of vicarious identification. Instead, the main characters are gentle, sensitive figures filled with longing, not unlike the protagonists of Yoshiya Nobuko's popular stories about schoolgirl desire in magazines for young women. In fact, the tastes of the boys in the story tend toward things young women might have liked as well. For instance, early in the story, one of the characters expresses his frustration that a teacher had taken away a prized photo of an actress in an all-female group. Not coincidentally, in the same year this story was published, the three-thousand-seat Takarazuka Grand Theater was completed at the end of the Hankyū train line that passed by the Kobe school where "R-chan and S no hanashi" takes place.[26] These references to the Takarazuka all-girl review no doubt helped establish a bond of familiarity and identification between the characters in the story and female readers of the magazine. One does find references to carnal desire among the characters, but that desire is typically not presented in a way that is explicit enough to impede female readers from identifying with it. If anything, Taruho has created a gentle, sentimental, and sometimes even humorous work that invites readers to identify with and understand the characters, not a work that throws up barriers that would compel the female reader to see the characters as some radically different "other." In short, the mode of representation in this story is fundamentally different from *ero, guro, nansensu* stories such as Ranpo's code-switching mystery novel *Kotō no oni,* which frequently presents its queer character as "strange" and at least temporarily limits the possibilities for empathetic identification. Given these facts, it is a suggestive coincidence that the main character has as his name the very same signifier, "S," that schoolgirls would use to describe same-sex relationships. Quite literally, the main character "S" occupies the same semiotic space as "sisterhood."

The work consists of eleven short sections, each of which describes an important moment in the relationship between the lead character S and the younger boy he admires, R-chan. (All characters in the story are identified only by an initial. The only exception is R-chan, who is sometimes identified by the initial of his surname, "T," and sometimes by the initial of his given name, "R," plus the diminutive suffix -*chan.*) Although the development of S's infatuation does give the work a sort of architectural development, the work is largely episodic, giving the story a fragmented, modernist feel. In fact, in the first publication of the story in the magazine *Josei,* Taruho gave it the English subtitle "A sentimental episode" as if to emphasize the episodic nature of the work. (The subtitle was dropped from later reprintings of the story, perhaps because the story consists of several episodes, rather than just one.)[27]

When the story begins, S is sitting outside school, admiring the ships, cranes, and machinery visible in the ports of Kobe below. S's appreciation of this panoramic view of "spectacular modernity" and "pristine nature" marks the protagonist of the story as a particularly sensitive, aesthetically aware young man, able to take pleasure in quiet moments of beauty and able to appreciate the sorts of transcendent beauty in modernity that Taruho saw as the hallmark of the "new arts." When S turns around and starts chatting with some other students, he sees R-chan pulling a lacy, peach-colored handkerchief from his pocket. Although this handkerchief strikes S as evidence of an advanced aesthetic sensibility, another boy begins ruthlessly teasing the boy with the handkerchief. He mocks R-chan, telling him how *"haikara"* it is and calling him various names: *"puriti shan"* (a macaronic combination of the English word "pretty" and the German word *"schön,"* which originally means "sweet" but in the slang of early twentieth-century Japan meant a "pretty boy" or "pretty lady"), *"naisu bōi"* (nice boy), and bishōnen (1:137–38). While none of these words are outright insults, the context renders them insulting by clearly indicating the name-caller sees him as diminutive and feminine.

The boy with the handkerchief has transgressed the unwritten rules of masculinity forbidding boys to have anything to do with pretty, sensitive things. The handkerchief, in effect, disrupts the idea of the masculinity as single, undifferentiated territory and disturbs the overly simplistic assumption boys must necessarily act in ways that conform to limiting norms of masculinity. To borrow the words of Judith Butler, the handkerchief points to the disjunction between sex and gender "in the face of cultural configurations of causal unities that are regularly assumed to be natural and necessary," thus dramatizing "the cultural mechanism of their fabricated unity."[28] Significantly, it is this incongruity between biological gender and gendered behavior that makes R-chan so interesting to S. This gender-bending jolt makes S pay attention to R-chan for the first time, and S identifies with R-chan as a fellow aesthetic visionary able to see past those limits forcing boys to act certain ways in the name of some arbitrary model of masculinity.

Unlike "Hana-megane," the story is narrated in the third person; however, most of the story is about S's feelings as he pines for R-chan. The result is that "R-chan to S no hanashi," despite the difference in narrative mode from "Hana-megane," still reproduces the textual formulation seen in "Hana-megane" and other, earlier Japanese texts in which an older boy admires the beauty of an attractive, younger bishōnen. Moreover, the difference in the boys' ages means they are in different grades and move in different circles. As a result, the two only have minimal opportunities to interact, and so for most of the story, he remains a mysterious beauty whose thoughts are sealed off from the reader's view. As the poet Sunaga Asahiko once commented,

Taruho's work treats adolescent boys as aesthetic *objets,* and this work is no exception.[29]

In "R-chan and S no hanashi," Taruho emphasizes the idea of the boy as a decorated surface by providing thorough descriptions of the things the boy wears and holds in his pockets and hands. In fact, the text shows an almost fetishistic interest in R-chan's clothing and accoutrements that at times seems greater than the physicality of the boy underneath. In the third section, the narration provides a long passage describing the movement of S's gaze over R-chan's body. Instead of focusing on the boy himself, his gaze lingers on his smartly shaped, perfectly positioned cap, his well-fitting clothes, and the cleanliness of his white shoes. The text states, "The carefully polished lace-up shoes, the green eraser-tipped pencils peeping from his pocket, the watch that encircled his pale wrist.... All of these things were a source of deep fascination for S, although he was at a loss as to why. They were ordinary things he saw all the time, but why had he not paid attention to them before?" (1:140) The textual gaze swirls around R-chan, taking in the things covering his body while paying little attention to boy's body itself. Over the course of the story, the reader learns remarkably little about the details of R-chan's appearance, other than that he had chic dimples and big eyes like a fashionably half-Japanese, half-Caucasian model, once again, like the figures in Takabatake Kashō's artwork.

This is perhaps not an inaccurate mode of depicting young love. Adolescent crushes, especially when those feelings have not yet manifested themselves in genital arousal, often involve almost fetishistic infatuations with the clothes, hairstyles, and so on of the beloved. At the same time, this mode of depiction is quintessentially Taruhoesque in that it depicts a profound emotional experience as arising from small yet noteworthy things. The textual gaze, in essence, reduces the adolescent male body to an aestheticized surface, whose interiority remains intriguingly out of view. It is the decorations upon this surface—the clothes, the pencils, and other accoutrements he carries—that provide the mechanism for inciting desire. It is also worth noting this particular mode of depicting the boy opens up a space for the reader to project his or her fantasies upon him. By describing R-chan's physicality only in general terms, the story opens the door for readers to create a mental image that might appeal to them. The only limits placed on the way the reader might imagine R-chan's appearance are the fashionably wide eyes and dimples that were closely aligned with the image of fashionable beauty in the early Shōwa period and likely to appeal to many young readers anyway.

The notion of the adolescent body as aestheticized surface reoccurs most dramatically in section 10 of the story. There, S daydreams about floating with R-chan to a secluded island and living with him in a castle that seems right out of a fairy tale. S imagines that in the castle, there are mirrors on every wall that multiply R-chan's image exponentially. S also daydreams about dressing his beloved in various costumes and photographing him with his Kodak. These choices of fantasies are telling ones. Mirrors do not allow any greater access to the mind or person one is admiring; instead, they merely serve as a mechanism to reflect or diffuse an image. In the mirror, R-chan would remain a flat surface, an enigmatic signifier that, in order to fulfill the scopophilia of the older boy's gaze, has merely been diffused across multiple rooms. Likewise, photographic images do not access the interiority of the boy but only provide a flat representation of the body that can be reproduced and possessed. R-chan is once again a moving object that is only incorporated into a system of meaning by the fantasies of the boy who observes him. In other words, he is an aestheticized object, and the only meaning read there is projected by some desiring other.

We see this most dramatically enacted in the tenth section when S literally uses the aestheticized object of the bishōnen's body as a screen onto which he projects his homoerotic desires. S imagines dressing R-chan in a series of costumes that have highly romantic and erotic overtones, including that of a handsome fairy-tale prince, an acolyte *(chigo)* in a Japanese temple, and a pageboy *(koshō)* serving his lord. The desire to dress T up indicates the degree to which S's desire is experienced in terms of aesthetics, but at the same time, the specific choice of these particular guises with their historical overtones reveals the romantic, homoerotic quality of S's admiration. Many Western fairy tales feature handsome princes who whisk their lovers away to fulfill all their worldly desires, and as mentioned in a previous chapter, so many stories were written about the homoerotic appeal of temple acolytes and beautiful young pageboys during the medieval and Edo periods that these had become associated with homoeroticism in the Japanese cultural imagination well before Taruho ever wrote this story. By specifically evoking these historical paradigms, Taruho is subtly drawing attention to the homoerotic overtones of S's seemingly "innocent" schoolboy desires, showing it is not easy to separate erotic urges and the high aestheticism filling the story.

In some of the most amusing passages of the story, Taruho makes it clear that by appreciating the aesthetics of the adolescent male body, he is not necessarily de-eroticizing it. In section 6 of the story, S memorizes R-chan's gym class so he can enjoy the sight of the younger boy at play, and one day as he stares out the broken window, "S was seized by an unbearable desire to reach out and touch the long curve that ran along the boy's back from the top of his delicate shoulders down to his waist" (1:145). The desire to touch R-chan is even stronger one day soon afterward when S goes to watch R-chan's gym class. He sees the boy try again and again to jump over a vaulting horse, but each time, the petite, nonathletic boy lands squarely on top of it like a cowboy straddling his steed. Enraptured by this sight, S thinks to himself, "Gee! How I'd love to be that vaulting horse . . . !" (1:146). The section ends on this humorous note, and the reader is left with the sexually suggestive image of S beneath the younger boy.

The most dramatic example of sexual overtones used for comic affect, however, comes at the end of the same story. S is off with his classmates engaging in the military practice required of the students. R-chan sneaks up to S, who is carrying a gun loaded with blanks. In what is the climactic scene of the story, S lets T shoot his big gun.

> "Want me to let you shoot?" S asked boldly.
> T's modern-looking eyes indicated his unspoken assent.
> "C'mon, follow me!" S jumped down a drop of about three feet and landed with a thud. He reached the skirmish, which was along a creek lined with willows. T was close behind, his face beaming. S loaded the gun and handed it to him.
> The boy raised it awkwardly as if it were difficult to handle. He paused for a moment and pulled the trigger.
> *BANG!!*
> It was S's first shot in the battle, but it was not his hand but that of the boy he loved that had discharged it. The shot's sharp report echoed across the brown fields. A flurry of paper from the discharged gun settled over the two boys. A puff of white smoke that smelled of gunpowder floated over their heads. (1:159–60)

The coyness of the younger boy's reactions, the shared intimacy of the moment, the phallic quality of the gun itself, and the benediction of white paper raining down after the shot all lend the passage unmistakable erotic overtones. To borrow the idea in René Magritte's modernist painting *La trahison des images (The Treachery of Images)*, which shows a pipe that is, according to the accompanying text, "not a pipe," this gun is not merely a gun.

In both "Hana-megane" and "R-chan to S no hanashi," one finds depictions of relatively innocent and romanticized worlds, full of youthful attractions between boys who live free from the demands of adult gender roles. As James Welker has noted, works that allow readers to identify with characters regardless of sex, age, or gender roles give readers a break from the limits arising "not just from patriarchy but from gender dualism and heteronormativity."[30] Such works provide the chance to fantasize about relationships outside of marriage and the strict gender roles promoted by mainstream society at the same time they help the reader understand "neither the body nor the psyche need be shackled by norms."[31] Certainly, this is the case with Taruho's work. Without resorting to heavy-handed political statements about the position of male–male desire and practice within modern society, Taruho has given his readers the chance to revel in an aestheticized world, where desires are controlled not by the heavy-handed, controlling scrutiny of educators and sexologists but only by the shyness and awkwardness of adolescents awakening to sexuality. In an era where many depictions of same-sex desire were often tainted with pathological language or circumscribed by a conservative sense of decorum, these works provide an unusually healthy model of adolescents learning about attraction, both in its indirect and more overtly erotic manifestations, allowing readers, regardless of their own sexual inclinations, to revel in a world of aestheticized desire.

## EXTRACURRICULAR PASSION

Both of the stories mentioned above take place within the world of the non-coeducational school where, whether educators and sexologists liked it or not, amorous and erotic desire had managed to find a place in school-boy culture. Taruho also wrote a handful of works from the 1920s that also involve the aesthetic and amorous appreciation of young men outside of schools, even though some of these still involve boys of school age. The first of these was "Kāru to shiroi dentō" (Karl and the white light) published in late 1924, only a month after "R-chan to S no hanashi." This is a brief work of only several flowery paragraphs describing a particular bishōnen named Karl. In fact, when first published, the work was given the explanatory subtitle "Watashi no sanbun shi" (My prose poem), indicating Taruho (or at least his editors) conceived of the short, fragmentary work as more closely akin to poetry than prose. It is clear the story is one about male–male attraction from the fact the narrator, who repeatedly describes himself as *boku* (a pronoun indicating a male speaker), waxes poetic about the beauty of another boy named Karl. Like "R-chan to S no hanashi," this story also appeared in a women's magazine, *Fujin gurafu* (Ladies' pictorial), showing Taruho's involvement in forging an aesthetic of homoerotic, adolescent desire that might also appeal to a female readership.

The brief text consists of a Taruhoesque blend of terse language, vivid images, and impassioned evocations of Karl's beauty, which the text suggests is peculiarly modern. Karl appears as a somewhat androgynous boy with large eyes and fair skin, which, when coupled with his Germanic name, suggests a foreign or biracial ethnic heritage:

> A green cloak is what suits Karl best. Moreover, his eyelashes, which look like those of a girl, and his new-style [*shinshiki*] eyes look especially charming, almost as if he is wearing a thin layer of make-up. It was a face that looked exactly like it had been weeping last night—a face that, as an artist friend of mine put it, has all "the grief of the delicate, white surface of a hardboiled egg someone has soiled with their dirty fingerprints." (1:69)

Taruho draws another connection between the boy's beauty and modernity in an imaginative comparison between the boy's face and the flickering, pale white light of an electric streetlamp. One of his friends, the "futurist artist A," commented to him, "The rhythm of that boy and the rhythm of the tungsten filament of a light bulb have the same oscillations. In other words, there is hardly a difference between them if you experience them both in terms of atmosphere" (1:69). As a result, whenever the narrator sees white electrical lamps at twilight, he would think of the boy's weeping face. He recalls coming home from the cinema, seeing an electric lamp, pointing to it and saying, "It looks just like you" (1:69–70). For contemporary readers who take for granted the streetlamps that dot the streets of every town and highway, the comparison between the streetlight and a boy's beauty may seem surprising, but electric streetlights had only started becoming common a short time before Taruho wrote this story, and so they represented to Taruho one sign of the modern material culture he found so appealing. The mention of futurism in this passage hints at Taruho's own interest in futurism since his days in grade school at Kwansei Gakuin, when he first read "The Futurist Manifesto" by F. T. Marinetti (1876–1944) in a book by the artist Kimura Shōhachi (1893–1958).[32] To Taruho, futurism represented a new means to describe the experience of modernity, and the mention of the boy's "rhythm" echoes the kind of language one finds in many futurist writings. In short, the fanciful simile comparing the boy's face to a flickering light manifests the sort of artistic perceptivity Taruho had advanced as the hallmark of the new arts in the essay "Watashi no tanbishugi," published earlier the same year.

The final paragraph makes the most explicit connection between modernity, aesthetic awareness, and the ability to appreciate the bishōnen's beauty:

> If you are a person who loves movies and whose heart races at the sobbing of the violins in an orchestra, and if you are a person who gets tears in your eyes at the sight of the red taillights on a car, then you will no doubt understand what I have tried to express here. And on those evenings in the city when all is blue, one will hear "Karl's lament" coming from the white lights trembling on the street corners under the sycamore trees. (1:70)

The narrator believes that not everyone can understand the sights he has described, for not everyone has an equal degree of aesthetic appreciation; only people who are moved by sensitive things will be able to comprehend the poignant beauty of a bishōnen like Karl. Not only does Taruho attempt to dispel the web of anxiety that educators, sexologists, and medical psychologists had woven around the appreciation of the same sex, he also argues that the appreciation of the charms of young men only belongs to those people of the modern age who possess an unusually high degree of sensitivity and worldliness. In his view, homoerotic appreciation was not perverse; it was, if anything, superior to more banal forms of heteronormative desire.

"Tsukehige" (The false mustache), published in *Shinchō* in 1927, is one of Taruho's most overtly erotic stories, and like "Kāru to shiroi dentō," it draws an explicit connection between modern culture—namely that of the cinema—and desire between adolescent boys. As in the tenth section of "R-chan and S no hanashi," it describes a series of increasingly erotic interactions involving dress-up and playacting, but this time, the boys are motivated by the desire to act out the sort of romantic scenes one might find in the movies. In this story, the body of the adolescent male literally serves as the screen upon which another projects desire. At the same time, this story is somewhat unusual in Taruho's oeuvre in that it breaks from the one-way pattern seen in other works and also gives an intimate glance at the feelings of the younger boy as well.

The unnamed protagonist, who is simply called the *shōnen* (the ado-lescent boy), happens to see a film with a vivid scene depicting a bunch of mounted soldiers standing at the base of a mountain and surrounded by a group of Native Americans. As they ride around and shoot, smoke pours from their guns and the Stars and Stripes waves in the background, and the boy finds himself overcome with the beauty of the cinematography. The brief scene that follows, however, is the one that stays with him. The soldiers are dead; their bodies have been stripped bare, and their corpses have been thrown into a pile so the soft, white fleshy parts of the bodies intermingle to the point one cannot tell what belongs to whom. What particularly piques the boy's excitement is the sight of one soldier about two-thirds of the way out of the pile, his body exposed and bent. Although he does not under-stand why, this particular shot fascinates him, and he thinks about it for days (1:189–90). Taruho never mentions the title of the film, but he appears to be referring to the 1913 film *The Massacre,* a twenty-minute-long dramatiza-tion of Custer's Last Stand directed by the American D. W. Griffith (1875–1948) and distributed by the Biograph Company.[33] *The Massacre* contains a scene that more or less matches the description, but the scene Griffith intended to be one of carnage designed to shock and galvanize the sym-pathies of American viewers, Taruho has turned into a scene charged with homoerotic potential.

The scene stays so firmly lodged in the boy's mind that back home, he secretly takes off most of his clothes and attempts to replicate the scene, trying to imagine how the soldiers must have felt. As he prostrates himself and bends his body, he imagines "being used as a toy" by the Indians, and he uses a mirror to help him view his own half-nude and bent body as he tries to get every detail just right (1:191). Right then, at the height of this eroti-cally charged game of make-believe, a young boarder, identified only by the third-person pronoun *kare* (he or him) happens to catch sight of him. The text explains that *kare* had been expelled from his previous school for hav-ing an affair with a married woman—a fact that positions him as having a greater degree of sexual knowledge and experience. The younger boy is at first mortified that he has been seen, but realizing he has nothing to lose, he goes to see *kare.* While sitting on the bed, *kare* pulls the boy close, rubs his cheek, gazes into his face, then begins to kiss him (1:193). Just then, how-ever, the caretaker calls them, and *kare* rushes out of the room.

A week later, *kare* orders the boy to remove the boy scout uniform he is wearing and to reenact the scene from the previous week. Each day, *kare* puts him in new positions, seating him suggestively on his lap or having him lie on the tatami where he can look at his body. Before long, however, the relationship takes an unexpected turn as *kare* also begins to participate in the games of dress-up and make-believe. One day, *kare* is dressed in a sky-blue military uniform with red stripes from some foreign country and tall boots of red leather. On his head is a helmet with a spear-shaped finial on top that his friend brought back for him as a souvenir from Germany. *Kare,* who had never struck the boy as particularly attractive before, begins to look more like a real foreign soldier, and the younger boy's interest grows ever stronger. Wondering where these "games" *(yūgi)* would take them, he decides to see them through to the very end (1:196). The boys, in other words, are both becoming increasingly involved in their world of fantasy, and their act of projection only helps their desires and level of intimacy to grow.

Before long, the fantasies the two enact grow increasingly specific. In the final, climactic scene of the work, *kare* sets the stage by telling the boy, "A young volunteer has fallen in the trenches on the northern French front and is illuminated by the moon. The stripes of the searchlights are criss-crossing overhead, and everywhere white smoke is rising from the shrapnel shells. It's too bad we cannot use fireworks. Sometime we'll have to look into how to do that . . ." (1:196). *Kare* ties a blindfold around the boy's eyes, and as the latter's heart races, *kare* carefully positions him, then steps back to admire his handiwork. A moment later, the boy hears the sound of leather boots, then feels *kare*'s legs against his as the scent of the "soldier," leather, and woolen cloth meets his nose. *Kare* pulls him up, and as the "the fourteen-year-old bride" trembles, he swoons as if he really is the unconscious soldier he is pretending to be. He feels *kare*'s mouth against his, and he realizes the older boy is wearing a false mustache—an addition that finally makes the cinematic scene complete. Right at this titillating, climactic moment, the story ends, leaving the rest to the reader's active imagination.

In the final section of "R-chan to S no hanashi," there is mention of a similar scene: "[S] had once read in a friend's book about a soldier who, after receiving a mortal wound at the hands of his enemy, died at the feet of the boy he loved. He planned to act out this climactic romance" in front of R-chan (1:156). Although "Tsukehige" does not mention the source of the fantasy, much less whether it came from a book or a film, *kare* is carefully directing a scene of exactly the same sort of intimacy between men as one lies at death's door. These cinematic moments drive the boys' fantasies, which they project onto each other's bodies through their elaborate dress-up games. In quite a literal sense, the surfaces of the characters' adolescent bodies become the screens upon which one another's fantasies are projected. As in "R-chan to S no hanashi," what evokes desire is not so much the body itself, but what appears on its surface. The act of seeing, emphasized over and over in the story, is all important; the aestheticizing gaze also has an eroticizing function. When viewed by another with similar inclinations, the clothes, boots, hat, and blindfold perform as fetishes, serving as the mechanism that opens desire and fosters intimacy.

At several points, people wander in on the boy's "games"; however, no one seems especially disturbed. Once, someone asks, "So what is it you do when you think no one else is here?" *Kare* simply responds, "It would be terrible if it was with a young lady" (1:194). *Kare* is, of course, just deflecting the prying eyes of the onlooker, but his words carry a larger implication, namely that playful relationships like his with another boy are harmless, whereas if it were with a woman, it would mean something else entirely. The story suggests that relationships between boys, even when tinged with eroticism, are of an entirely different category than cross-sex relationships, which as *kare* knew first-hand, could land a schoolboy in significant trouble.

## RECOUPING SAME-SEX DESIRE

As mentioned in the introduction to this book, in 1921, right about the same time Taruho began his career as a writer, Ozaki Shirō wrote that "the way of bishōnen" *(bishōnendō)* had largely faded away as a result of the rise of the notion of "perverse sexual desire," which described "same-sex love" as an inevitable consequence of deeply implanted instincts. He stated, however, "as our artistic lives as Japanese gradually grow fuller and approach completion, a new practice of the worship of the beautiful young boys must arise in response to our deeply seated desires."[34] With their idealizing worship of boyish beauty, Taruho's stories represent a development in the "worship of the bishōnen" Ozaki had envisioned just a few years earlier. By emphasizing the aesthetic, almost innocent side to schoolboy love, Taruho recuperates the appreciation of boyish beauty from the rhetoric of sexology, which treats adolescent male desire as a force deleterious to adolescent development. In focusing the textual gaze on surface details and describing his characters in a way that hovers around the surface of the body, the text refuses to give into the sexology's tendency to drive inward and search for the "truth" of same-sex eroticism within the inner psychology of the individual. In other words, the focus on surface detail resists the tendency of much early Shōwa-period literature to account for homoerotic desire within the interior psychology of the characters.

Although one finds occasional use of pseudoscientific words borrowed from German, English, and Latin in Taruho's writing, his early work shows an almost blissful ignorance of the ideas presented in sexological literature. This does not mean, however, Taruho had no exposure to sexological ideas; in fact, his writings make it clear he was aware of them. Nowhere can this be better seen than when he uses the surname of the famous European sexologist Richard von Krafft-Ebing in the phrase *"kurafuto-ebing-teki"* (Krafft-Ebing-ish) to describe scenes displaying a degree of mysterious homoerotic appeal. Krafft-Ebing, of course, was the author of one of the foundational texts of European sexology, namely *Psychopathia sexualis,* which attempted to catalogue various sorts of sexual behavior into individual categories. By the time Taruho was writing, this work had been translated into Japanese twice, first in 1894 and again in 1913, and had attracted the attention of numerous writers, including Tanizaki Jun'ichirō, who drew on it for inspiration in his own works.[35]

Taruho explains his own use of the word *kurafuto-ebing-teki* in "Aru kōji no hanashi" (The story of a certain alleyway) published in *Shinchō* in 1924:

> I, who ordinarily went out of my way not to pay any attention to girls,
> and a few of my friends who were in the know, used this strange
> adjective as part of our own secret language. We had coined it from
> the proper name on the blue cover of a certain book we had managed
> to get our hands on somewhere. For instance, we would use it as an
> adjective to refer to the special feeling produced by the gaze of an
> adolescent boy, the glimpse of a red sweater peeking out the sleeve
> of his jacket, or perhaps even the boy's entire appearance. Still one
> other condition for its use is that we would use it in ways that did not
> fail to take account of the circumstantial, scenic, unfortunate, or even
> criminal quality of what we were trying to describe. (3:102)

The use of Krafft-Ebing's name in conjunction with same-sex desire comes from the fact that in its later editions, one-third to one-half of *Psychopathia sexualis* consisted of descriptive case studies about same-sex desire. In Taruho's terminology, things that are *kurafuto-ebing-teki* involved a titillating form of beauty that was all the more arousing because it was compromised by a hint of sadness, imperfection, or even danger. We see this in the description of the face of Karl, the attractive bishōnen in "Kāru to shiroi dentō": "It was a face that looked exactly like it had been weeping last night—a face that, as an artist friend of mine put it, has all 'the grief of the delicate, white surface of a hardboiled egg someone has soiled with their dirty fingerprints.' In it, there was something both highbrow and Krafft-Ebing-ish" (1:69). A similarly complicated blend of aesthetics can be seen in Taruho's description of the feelings he once experienced when reading a homoerotic exchange scrawled on the wall of a public toilet. In the 1925 essay "WC," Taruho states that the feeling the graffiti provoked in him had nothing to do with the kind of feeling that pretty young women would evoke. Instead, the graffiti provoked far more complicated feelings—feelings that hinted at something "more eternal, more metaphysical," but at the same time, that gave him a taste of "Krafft-Ebing-ish" baseness. These contradictory feelings filled his mind with thoughts of "a young boy's face, so pale it seemed to be covered in powder, burying his cheeks in the collar of a green cloak," and sent his heart soaring "far higher than the red wings of Art Smith's airplanes" (1:188). Once again, the word *kurafuto-ebing-teki* describes something imperfect and perhaps even vulgar, yet for Taruho, this quality only highlights the homoerotic appeal of the object it describes.

Taruho's idiosyncratic use of Krafft-Ebing's name is humorous, but it also reveals a somewhat more subversive politics at work. Krafft-Ebing's project in classifying sexual interests, desires, and practices was ultimately to study them for the purposes of diagnosing and perhaps even eradicating them; Taruho, however, uses Krafft-Ebing's name to describe and even *celebrate* same-sex desire. By using his name as a "code word" for something with a special homoerotic appeal, Taruho essentially undermines the intent of Krafft-Ebing and sexology more generally. Through exactly this kind of comical turn of phrase, his literature, by merit of its very lightness, engages in a concerted struggle with modern sexology over the meaning and implications of male–male desire. His clever turns of phrase and unusual metaphors forge a connection between wit, high aesthetic acuity, and homoerotic desire that flagrantly disregards the negative and pathologizing rhetoric of same-sex attraction Japanese sexologists had helped to put in place around the turn of the century.

Although Taruho was probably the most forthright advocate of male–male desire and attraction in the literary circles of the 1920s, he began to turn his attention to other subjects at the beginning of the 1930s. Most of

Taruho's writing over the next decade turns to other subjects, such as airplanes, astronomy, science, aesthetics, and film. Bishōnen continue to populate the pages of his writing, but no works from the 1930s and 1940s give the same extended treatment to adolescent desire one finds in the burst of works on boyish love published during the 1920s. This has to do partly with Taruho's personal circumstances and partly with the circumstances of the nation as a whole. In 1932 he returned to his childhood home of Ashiya in Kansai, and although he published a few stories, such as the relatively surreal "Kokoa-yama kidan" (The strange tale of Mount Cocoa), which appeared in *Shin seinen* in 1933, he soon entered a long dry spell in which he wrote little other than short essays for minor magazines. After the death of his father in 1934, he started a used-clothing store, which occupied much of his time, and by 1936, he was publishing nothing at all, partly because he had succumbed to a reliance on alcohol.

After returning to Tokyo at the end of 1936, he did resume publishing, but this time, historical circumstances intervened to silence his literary output. Because of the outbreak of full-fledged war in China with the Marco Polo Bridge Incident in 1937, there seemed to be far less space in the literary journals for the light, aestheticized, consciously apolitical literature Taruho had spent much of his career writing. In 1938, he published only two stories, one of which was the story "Fevaritto" (Favorite), a light and seemingly innocuous story that represented a return to the star-studded, surreal stories of his debut over a decade before. As the mechanisms of censorship grew increasingly strict, Taruho fell silent, waiting for the dawn of a new era in which he might be able to broach the subjects he cared about once again.

# Conclusion

*Postwar Legacies*

T HE WRITINGS OF Kaita, Ranpo, and Taruho lie at the center of a long, ongoing, multifaceted cultural dialogue in early twentieth-century Japan about the meaning of male–male love and eroticism—a dialogue given new urgency by the proliferation of sexological and psychological writings as well as the spread of the notion that certain forms of sexuality were unhealthy and even uncivilized. Caught up in the midst of this dialogue, these three writers responded in their own respective ways and developed different modes of representation as they explored and attempted to work out for themselves and their readers the significance and nature of love between men.

At the same time, it is clear from the relatively diverse representations in their writing that what male–male desire signified to them at any given moment had as much (if not more) to do with other personal, thematic, and genre-related concerns as with the kinds of discourse circulating in society at large. As a result, Kaita, Ranpo, and Taruho's treatments of the subject are not flat works that can easily be pigeonholed as simply representing one view of same-sex desire or another. Instead, they are complicated, idiosyncratic engagements with not just the rhetoric of "same-sex love," but also with a wider array of themes including art, friendship, decadence, aesthetics, and even the nature of modernity itself.

Although Kaita did not live long enough to see the war years or their aftermath, Ranpo and Taruho did continue over subsequent decades to engage with the subject in various ways. As mentioned at the end of the last chapter, the rising tide of war during the late 1930s led Japanese censors to be less accepting of the kinds of light-hearted, playful, and even subtly subversive literature that had flourished before the outbreak of full-fledged war with China in 1937. Censors did not crack down immediately on representations of sexuality—their eyes focused first and foremost on antiwar sentiments and expressions of political discontent—but the intense desire of editors to publish subjects related to the national emergency crowded from their pages the kinds of writing Ranpo and Taruho had published during the more liberal atmosphere of the 1920s and early to mid-1930s.[1] By the time the U.S.-Japan war began in late 1941, nationalism had reached such fervor that unless authors were willing to cater to the increasingly fascistic demands of the publishing industry and the jingoistic tastes of the public, they found few outlets in which to publish. As paper shortages worsened over the course of the war, there was little space left in publications for overt explorations of sexuality in any form, heteronormative or not.

Although forums for publishing on such subjects did die away temporarily, the desire to read about such subjects did not. When World War II came to an end and Japan began its long process of recovery in the 1940s, there was a virtual explosion of lowbrow magazines appealing to a mass audience eager for erotic stories and pornography. Provided there was no mention of fraternization between Japanese women and American GIs, Occupation censors did relatively little to stop the small flood of erotic stories, columns, and photo exposés publishers created to feed the hunger of a population that had gone without for years. Popularly known as "*kasutori* magazines" (named after the cheap, low-grade alcohol known as *kasutori shōchū*), these magazines were printed on cheap paper and went in and out of print with amazing rapidity. As historian John Dower has pointed out, *kasutori shōchū* is said to put one under the table with only three cups, thus ending a drinking spree; the name *kasutori* was, therefore, appropriate for a category of magazine that rarely made it past three issues.[2] These magazines were typically written for a male audience, presented many images of scantily clad women on their covers, and offered a variety of titillating stories, photographs, and articles about unusual subjects that hearkened back to the "curiosity-seeking" prewar *ryōki* press discussed in chapter 3. Not coincidentally, one of the popular, early *kasutori* magazines was called *Ryōki*. In its inaugural issue, the editors stated they had "not the slightest intention of presuming to enlighten or educate our readers. Our only wish is for you to enjoy the magazine in those moments of rest when you have become exhausted in body and spirit from the tasks of building a nation of peace. And when you have drawn from it a moment's pleasure, then simply throw it away."[3] Several later magazines with similar titles, including *Ōru ryōki* (All curiosity-hunting), *Sei ryōki* (Sex curiosity-hunting), *Ryōki zeminaru* (Curiosity-hunting seminar), professed a similar agenda and helped to revive the cultural sensibility of *ero, guro, nansensu* that had flourished before the era of heavy censorship and nationalism.[4] As Mark McLelland has discussed in detail, however, the work in *kasutori* magazines was not just a simple replaying of what one saw in the 1930s. One sees reflections of the current occupation-era zeitgeist almost constantly in the Westernized images of women's fashion, discussions of changing gender roles and sexual minorities, and new slang referring to dating practices and sexual behavior.[5]

By the time the U.S. occupation ended in 1952, several of these popular, pulpy magazines were able to maintain a better publication record, staying afloat for years at a time. Among them were the widely circulated magazines *Ningen tankyū* (Human explorations, 1950–53), *Amatoria* (1951–55), *Fūzoku kagaku* (Sex-customs science, 1953–55), and *Fūzoku zōshi* (Sex-customs storybook, 1953–55). As hinted by the identical subtitle of *Ningen tankyū* and *Amatoria,* "Bunkajin no sei kagaku shi" (A magazine of sexual science for cultivated people), these magazines attempted to preserve a façade of respectability even while discussing various forms of sexuality, including male–male eroticism, in a titillating format. The attempt to frame discussions of so-called "perverse sexuality" in broad cultural terms, especially those of science and psychology, involved adopting (at least on the surface) a rhetorical mode not unlike those of the prewar magazines that dealt with same-sex desire as a subject of curiosity. Even more than the first generation of postwar *kasutori* magazines, this second generation of what McLelland has called "the perverse press" dedicated itself to publishing on a full range of erotic practices, including male homoeroticism, female homoeroticism, prostitution, nymphomania, sadism, and masochism. Few writers for these journals claimed any kind of training or degrees that might give them an official kind of authority; many were young essayists and reporters who gathered knowledge from real-life explorations, their own reading, and a dash of sensationalizing imagination.[6] To supplement these lesser known figures, however, editors sometimes invited popular authors, psychologists, and journalists to contribute their works, thus lending an air of authority to the magazine while helping to sell issues.

Given that Ranpo had written so often about love and eroticism between men before the war, it is not surprising editors would approach him to contribute to these journals. At first, Ranpo appears to have been reluctant to publish with the postwar "perverse press." When Ranpo did cede and finally write for them, however, his contribution was of a somewhat more personal type, having more to do with his friendship with Iwata Jun'ichi, who had died in 1945, than the history of male love in general. For the May 1952 issue of *Ningen tankyū*, a special issue on self-published books having to do with eroticism, Ranpo described his friendship with Iwata, their light-hearted competition for bibliographical sources about same-sex love, and Iwata's passionate dedication to examining these sources (22:44–51). Ranpo notes that Iwata's dedication produced a number of articles, including the still only partially published study *Honchō nanshoku kō* (Thoughts on male love in our kingdom). Ranpo mentions he hoped to serialize the remainder of *Honchō nanshoku kō* in *Ningen tankyū*, and sure enough, the editors picked it up for the following issue, kicking off the serialization with an introductory essay by Ranpo.[7] Neither of Ranpo's two essays for *Ningen tankyū*, however, gives any indication he was continuing to dedicate any time to his bibliographic inquiries into same-sex desire. If anything, he seems to have abandoned the idea of further research, leaving it to a new generation of postwar investigators.

Nonetheless, it is clear people in the postwar period did continue to look up to Ranpo as an authority figure on various forms of nonheteronormative desire. In 1948, an article about the beauty of male love appeared under Ranpo's name in the small journal *Senryūsai* (Festival of humorous verse), published in Chiba Prefecture, but the Ranpo scholar Naka Shōsaku has determined this was the work of a ghostwriter.[8] This was not the only instance of a writer trying to cash in on Ranpo's reputation as a researcher on queer desire. In January 1969 (a few years after Ranpo's death in 1965), an author calling himself "Egawa Ranzō" published an article in *Kidan kurabu* (Club for strange stories) describing the attributes of various types of underwear and the physical sensations they provoke. In fact, this author comments he would like to purchase some thin, tight, supportive underwear of high-quality elastic; he has heard such things are available in stores for "gay boys" *(gei bōi)* in America.[9] The author's pen name is remarkably close to Ranpo's own name; two of the characters are the same, and the final character *po*, meaning "walk," has been cleverly replaced with *zō*, meaning "run." Indeed, the similarity between the names would make it virtually impossible for any Japanese reader to miss the fact the author was adopting a literary guise that mimicked that of Ranpo. Two months later, in March, an article about the beauty of tattoos appeared in *Kitan kurabu,* by someone calling himself "Edogawa Ranzō"—a name that mimics Ranpo's name even more closely. This article responds to the current popularity of yakuza films, noting the appeal of tattoos on tough bodies, yet it also argues tattoos have a long history in Japan and appear in many appealing forms on both men and women.[10] Once again, it is clear the author was drawing on the popular image of Ranpo as a writer attracted to what some might consider "off-color" displays of eroticism.

In fact, other than the roundtable discussion with Taruho and two postwar essays about Iwata Jun'ichi and his work, Ranpo did not write openly about love between men in the postwar period. Instead, it seems he sublimated his interest in male–male desire into the postwar novels he wrote for an adolescent audience. In the postwar period, Ranpo wrote numerous novels featuring his detective hero Akechi Kogorō and the leader of the Boy's Detective Club (Shōnen Tanteidan), the adolescent Kobayashi. Interestingly, Kobayashi had made his first appearance a couple of decades earlier in the novel *Kyūketsuki* (The vampire), serialized in the newspaper *Hōchi shinbun* in 1930, the year that marked the height of Ranpo's bibliographic research into male–male desire. In that novel, Kobayashi is described as an attractive "thirteen- or fourteen-year-old with cheeks like apples" (7:49)—an explanation that recalls Ranpo's idealizing essays about the love of boys and perhaps even the ruddy-cheeked youth in Kaita's painting hanging in Ranpo's study.

In 1949 Ranpo brought Kobayashi back to center stage with *Seidō no majin* (The magic man of bronze), serialized in the magazine *Shōnen* (Youth). In a short essay published as an afterword to the novel, Ranpo describes the relationship between the two heroes:

> Kobayashi is smart and quick as a squirrel, so he is an important, even indispensable helper for the detective Akechi. For that reason, our detective hero loves Kobayashi as if Kobayashi were his own protégé. The boy respects his mentor from his very core, and is as close to Akechi as if Akechi were his father or older brother. . . .
>
> Young Kobayashi would gladly walk through fire for his *Sensei.* If the detective Akechi thought Kobayashi was in danger, he would gladly risk his life to go to Kobayashi's rescue. That's how deep the love is that binds them. All they have to do is look in one another's eyes without saying a word to know immediately what the other is thinking. For that reason, the two can pick up in the twinkling of an

eye and work together so shrewdly it leaves onlookers speechless in astonishment.

Ah, what an enviable relationship between mentor and protégé! If the two just put their minds together and act, they're no match for any thief or man of mystery. Japan's finest detective hero and Japan's finest adolescent assistant—that's who they are![11]

Clearly, Ranpo envisions the relationship between Akechi and his sixteen-year-old protégé Kobayashi as a form of powerful, homosocial love. In fact, the homosocial relationship between Akechi and Kobayashi is so intimate that Ranpo fans have often commented that it must mask a homoerotic attraction; however, their relationship never develops an overtly homoerotic dimension—not surprising considering the novels were for an adolescent audience.[12] Still, one could argue the depiction of a powerful, idealized homosocial relationship, by expressly avoiding any hint of homoeroticism, echoes the split within the spectrum of heterosexual desire seen so often in Ranpo's prewar writing, which had argued that youthful, platonic expressions of same-sex love represents a powerful and even socially productive emotion, but those feelings are of a different nature than homoerotic passion.

Inagaki Taruho, by contrast, was more vocal in the postwar period about homoerotic love. After publishing his summary of the *Kuiin* roundtable with Ranpo as "E-shi to no isseki" in 1951, Taruho began writing a number of longer, essayistic treatments about the meaning and aesthetic implications of same-sex desire and eroticism. These include the 1954 book *A-kankaku to V-kankaku* (The A-sensibility and the V-sensibility) and a series of essays he started in 1958 but reworked multiple times before finally publishing them as *Shōnen'ai no bigaku* (The aesthetics of the love of boys) in 1968. Both books describe the historical, psychological, and metaphysical ramifications of the love of beautiful boys in an eclectic blend of ideas culled from history, Freudianism, pop psychology, and existentialism. In 1969 *Shōnen'ai no bigaku* was selected along with a work by Inoue Yasushi (1907–91) as co-winner of the first Japanese Literary Grand Prize (Nihon Bungaku Taishō), a newly created award to promote sales of contemporary Japanese literature. This award, plus a six-volume collection of his work released in 1969, helped to spark a wave of interest in Taruho's work, which found a new, affirming audience interested in considering the relationship between eroticism, especially its nonheteronormative forms, in relation to larger questions about culture, psychology, and daily existence. In this way, Taruho joined

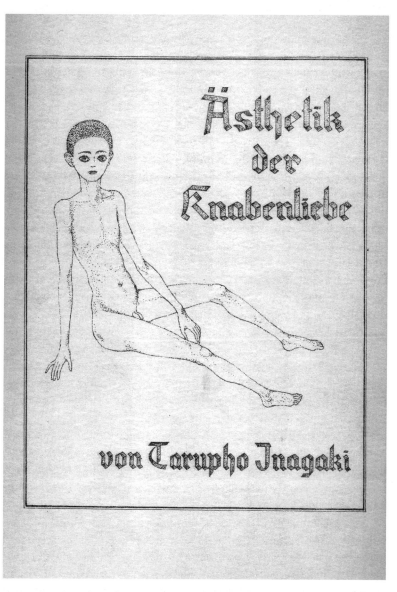

Cover of Taruho's *Shōnen'ai no bigaku* (The aesthetics of the love of boys) with an illustration by Kameyama Iwao (1907–89). In the nineteenth and early twentieth centuries, the Japanese gathered much of their medical and psychological knowledge from German and Austrian texts. The German translation of Taruho's title not only gives his work an air of authority, it also situates it in relation to a long lineage of German-language psychological and sexological texts. Collection of the author.

the ranks of a number of thinkers such as Jean-Paul Sartre (1905–80), Georges Bataille (1897–1962), Herbert Marcuse (1898–1979), and Shibusawa Tatsuhiko (1928–87) who urged a fundamental reconsideration of the meaning of eroticism and earned an impassioned following among young Japanese readers in the late 1960s and 1970s.

Taruho's postwar essays tend to be less anecdotal and more belletristic than the prewar works; however, like the early works, they also argue same-sex eroticism represents a path to profound aesthetic experiences. In them, Taruho claims the "A-sensibility"—that feeling he believed to be manifested in same-sex eroticism—is an essential quality in the production of original, visionary art, and the appreciation of young boys represented a means to plug into the eternal, atmospheric, inspiring energy circulating around humanity. He argues this based on an iconoclastic and often humorous reading (perhaps a purposeful *mis*reading) of Freud, in which Taruho claims the anus, the home and origin of the "A-sensibility," is fundamentally connected to production, given its role as the endpoint of the digestive tract and an orifice that produces a certain kind of sexual pleasure disassociated from procreation. The body, he suggests, is basically the end point of a long tube that opens to the universe through the mouth and ends with the anus, where humanity returns its own products to the world. For Taruho, the vagina and the penis are not directly related to this productive tube; if anything, they are distractions that do not participate in the grand drama of ingesting, digesting, transformation, and reproduction.[13]

No doubt, one should trouble this association between the anus and creativity and the leap he makes in connecting these to the appreciation of young men. In fact, little of his work describing concrete examples of attraction to young men implies that the characters experience an overt desire to engage in anal eroticism, thus implying the connection between homoerotic attraction and anal eroticism is not even consistent within his own work. What is important to note, however, is that as in his prewar work, Taruho is attempting to create a new, radical paradigm in which nonheteronormative forms of attraction do not occupy a peripheral position as a psychological aberration or marginal form of sexuality. He takes to task the common assumption that male homoeroticism is nonprocreative and therefore nonproductive; meanwhile, he turns the dynamics of Freud, who hypothesized that anal eroticism represented a perversion of the default heterosexual drives, on its head.

One might posit Taruho's postwar essays perform a radical political act not only by validating nonheteronormative desire, but also by insisting the attraction to young men, so often maligned in modern Japanese society as marginal or perverse, is actually *more* closely associated with the production of culture than other forms of desire that Japanese society readily endorses. In short, he inverts the entire paradigm of thinking about erotic desire, moving an attraction to young boys from a place at the fringes of society to a position at the center of culture. In the final year of his life, Taruho published a new, self-annotated, deluxe version of Ihara Saikaku's late seventeenth-century *Nanshoku ōkagami (The Great Mirror of Male Love)*, a collection that features stories about older men *(nenja)* loving younger *wakashu* and bishōnen.[14] Although Saikaku had been considered a giant of Japanese literature for most of the twentieth century, this collection had received far less critical and popular attention than other works such as *Kōshoku ichidai onna (The Life of an Amorous Woman)* and *Kōshoku gonin onna (Five Women Who Loved Love)* that focus primarily on cross-sex eroticism. By editing this new edition, Taruho helped it bring to the attention of an audience that likely knew little about it. Once again, Taruho was attempting to move the appreciation of young men from a peripheral position to one of significant historical and cultural importance.

Although Kaita, Ranpo, and Taruho each touched on similar themes, the readership they earned in the postwar period differed a great deal. Although Kaita's fame as a painter never diminished significantly, his literary works received a revival of attention, especially among poets, when they were edited by the prominent poet Yamamoto Tarō and reissued in a single-volume collection in 1963. Taruho continued to publish until his death in 1977, earning a dedicated following among literary figures, artists, intellectuals, scholars, and readers of a relatively artistic bent. Ranpo wrote for a popular audience, and therefore always had a broad readership, especially in the postwar period when his Boy's Detective Club series for adolescent readers made him even more of a household name than he had been previously. Despite the different readerships, however, all three of these authors remained well known for their representations of beautiful young boys and love between men, inspiring numerous essayists, visual artists, and manga authors to reflect upon their work in their own creations.

## MANGA LEGACIES

In the 1970s there was a blossoming of writing about male homoeroticism, as urban queer men who participated in the homosexual subculture of Tokyo and other major cities began writing about their own experiences for

magazines such as *Barazoku* (Tribe of roses, 1971–2004), the first successful, long-running commercial magazine for men-loving men. In this and the
many other magazines that followed in the years to come, ordinary men
wrote about their own lives, reacting to some of the images that had come
before them and documenting their own lives and fantasies.[15]

Still, one of the most visible engagements with the subject of male homoeroticism, especially love between schoolboys, came not within the queer
magazines, which were read by a relatively small segment of the population,
but within the wildly popular world of manga. Love between young men,
especially between school-age boys, became a major theme of girl's comics
in the 1970s when an influential group of female manga artists known as the
"24-nen-gumi" (The 24s) began writing stories about the subject for a young
female readership. (All of these artists were born around the year Shōwa
24, which corresponds to 1949 in the Gregorian calendar. For that reason,
the 24-nen-gumi has sometimes been translated in English as the "Fabulous
Forty-Niners.") Although the theme had surfaced in smaller, privately produced manga zines, it emerged as a major theme in the works of the 24-
nen-gumi artists.

As briefly mentioned in the introduction, one of the undisputed master-
pieces of the genre was *Kaze to ki no uta* (The song of the wind and the
trees, serialized 1976–84) by Takemiya Keiko (1950–).[16] Set in the late
nineteenth century in a remote, wind-swept all-male school outside Arles,
France, *Kaze to ki no uta* tells the story of the relationship between the often
self-destructive protagonist Gilbert, who possesses a deeply wounded psyche and employs homoeroticism as a way to manipulate others, and the half-
gypsy Serge, who attempts to understand and help Gilbert and develops
complicated feelings in the process. Although Gilbert is a boy, he is drawn
with silky blond curls, a slender figure, and an apparent lack of male genitalia (judging from the occasional bed scene)—all characteristics that invite
readers to see him as highly feminized. In this way, the artwork sets up a
dichotomy between him and the more traditionally boyish Serge that, while
not replicating heterosexual tension directly, maps a sort of difference onto
the bodies of the characters. As numerous cultural critics have pointed out,
the use of such gender-bending techniques opens channels of identification between female readers and the male characters, while still allowing
readers to fantasize about relationships other than the heterosexual norms.[17]
As Midori Matsui notes, the popularity of male homoeroticism in girls'
comics shows Japanese girls' identification with a "fictitious category which,

embodying the principle of pure play (fantasy), contests the socially deter-mined definitions and parameters of sexuality."[18]

Interestingly, Takemiya recalls that about five years before she started seri-alizing *Kaze to ki no uta,* she happened to read Taruho's *Shōnen'ai no bigaku* about the beauty of the adolescent male body, and it struck her as giving voice to many ideas that had occupied her but that she had been unable to articu-late herself. She has noted this encounter with Taruho's writing was critical in helping her to believe in herself and to continue to create manga.[19] In a recent interview, Takemiya was even more direct, stating that the very idea of pro-ducing a manga about the love between boys in a European boarding school came directly from Taruho's *Shōnen'ai no bigaku* and its many mentions of the eroticism of young boys in British schools at the turn of the century.[20]

The work of Takemiya and her one-time roommate and fellow manga artist Hagio Moto helped give rise to an entire subgenre of comics popu-larly known as *shōnen'ai,* from the word meaning "the love of boys." In fact, the critic Ishida Minori has argued that the entire name of this subgenre was borrowed directly from Taruho's *Shōnen'ai no bigaku,* which inspired Take-miya and other manga artists.[21] More recently, *shōnen'ai* comics have also come to be known as *bōizu rabu* (boys' love) comics. Like Taruho's early novels from the 1920s and like Takemiya's manga, the manga belonging to this subgenre feature bishōnen with lithe bodies, large and expressive eyes, and long hair that gives them romantic and often pensive looks. Not just the styling of the characters is highly romanticized, but the plotlines are as well. They often emphasize love at first sight, brief but powerful connections, and, in many cases, doomed relationships that end with separation or even death.

Because both partners in these stories are male, there is no overt differ-ence in biological gender; however, as in *Kaze to ki no uta,* manga authors typically replace this sort of difference with other sorts of difference: body type, size, age, or aggressiveness. One of the major conventions of boys' love manga becomes the presence of a boy who is more sexually aware and aggressive (usually as the result of being older, stronger, or more worldly) and a boy who plays a more passive role in the relationship (usually because he is younger or more feminine). Still, as Ishida Minori notes, many *shōnen'ai* manga are created in ways that allow readers to identify with multiple char-acters, as the focus of attention shifts from one character to another, inviting the reader into the private, inner worlds of multiple figures in the story. As a result, *shōnen'ai* manga, like the affections described in Taruho's work, are typically not about a unidirectional affection in which one man loves a boy;

there is a fluid circulation of desire between reader and characters, as the reader is invited into the world of the text to identify with multiple subject positions. There is a slipperiness in the meaning of *shōnen'ai* in these comics; on one hand, it means "loving a boy," in that the manga tell stories in which boys are the objects of affection, yet at the same time, it could also mean "boys loving," in that boys occupy the position of subject as well.[22]

In the 1980s there was a radical shift in the production of manga as new printing and home publishing technology made it possible for independent artists and manga fans to produce and market their own work. The works produced by independent readers outside of the ordinary operations of publishing were known as *dōjinshi* (a word which formerly referred to the magazines and booklets created and circulated privately in small groups of readers), and producers and fans of these independent manga gathered in conventions to exchange ideas and sell their work. As Sharon Kinsella has noted, the amateur manga movement had exploded by the early 1990s when a quarter million artists and fans gathered at the Comic Market (Komikku Māketto), which had quickly grown into the most important and systematic of these conventions since its founding in 1975.[23] More recently, the Internet has allowed independent artists to bypass even the structures of the Comic Market and sell their work directly to the public. The result was a virtual explosion of homemade manga as young women, mostly in their late teens and early twenties, began to produce and market their own stories.

One of the most important developments in these amateur manga was the development of a rich genre of parody that takes preexisting characters and plot lines, then reinterprets them in ways that diverge from the original work. Although Kinsella notes some people decry these parodies as derivative and less interesting than other manga, some have seen them as a creative means of refashioning and ultimately taking control of elements of culture and ideology handed to them from on high by mainstream authors, artists, and publishers.[24] From the point of view of scholars interested in the circulation of individual works and ideas, the relatively democratic subgenre of *dōjinshi* provides a valuable resource showing how ideas, plots, and characters have been reinterpreted to suit the desires of individual manga artists reflecting on what came before.

Artists working in this parodic genre did not just turn to other manga for inspiration; they also drew on more "traditional" genres of literature as well, reinterpreting motifs, themes, and plots from novels and short stories they found particularly appealing. It is perhaps not surprising that some manga artists turned to Ranpo, Taruho, and Kaita for inspiration, since all had written so often about love between young men—the major staple of this significant subgenre of women's comics. One particularly interesting example of a *dōjinshi* based on these authors' work is *Negachibu kotō no oni* (Negative demon of the lonely isle, 1993) by Hirano Ayu. Born in Hiroshima Prefecture, Hirano started her career by self-publishing, but she has since gone on to a successful career publishing humorous manga, most notably the long-running series *Rajikaru hosupitaru* (Radical hospital), which started serialization in 1998 and continued for nearly a decade. *Negachibu kotō no oni*, which is drawn in a relatively rough, naïve style compared to that of many other professional manga artists, represents a thorough and careful reworking of Ranpo's novel *Kotō no oni*. In fact, the word "negative" in the title refers to a photographic negative, suggesting Hirano wanted to look at the story from a profoundly different perspective, reversing ideas in the original text. In the introduction, Hirano says she wrote this particular *dōjinshi* as a purposeful misreading of *Kotō no oni* (a novel she particularly loved) as a love story. She asks her readers to excuse her for putting on the back burner the "search for strange beauty and the bizarre one finds in Ranpo's works" while instead focusing on the homoerotic relationship between the two main characters.[25]

Although *Negachibu kotō no oni* draws inspiration from Ranpo's novel, Hirano has largely abandoned the structure of the original and instead presented a series of episodes she has either recreated or drawn from her imagination. From the first pages alone, it is immediately clear Hirano has inserted the Moroto–Minoura relationship into the archetypal boy's love relationship of an older, more worldly boy who puts the moves on a somewhat passive, beautiful, younger boy. Moroto is a debonair, masculine fellow who is much taller and more powerful than Minoura, who is smaller and more boyish. Most of the book consists of a series of loosely ordered flashbacks to various moments in their adventure together, which Hirano has peppered with humorous references to contemporary culture to make the reader smile. For instance, when the character Moroto talks about the traumatic rape by his mother that turned him away from women forever, he shudders and comments that his mother kept doing "terrible things like you would see on one of those CBS specials."[26] In this way, Hirano takes the events Ranpo included to create an "erotic, grotesque" atmosphere and makes them the stuff of humor, thus subverting the effect of the original altogether and highlighting the potentially campy qualities latent within Ranpo's text.

Cover of Hirano Ayu's *Negachibu kotō no oni* (Negative demon of the lonely isle,
1993), a parodic reinterpretation of Ranpo's *Kotō no oni* as a romance between the
handsome Moroto (pictured on top) and the younger Minoura (pictured below).
Collection of the author.

The climactic moment when Moroto and Minoura are lost in the dark cave together and Moroto begins to force himself on his reluctant friend is also retold in a humorous fashion. Although Minoura has been reluctantly shying away with nervous beads of sweat running down his face, he suddenly does a coy about-face, blushes, and says, "Well, things have their proper order, you know? Look, how about starting with a kiss on the hand . . ." Moroto thinks to himself, "You say such girly little things . . . ," takes off his jacket, and forces himself on Minoura. The next frame is black, as if the "camera" recording the event has shut off. Superimposed on the blackness are words similar to those in Ranpo's novel: "Moroto Michio is no longer a person of this world. I am afraid of embarrassing the dead. I will refrain from writing at any length about the sorts of things that happened." In the next frame, however, the "lights" go back on, and the reader sees a bold shot of Moroto wedging himself between the legs of Minoura and kissing him passionately. Above his head is a text bubble that emphatically states, "I don't care! Go ahead and write all about it! Put it all out there! Go ahead!" In the next frame, a servant shows up, making a big peace sign with his hands as if stepping into a photograph. Moroto gasps and holds up his pants as tears well in his eyes; meanwhile, Moroto curses the servant, calling him an "idiot" for showing up at just the wrong time.[27] Soon afterward, Minoura realizes his hair has gone white as a result of the encounter in the cave, and he dejectedly comments on his appearance. Moroto steps back, strikes an absurdly romantic pose, and says, "Marie Antoinette! I will call you Antoinette-*sama!*" As he speaks, he is surrounded by roses, a visual motif that appears often in manga at climatic, romantic scenes.[28] The roses and the mention of Marie Antoinette serve as an indirect reference to a highly aestheticized, even rococo manga in which she appears as a major character: Ikeda Riyoko's (1947–) *Berusaiyu no bara* (The rose of Versailles), which started serialization and 1972 and went on to become one of the best selling girls' comics of all time.[29]

What is important to note is that once again, Hirano has taken a scene written to shock and fascinate curious readers with its titillating "perversity" and instead inserted it into a routine seemingly right out of a romantic comedy. Readers no longer see Moroto's advances as scandalous or outrageous; instead, he is the enterprising lover whose attempts to get his beloved are frustrated in ridiculous ways by the vagaries of circumstance. Same-sex love is not described as something incomprehensible or difficult to fathom. In fact, the manga contains several relatively serious passages that present

Moroto in a way that makes him entirely sympathetic to the audience. For instance, in one long aside to the reader, Hirano writes, "Even if you are not a homosexual, Moroto's dilemma is entirely understandable, isn't it? It is the same pattern you see when a man is told, 'Let's just be friends, okay?'"[30]

Likewise, Minoura's back-and-forth, sometimes flirtatious, sometimes reticent responses to Moroto's advances also neutralize the anxiety Ranpo works into the original novel. In fact, at the end of Hirano's retelling, Minoura imagines Moroto has come back to him out of love. A few moments later, he realizes Moroto's return is nothing but a dream, and the vision he had seen was Moroto's soul calling out to him from his deathbed. The final pages show Minoura tearfully thinking, "Even now, sometimes in the darkness, I can feel Moroto's certain warmth and nostalgic aroma holding me. Perhaps this is just my imagination, but there is nothing mysterious, frightening, or unpleasant about it."[31] This ending invites the readers to sympathize with Minoura, and to feel the pleasant warmth of true love, a sensation many adolescent readers of this *dōjinshi* no doubt also yearned to experience.

Of course, the differences in Ranpo's and Hirano's versions of the story are partly due to the fact that Hirano's is a parody, but the differences also reflect a sea change in understandings of male homoeroticism between the years these two versions were written. Attitudes toward homosexuality have shifted so that younger women born in the last quarter of the twentieth century feel more curiosity and interest in queer men than antipathy or concern. One survey published in the *Asahi shinbun* in January 1998 asks "Do you agree or disagree with the statement that homosexuality is one way of loving?" Twenty-eight percent of respondents agreed it was a meaningful way of loving, whereas 65 percent did not. Significantly, however, a majority of all women under age thirty-five supported the statement, showing that attitudes toward same-sex eroticism are shaped in large part by age and gender.[32] Mark McLelland has argued that boys' love manga, television shows, novels, films, and other cultural media consumed by young women have shaped a gay-positive attitude, even leading them to believe gay men are romantic, comforting figures who can interact with women with none of the complications of sexual tension.[33] Elsewhere, McLelland cites Ōtsuka Takashi, the host of a gay spot on a mainstream television show during the late 1970s, as stating that up to 80 percent of his viewer mail was from young women who thought "gays are lovely"—an impression based principally on boys' love manga.[34] For younger women who grew up reading these manga, homoerotic desire, if anything, represents a sort of strong, passionate love that exists outside of the boundaries of marriage, procreation, and other institutions of heterosexuality. Not surprisingly, many boys' love manga reflect the assumption that the men who experience it are even more sensitive and romantically determined than heterosexual men.

One sees another romanticized representation of same-sex love in *Ippon no garansu* (A tube of garance), a 1994 *dōjinshi* published under the pseudonym Nobi Nobita (1967–). At the time she published *Ippon no garansu*, Nobi (who also publishes under the name Enomoto Nariko) was an aspiring manga artist publishing with the *dōjinshi* group Gekkō Tōzoku (Moonlight Thieves), but since then, she has gone on to release numerous volumes of comics with some of Japan's most important publishers, including a contemporary adaptation of Natsume Sōseki's classic Japanese novel *Kokoro* (1914), which describes the powerful homosocial bonds between an older man and his student.[35] *Ippon no garansu* takes its title from a line in a poem Murayama Kaita wrote during his days as an art student. In it, Kaita describes the intense, sensual pleasure he derives from a tube of the deep, red paint derived from madder flowers (*garance* in French), and uses the color as a metaphor for his passionate approach to art and life. The quotes from "Ippon no garansu" are interspersed with quotes from another Kaita poem "Juketsu" (Engorged with blood) that describes the intense, gaudy beauty of a thistle, which he imagines to be swollen with blood. If one thinks of the thistle in "Juketsu" as a metaphor for an erect phallus, the poem takes on a distinct homoerotic subtext. Clearly aware of this, Nobi uses passages from "Juketsu" like a recurring mantra in the homoerotic scenes in her manga.

*Ippon no garansu* is typical of many *dōjinshi* that show a relative lack of narrative structure and that have been described by the word *yaoi*, an acronym made up of the initial letters of three phrases meaning "no build-up" (*YAma nashi*), "no foreclosure" (*Ochi nashi*), and "no meaning" (*Imi nashi*).[36] In fact, *Ippon no garansu* hardly has any story at all; the forty-page manga just presents a number of loosely organized, somewhat surreal scenes that take place between two boys living in contemporary times. The very looseness of this structure, however, gives it a poetic quality, as the scenes hang without clear resolution, resonating in the reader's mind. What story there is begins with Tobikage, a trim school-aged boy, coming to the window of his slightly larger and apparently older friend Shūichi, covered with blood from a fight. As he stares at the boy's red wounds, Shūichi thinks of lines from Kaita's poems "Ippon no garansu" and "Juketsu," making an association between his friend's bloody body and the enticingly beautiful but

一本のガランス

野火ノビタ◆月光盗賊

Cover of Nobi Nobita's *Ippon no garansu* (A tube of garance, 1994), a *yaoi* manga that incorporates passages from Kaita's poetry in a melodramatic story of two adolescent male lovers. Collection of the author.

dangerously thorny flower of a thistle. He is jealous that this "flower" will be given to a girl and not to him. Later, Shūichi goes off to see Tobikage on a battlefield where he sits, inexplicably holding a samurai sword. He uses Tobikage's blade to cut himself, then forces himself onto Tobikage, who responds by wounding Shūichi. The conversation that ensues makes it clear Tobikage has already given his girlfriend his "flower," but at the end of the short manga, Tobikage gives himself over to Shūichi, explaining he is doing so in order for Shūichi to see his blood. The cover of the manga shows Shūichi tenderly embracing Tobikage from behind, and Tobikage holding up a big sword covered with bright red blood—an image that almost certainly takes place after Shūichi's "sword" penetrates Tobikage's body. Metaphorically, the exchange of blood comes to represent the utmost in devotion as the boys consummate their blood pact.

Further proof of the aesthetic connections between early twentieth-century writing and the contemporary work of girls' comics can be found in the manga adaptation of Inagaki Taruho's 1924 essayistic story "Kāru to shiroi dentō" (Karl and the white light) by the contemporary manga artist Hatoyama Ikuko (1968–), originally from Yokohama. Hatoyama has made a career of drawing sensitive images of beautiful young men in a style blending early twentieth-century aesthetics with the visual language of manga. The resulting images have a vintage, steampunk sensibility. Although she has produced several manga novels, these have been distributed not through the principal channels of manga production, but through smaller publishers specializing in manga that have a more overtly artistic bent.

Hatoyama's manga adaptation of Taruho's story appeared in a 2006 special issue of the literary criticism journal *Yuriika* (Eureka) dedicated to Taruho.[37] Of the manga adaptations discussed so far, Hatoyama's is the most faithful to the original. Only several pages long, it maintains the brevity of the original, which is little more than a few paragraphs, and most of the text comes verbatim from Taruho's writing. The narrator's discussions about Karl's beauty are superimposed over images of him drawn from three-quarter angles and profiles that suggest that at least part of the time, we are seeing Karl through the eyes of the narrator. Karl's appearance is more naturalistic than one might see in many commercially produced manga, but his large eyes and thin nose still show a nod to manga conventions. Interestingly, Hatoyama has drawn the narrator (the smoker in the Figure) so he is taller and older than Karl. Although Taruho's text does not indicate the relative age of the narrator vis-à-vis Karl, Hatoyama has followed the convention of

Excerpt from Hatoyama Ikuko's manga adaptation of Taruho's short story "Kāru to shiroi dentō" (Karl and the white light). The narrator says to Karl, "It looks just like you," and at the bottom of the page, he thinks to himself, "I've taken quite a liking to that face." Copyright Ikuko Hatoyama 2006–10.

boys' love manga by positioning the narrator as the older and more worldly boy, and Karl as the younger boy who is the object of affection. Unlike less subtle manga, the relationship between the two is never consummated. In this way, it is faithful to Taruho's understated original, but it does find a way to end with a romantic image reminiscent of mainstream boys' love manga. As the narrator walks through the darkness of the city, he looks up and sees an electric streetlamp shining in the darkness. In the penultimate frame, one sees the glowing filaments of the electric lamp with Karl's image superimposed over it, as though one is seeing the hallucination through the narrator's eyes. The final frame shows a close-up of Karl, still superimposed over the bulb, weeping and looking every bit the sensitive, romantic hero.

Ultimately, the reason the manga of Hirano Ayu, Nobi Nobita, and Hatoyama Ikuko are so important for the purposes of this study is that they show a concrete line of connection between the homoerotic appreciation of boyish beauty forged in the writings of the early twentieth century and the boys' love manga produced several decades later. These manga prove that contemporary artists are not working within a vacuum, unaware of the representations of homoerotic love in the writing preceding them; indeed, those representations sometimes serve as the point of departure for new creative works on the subject of boys' love. Even when not directly referencing those works, however, *shōjo manga* and their representations of homoerotic desire seem to partake of a palate of aesthetics created by early twentieth-century writers such as Kaita and Taruho, who saw homoerotic appreciation of boyish beauty as an intense aesthetic experience and a sign of deep, personal feelings that could define one's experience as an individual.

Of course, *shōjo manga* do not portray the entire range of male homoeroticism; they focus on highly romanticized stories, which do not necessary match the real, lived experience of many queer men living in Japan today. As McLelland has pointed out, many Japanese gay men do not necessarily feel as if manga represent the reality of their own experiences; indeed, many of my own friends and colleagues in the Japanese gay world have commented they do not feel the slender, thin, aestheticized images of bishōnen in girls' comics reflect themselves, nor the objects of their desires.[38] It is no surprise that gay male manga artists such as Tagame Gengoroh (1964–), Matsuzaki Tsukasa, and Jiraiya (1967–), who started by contributing shorter manga to gay magazines, have in recent years been producing their own full-length manga that map out their own erotic fantasies, explore contemporary gay life in Japan, and negotiate the possibilities of same-sex desire from their own perspectives. In most cases, these artists depict entirely different sorts of characters than one finds in girls' manga—athletic, muscular, and butch men more likely to appeal sexually to the queer male readership buying their manga.

As Japan's sexual minorities become more visible to mainstream society by writing their own novels, drawing their own manga, creating their own films, presenting their own ideas, and voicing their own opinions, the numbers of works probing the meaning, significance, and implications of same-sex eroticism will only grow. No doubt, these writers will refer to, modify, and perhaps even reject the literary traditions and kinds of representations of same-sex love and eroticism examined within this book. It is exciting to anticipate what new representations and ideas will come as Japan's queer world moves forward to embrace the future.

# Acknowledgments

It was several years ago on a warm afternoon in the book-filled study of the brilliant poet Takahashi Mutsuo that I first heard the name Murayama Kaita in a conversation about erotic desire and poetry. Since it was this bit of karma that eventually led me to the topic of this book, it is only appropriate I begin by thanking Mr. Takahashi. Over the years, he has been a great source of knowledge about Japanese stylistics and poetic history, and his wisdom and friendship have encouraged me in more ways than he will probably ever realize.

The members of my dissertation committee at Ohio State University, Richard Torrance and Naomi Fukumori, were instrumental in helping me think about the subject of this book several years ago when this project was first beginning. My biggest debt, however, is to my advisor, William J. Tyler, whose wise and gracious touch is evident on nearly every page. It is my greatest regret he did not live long enough to see the publication of this book. Bill Tyler was an extraordinary scholar, author, and translator who wrote not just with an amazing eye for detail but also with great elegance. He will always remain a profound inspiration.

I am grateful to MEXT (the Japanese Ministry of Education, Culture, Sports, Science, and Technology), The Ohio State University, and the International Research Center for Japanese Studies for their generous support while I worked on this project as a graduate student. The final stages of writing were made possible through Western Michigan University's Faculty Research and Creative Activities Award. The gracious guidance and incredibly vast erudition of Suzuki Sadami was instrumental in the early days of this project and once again while I was doing the final polishing of the manuscript, back again at the International Research Center for Japanese Studies, where I spent the 2009–10 academic year as a visiting research fellow. Professor Suzuki is a living, breathing encyclopedia, unmatched in his knowledge of twentieth-century literary and cultural history, and his inspiration shaped this text in many significant ways. I am also grateful for the counsel of the brilliant cultural historian Inaga Shigemi, as well as to the members of the center's research group on the history of sexual desire. Inoue Shōichi, Furukawa Makoto, Saitō Hikaru, and Mitsuhashi Junko responded to my thoughts about this project with great enthusiasm and several helpful suggestions.

The largest collection of Kaita's works and original manuscripts is housed in the Mie Prefectural Art Museum in Tsu, and I thank curator Ikuta Yuki not just for giving me access to their manuscripts and library but also for her continuing friendship over the years. I will never forget our trip through the same islands in southern Mie Prefecture that Edogawa Ranpo and Iwata Jun'ichi had visited so many years before—a trip that inspired Ranpo to write *Kotō no oni,* one of the novels I examine in this book. Many scholars and fans of Kaita, Ranpo, and Taruho gave me great encouragement as I worked on this project. I am deeply grateful to Aizawa Keizō, Fukushima Yasuki, Sasaki Teru, Hayashi Michiko, Sunaga Asahiko, Naka Shōsaku, Mark McLelland, and James Welker for providing both materials and inspiration essential for the production of this book.

The following individuals and organizations have been a great help in securing permissions for the illustrations in this book, and for this they deserve special gratitude: Ranpo's grandson Hirai Kentarō, Iwata Junko of the Toba Minato-Machi Bungakukan in Mie, Koike Tomoko of the Setagaya Literary Museum in Tokyo, Arayashiki Tōru and Hayashi Michiko of the Pola Art Museum in Kanagawa, Kuboichi Seiichirō of the Shinano Drawing Museum in Nagano, and Kaneko Yukari of the Takemura Eitarō Memorial Museum in Yamanashi. I am particularly obliged to Inagaki Miyako, the stepdaughter of Inagaki Taruho and executor of his estate. Over the past several years she has been a valuable informant about Taruho's life as well as a dear friend whose long, lively conversations made my years in Kyoto a great deal of fun.

Jim Reichert and the anonymous reviewer for the University of Minnesota Press provided extremely valuable suggestions that helped give this book its final shape. Sue Breckenridge did a fine job with the copyediting, catching many infelicities and ironing out countless wrinkles inadvertently left behind in my sentences. I am deeply grateful for their many insightful and constructive suggestions that made this manuscript much better than it would have been otherwise. Any shortcomings are, needless to say, still entirely my own. I thank my editor, Jason Weidemann, at the University of Minnesota Press for his unwavering support of this project. As we ushered this manuscript through the many stages of the publication process, our relationship slowly evolved from that of editor and author into that of two friends.

During the long process of working on this book, I have incurred debts to more people than I can possibly name here. Among them, I extend my sincerest and most heartfelt thanks to David Feaster, Suzuki Yasuko, Iwai Shigeki, Ōmori Kyōko, William Gardner, Alisa Freedman, Angela Yiu, Christopher Scott, Julia Bullock, Micah Auerbach, Tanaka Atsusuke, Miyata Hotsue, the Iwane family, Itō Hiromi, Arai Takako, Stephen Miller, Judith Rabinovitch, Anthony and Gemma Ybarra, Cindy Bowers, Bill Dreger, Judy Dutson, and Drew Banbury. I am also grateful to my colleagues at Western Michigan University who provided models of how to balance teaching, research, and the many other seemingly endless demands of our impossibly hectic lives. For this, I thank Cynthia Running-Johnson, Steve Covell, Takashi Yoshida, Rika Saito, Priscilla Lambert, Todd Kuchta, Lisa Minnick, Rand Johnson, David Kutzko, Mustafa Mughazy, Michitoshi Soga, and my colleagues in the Department of Foreign Languages and at Soga Japan Center at WMU for their support behind the scenes while I was writing this book.

I dedicate this book to my parents, Wib and Janet Angles, and my ninety-two-year-old grandfather, John Young, who have always been a source of encouragement and love, even when life's twists and turns sometimes took me quite far from home. I thank them for letting a starry-eyed fifteen-year-old who had barely been outside the American Midwest go to a small town in rural southwestern Japan, thus sparking a passion that has now lasted two and a half decades.

# Notes

INTRODUCTION

All translations, unless otherwise noted, are by the author.

1. Hagio, *Tōma no shinzō*, and Takemiya, *Kaze to ki no uta*.
2. Angles, "Penisism and the Eternal Hole."
3. Foucault, *The History of Sexuality*, 17–49.
4. Pflugfelder, *Cartographies of Desire*.
5. Ibid., 193.
6. Reichert, *In the Company of Men*.
7. Edogawa, *Edogawa Ranpo suiri bunko*, 60:91.
8. I have used the words "same-sex love" within quotation marks to refer to the medico-scientific understanding of male–male and female–female desire that arose in the late nineteenth century. The reason is that there were numerous different terms in Japanese used to describe roughly the same concept, including *dōsei kōsetsu* (same-sex intercourse), *dōsei-teki shikijō* (same-sex erotic lust), *dōsei-teki jōkō* (same-sex sexual intercourse), *dōseiyoku* (same-sex desire), *dōseikan seiyoku* (sexual desire among the same sex), *dōsei ren'aishō* (same-sex love syndrome), and *dōsei sōshinshō* (same-sex love illness).
9. Schalow, introduction, 4.
10. Furukawa, "The Changing Nature of Sexuality," 115.
11. Pflugfelder, *Cartographies of Desire*, 268–69. For one example, see the widely circulated book by Habuto and Sawada, *Hentai seiyoku ron*, 115–53.
12. For an extensive discussion of sex education and its relationship to social control, see Frühstück, *Colonizing Sex*, 55–82.
13. Habuto, *Seiten*, 290.
14. Habuto and Sawada, *Hentai seiyoku ron*, 301–7.
15. Pflugfelder, *Cartographies of Desire*, 158–62.
16. Ibid., 147. It is tempting to assume that the law arose from concern about making Japan more "civilized," but Pflugfelder argues that in formulating this part of

the legal code, the Japanese drew on contemporary Qing dynasty Chinese and pre-Napoleonic French law (ibid., 171–72; see also Furukawa, "The Changing Nature of Sexuality," 109–10).

17. Sedgwick, *Epistemology of the Closet*, 45. Also see Halperin, *How to Do the History of Homosexuality*, 10–11.

18. Sedgwick, *Epistemology of the Closet*, 45.

19. Ibid., 47.

20. Reichert, review of *Cartographies of Desire*, 225.

21. *"Kaita no utaeru* by Murayama Kaita," 1.

22. Arishima, *Arishima Takeo zenshū*, 8:407.

23. Kusano, *Murayama Kaita*, 43–56.

24. Nakano, "Uta no wakare," 281.

25. Itō Ken, *Hentai sakka shi*, 19.

26. Ranpo includes three variants of this advertisement in his personal scrapbook: Edogawa Ranpo, *Harimaze nenpu*, 200.

27. Ibid., 235.

28. Ibid., 359.

29. Mishima, *Sakka ron*, 92.

30. Mori Ōgai, *Ōgai zenshū*, 5:83–179. Historian Donald Roden translates the terms *kōha* and *nanpa* as "roughneck" and "softie" respectively (Roden, *Schooldays in Imperial Japan*). Pflugfelder translates them as "roughneck" and "smoothie," which he sees as more symmetrical than Roden's choice of words (Pflugfelder, *Cartographies of Desire*, 214–17). A 1972 translation of the novel by Kazuji Ninomiya and Sanford Goldstein gives the terms "queer" and "masher" (Ogai, *Vita Sexualis*).

31. Pflugfelder, *Cartographies of Desire*, 119–226; Reichert, *In the Company of Men*, 199–226.

32. Roden, *Schooldays in Imperial Japan*, 141.

33. Ranpo, *Edogawa Ranpo zenshū*, 16:14–19.

34. See Yamazaki's *Yamazaki Toshio sakuhin shū* (Collected works of Yamazaki Toshio), Kawabata Yasunari's "Shōnen" (Adolescent boys), Hori Tatsuo's "Moyuru hō" ("Les Joues en Feu"), and Tachibana Sotō's "Nanshoku monogatari" (Tales of male love).

35. Isoda, *Kindai no kanjō kakumei*.

36. Saeki, *Ren'ai no kigen;* Saeki, "From *Iro* (Eros) to *Ai=Love*," 71–82.

37. Tyler, review of *In the Company of Men*, 559.

38. Ozaki, "Bishōnen no kenkyū," 540.

39. Silverberg, *Erotic Grotesque Nonsense*.

40. "Shini e to 'Shi no shima,'" 6.

41. Pflugfelder, *Cartographies of Desire*, 290.

42. Angles, "Seeking the Strange," 118–24.

43. Pflugfelder, *Cartographies of Desire*, 290–91.

44. Love, *Feeling Backward*, 37.

45. Jagose, *Queer Theory*, 72–83.

46. Halperin, *How to Do the History of Homosexuality,* 14.

47. Ibid., 17.

48. For biographical information about Kaita, see Kusano Shinpei's biography *Murayama Kaita* as well as Harada, "Kaita den"; Hasegawa, "Chizome no rappa fuki-narase"; and Itō Kyō, "Nenpu."

49. Ono, *Warera wa Ranpo tanteidan,* 152–54. For a series of anecdotes about Ranpo's visits to gay bars, see Heiji, "Edogawa Ranpo to 'Kare.'"

50. Despite his enormous stature in the world of popular Japanese literature, sur-prisingly, no full-length biography of Ranpo has yet been written. Almost all studies of Ranpo rely primarily on his own autobiographical writings, which treat the subject of his sexual desires gingerly. The best autobiographical sources on Ranpo are his *Harimaze nenpu* (Scrapbook chronology), and his memoir, *Tantei shōsetsu yon-jū-nen* (Forty years of detective fiction). Other sources of biographical information about Ranpo include Ranpo's son Hirai Ryūtarō's memoir *Utsushiyo no Ranpo* (Ranpo in this world), Ranpo's relative Matsumura Tami's memoir, *Ranpo ojisan* (Uncle Ranpo), the Kawade Shobō Shinsha collection of articles simply entitled *Edogawa Ranpo,* and the volume Suzuki Sadami and Matsuyama Iwao have edited for the Shinchō Nihon Bungaku Arubamu series. Naka Shōsaku at the Nabari Shiritsu Toshokan has created several resources about Ranpo's life and work that are indispensable for any Ranpo researcher: *Ranpo bunken dēta bukku* (Ranpo bibliographic data book), *Edogawa Ranpo shippitsu nenpu* (Chronology of Edogawa Ranpo's writing), *Edogawa Ranpo chosho mokuroku* (Index of Edogawa Ranpo's writing), and *Edogawa Ranpo nenpu shūsei* (Edogawa Ranpo, a compiled chronology).

51. Takahashi Mutsuo, personal communication.

52. On his married life, see Inagaki Shiyo, *Otto Inagaki Taruho.* Published six years before Taruho's death, this memoir by his wife remains the only major biographical work about him so far, but it tells relatively little about his premarital life, the period on which this study focuses. One additional especially helpful resource about Taruho's life is the collection of articles *Inagaki Taruho,* published in 1993 by Kawada Shobō Shinsha.

53. Reichert, "Representations of Male–Male Sexuality in Meiji-Period Litera-ture," 11–18.

54. One sees this most dramatically in his discussions of the biography of the kabuki actor Sawamura Tanosuke, which reworks conventions of the poison-woman narratives so popular in the late Meiji period (Reichert, *In the Company of Men,* 36–64).

55. Pflugfelder, *Cartographies of Desire,* 5.

56. Edogawa and Inagaki, "Dōseiai no risō to genjitsu," 31. The literature of the Taishō and early Shōwa periods contains a number of provocative representations of love between women, especially schoolgirls, by authors as diverse as Yoshiya Nobuko (1896–1973), the author of the collection of short stories *Hana monogatari* (Flower tales); Tamura Toshiko (1884–1945), the author of the novella "Akirame" (Giving up); and Osaki Midori (1896–1971), author of the novella "Dai-nana kankai hōkō" (Wandering in the seventh realm).

57. Sedgwick, *Between Men,* 1–6.

58. Karatani, "The Discovery of the Child," 115.

59. Tanizaki, *Tanizaki Jun'ichirō zenshū,* 1:143–85; for Anthony Chambers's English translation, see Tanizaki, *The Children.*

60. Hunter, *The Emergence of Modern Japan,* 193–94; Jansen, *The Making of Modern Japan,* 537–48.

61. I recall having drinks in 2001 with a long retired professor who had himself been a schoolboy in the early Shōwa period. When I told him about my research interests, he advised me that it was fine to talk about, and even practice, male homoeroticism in one's youth, but when one grew up, that was no longer an appropriate topic of conversation, and he urged me to change my field of study for the sake of decorum.

## 1. Blow the Bloodstained Bugle

1. Soon after Kaita's death, Yamazaki Shōzō (1896–1945), a close friend and a fellow art student, collected Kaita's verse, diary, and letters for publication in the volume Murayama, *Kaita no utaeru* (Songs of Kaita). The following year, the same publisher published a second collection, containing Kaita's mystery-adventure stories, fragmentary manuscripts for plays, fantasies, diary entries, and two final testaments, as well as eulogistic remembrances by friends, fellow artists, and classmates: Murayama Kaita, *Kaita no utaeru sono go oyobi Kaita no hanashi* (Songs of Kaita continued, plus remembrances of Kaita). (From here onward, the title of this book will be abbreviated as *Kaita no utaeru sono go.*) Among them were the reminiscences of Kaita's cousin Yamamoto Kanae, a leading figure in the Nihon Bijutsuin and the artistic world of that time. In the mid-1910s, Kanae had played the role of mentor, urging his cousin to pursue art and even arranging for his young protégé to study art in Tokyo. See Kosaki, *Yamamoto Kanae hyōden.* According to Kaita's Tokyo roommate, the artist Mizuki Shin'ichi (1892–1988), Kanae also played an instrumental role in arranging for the posthumous publication of Kaita's works from the publishing house Ars, which was run by Kanae's brother-in-law, Kitahara Tetsuo (1892–1957). See Mizuki, "Akutagawa Ryūnosuke no yūjō."

2. For one of the later versions, see Mori Ōgai, *Omokage,* 105–67.

3. Keene, *Dawn to the West,* 2:218.

4. For instance, Anna Balakian draws a trajectory through the development of literature that begins with romanticism and passes through symbolism to arrive at surrealism (Balakian, *The Symbolist Movement,* 14).

5. Ibid., 70–71. Also see Cornell, *The Symbolist Movement,* 42.

6. Nicholls, *Modernisms,* 32.

7. Rimbaud, *Collected Poems,* 6 (emphasis in the original).

8. According to Earl Jackson, the word *shōchō* was first given a meaning corresponding to the word "symbol" in 1884 when political philosopher Nakae Chōmin (1847–1900) used it to translate the word *symbole,* which had appeared in *L'esthétique (The Aesthetic)* by Eugène Véron (1825–1879). Ueda Bin had been writing about the symbolists for some time before he used the word *shōchōha* in a 1904 article. See Jackson, "The Heresy of Meaning," 563–64.

9. Ueda, *Kaichōon*, 169–264.

10. Quoted in Keene, *Dawn to the West*, 2:228.

11. Ibid., 2:227.

12. *Kaichōon* was not exclusively dedicated to symbolist poetry. In fact, it included verses by figures as diverse as Sappho and William Shakespeare; however, it was the translations of French poems that had the greatest impact on the Japanese literary world.

13. Nicholls, *Modernisms*, 42. In a discussion of Mallarmé, whom Balakian believes to have set the tone of decadence in late nineteenth-century symbolist poetry, she writes, "'Symbolist and Decadent!' Too often histories of literature suggest that the famous 'and' is really an 'or.' But the 'and' is truer than the 'or,' and any suggestion of a duality is in truth a fallacy. The one could not exist without the other, and Mallarmé proves it from the very start by his own existence, in his writings as in his conversations" (Balakian, *The Symbolist Movement*, 81–82).

14. Kitahara Hakushū, *Hakushū zenshū*, 1:6.

15. "*Kaita no utaeru* by Murayama Kaita," 1.

16. Itō Kyō, "Nenpu," 172.

17. Iida Shizue, *Fūka*, 8.

18. Kaita is known to have sent six postcards to Oto in the decade between 1907 and 1917. Some of these are housed in the Ōgai Memorial Hongō Library (Ōgai Kinen Hongō Toshokan).

19. On Kaita's name, see Iida Shizue, *Fūka*, 8. For the mention of the Murayama children in Ōgai's diary, see Mori Ōgai, *Ōgai zenshū*, 35:467.

20. Mori Oto, *Chichi toshite no Ōgai*, 36, 149–50, 225–26.

21. Quoted in Noda, "'Pan no kai' no tanbiha shijin no tanjō," 314.

22. Unless otherwise noted, all references to the work of Murayama Kaita will be to the 1997 edition of Murayama, *Murayama Kaita zenshū* (The complete works of Murayama Kaita). Page numbers will appear in parentheses in the text.

23. Isoda, *Kindai no kanjō kakumei*.

24. In describing Kaita's early life in *Kaita no utaeru* and its sequel, Yamamoto Jirō, Yamazaki Shōzō, and Imazeki Keiji refer to Inō as either "Y" or "I." In the early twentieth century, many editors and writers added a Y to Japanese words beginning in an E or I; for instance, one often finds the city of Edo romanized as "Yedo."

25. Yamamoto Jirō, "Kaita no shi," 401–9. Kaita's mother's maiden name was Yamamoto, and therefore, Kaita had many relatives with this surname, such as his cousin, Yamamoto Kanae. Yamamoto Jirō, however, was not a blood relative.

26. Sasaki, *Ennin Murayama Kaita*, 67–70.

27. Imazeki and Yamazaki, "Murayama Kaita ryakuden," final section, 1. The first edition of *Kaita no utaeru* paginates each section anew, but a later reprinting from 1927 has continuous pagination.

28. Yamamoto Jirō, "Kaita no hatsukoi," 302.

29. Ibid., 300.

30. The friend who called his name may have been Hayashi Tatsuo (1896–1984), a younger schoolmate who later in life became a prominent intellectual historian. In a

series of biographical interviews, Hayashi recalls his older classmate's passion for the "incredible *bishōnen*" Inō. Hayashi says that because he lived on a rise directly above Inō's home, Kaita would frequently come and chat merely as an excuse to stare at Inō's house below (Hayashi Tatsuo, *Shisō no doramaturgii*, 144–45, 148–49).

31. Yamamoto Jirō, "Kaita no hatsukoi," 302.

32. Yamazaki Shōzō, "Saisho atta toki no Kaita," 308.

33. Childs, "Chigo Monogatari"; Childs, "Rethinking Sorrow"; Iwata Jun'ichi, "Nanshoku ishō shū," 281–88; Pflugfelder, *Cartographies of Desire*, 74–75.

34. Iwata Jun'ichi, "Nanshoku ishō shū," 281.

35. Takahashi Mutsuo, *Seishun o yomu*, 235.

36. For a discussion of the literary idioms shared by the work of Kaita, Hakushū, and his friends, see Higashi, "Aka no Kaita, aka no Hakushū," 148–54.

37. Kitahara, *Hakushū zenshū*, 2:84.

38. Itō Shinkichi, Itō Sei, and Inoue Yasushi, *Doi Bansui, Susukida Kyūkin, Kanbara Ariake, Miki Rofū*, 305.

39. The image of the silver flute, which appears in "Nigiyaka na yūgure" and the diary entries about Kaita's trips to Inō's home, is a particularly common motif used to express melancholy in Hakushū's work. See, for instance, Kitahara, *Hakushū zenshū*, 6:14.

40. Murayama, *Murayama Kaita ten*, 181. Incidentally, the pink love letter shows no signs of ever having been folded to fit in an envelope, and it remained with Kaita's sketches and writings until its purchase in 1992. Judging from these facts, it seems to have never been sent.

41. Satō Akira, *Funsui shi kenkyū*, 381–83.

42. Kitahara, *Hakushū zenshū*, 1:92–93.

43. Ibid., 2:86.

44. Takahashi Mutsuo, "Chi no teki mote," 70–71.

45. Kitahara, *Hakushū zenshū*, 1:6.

46. See Yosano and Yosano, *Tekkan Akiko zenshū*, 2:77–125, and Ishikawa, *Takuboku zenshū*, 1:1–104. Selections from Yosano Akiko's *Midaregami* are available in several translations, including those by Sanford Goldstein and Seishi Shinoda in Yosano, *Tangled Hair*; by Edward Cranston in Yosano, "Carmine-Purple"; and by Janine Beichman in her book *Embracing the Firebird*. On Akiko's contributions to modern Japanese poetry, see Beichman's book and Morton's insightful chapter "The Birth of the Modern." Ishikawa Takuboku's poetry is also available in several translations, including those by Carl Sesar in Ishikawa, *Poems to Eat*; by Sanford Goldstein and Seishi Shinoda in Ishikawa, *Romaji Diary and Sad Toys*; and by Tamae Prindle in Ishikawa, *On Knowing Oneself Too Well*.

47. Quoted in "*Kaita no utaeru* by Murayama Kaita," 1.

48. Tamaki Tōru, *Shōwa tanka made*, 6.

49. The original Japanese is provided for this and other tanka poems in this chapter. Because tanka poems are short and dense, and often involve word play, it is common practice in English-language studies to provide the original when giving a translation.

In addition, it is difficult to locate tanka poems in collections, since typically authors write many of them and they do not have individual titles.

50. Japanese has many possible words that could have filled the missing words, including *dankon* (男根), *inkei* (陰茎), and the slang *chinboko* (ちんぼこ), all of which are different ways to refer to the male member. Unfortunately, because so little remains of the third poem, it is difficult to guess the word Kaita used.

51. Yamamoto Tarō, the editor of Kaita's complete works, suggests that the missing words might be *saru* (猿), meaning "monkeys," and *gunjin* (軍人), meaning "soldiers" (64). "Monkeys" is certainly derogatory enough that editors might have removed it, but the word "soldiers" in the final line is not offensive. More insulting words, however, like *ahō* (阿呆), *baka* (馬鹿), or *gusha* (愚者), all of which deride the addressee's intelligence, better fit the context.

## 2. Treading the Edges of the Known World

1. Nakajima, *Nihon suiri shōsetsu shi*, 1:187. The stories all appear in Kaita's collection of posthumous works *Kaita no utaeru sono go* under the rubric *kaiki shōsetsu*.

2. Suzuki Sadami, "Kaita no jidai," 165.

3. Yamamoto Kanae, *Yamamoto Kanae no tegami*, 68.

4. For my translation of the story, see Murayama, "The Bust of the Beautiful Young Salaino," 66–69.

5. On Leonardo and Salaino's relationship, see Clark, *Leonardo da Vinci*, 58–59.

6. In 1910, Sigmund Freud (1859–1939) wrote the article "Leonardo da Vinci and a Memory of His Childhood," which was particularly influential in spreading the image of Leonardo as a homosexual in the West. Freud draws on several facts from Leonardo's life to speculate about Leonardo's sexual orientation: the charge that Leonardo had engaged in "immoral" acts with a model of ill repute in 1476, a statement in Leonardo's notebooks expressing revulsion for heterosexual coupling, the closeness of his relationships with his students, and a perceived androgyny in some of his paintings (Freud, *Leonardo da Vinci and a Memory of His Childhood*, 57–137). Even though this article was widely read in the West, Kaita could not have read it. The article was first translated into English in 1916, and given Kaita's lack of familiarity with German, it is impossible that he could have read it before writing "Bishōnen Saraino no kubi" in late 1913 or early 1914.

7. *The Renaissance* was published in book form in Japanese twice during the Taishō period, first in 1915 by Tanabe Jūji as *Bungei fūkō*, then again in 1921 by Sakuma Masakazu as *Runesansu*. Pater's work was well known in Taishō-period Japan even before Tanabe's translation; in fact, one character in Tanizaki Jun'ichirō's novella *Konjiki no shi* (A golden death), which was serialized for two weeks in a Tokyo newspaper in December 1914, discusses it in the midst of a conversation on aesthetics (Tanizaki, *Tanizaki Jun'ichirō zenshū*, 2:479).

8. Pater, *The Renaissance*, 91–92.

9. In one of the earliest biographies of Leonardo, Giorgio Vasari describes a remarkably realistic image of the Medusa painted by the master (Vasari, *The Lives of*

*the Artists,* 288). After 1540, when the Medusa hung in the Palazzo della Signora, it vanished. The mistaken connection between the painting of a Medusa in the Uffizi and the one described in Vasari's biography dates to the late eighteenth century. See Turner, *Inventing Leonardo,* 114–17.

10. Pater, *The Renaissance,* 82. Hans Christian Andersen's novel *The Improvisatore,* which Kaita read and loved in Mori Ōgai's famous translation *Sokkyō shijin,* also describes this painting, emphasizing the horrifying beauty in the work: "Leonardo da Vinci has painted a Medusa's head, which is in the gallery at Florence. Everyone who sees it is strangely captivated by it, and cannot tear themselves away. It is as if the deep, out of froth and poison, had formed the most beautiful shape—as if the foam of the abyss had fashioned a Medician Venus" (Andersen, *The Improvisatore,* 94).

11. Ross, *The Rest Is Noise,* 3.

12. *Salome* appeared in Mori Rintarō [Ōgai]'s 1910 collection *Zoku hitomakumono* (More one-act plays), which was then combined with an earlier collection of plays to produce Mori Rintarō [Ōgai]'s 1912 collection *Hitomakumono* (One-act plays). A detailed summary of Wilde's play also appeared in the following book, which was designed for younger audiences, perhaps around Kaita's age: Araki, *Kindai geki monogatari,* 1:184–96.

13. Murayama, *Murayama Kaita ten,* 181.

14. Ogawa, *Sekai bijutsu shi,* 1:190–91.

15. Iwamura, *Seiyō bijutsu shiyō,* 79.

16. Vasari, *The Lives of the Artists,* 293. For the development of Leonardo's hagiography in Europe, see Turner, *Inventing Leonardo.*

17. Ueda, "Reonarudo da Winchi (Jo)," 5.

18. Ibid., 1.

19. Ibid., 2.

20. Takayama, "Tensai ron." In 1895 and 1896 a number of prominent cultural and literary figures wrote articles about the theory of genius, but Chogyū's piece is one of the best known.

21. Sasaki, *Ennin Murayama Kaita,* 61–66. About the use of the nickname Mona Lisa for Sasa Sao, see Yamamoto Sanzō, "Kaita to obasan," 322–23. For a history of the famous painting and the research on it, see Satō Michiko, "Murayama Kaita 'Kosui to onna' o megutte," 124–31.

22. Nakajima, *Nihon suiri shōsetsu shi,* 1:184–85.

23. Shunrō entered the publishing company Hakubunkan at the introduction of the author Iwaya Sazanami and served as a lead reporter for *Shajitsu gahō* (Graphic pictorial), a magazine that featured photos and stories about the Russo-Japanese War. The magazine ceased publication in 1907. The following year, Shunrō joined the editorial crew of *Bōken sekai.* Shunrō is best remembered in Japan for his important role in developing the "adventure story" into an independent genre of children's fiction.

24. Under the pseudonym Kosugi Hōan, Misei would in future years also become well known for his oil paintings on Japanese and Chinese themes and his tanka poetry.

25. Higashi, "Tare ka ibari suru," 178.

26. Pflugfelder, *Cartographies of Desire*, 203.

27. On *Shizu no odamaki*, see Reichert, *In the Company of Men*, 17–35.

28. Ozaki, "Bishōnen no kenkyū," 540. The popular association notion of Satsuma as a den of male–male eroticism circulated not just in Japan but in the West as well. In 1902 the author of children's fiction Iwaya Sazanami (1870–1933), who was teaching in Germany, was asked to contribute an article to the annual publication of the Wissenschaftlich-humanitäre Komitee (Scientific-Humanitarian Committee), which had been founded by Magnus Hirschfeld five years earlier. The result was Iwaya, "Nan-šo-k,'" 265–71. This article describes Satsuma as a place where male–male eroticism was practiced extensively. The British socialist critic Edward Carpenter (1844–1929) draws on Iwaya's article in his chapter about same-sex eroticism in *Intermediate Types among Primitive Folk*, which quotes Iwaya as stating that male–male desire "has spread more widely in the Southern part [of Japan] than in the Northern provinces. There are regions where the general public knows nothing of it. On the other hand, in Kyushu, and especially in Satsuma, it is from of old very wide spread." Like other writers who emphasized a connection between martial prowess and the practice of male–male desire, Iwaya states that one possible reason is that Satsuma natives "prize courage and manliness so very highly." He states that it is common to hear "that the population in those provinces where the love of youths prevail is more manly and robust, while in regions which are void of it the people are softer, more lax, and often more dissolute." See Carpenter, *Intermediate Types among Primitive Folk*, 148.

29. Habuto and Sawada, *Hentai seiyoku ron*, 345.

30. Ōtsuki, *Ren'ai seiyoku no shinri to sono bunseki shochi hō*, 228.

31. For my translation of the story, see Murayama, "The Diabolical Tongue."

32. Freud, *The Interpretation of Dreams*, 354–56.

33. Hamada, "Murayama Kaita no tantei shōsetsu," 207–10.

## 3. The Appeal of the Strange

1. Silverberg, *Erotic Grotesque Nonsense*, 4.

2. Ibid., 33.

3. Silver, *Purloined Letters*, 132–37.

4. Jacobowitz, introduction, xxii–xxiii.

5. On the history of the Japanese crime and mystery fiction, see the three-volume Nakajima, *Nihon suiri shōsetsu shi*, and Itō Hideo's four books, *Meiji no tantei shōsetsu*, *Taishō no tantei shōsetsu*, *Shōwa no tantei shōsetsu*, and *Kindai no tantei shōsetsu*. In English, see Omori, "Detecting Japanese Vernacular Modernism"; Silver, *Purloined Letters*; and the excellent study Kawana, *Murder Most Modern*.

6. Unless otherwise noted, all references to the works of Ranpo will be to *Edogawa Ranpo zenshū*, the 1978–79 edition of Ranpo's complete works published by Kōdansha. Volume and page numbers will appear in parenthesis in the text. For my English translation of "Ni-sen dōka," see Edogawa, "The Two-Sen Copper Coin."

7. Kozakai, "'Ni-sen dōka' o yomu," 264–65.

8. For example, see Minami, "Nihon modanizumu ni tsuite," 7–9; Suzuki Sadami, "Eroticism, Grotesquerie, and Nonsense in Taishō Japan," 41–53.

9. Two works that have been particularly useful in interpreting the literature created during the fad for *ero, guro, nansensu* as reflecting social currents and ideological trends are Suzuki Sadami's books *Shōwa bungaku no tame ni* and *Modan toshi no hyōgen*. Another provocative study published at just the moment this book went to press is Driscoll, *Absolute Erotic, Absolute Grotesque*.

10. Nakayama, *Modan-go manga jiten*, 635.

11. Gendai henshūkyoku, *Gendai shingo jiten*, 474–75.

12. *Yomiuri shinbun*, November 3, 1929, morning edition, 1.

13. Satō Giryō, *Gendai ryōki sentan zukan*.

14. On the term *ryōki*, its use, and the connections that Shōwa-period commentators drew between *ryōki* and modern existence, see Angles, "Seeking the Strange."

15. Nakayama, *Modan-go manga jiten*, 635.

16. Kojima, *Bunruishiki modan shin yōgo jiten*, 142. This volume does not contain an entry for *ryōki*.

17. Gendai henshūkyoku, *Gendai shingo jiten*, 474–75.

18. Hayasaka and Matsumoto, *Sentango hyakka jiten*, 392.

19. For a complete translation by Seth Jacobowitz, see Edogawa Rampo, *The Edogawa Rampo Reader*, 43–80. The translations of the quotations that appear here, however, are my own.

20. Tanizaki, *Tanizaki Jun'ichirō zenshū*, 1:247–70. For a translation by Anthony Chambers, see Tanizaki, "The Secret," 47–68.

21. For a translation by Ian Hughes, see Edogawa Rampo, *The Black Lizard and Beast in the Shadows*, 175–277.

22. Hosoma, *Asakusa jū-ni-kai*.

23. The story has been translated into English twice: first by James B. Harris in Rampo Edogawa, *Japanese Tales of Mystery and Imagination*, 195–222, then by Michael Tangeman in Edogawa, "The Man Traveling with the Brocade Portrait," 376–93.

24. Quoted in Inoue, *Ai no kūkan*, 46.

25. Ibid., 45–49.

26. Inagaki Taruho, "Shōnen tokuhon," 61.

27. Kataoka, "Rōkō," <Sōsaku> 3.

28. Hamao, "Dōseiai kō," 140–41. The Andō Kōsei passage is quoted in Furukawa, "The Changing Nature of Sexuality," 106. In another anecdote about eroticism in public places, Hamao relates the following humorous story: "A certain young policeman was walking through XXX Park when a certain foreigner called to him, saying 'Keikan, keikan!' When he looked, he saw that the foreigner had a five-yen bill in his hand and was making an odd gesture. At that point, the officer realized that what the foreigner was calling out was not the word *keikan* meaning 'police' [but the homophone meaning 'sodomy']." The name of the park has been blocked out by *fuseji*, but because there are three characters missing, it seems clear that the name of the park is Hibiya, which is written with three characters ( 日比谷 ).

29. See Ranpo's article "Asakusa shumi" (A taste for Asakusa, 16:21–25), published in *Shin seinen* in 1926, and his memoirs (20:109–12). Long descriptions of Asakusa Park appear in the beginnings of *Yami ni ugomeku* (2:182–83) and "Monoguramu" ("The Monogram," 2:267–68), both published in 1926.

30. "Shin'ya no Asakusa ni runpen to kataru Edogawa Ranpo-shi."

31. Silverberg, "Constructing Japanese Cultural History," 123–24.

32. Silver, *Purloined Letters,* 166. Other commentary on this novel includes Pflugfelder, *Cartographies of Desire,* 314–15; Reichert, "Deviance and Social Darwinism," 113–41; Taguchi, "*Kotō no oni* ron," 109–14; and Tsuikawa, "Shōsetsu no naka no dōseiai," 39–45.

33. Reichert, "Deviance and Social Darwinism," 120. Reichert has also published a modified version of this article that does not include this quote: Reichert, "Disciplining the Erotic-Grotesque in Edogawa Ranpo's *Demon of the Lonely Isle.*"

34. Ibid., 122.

35. One contemporary edition of the text that shows the way the novel was serialized appears in the Edogawa Ranpo Series 1 published by Sōgen Suiri Bunko in 1987 (see Edogawa, *Kotō no oni*). This edition includes the illustrated headings at the beginning of each installment of the story and the illustrations that accompanied the story.

36. Because the names of many of the characters are unusual, I have referred to the *furigana* glosses in the magazine *Asahi*. Several other English-language studies of *Kotō no oni* contain other readings of these names, no doubt due to their rarity.

37. The line break is present in the first publication of the text in Edogawa, *Kotō no oni, Asahi* 1, no. 1 (January 1929): 120.

38. The Toba Minato Machi Bungakukan (The Toba Porttown Literary Museum) has in its collection a copy of a short home movie that Ranpo shot while visiting Iwata Jun'ichi. On a trip to the Shinjūshima (Pearl Island) in Toba Bay, Ranpo filmed a series of extreme close-up shots that show the bodies of the island's diver women in extreme, almost grotesque detail. It seems possible that the uncomfortably exaggerated bodies he captured on film there could have inspired the visions of the grotesquely deformed people that appear in *Kotō no oni* or his 1926–27 novella *Panorama-tō kidan* (The strange tale of Panorama Isle), which contains a scene featuring the oddly exaggerated body of a female diver.

39. Edogawa, *Kotō no oni, Asahi* 1, no. 2 (February 1929): 286.

40. Edogawa, *Kotō no oni, Asahi* 1, no. 5 (May 1929): 132–33.

41. Iwata Jun'ichi's granddaughter Iwata Junko draws upon this essay, plus her grandfather's unpublished letters, diaries, and other writings, to build a fictionalized account of the relationship in her novel *Ni seinen zu* (Portrait of two young men). This novel describes Iwata as being madly in love with Ranpo, while Ranpo does not return his affections. In a conversation I had with Iwata Junko in July 2010, she mentioned that in researching the novel, she could find no conclusive proof that would indicate the relationship between Iwata and Ranpo spilled over into the homoerotic, but there was no question that their friendship contained a very special dimension (Iwata Junko, personal communication, July 9, 2010). In its attempt to draw some parallels between

the novel *Kotō no oni* and Ranpo and Iwata's real-life relationship, *Ni seinen zu* does note a number of similarities between the two men and the characters in *Kotō no oni*. In the novel, there is a six-year age difference between Moroto and Minoura, just like that between Ranpo, who was born in 1894, and Iwata, who was born in 1900. Moreover, Iwata was from Toba in the southern Kii Peninsula, the same reigion Moroto's bizarre island was located, and Ranpo was, like Minoura, a visitor from elsewhere (Iwata Junko, *Ni seinen zu*, 178).

42. For Takenaka's illustrations of the scene, see Edogawa, *Kotō no oni*, 354–55, 364–65. On these images and their role in constructing the text, see Reichert, "Deviance and Social Darwinism," 123–26, and Reichert, "Disciplining the Erotic-Grotesque," 362–65.

43. Andersen, *The Improvisatore*, 10–11; Mori Ōgai, *Ōgai zenshū*, 2:228–29.

44. Andersen, *The Improvisatore*, 11; Mori Ōgai, *Ōgai zenshū*, 2:229.

45. Reichert, "Deviance and Social Darwinism," 134.

## 4. (Re)Discovering Same-Sex Love

1. Dinshaw, *Getting Medieval*, 1.

2. Ibid., 21.

3. Love, *Feeling Backward*, 37.

4. On Hamao's past, see Itō Hideo, *Kindai no tantei shōsetsu*, 277–96; Nakajima, *Nihon suiri shōsetsu shi*, 3:11–17, 42–47; Ōuchi, "Hamao Shirō no hito to sakuhin," 1:525–38, 2:607–20; Angles, "Hamao Shirō's 'The Execution of Ten'ichibō,'" 307–10.

5. Hamao, "Hentaisei no hanzai ni tsuite," 277–82. See also Hamao, "Hentai satsujin kō," 190–205.

6. Hamao, "Hentaisei no hanzai ni tsuite," 281.

7. Pflugfelder, *Cartographies of Desire*, 159–69.

8. Quoted in ibid., 170. See also Furukawa, "The Changing Nature of Sexuality," 110.

9. Habuto and Sawada, *Hentai seiyoku ron*, 106.

10. Hamao, "Dōseiai kō," 137.

11. Ibid., 136.

12. Carpenter, *The Intermediate Sex*, 192.

13. Hamao, "Dōseiai kō," 138.

14. Ibid., 137.

15. Ibid., 139.

16. Ibid. The argument that same-sex desire goes hand-in-hand with pedagogical relationships appears in a slightly less problematic form in Carpenter's *The Intermediate Sex* (222), which discusses at great length the importance of same-sex bonds in education.

17. Hamao, "Dōseiai kō," 138.

18. Ibid., 141–42.

19. Ibid., 142.

20. Hamao, "Futatabi dōseiai ni tsuite," 58–59.

21. On the power relations inherent in medical and popular sexological discourse, see Pflugfelder, *Cartographies of Desire,* 296.

22. Hamao, "Futatabi dōseiai ni tsuite," 60.

23. Ibid., 62.

24. Ibid. (emphasis in the original).

25. Carpenter, *The Intermediate Sex,* 211.

26. Hamao, "Futatabi dōseiai ni tsuite," 63.

27. Carpenter, *The Intermediate Sex,* 211–12.

28. Hamao, *Kare ga koroshita ka?* 73.

29. Hamao, "Madamu no satsujin," 340–53.

30. Hamao, "Akuma no deshi," *Hamao Shirō shū,* 83–124.

31. Ibid., 86.

32. Ibid., 91–92.

33. Ibid., 94.

34. Vincent, "Hamaosociality."

35. Hamao, "Akuma no deshi," *Shin seinen,* 168–98.

36. Hamao, "Futatabi dōseiai ni tsuite," 64–65.

37. Carpenter, *The Intermediate Sex,* 186.

38. Ibid., 187.

39. Ibid., 237.

40. Ibid., 238.

41. Yamakawa then republished the work in book form in 1919 as Carpenter, "Dōsei no ai."

42. Carpenter, *Ioläus.*

43. Carpenter, *Intermediate Types among Primitive Folk,* 9.

44. Ibid., 146–47.

45. Karsch-Haack, "Das gleichgeschlechtliche Leben der Ostasiaten Kulturvölker," 111–13.

46. Bakin's edition appears with a postscript by him in Kyokutei, "Mokuzu monogatari," 380–95. Also see Shokusanjin [Ōta Nanpo], "Amayo monogatari," 411–32. Ranpo mentions that the popular writer Ryūtei Tanehiko (1783–1842) also owned a version of the story (17:59).

47. Ihara, "Nanshoku ōkagami," 398–406; Ihara, *The Great Mirror of Male Love,* 143–50. Ranpo eventually bought a copy of *Nanshoku giri monogatari* published after 1640. A facsimile of Ranpo's personal copy is available as *Nanshoku giri monogatari,* 1–106.

48. Edogawa, "Shudō mokuzuzuka," 320–26. In later reprintings, the word *shudō* was dropped from the title, which became simply "Mokuzuzuka" (Mokuzu mound). My discussion of this essay builds upon an earlier exploration of this subject in Angles, "Haunted by the Sexy Samurai," 101–9.

49. Derrida, *Specters of Marx,* 37–48.

50. Brown, *Politics Out of History,* 150.

51. De Certeau, *The Writing of History,* 2.

52. Freccero, *Queer/Early/Modern*, 80.

53. Ibid., 101.

54. Habuto and Sawada, *Hentai seiyoku ron*, 320–24.

55. The essay "Dōseiai bungaku shi: Iwata Jun'ichi-kun no omoide," published in 1952, contains a list of old volumes in his collection (22:48).

56. Edogawa, *Edogawa Ranpo suiri bunko*, 60:91.

57. Ranpo contains a partial list of Western works he found in 22:46. The list contains many now-famous nineteenth-century and early twentieth century treatises on the subject, including works by Ulrichs, Krafft-Ebing, Hirschfeld, and Karsch-Haack.

58. Iwata's son has asserted that a number of drawings commonly believed to be by Yumeji are actually the work of his young protégé (Iwata Sadao, "Bōfu Iwata Jun'ichi," 57).

59. Iwata's granddaughter has provided a highly fictionalized account of the meeting in Iwata Junko, *Ni seinen zu*, 9–25, but the details of Iwata's earliest encounter with Ranpo are unknown.

60. The entry of Iwata's diary which describes this meeting is quoted in Iwata Kyōnosuke [Iwata Sadao], "Tōkyō Hongō 'Ise Sakae Ryokan' no yoru," 28. The diary entry was dated November 13, 1925.

61. Edogawa, "Iwata Jun'ichi-kun no sashie," 2.

62. Edogawa, *Edogawa Ranpo suiri bunko*, 60:89.

63. Ibid., 60:91.

64. The estates have not yet granted researchers access to the letters. In late November 2001, when Iwata's son discussed their existence to the press, a number of Japanese newspapers ran stories about them. See "Dōseiai kenkyū"; "Edogawa Ranpo no shokan"; Hayashi Mikihiro, "Edogawa Ranpo." Iwata's son has since passed away, but his granddaughter, Iwata Junko, has mentioned to me that the letters are somewhat businesslike and do not provide a great deal of insight into the personal relationship between the two writers, yet she hopes to publish them, along with Iwata's diaries, at some point in the future (Iwata Junko, personal communication, July 9, 2010).

65. Minakata and Iwata, *Minakata Kumagusu nanshoku dangi*. Selections have been translated by William F. Sibley as Minakata and Iwata, "Morning Fog," 134–71.

66. Iwata Jun'ichi, *Honchō nanshoku kō*. Parts of this book have been translated in Watanabe and Iwata, *The Love of the Samurai*.

67. This title refers to *Iwatsutsuji (Wild Azaleas)*, an anthology of Japanese verse on male–male desire compiled by Kitamura Kigin (1624–1705). For a translation by Paul Schalow, see Kitamura Kigin, "Wild Azaleas," 97–124.

68. With an introduction from Ranpo, the bibliography started to appear in the magazine *Kisho* (Rare books), but the magazine went out of print in the middle of serialization. Thanks again to Ranpo's help, Iwata's bibliography finally appeared in its entirety as *Nanshoku bunken shoshi* (Bibliography of resources on male love), published in 1956.

69. For more on Kaita's influences on Ranpo's writing, see Angles, "Writing the Love of Boys," 163–67.

70. Kaita's work appeared in the first annual Nika exhibition in 1914, the first Nihon Bijutsuin Shūsaku Ten (Japan Art Institute Study Exhibition) in 1915, and the second Saikō Nihon Bijtsuin-ten (Restored Japan Art Institute Exhibition) in 1915. All of these exhibitions were held in Ueno. *Ni shōnen zu* did not appear in any of them, however. The first public showing of this painting was apparently a posthumous, commemorative exhibition organized by Kaita's friends and held November 11–30, 1919, in Jinbochō, Tokyo. In describing this exhibition, an art critic for the *Yomiuri shinbun* (Yomiuri News) put this watercolor at the top of a list of Kaita's work ("Kioku ni atai suru Kaita shi no geijutsu"). The catalogue for the exhibition shows that it was in the private collection of a certain Mr. Hayada at the time (*Murayama Kaita isaku tenrankai mokuroku*, 78).

71. Yoshida, "Bundan kōgengaku," 144–46.

72. Yanase, "Murayama Kaita-kun," unpag.

73. Sasaki, *Ennin Murayama Kaita*, 85–89.

74. Yamamoto Jirō, "Kaita no hatsukoi," 302.

75. Ranpo surmises the passage consists of some random jottings or Yamamoto's reconstitution of something Kaita once told him, but their exact origin is unclear. The passage appears nowhere in Kaita's extant works, only in Yamamoto Jirō's reminiscences.

76. Yamamoto, "Kaita no hatsukoi," 301.

77. Sasaki Teru suggests that the flora and the clothing indicate the scene is in late summer or early autumn (Sasaki, *Ennin Murayama Kaita*, 85–86).

78. This short essay appeared in the first edition of *Tantei shōsetsu yon-jū-nen* (Forty years of detective fiction), where it was written in small font and enclosed in a box. Ranpo was famous for hating blank pages in his books. When publishers returned to him galleys of his essays, he would sometimes write short essays to fill pages that had only a few lines on them. This essay was one of those space-fillers (Edogawa, *Tantei shōsetsu yon-jū-nen*, 196).

79. Sunaga, "Shōnen," 44.

80. Furukawa, "Ranpo to dōseiai," 120.

81. Habuto and Sawada, *Hentai seiyoku ron*, 314.

82. Matsunaga, "Yume to seisei," 255–58.

83. For a complete translation by Seth Jacobowitz, see Edogawa, *The Edogawa Rampo Reader*, 173–80. The quotations that appear here, however, are my own translations.

84. Furukawa, "Edogawa Ranpo no hisoka naru jōnetsu," 62.

85. Ranpo later revised the title of the essay to simply "Ren'ai funōsha" (Impotent in love).

86. Not coincidentally, the historian of sexuality Inoue Shōichi finds it was in the early Shōwa period that Japanese women began to wear Western-style underwear for fear of people glimpsing their genitals under their dresses or through the opening of a kimono (Inoue, *Pantsu ga mieru*).

87. In 1935 Musei had written an article for *Shin seinen* called "Edogawa Ranpo-shi no shikyō o kiku" (Inquiring after Mr. Edogawa Ranpo's state of mind). In it, he notes

an apparent contraction between Ranpo's soft, even slightly feminine personal demeanor and the horrifyingly bloody scenes in his novels. He states that the reason for this probably lies in "perverse psychology" *(hentai shinri)*, or more specifically, Ranpo's "perverse sexual desires" *(hentai seiyoku)*. He speculates that Ranpo "probably has more feminine traits than the ordinary person not just in his face, but also in his heart." Musei does not speculate outright that Ranpo prefers sleeping with men, but this is clearly what he is insinuating. Musei was probably trying to amuse his audience by applying the label of "perverse psychology" that often appears in Ranpo's novels to the author himself, but at the same time, his article reflects the kinds of speculations that most likely went through the minds of many fans who had read Ranpo's autobiographical essays (Tokugawa, "Edogawa Ranpo-shi no shikyō o kiku," 285–88).

88. Gide, *If It Die . . .* , 116. Critic Paul Robinson states that in this scene Gide "points, almost too obviously, to his secret destiny" as a man who loves men (Robinson, *Gay Lives,* 190).

89. Sunaga Asahiko finds it an "interesting" coincidence that Ranpo wrote *Kare* about the same time he began writing his numerous articles about *dōseiai* in literature (Sunaga, "Ranpo no hisoka naru jōnetsu," 185). Ultimately, however, it is unclear whether the "certain incident having to do with sexual desire" that caused Ranpo to quit writing necessarily had to do with male–male eroticism. It could have also had to do with other sexual feelings or acts, such as masturbation. (Gide's autobiography, which inspired Ranpo to try writing his, describes in some detail his discovery of masturbation and his feelings regarding the act, so it is not impossible that Ranpo considering writing about a similar subject but decided in the end not to.)

90. The editions he purchased were the fifteen-volume *Seishin bunseki taikei* (Survey of psychoanalysis), translated by Yasuda Tokutarō, Marui Kiyoyasu, Masaki Fujokyū, et al., and published in 1929–33, and the ten-volume *Furoido seishin bunseki-gaku zenshū* (Complete works of Freud's psychoanalysis), translated by Ōtsuki Kenji, Hasegawa Seiya, Yabe Yaekichi, et al., and published in 1930–33.

91. "Edogawa Ranpo to no shinkō," 51.

92. Ranpo would write again about Symonds multiple times, most notably in "Hoittoman no hanashi" (About Whitman), an essay for *Shin seinen* that describes Symonds's correspondence with Walt Whitman (17:63–66); in "Shimonzu, Cāpentā, Jīdo," a 1936 essay for an encyclopedia of world literature (17:66–68); and in an extended passage in his memoirs (20:283–85). Symonds's name also appears briefly in numerous other essays, such as the 1940 essay "Shosai no tabi" (Travels in my study, 17:53).

93. Symonds and Brown, *John Addington Symonds.* Another major source was Babington, *Bibliography of the Writings of John Addington Symonds.*

94. Symonds describes the purpose of his memoirs in the unexpurgated version found in Symonds, *The Memoirs of John Addington Symonds,* 182–83.

95. Ibid., 77.

96. Symonds, *In the Key of Blue,* 76. Ranpo read the essay in a translation by Tanabe Jūji (1884–1972).

97. Symonds, *The Life of Michelangelo Buonarotti*.

98. Symonds, *Studies of the Greek Poets*, 64.

99. Traubel, *With Walt Whitman in Camden*, 75–76.

100. Ibid., 202–5, 288, 387–88, 457–60.

101. Symonds, *A Problem in Modern Ethics*. Symonds does not include the entire letter. For the entire text, see Whitman, *Selected Letters of Walt Whitman*, 282–83.

102. The fact that Symonds essentially agreed with Whitman (at least on paper) is clear from his response. On September 5, 1890, he wrote to Whitman, "I am not surprised; for this indeed is what I understood to be your meaning, since I have studied Leaves of Grass in the right way—interpreting each part by reference to the whole and in the spirit of the whole. The result of this study was that the 'adhesiveness' of comradeship had no interblending with the 'amativeness' of sexual love." Still, Symonds goes on to point out that eroticism and camaraderie could spill into one another: "Yet you must not think that the 'morbid inferences,' which to you 'seem damnable,' are quite 'gratuitous' or outside the range of possibility." He points out that the feelings Whitman describes are like those of the early Greeks with their "enthusiasm of comradeship in arms" and like those of the "certain percentage (small but appreciable) of male beings" who are born with "inverted" tendencies. Still, in the end, Symonds emphasizes that one should think of homosocial camaraderie and homoeroticism as separate entities: "I am so profoundly convinced that you are right in all you say about the great good which is to be expected from Comradeship as you conceive it, and as alone it can be a salutary human bond, that the power of repudiating those 'morbid inferences' authoritatively—should they ever be made seriously or uttered openly, either by your detractors of by the partizans of some vicious crankiness—sets me quite at ease as to my own course" (Symonds, *The Letters of John Addington Symonds*, 3:493).

103. Diogenes Laertius, *Lives of Eminent Philosophers*; Athenaeus of Naucratis, *The Deipnosophists*.

104. Paton, "Strato's 'Musa Puerilis,'" 280–413.

105. Ibid., 287.

106. Symonds, *Studies of the Greek Poets*, 525.

107. Edogawa, *Edogawa Ranpo suiri bunko*, 60:44–45.

108. Paton, "Strato's 'Musa Puerilis,'" 289.

109. Halperin, *How to Do the History of Homosexuality*, 17.

110. This story has been translated twice, first by James Harris in Edogawa, *Japanese Tales of Mystery and Imagination*, 67–88, and later by Michael Tangeman in Edogawa, "The Caterpillar," 406–22.

111. Reprinted as Edogawa and Inagaki, "Dōseiai no risō to genjitsu." For Ranpo's comments on the conversation, see 22:46.

5. Uninscribing the Adolescent Body

1. The quote comes from Taruho's own notes in Edogawa, "Hagiwara Sakutarō to Inagaki Taruho," 275. Hagiwara, who thought of himself as somewhat of a misanthrope, describes his unusually close friendship with Taruho and his circle of

decadent and nihilistic poet friends in Hagiwara, "Maruyama Kaoru to Kinumaki Seizō," 278–81.

2. Edogawa, "Hagiwara Sakutarō to Inagaki Taruho," 273.

3. Ibid., 274.

4. Reprinted as Edogawa and Inagaki, "Dōseiai no risō to genjitsu," 26–33.

5. See Taruho's added comments in Edogawa, "Hagiwara Sakutarō to Inagaki Taruho," 274.

6. Omuka, *Taishō-ki shikō bijutsu undō no kenkyū*, 188–97, and Omuka, "Dai-ni-kai mirai-ha bijutsu kyōkai ten (1921-nen kaisai) to shijin-tachi." Hirato Renkichi's 'Nihon mirai-ha sengen undō' (Manifesto of the Japanese Futurist Movement) was displayed at the door. On Hirato's brand of futurism, see Hirata, *The Poetry and Poetics of Nishiwaki Junzaburō*, 133–34; Sas, "Subject, City, Machine," 204–13; and Gardner, *Advertising Tower*, 93–94.

7. Inagaki Taruho, *Inagaki Taruho zenshū*, 1:3–43. Subsequent references to Taruho's complete works will appear in the body of the text with the volume and page numbers in parentheses. For Tricia Vita's English translation of *Issen ichi-byō monogatari*, see Inagaki Taruho, *One Thousand and One-Second Stories*.

8. Sas, "Subject, City, Machine," 217.

9. Takahashi Yasuo, "Kyōshū no genten," 6–7.

10. Kurutz, "The Only Safe and Sane Method . . ."

11. Takahashi Yasuo, "Kyōshū no genten," 11.

12. Takahashi Nobuyuki, "'Utsukushiki gakkō' o megutte," 8–9.

13. Portions of the following discussion about Taruho's brand of modernism and its relationship to homoeroticism build on Angles, "Queer Nonsense," 95–114.

14. Baudelaire, *Œuvres complètes*, 2:685. Also see Sheppard, *Modernism—Dada—Postmodernism*, 2; and Nicholls, *Modernisms*, 5.

15. Tyler, "Making Sense of *Nansensu*," 9.

16. Takahashi Nobuyuki, "'Utsukushiki gakkō' o megutte," 13.

17. For my translation of the story, see Inagaki Taruho, "Pince-Nez Glasses."

18. For some representative images by Takabatake, see the Web page of the Yayoi Museum in Tokyo (http://www.yayoi-yumeji-museum.jp/about/yayoi/collection.html) and the book *Takabatake Kashō: Bishōnen, bishōjo gen'ei*.

19. In this essay Taruho noted that he lived close to Takabatake Kashō in Tokyo and even had a mutual friend, but they had not met by the time Taruho wrote this essay.

20. Uno, "Aidoku suru ningen," 65. A photo of Taruho's own pince-nez glasses adorns the back cover of Korona Bukkusu Henshūbu's *Inagaki Taruho no sekai* (The world of Inagaki Taruho) published by Heibonsha in 2007.

21. For my translation of the story, see Inagaki Taruho, "The Story of R-chan and S."

22. On the terms used to describe love between schoolgirls in journalism and literature, see Pflugfelder, "'S' Is for Sister," 136–38; and Michiko Suzuki, "Writing Same-Sex Love," 577. For a study examining the ways that relationships between women

were viewed in the press after two well-known Takarazuka actresses committed suicide, see Robertson, "Dying to Tell," 9–11. Although Robertson's study does not focus exclusively on schoolgirl relationships, it does describe the language that women and others used to talk about passionate relationships between women.

23. On the representations of nonheteronormative desire in this and other works by Yoshiya Nobuko, see Michiko Suzuki's excellent work, "Writing Same-Sex Love," 575–99.

24. Tsurumi, "Sono toki no ketsudan," 324.

25. Pflugfelder, *Cartographies of Desire*, 248.

26. For more on the history of the theater and the role it played in the cultural life of Japan both in the era of modernism and in more contemporary times, see Robertson, *Takarazuka*.

27. Interestingly, Taruho added a classical Chinese epigraph by the Tang-dynasty poet Bo Juyi to later editions of the story. It reads, "A candle at our backs, together we are moved to pity by the deep night moon / Standing amongst the flowers, we yearn for the spring of our youth" (1:135). Although it creates a sentimental mood appropriate for this story of youth remembered, the epigraph comes from a poem, heavy with political overtones, in which Bo Juyi and his friend remember their youth before their political exile. Taruho has excised the political implications of the poem in favor of sentimentality, just as he has excluded any hint of an overtly political theme in the main body of "R-chan to S no hanashi" itself. For the full text of the poem, see Tanaka, *Haku Rakuten*, 24–25.

28. Butler, *Gender Trouble*, 138.

29. Sunaga, *Bishōnen Nihon shi*, 300.

30. Welker, "Beautiful, Borrowed, and Bent," 843. Welker is writing in particular about *shōjo manga* depicting male–male love.

31. Ibid., 866.

32. Kimura, *Mirai-ha oyobi rittai-hai no geijutsu*. On Taruho's reading about futurism, see Omuka, "Dai-ni-kai mirai-ha bijutsu kyōkai ten (1921-nen kaisai) to shijin-tachi," 297.

33. Included in Griffith, *Biograph Shorts*. In *The Massacre*, the soldiers are more fully clothed than in the descriptions within Taruho's story, but because he was writing in an era without videotape or digital reproduction, flaws in recollection, especially in recalling a scene that was no more than a few seconds long, may be inevitable.

34. Ozaki, "Bishōnen no kenkyū," 540.

35. It is commonly believed the first translation of Krafft-Ebing's work was banned by censors; however, Saitō Hikaru, a scholar of the history of sexuality, suggests this may be merely a legend, and he points to the existence of a second printing as proof (Saitō, "Hentai seiyoku shinri kaisetsu," 5).

CONCLUSION

1. On the mechanisms of censorship at this time, see Rubin, *Injurious to Public Morals*, 227–78.

2. Dower, *Embracing Defeat,* 148–49. The Japanese words for "three cups" and "three issues" are homophonic, both pronounced *sango,* thus allowing a double meaning for the phrase *sangome de tsubureru* (go under by the third).

3. Quoted in Rubin, "From Wholesomeness to Decadence," 81–82.

4. See Dower, *Embracing Defeat,* 149–50.

5. McLelland, *Queer Japan from the Pacific War to the Internet Age,* 60–66.

6. Ibid., 70–71.

7. Reprinted as Edogawa, "Honchō nanshoku kō ni tsuite," unpag.

8. Naka, *Edogawa Ranpo shippitsu nenpu,* 123.

9. Egawa Ranzō, "Kokan shitagi," 247. I thank Mark McLelland for sharing this and the other articles from *Kitan kurabu.*

10. Edogawa Ranzō, "Shisei sanka," 236.

11. Reprinted in Ōgon Dokuro no Kai, *Shōnen tanteidan dokuhon,* 140–41.

12. Ibid., 142–43; Setagaya Torikku Kenkyūkai, "Kobayashi shōnen wa tensai gaka no e ga moderu," 191–93; Shibusawa, "Ranpo bungaku no honshitsu," 405; Sunaga, *Bishōnen Nihon shi,* 303; and Terayama, "Shōnen tanteidan dōsōkai," 125–26.

13. Many scholars have attempted to make sense of Taruho's amusing and often contradictory theory of the "A-sensibility" and its relationship to the "P-sensibility" and the "V-sensibility." Among them, I have found the following two particularly helpful: Takahashi Mutsuo, *Otoko no kaibōgaku,* 48–51, and Takahara, *Muku no chikara,* 110–41. One of the reasons that Taruho's "theoretical" works are so challenging is that Taruho makes fleeting reference to an enormous number of scholars, historical events, and ideas, but provides no scholarly apparatus to cite those ideas or where they come from. Inagaki Miyako, Taruho's stepdaughter, has mentioned to me that Taruho kept almost no books in the house. He would borrow books from her, from friends, or from the library, and read then return them. Later, as he wrote, he would draw on the ideas of others solely from memory and thus did not always represent them accurately. As a result, when Taruho misrepresents an idea, it is sometimes difficult to know whether he was purposely being facetious or not. The fundamental point, however, remains that Taruho's text represents a playful, almost surreal amalgamation of ideas that valorize forms of desire and eroticism typically relegated to the periphery of respectability.

14. Inagaki Taruho, *Taruho han nanshoku ōkagami.*

15. Mark McLelland has pioneered the valuable work of examining the rise of a homosexual subculture in Tokyo, the journals they produced, and the images of masculinity and same-sex love presented within them. Particularly useful is the chapter "The Development of a *Homo* Subculture" in McLelland, *Queer Japan from the Pacific War to the Internet Age,* 127–57.

16. See Toku, "Shojo Manga! Girls' Comics!" 27.

17. See McLelland, *Male Homosexuality in Modern Japan,* 82–84, and Welker, "Beautiful, Borrowed, and Bent," 855–57.

18. Matsui, "Little Girls Were Little Boys," 179.

19. Takemiya, "Tsuki," 32.

20. Ishida, *Hisoyaka na kyōiku*, 284.

21. Ibid., 88–92. James Welker has investigated the historical rise of the word *shōnen'ai* and the complicated routes through which it came to be used as a signifier indicating a form of erotic desire as well as a specific subgenre of *shōjo manga* in Welker, "Transfiguring the Female," 126–37.

22. Ishida, *Hisoyaka na kyōiku*, 98.

23. Kinsella, *Adult Manga*, 108–10. The 2008 Comic Market, held December 28–30, had 35,000 registered circles (out of 49,000 who applied) and around 510,000 attendees. See Welker, "Transfiguring the Female," 71.

24. Kinsella, *Adult Manga*, 117–19.

25. Hirano, *Negachibu kotō no oni*, 4.

26. Ibid., 10. CBS stands for Chūō Broadcasting Service, a major Japanese televion channel.

27. Ibid., 64–65.

28. Ibid., 69.

29. See Shamoon, "Revolutionary Romance."

30. Hirano, *Negachibu kotō no oni*, 96.

31. Ibid., 102.

32. The survey is discussed in McLelland, *Male Homosexuality in Modern Japan*, 70. The results of this survey reflect my own experience telling friends and acquaintances in Japan about my own preference for men. Women are often far more curious than men, and on several occasions, young women have told me that after reading so many boys' love manga, they were happy finally to meet a gay man in person.

33. Ibid., 89–109.

34. McLelland, *Queer Japan from the Pacific War to the Internet Age*, 147.

35. The artist published the manga adaptation of *Kokoro* as Enomoto Nariko, the name she uses for her work about young men and women. (According to her Web site, she uses the penname Nobi Nobita for her *dōjinshi*, her boy's love manga, and critical work.) On the homoerotic subtext of *Kokoro*, see Iida Yūko, *Karera no monogatari*, 256–76; Dodd, "The Significance of Bodies in Sōseki's *Kokoro*," 473–98.

36. See Kinsella, *Adult Manga*, 113–18. The word *yaoi* has been used more generally to refer to the entire subgenre of boy's love comics, but the word *yaoi* has, in recent years, seemed to be less popular than the terms *shōnen'ai* and *bōizu rabu*. Because of its connection with boy love, people sometimes suggest other spurious etymologies such as "YAmete! Oshiri ga Itai!" (Cut it out! My ass hurts!) or "YAru, Okasu, Ikaseru" (Fuck [him], rape [him], make [him] cum). See Vincent, "A Japanese Electra and Her Queer Progeny," 77; and Welker, "Transfiguring the Female," 141.

37. Hatoyama, " Kāru to shiroi dentō," 263–69.

38. McLelland, *Male Homosexuality in Modern Japan*, 84–86.

# Bibliography

"Akuseiyoku kyōsei gō" (Issue on correcting bad sexual desire). Spec. issue of *Bukyō sekai* (World of heroism) 7, no. 6 (1919).

Andersen, Hans Christian. *The Improvisatore.* Translated by Mary Howitt. New York: Hurd and Houghton, 1869.

Angles, Jeffrey. "Hamao Shirō's 'The Execution of Ten'ichibō.'" *Critical Asian Studies* 37, no. 2 (2005): 305–21.

———. "Haunted by the Sexy Samurai: Ranpo's Mobilization of the Queer Past in 'Shudō mokuzuzuka.'" In *Literature and Literary Theory: Proceedings of the Association for Japanese Literary Studies,* edited by Atsuko Ueda and Richard Okada, 101–9. West Lafayette, Ind.: Association of Japanese Literary Studies, 2008.

———. "Penisism and the Eternal Hole: (Homo)Eroticism and Existential Exploration in the Early Poetry of Takahashi Mutsuo." *Intersections: Gender, History and Culture in the Asian Context.* 2006. http://intersections.anu.edu.au/issue12/angles.html.

———. "Queer Nonsense: Aestheticized Homoeroticism in Inagaki Taruho's Early Stories." *Japan Forum* 21, no. 1 (2009): 95–114.

———. "Seeking the Strange: *Ryōki* and the Navigation of Normality in Interwar Japan." *Monumenta Nipponica* 63, no. 1 (2008): 101–41.

———. "Writing the Love of Boys: Representations of Male–Male Desire in the Literature of Murayama Kaita and Edogawa Ranpo." PhD dissertation, Ohio State University, 2004.

Araki Shūichi. *Kindai geki monogatari* (Tales from modern plays). Tokyo: Dai Nippon Tosho, 1913.

Arishima Takeo. *Arishima Takeo zenshū* (The complete works of Arishima Takeo). 16 vols. Tokyo: Chikuma Shobō, 1979–1988.

Athenaeus of Naucratis. *The Deipnosophists.* Translated by Charles Burton Gulick, Loeb Classical Library 204, 208, 224, 235, 274, 327, and 345. Cambridge, Mass.: Harvard University Press, 1927.

Babington, Percy L. *Bibliography of the Writings of John Addington Symonds.* London: J. Castle, 1925.

Balakian, Anna. *The Symbolist Movement: A Critical Appraisal.* New York: New York University Press, 1977.

Baudelaire, Charles. *Œuvres complètes.* Edited by Claude Pichois. Paris: Pléiade, 1976.

Beichman, Janine. *Embracing the Firebird: Yosano Akiko and the Birth of the Female Voice in Modern Japanese Poetry.* Honolulu: University of Hawai'i Press, 2002.

Brown, Wendy. *Politics Out of History.* Princeton: Princeton University Press, 2001.

Butler, Judith. *Gender Trouble: Feminism and the Subversion of Identity.* New York: Routledge, 1990.

Carpenter, Edward. "Chūseiron" [translation of *The Intermediate Sex*]. Translated by Yamakawa Kikue. *Safuran* 1, no. 3 (1914): 1–22; no. 4: 130–153; no. 5: 55–76.

———. "Dōsei no ai" (Same-sex love [translation of *The Intermediate Sex*]). Translated by Yamakawa Kikue. In *Josei chūshin to dōseiai* (Double suicides between women and same-sex love), edited by Sakai Toshihiko, 165–256. Tokyo: Ars, 1919.

———. *The Intermediate Sex: Selected Writings.* London: GMP, 1984.

———. *Intermediate Types among Primitive Folk.* London: George Allen and Unwin, 1919. Reprint, New York: Arno Press, 1975.

———, ed. *Ioläus: An Anthology of Friendship.* New York: Mitchel Kennerley, 1917. Reprint, New York: Pagan Press, 1982.

Childs, Margaret H. "Chigo Monogatari: Love Stories or Buddhist Sermons?" *Monumenta Nipponica* 35, no. 2 (1980): 127–51.

———. "Rethinking Sorrow: Revelatory Tales of Late Medieval Japan." 31–52. Ann Arbor, Mich.: Center for Japanese Studies, 1991. Reprint, "The Tale of Genmu." In *Partings at Dawn: An Anthology of Japanese Gay Literature,* edited by Stephen D. Miller, 36–54. San Francisco: Gay Sunshine Press, 1996.

Clark, Kenneth. *Leonardo da Vinci.* Rev. ed. London: Penguin, 1967.

Cornell, Kenneth. *The Symbolist Movement.* New Haven: Yale University Press, 1951.

De Certeau, Michel. *The Writing of History.* Translated by Tom Conley. New York: Columbia University Press, 1988.

Derrida, Jacques. *Specters of Marx: The State of the Debt, the Work of Mourning, and the New International.* Translated by Peggy Kamuf. New York: Routledge, 1994.

Dinshaw, Carolyn. *Getting Medieval: Sexualities and Communities, Pre- and Postmodern.* Durham: Duke University Press, 1999.

Diogenes Laertius. *Lives of Eminent Philosophers.* Translated by R. D. Hicks, Loeb Classical Library 184 and 185. Cambridge, Mass.: Harvard University Press, 1925.

Dodd, Stephen. "The Significance of Bodies in Sōseki's *Kokoro*." *Monumenta Nipponica* 53, no. 4 (1998): 473–98.

"Dōseiai kenkyū, Edogawa Ranpo no tegami, Toba no Iwata-san kōkai" (Research on same-sex love, Edogawa Ranpo's correspondence with Mr. Iwata from Toba). *Asahi shinbun,* November 28, 2001, 8.

Dower, John. *Embracing Defeat: Japan in the Wake of World War II.* New York: W. W. Norton, 1999.

Driscoll, Mark. *Absolute Erotic, Absolute Grotesque: The Living, Dead, and Undead in Japan's Imperialism, 1895–1945.* Durham: Duke University Press, 2010.

Edogawa, Rampo. *Japanese Tales of Mystery and Imagination.* Translated by James B. Harris. Rutland, Vt.: Charles E. Tuttle Co., 1956.

Edogawa Rampo. *The Black Lizard and Beast in the Shadows.* Translated by Ian Hughes. Fukuoka: Kurodahan Press, 2006.

——. *The Edogawa Rampo Reader.* Translated by Seth Jacobowitz. Fukuoka: Kurodahan Press, 2008.

*Edogawa Ranpo.* Shin bungei dokuhon (New readers on art and letters). Tokyo: Kawade Shobō Shinsha, 1992.

Edogawa Ranpo. "The Caterpillar." Translated by Michael Tangeman. In *Modanizumu: Modernist Fiction from Japan, 1913–1938,* edited by William J. Tyler, 406–22. Honolulu: University of Hawai'i Press, 2008.

——. *Edogawa Ranpo suiri bunko* (Edogawa Ranpo detection paperbacks). 60 vols. Tokyo: Kōdansha, 1987–89.

——. *Edogawa Ranpo zenshū* (The complete works of Edogawa Ranpo). 25 vols. Tokyo: Kōdansha, 1978–79.

——. "Hagiwara Sakutarō to Inagaki Taruho" (Hagiwara Sakutarō and Inagaki Taruho). In *Taruho jiten: Taruho Mantra* (Taruho dictionary: Taruho mantra), 273–78. Tokyo: Ushio Shuppan, 1970.

——. *Harimaze nenpu* (Scrapbook chronology). Tokyo: Tōkyō Sōgensha, 2001.

——. "Honchō nanshoku kō ni tsuite" (About thoughts on male love in our kingdom). In *Honchō nanshoku kō* (Thoughts on male love in our kingdom), edited by Iwata Sadao, unpag. Toba: Iwata Sadao, 1974.

——. "Iwata Jun'ichi-kun no sashie" (The illustrations of Iwata Jun'ichi). In *Taishū bungaku geppō* (Monthly bulletin of popular literature) 5, no. 2. Tokyo: Heibonsha, 1927.

——. "J. A. Shimonzu no hisoka naru jōnetsu" (The secret passion of J. A. Symonds). *Seishin bunseki* (Psychoanalysis) 1 (1933), no. 1: 16–26; no. 2: 27–39; no. 4: 60–69; no. 6: 34–42.

——. *Kotō no oni* (The demon of the lonely isle), Edogawa Ranpo Series 1. Tokyo: Sōgen Suiri Bunko, 1987.

——. "The Man Traveling with the Brocade Portrait." Translated by Michael Tangeman. In *Modanizumu: Modernist Fiction from Japan, 1913–1938,* edited by William J. Tyler, 376–93. Honolulu: University of Hawai'i Press, 2008.

——. "Shudō mokuzuzuka" (Mokuzu mound commemorating the way of the youth). *Bungei shunjū* (Literary arts spring and autumn) 16, no. 9 (1936): 320–26.

——. *Tantei shōsetsu yon-jū-nen* (Forty years of detective fiction). Tokyo: Tōgensha, 1961.

——. "The Two-Sen Copper Coin." Translated by Jeffrey Angles. In *Modanizumu: Modernist Fiction from Japan, 1913–1938,* edited by William J. Tyler, 270–89. Honolulu: University of Hawai'i Press, 2008.

Edogawa Ranpo and Inagaki Taruho. "Dōseiai no risō to genjitsu" (The ideals and reality of same-sex love). *Barazoku* (Tribe of roses) 228 (1992): 26–33.

"Edogawa Ranpo no shokan, yūjin no sashie gaka ni 87-tsū, hansū 'dōseiai' shiryō" (Edogawa Ranpo's correspondence, 87 letters to his friend the illustrator, half dedicated to documents on "same-sex love"). *Yomiuri shinbun*, November 29, 2001, 34.

"Edogawa Ranpo to no shinkō" (Friendship with Edogawa Ranpo). In *Takahashi Tetsu*, 151. Shin bungei dokuhon (New readers on art and letters). Tokyo: Kawade Shobō Shinsha, 1993.

Edogawa Ranzō. "Shisei sanka" (Odes of praise for the tattoo). *Kitan kurabu* (March 1969): 236.

Egawa Ranzō. "Kokan shitagi" (Underwear in the crotch). *Kitan kurabu* (1969) no. 1: 246–47.

Enomoto Nariko. *Kokoro.* Tokyo: Shōgakkan, 2005.

Foucault, Michel. *The History of Sexuality: An Introduction.* Translated by Robert Hurley. New York: Random House, 1990.

Freccero, Carla. *Queer/Early/Modern.* Durham: Duke University Press, 2006.

Freud, Sigmund. *Furoido seishin bunsekigaku zenshū* (Complete works of Freud's psychoanalysis). Translated by Ōtsuki Kenji, Hasegawa Seiya, and Yabe Yaekichi. 10 vols. Tokyo: Shun'yōdō, 1930–33.

———. *Seishin bunseki taikei* (Survey of psychoanalysis). Translated by Yasuda Tokutarō, Marui Kiyoyasu, Masaki Fujokyū, et al. 15 vols. Tokyo: Ars, 1929–33.

———. *The Interpretation of Dreams.* Translated by James Strachey. In The Standard Edition of the Complete Psychological Works of Sigmund Freud. London: Hogarth Press, 1953.

———. *Leonardo da Vinci and a Memory of His Childhood.* Translated by Alan Tyson. In The Standard Edition of the Complete Psychological Works of Sigmund Freud. London: Hogarth Press, 1957.

Frühstück, Sabine. *Colonizing Sex: Sexology and Social Control in Modern Japan.* Berkeley: University of California Press, 2003.

Furukawa Makoto. "The Changing Nature of Sexuality: The Three Codes Framing Homosexuality in Modern Japan." Translated by Angus Lockyer. *U.S.–Japan Women's Journal: English Supplement* 7 (1994): 98–127.

———. "Edogawa Ranpo no hisoka naru jōnetsu" (The secret passion of Edogawa Ranpo). *Kokubungaku: Kaishaku to kanshō* (Japanese literature: Interpretation and Appreciation) 59, no. 12 (1994): 59–64.

———. "Ranpo to dōseiai" (Ranpo and same-sex love). *Bessatsu taiyō* (Supplement to "The sun") 88 (1994): 120.

Gardner, William O. *Advertising Tower: Japanese Modernism and Modernity in the 1920s.* Cambridge, Mass.: Harvard East Asia Center, 2006.

Gendai Henshūkyoku, ed. *Gendai shingo jiten* (Dictionary of modern, new words). Tokyo: Dai Nippon Yūbenkai Kōdansha, 1931. Reprint, Tokyo: Ōzorasha, 1995.

Gide, André. *If It Die . . . : An Autobiography.* Translated by Dorothy Bussy. New York: Vintage International, 2001.

Griffith, D. W. *Biograph Shorts: Griffith Masterworks, Twenty-Three Complete Films.* New York: Kino Video, 2002. DVD.

Habuto Eiji. *Seiten* (The laws of sex). Tokyo: Tōkyō Shoin, 1926.

Habuto Eiji and Sawada Junjirō. *Hentai seiyoku ron* (On perverse sexuality). Tokyo: Shun'yōdō, 1915.

Hagio Moto. *Tōma no shinzō* (The heart of Thomas). Tokyo: Shōgakukan Bunko, 1995.

Hagiwara Sakutarō. "Maruyama Kaoru to Kinumaki Seizō" (Maruyama Kaoru and Kinumaki Seizō). In *Taruho jiten: Taruho Mantra* (Taruho dictionary: Taruho mantra), 278–82. Tokyo: Ushio Shuppan, 1970.

———. "Neko-machi" (The town of cats). In *Hagiwara Sakutarō shishū* (Poetry of Hagiwara Sakutarō). Gendai shi bunko (Modern poetry paperbacks) 1009, 112–24. Tokyo: Shichōsha, 1975.

———. "The Town of Cats." Translated by Jeffrey Angles. In *Modanizumu in Japanese Fiction: An Anthology of Modernist Prose from Japan, 1914–1938,* edited by William J. Tyler, 542–53. Honolulu: University of Hawai'i Press, 2008.

Halperin, David M. *How to Do the History of Homosexuality.* Chicago: University of Chicago Press, 2002.

Hamada Yūsuke. "Murayama Kaita no tantei shōsetsu: Edogawa Ranpo kara no shikaku" (The detective fiction of Murayama Kaita: The perspective from Edogawa Ranpo). *Yuriika* (Eureka) 31, no. 7 (1999): 204–11.

Hamao Shirō. "Akuma no deshi" (The devil's apprentice). In *Hamao Shirō shū* (Collected works of Hamao Shirō), edited by Kitamura Kaoru, 83–124. Tokyo: Sōgen Suiri Bunko, 1995.

———. "Akuma no deshi." *Shin seinen* (New youth) 10, no. 5 (1929): 168–98.

———. "Dōseiai kō" (Thoughts on same-sex love). *Fujin saron* (Housewife's salon) 2, no. 9 (1930): 136–42.

———. "Futatabi dōseiai ni tsuite" (More on same-sex love). *Fujin saron* (Housewife's salon) 2, no. 11 (1930): 58–65.

———. "Hentai satsujin kō" (Thoughts on perverse crime). *Shin seinen* (New youth) 11, no. 6 (1930): 190–205.

———. "Hentaisei no hanzai ni tsuite" (On crimes of a perverse nature). *Shin seinen* (New youth) 9, no. 12 (1928): 277–82.

———. *Kare ga koroshita ka?* (Did he kill?). In *Hamao Shirō shū* (Collected works of Hamao Shirō), edited by Kitamura Kaoru, 9–81. Tokyo: Sōgen Suiri Bunko, 1985.

———. "Madamu no satsujin" (Murders for madam). *Asahi* (Morning sun) 3, no. 6 (1931): 340–53.

———. "Shisha no kenri" (The rights of the dead.) In *Hamao Shirō shū* (Collected works of Hamao Shirō), edited by Kitamura Kaoru, 125–74. Tokyo: Sōgen Suiri Bunko, 1985.

Harada Hikaru. "Kaita den" (Biography of Kaita). *Yuriika* (Eureka) 31, no. 7 (1999): 140–53.

Hasegawa Ryūsei. "Chizome no rappa fukinarase: Murayama Kaita no michikai seigai ni tsuite" (Blow the blood-stained bugle: On Murayama Kaita's short life). *Yuriika* (Eureka) 31, no. 7 (1999): 154–61.

Hatoyama Ikuko. "Kāru to shiroi dentō" (Karl and the white light). *Yuriika* (Eureka) 38, no. 11 (2008): 263–69.

Hayasaka Jirō and Matsumoto Gorō, eds. *Sentango hyakka jiten* (Encyclopedia of cutting-edge words). Tokyo: Sentansha, 1931. Reprint, Tokyo: Ōzorasha, 1995.

Hayashi Mikihiro. "Edogawa Ranpo: Yūjin no minzokugakusha to nanshoku kenkyū, shokan shokōkai" (Edogawa Ranpo: A short presentation of his correspondence on the research of male love with his friend, an anthropologist). *Mainichi shinbun*, November 27, 2001.

Hayashi Tatsuo. *Shisō no doramaturgii* (The dramaturgy of ideology). Heibonsha raiburarii (Heibonsha library) 2. Tokyo: Heibonsha, 1993.

Heiji Tai. "Edogawa Ranpo to 'Kare'" (Edogawa Ranpo and "him"). *Fuzoku kitan* (Strange tales of sex customs) (1971) no. 3: 198–201; no. 4: 198–202; no. 5: 198–203.

Higashi Shunrō. "Aka no Kaita, aka no Hakushū" (Red Kaita, red Hakushū). In *Korekushon mangekyō: Yattsu no hako no nanatsu no hanashi* (Collection kaleidoscope: Seven stories in eight boxes), edited by Mie Kenritsu Bijutsukan, 148–54. Tsu: Mie Kenritsu Bijutsukan, 1998.

———. "Tare ka ibari suru" (Who is urinating?) *Yuriika* (Eureka) 31, no. 7 (1999): 172–82.

Hirai Ryūtarō. *Utsushiyo no Ranpo* (Ranpo in this world). Tokyo: Kawade Shobō Shinsha, 2006.

Hirano Ayu. *Negachibu kotō no oni* (Negative demon of the lonely isle). Self-published, 1993.

Hirata, Hosea. *The Poetry and Poetics of Nishiwaki Junzaburō: Modernism in Translation.* Princeton: Princeton University Press, 1993.

Hori Tatsuo. "Les Joues en Feu." Translated by Jack Rucinski. In *The Shōwa Anthology: Modern Japanese Short Stories 1929–1984,* edited by Van C. Gessel and Tomone Matsumoto, 28–37. New York: Kodansha International, 1985.

———. "Moyuru hō" (Les joues en feu). In *Hori Tatsuo zenshū* (The complete works of Hori Tatsuo), vol. 1, 207–22. Tokyo: Chikuma Shobō, 1977.

Hosoma Hiromichi. *Asakusa jū-ni-kai: Tō no nagame to "kindai" no manazashi* (The Asakusa twelve stories: Looking from the tower and gazing upon "modernity"). Tokyo: Seidōsha, 2001.

Hunter, Janet E. *The Emergence of Modern Japan: An Introductory History since 1853.* New York: Longman, 1989.

Ihara Saikaku. *The Great Mirror of Male Love.* Translated by Paul Gordon Schalow. Stanford: Stanford University Press, 1990.

———. "Nanshoku ōkagami" (The great mirror of male love). In *Ihara Saikaku shū 2* (Collection of the work of Ihara Saikaku 2), 289–591. Tokyo: Shōgakkan, 1996.

Iida Shizue. *Fūka* (Wind flowers). Tokyo: Shinpūsha, 1998.

Iida Yūko. *Karera no monogatari: Nihon kindai bungaku to jendā* (Their male tales: Modern Japanese literature and gender). Nagoya: Nagoya Daigaku Shuppankai, 1998.

Imazeki Keiji and Yamazaki Shōzō. "Murayama Kaita ryakuden" (An abbreviated biography of Murayama Kaita). In *Kaita no utaeru* (Songs of Kaita), final section, 1–5. Tokyo: Ars, 1920.

Inagaki Shiyo. *Otto Inagaki Taruho* (My husband Inagaki Taruho). Tokyo: Geijutsu Seikatsusha, 1971.

*Inagaki Taruho*. Shin bungei dokuhon (New readers on art and letters). Tokyo: Kawade Shobō Shinsha, 1993.

Inagaki Taruho. *Inagaki Taruho zenshū* (The complete works of Inagaki Taruho). 13 vols. Tokyo: Chikuma Shobō, 2000–2001.

———. *Momoiro no hankachi* (Peach-colored handkerchief). Tokyo: Gendai Shichōsha, 1974.

———. *One Thousand and One-Second Stories*. Translated by Tricia Vita. Sun and Moon Classics 139. Los Angeles: Sun and Moon Press, 1998.

———. "Pince-Nez Glasses." Translated by Jeffrey Angles. *Harrington Gay Men's Fiction Quarterly* 7, no. 1 (2005): 3–12.

———. "Shōnen tokuhon: Essei-fū na sōsaku" (Youth reader: A creative work in the style of an essay). In *Shōnen tokuhon* (Youth reader), 46–72. Tokyo: Ushio Shuppan, 1986.

———. "The Story of R-chan and S." Translated by Jeffrey Angles. In *Modanizumu: Modernist Fiction from Japan, 1913–1938*, edited by William J. Tyler, 358–75. Honolulu: University of Hawai'i Press, 2008.

———. *Taruho han nanshoku ōkagami* (Taruho's edition of "The great mirror of male love"). Tokyo: Kadokawa Shoten, 1977.

Inoue Shōichi. *Ai no kūkan* (Spaces for making love). Kadokawa sensho (Kadokawa selected books) 307. Tokyo: Kadokawa Shoten, 1999.

———. *Pantsu ga mieru: Shūchishin no gendaishi* (Your panties are showing: A contemporary history of embarassment). Asahi sensho (Asahi selected books) 700. Tokyo: Asahi Shinbunsha, 2003.

Ishida Minori. *Hisoyaka na kyōiku: "Yaoi bōizurabu" zenshi* (An unobtrusive education: A prehistory of "Yaoi boy's love"). Kyoto: Rakuhoku Shuppan, 2008.

Ishikawa, Takuboku. *Poems to Eat*. Translated by Carl Sesar. Tokyo: Kodansha International, 1968.

———. *Romaji Diary and Sad Toys*. Translated by Sanford Goldstein and Seishi Shinoda. Rutland, Vt.: Tuttle, 1985.

Ishikawa Takuboku. *On Knowing Oneself Too Well*. Translated by Tamae K. Prindle. Baltimore: Syllabic Press, 2010.

———. *Takuboku zenshū* (The complete works of Takuboku). 8 vols. Tokyo: Chikuma Shobō, 1967–68.

Isoda Kōichi. *Kindai no kanjō kakumei* (The modern revolution of feeling). Tokyo: Shinchōsha, 1987.

Itō Hideo. *Kindai no tantei shōsetsu* (Modern detective fiction). Tokyo: San'ichi Shobō, 1994.

———. *Meiji no tantei shōsetsu* (Meiji detective fiction). Tokyo: Shōbunsha, 1986.

———. *Shōwa no tantei shōsetsu: Shōwa gannen-Shōwa ni-jū-nen* (Shōwa detective fiction: From the first year of the Shōwa era to the twentieth year). Tokyo: San'ichi Shobō, 1993.

———. *Taishō no tantei shōsetsu: Ruikō, Shunrō kara Ranpo, Eiji made* (Taishō detective fiction: From Ruikō and Shunrō to Ranpo and Eiji). Tokyo: San'ichi Shobō, 1991.

Itō Ken. *Hentai sakka shi* (A history of perverse authors). Tokyo: Bungei Shiryō Kenkyūkai, 1926.

Itō Kyō. "Nenpu" (Chronology). In *Murayama Kaita ten: Seitan 100-nen* (An exhibition of Murayama Kaita: 100th anniversary of his birth), edited by Mie Kenritsu Bijutsukan, 166–73. Tsu: Mie Kenritsu Bijutsukan, 1997.

Itō Shinkichi, Itō Sei, and Inoue Yasushi, eds. *Doi Bansui, Susukida Kyūkin, Kanbara Ariake, Miki Rofū*. Nihon no shiika (Japanese poetry) 2. Tokyo: Chūō Kōronsha, 1968.

Iwamura Tōru. *Seiyō bijutsu shiyō: Itari kaiga no bu* (Essentials of western art: Italian painting). Tokyo: Shūzanbō Shoten, 1904.

Iwata Jun'ichi. *Honchō nanshoku kō* (Thoughts on male love in our kingdom). Toba: Iwata Sadao, 1974.

———. *Nanshoku bunken shoshi* (Bibliography of resources on male love). Tokyo: Koten Bunko, 1956. Reprint, Toba: Iwata Sadao, 1973.

———. "Nanshoku ishō shū" (Collection of notes on male love). In *Nanshoku bunken shoshi* (Bibliography of resources on male love), 281–88. Toba: Iwata Sadao, 1973.

Iwata Junko. *Ni seinen zu: Ranpo to Iwata Jun'ichi* (Portrait of two young men: Ranpo and Iwata Jun'ichi). Tokyo: Shinchōsha, 2001.

———. Personal communication. July 9, 2010.

Iwata Kyōnosuke [Sadao]. "Tōkyō Hongō 'Ise Sakae Ryokan' no yoru: Ranpo to Iwata Jun'ichi no dōseiai bunken no kenkyū" (An evening at the "Ise Sakae Inn" in Hongō, Tokyo: Ranpo and Iwata Jun'ichi's research into bibliographic sources on same-sex love). *Bungei zuihitsu* (Essays on arts and letters) 39 (2001): 38.

Iwata Sadao. "Bōfu Iwata Jun'ichi" (My late father Iwata Jun'ichi). In *Takehisa Yumeji, sono deshi: Iwata Jun'ichi gabunshū—Eiri man'yōshū* (Takehisa Yumeji's disciple: A collection of the artwork of Iwata Jun'ichi—an illustrated ten thousand leaves), 53–71. Tokyo: Ōfūsha, 1979.

Iwaya Sazanami [Suweyo-Iwaya]. "Nan-šo-k' (die Päderastie in Japan)." *Jahrbuch für sexuelle Zwischenstufen* 4 (1902): 265–71.

Jackson, Earl, Jr. "The Heresy of Meaning: Japanese Symbolist Poetry." *Harvard Journal of Asiatic Studies* 51, no. 2 (1991): 561–98.

Jacobowitz, Seth. Introduction to *The Edogawa Rampo Reader*, xv–xlvii. Fukuoka: Kurodahan Press, 2008.

Jagose, Annamarie. *Queer Theory: An Introduction*. New York: New York University Press, 1996.

Jansen, Marius B. *The Making of Modern Japan.* Cambridge, Mass.: Belknap Press of Harvard University Press, 2000.

"*Kaita no utaeru* [Songs of Kaita] by Murayama Kaita." Advertisement. *Yomiuri shinbun,* October 8, 1920, 1.

Karatani Kōjin. "The Discovery of the Child." Translated by Ayako Kano and Eiko Elliot. In *Origins of Modern Japanese Literature,* edited by Brett DeBary, 114–35. Durham: Duke University Press, 1993.

Karsch-Haack, Ferdinand. *Das gleichgeschlechtliche Leben der Ostasiaten Kulturvölker: Chinesen, Japaner, Koreer. Forschungen über glesichgeschlechtliche Liebe.* Munich: Seitz and Schauer, 1906.

Kataoka Teppei. "Rōkō" (Squalid alleyways). *Chūō kōron* (Central review) 49, no. 6 (1934): Sōsaku section, 1–41.

Kawabata Yasunari. "Shōnen" (Adolescent boys). In *Kawabata Yasunari zenshū* (The complete works of Kawabata Yasunari), vol. 10, 141–225. Tokyo: Shinchōsha, 1980.

Kawana, Sari. *Murder Most Modern: Detective Fiction and Japanese Culture.* Minneapolis: University of Minnesota Press, 2008.

Keene, Donald. *Dawn to the West: Japanese Literature of the Modern Era.* 2 vols. New York: Holt, Rinehart, and Winston, 1984.

Kimura Shōhachi. *Mirai-ha oyobi rittai-hai no geijutsu* (The art of the futurists and cubists). Kindai shichō sōsho (Library of modern new trends). Tokyo: Tengendō, 1915.

Kinsella, Sharon. *Adult Manga: Culture and Power in Contemporary Japanese Society.* Honolulu: University of Hawai'i Press, 2000.

"Kioku ni atai suru Kaita shi no geijutsu" (The artwork of Mr. Kaita, a man who deserves to be remembered). *Yomiuri shinbun,* November 18, 1919, 7.

Kitahara Hakushū. *Hakushū zenshū* (The complete works of Hakushū). 40 vols. Tokyo: Iwanami Shoten, 1984–1988.

Kitamura Kigin. "Wild Azaleas." Translated by Paul Gordon Schalow. In *Partings at Dawn: An Anthology of Japanese Gay Literature,* edited by Stephen D. Miller, 97–124. San Francisco: Gay Sunshine Press, 1996.

Kojima Tokuya. *Bunruishiki modan shin yōgo jiten* (A dictionary of new, modern words divided by area). Kyōbunsha, 1931. Reprint, Tokyo: Ōzorasha, 1995.

Korona Bukkusu Henshūbu, ed. *Inagaki Taruho no sekai: Taruhosukōpu* (The world of Inagaki Taruho: Taruhoscope). Corona Books 132. Tokyo: Heibonsha, 2007.

Kosaki Gunji. *Yamamoto Kanae hyōden* (A critical biography of Yamamoto Kanae). Nagano: Shinanoji, 1979.

Kozakai Fuboku. "'Ni-sen dōka' o yomu" (Reading "The two-sen copper coin"). *Shin seinen* (New youth) 4, no. 5 (1923): 264–65.

Krafft-Ebing, Richard von. *Hentai seiyoku shinri* [translation of *Psychopathia sexualis*]. Tokyo: Dai Nihon Bunmei Kyōkai, 1913.

———. *Shikijōkyō hen* [translation of *Psychopathia sexualis*]. Translated by Nihon Hōigakkai. Tokyo: Nihon Hōigakkai, 1894.

Kurutz , Gary F. "The Only Safe and Sane Method. . . . The Curtiss School of Aviation." *Journal of San Diego History* 25, no. 1 (1979): 26–59.

Kusano Shinpei. *Murayama Kaita.* Tokyo: Nichidō Shuppanbu, 1976. Reprint, *Waga Kaita* (My Kaita), in *Kusano Shinpei zenshū* (The complete works of Kusano Shinpei), vol. 6, 327–564. Tokyo: Chikuma Shobō, 1981.

Kyokutei Bakin. "Mokuzu monogatari" (Tale of weeds in the sea). In *Enseki jisshu* (Ten types of worthless things valued as precious), edited by Iwamoto Sashichi, 380–95. Tokyo: Higashi Shuppan, 1976.

Love, Heather. *Feeling Backward: Loss and the Politics of Queer History.* Cambridge, Mass.: Harvard University Press, 2007.

Matsui, Midori. "Little Girls Were Little Boys: Displaced Femininity in the Representation of Homosexuality in Japanese Girls' Comics." In *Feminism and the Politics of Difference,* edited by Sneja Gunew and Anne Yeatman, 177–96. Boulder, Colo.: Westview, 1993.

Matsumura Tami. *Ranpo ojisan: Edogawa Ranpo ron* (Uncle Ranpo: On Edogawa Ranpo). Tokyo: Shōbunsha, 1992.

Matsunaga Goichi. "Yume to seisei" (Dreams and creation). In *Edogawa Ranpo zenshū* (The complete works of Edogawa Ranpo), vol. 22, 255–58. Kōdansha, 1979.

McLelland, Mark. *Male Homosexuality in Modern Japan: Cultural Myths and Social Realities.* Richmond, Surrey: Curzon, 2000.

———. *Queer Japan from the Pacific War to the Internet Age.* Oxford: Rohan and Littlefield Publishers, 2005.

Minakata Kumagusu and Iwata Jun'ichi. *Minakata Kumagusu nanshoku dangi: Iwata Jun'ichi ōfuku shokan* (Minakata Kumagusu's talks on male love: His two-way correspondence with Iwata Jun'ichi). Edited by Hasegawa Kōzō and Tsukikawa Kazuo. Tokyo: Yasaka Shobō, 1991.

———. "Morning Fog (Correspondence on Gay Lifestyles)." Translated by William F. Sibley. In *Partings at Dawn: An Anthology of Japanese Gay Literature,* edited by Stephen D. Miller, 134–71. San Francisco: Gay Sunshine Press, 1996.

Minami Hiroshi. "Nihon modanizumu ni tsuite" (On Japanese modernism). *Gendai no esupuri* (The contemporary esprit) 188 (1983): 7–9.

Mishima Yukio. *Sakka ron* (On authors). Tokyo: Chūō Koronsha, 1970.

Mizuki Shin'ichi. "Akutagawa Ryūnosuke no yūjō" (My friendship with Akutagawa Ryūnosuke). In "Geppō" (Monthly bulletin) 24, supplement to vol. 24 of *Akutagawa Ryūnosuke zenshū* (The complete works of Akutagawa Ryūnosuke), 9–14. Tokyo: Iwanami Shoten, 2008.

Mori, Ogai. *Vita Sexualis.* Translated by Kazuji Ninomiya and Sanford Goldstein. Rutland, Vt.: Charles E. Tuttle Co., 1972.

Mori Ōgai. *Ōgai zenshū* (The complete works of Ōgai). 38 vols. Tokyo: Iwanami Shoten, 1971–75.

———. *Omokage* (Vestiges). In *Meiji Taishō yakushi shū* (Collection of translated verse from the Meiji and Taishō periods), 105–67. Tokyo: Kadokawa Shoten, 1971.

Mori Oto. *Chichi toshite no Ōgai* (Ōgai as my father). Chikuma sōsho (Chikuma library) 159. Tokyo: Chikuma Shobō, 1969.

Mori Rintarō [Ōgai]. *Hitomakumono* (One-act plays). Tokyo: Momiyama Shoten, 1912.

———. *Zoku hitomakumono* (More one-act plays). Tokyo: Ifūsha, 1910.

Morton, Leith. "The Birth of the Modern: Yosano Akiko and Tekkan's Verse Revolution." In *Modernism in Practice: An Introduction to Postwar Japanese Poetry,* 11–33. Honolulu: University of Hawai'i Press, 2004.

Murayama Kaita. "The Bust of the Beautiful Young Salaino." Translated by Jeffrey Angles. In *Modanizumu: Modernist Fiction in Japan, 1914–1938,* edited by William J. Tyler, 66–69. Honolulu: University of Hawai'i Press, 2008.

———. "The Diabolical Tongue." Translated by Jeffrey Angles. In *Kaiki: Weird Tales from Japan.* Vol. 3, *Tales of the Metropolis,* edited by Higashi Masao. Fukuoka: Kurodahan Press, in press.

———. *Kaita no utaeru* (Songs of Kaita). Edited by Yamazaki Shōzō. Tokyo: Ars, 1920.

———. *Kaita no utaeru sono go oyobi Kaita no hanashi* (Songs of Kaita continued, plus remembrances of Kaita). Edited by Yamamoto Jirō. Tokyo: Ars, 1921.

———. *Murayama Kaita ten: Seitan hyaku-nen* (An exhibition of Murayama Kaita: 100th anniversary of his birth). Edited by Mie Kenritsu Bijutsukan. Tsu: Mie Kenritsu Bijutsukan, 1997.

———. *Murayama Kaita zenshū* (The complete works of Murayama Kaita). Edited by Yamamoto Tarō. Rev. 2nd ed. Tokyo: Yayoi Shobō, 1997.

———. "Satsujin gyōja" (The murdering ascetic). *Bukyō sekai* (World of heroism) 4, no. 5 (1914): 45–55.

*Murayama Kaita isaku tenrankai mokuroku* (Catalogue from the posthumous exhibition of the works of Murayama Kaita). Tokyo: Kabutoya Gadō, 1919.

Naka Shōsaku, ed. *Edogawa Ranpo chosho mokuroku* (Index of Edogawa Ranpo's writing). Edogawa Ranpo rifarensu bukku (Edogawa Ranpo reference book) 3. Nabari: Nabari Shiritsu Toshokan, 2003.

———. "Edogawa Ranpo nenpu shūsei" (Edogawa Ranpo, a compiled chronology). *Nabari ningai kyō* (The unethical mirror of Nabari). 2000. http://www.e-net.or.jp/ user/stako/ED1/E04-00.html.

———, ed. *Edogawa Ranpo shippitsu nenpu* (Chronology of Edogawa Ranpo's writing). Edogawa Ranpo rifarensu bukku (Edogawa Ranpo reference book) 2. Nabari: Nabari Shiritsu Toshokan, 1998.

———, ed. *Ranpo bunken dēta bukku* (Ranpo bibliographic data book). Edogawa Ranpo rifarensu bukku (Edogawa Ranpo reference book) 1. Nabari: Nabari Shiritsu Toshokan, 1997.

Nakajima Kawatarō. *Nihon suiri shōsetsu shi* (A history of Japanese mystery fiction). 3 vols. Tokyo: Tōkyō Sōgensha, 1993–1996.

Nakano Shigeharu. "Uta no wakare" (A farewell to verse). In *Hayama Yoshiki, Kobayashi Takiji, Nakano Shigeharu shū* (Collected works of Hayama Yoshiki, Kobayashi Takiji, and Nakano Shigeharu), 279–320. Tokyo: Chikuma Shobō, 1954.

Nakayama Yūgorō, ed. *Modan-go manga jiten* (Illustrated dictionary of modern words). Tokyo: Rakuyō Shoin, 1931. Reprint, Tokyo: Ōzorasha, 1995.

*Nanshoku giri monogatari, tsuki shudō monogatari* ("Tales of male love and obligation," followed by "Tales of the way of the youth"). Edited by Yoshida Kōichi. Koten bunko 101. Tokyo: Koten Bunko, 1955.

Natsume Sōseki. *Ten Nights of Dream and Our Cat's Grave.* Translated by Sankichi Hata and Dofu Shirai. Tokyo: Tokyo News Service, 1934.

———. "Yume jūya" (Ten nights of dream). In *Sōseki zenshū* (Complete works of Sōseki), vol. 12, 99–130. Tokyo: Iwanami Shoten, 1994.

Nicholls, Peter. *Modernisms: A Literary Guide.* Berkeley: University of California Press, 1995.

Nobi Nobita. *Ippon no garansu* (A tube of garance). Gekkō Tōzoku [Self published], 1994.

Noda Utarō. "'Pan no kai' no tanbiha shijin no tanjō" ("The Pan Society" and the birth of the aesthetic poets). In *Kōza Nihon gendai shishi* (Lectures on the history of contemporary Japanese poetry), edited by Murano Shirō, Seki Ryōichi, Hasegawa Izumi, and Hara Shirō, 305–33. Tokyo: Ubun Shoin, 1973.

Ogawa Ginjirō, ed. *Sekai bijutsu shi* (History of the world's art). Vol. 1 of Teikoku hyakka zensho (Complete encyclopedic works of the empire) 143. Tokyo: Hakubunkan, 1905.

Ōgon Dokuro no Kai. *Shōnen tanteidan dokuhon: Ranpo to Kobayashi shōnen to kaijin ni-jū mensō* (A boy's detective club reader: Ranpo, the adolescent Kobayashi, and the mystery man of twenty faces). Tokyo: Jōhō Sentā Shuppan, 1994.

Omori, Kyoko. "Detecting Japanese Vernacular Modernism: *Shinseinen* Magazine and the Development of the Tantei Shōsetsu Genre." PhD dissertation, Ohio State University, 2003.

Omuka Toshiharu. "Dai-ni-kai mirai-ha bijutsu kyōkai ten (1921-nen kaisai) to shijin-tachi: Inagaki Taruho, Hirato Renkichi, Ogata Kamenosuke, Hagiwara Kyōjirō" (The second futurist art exhibition [held in 1921] and the poets Inagaki Taruho, Hirato Renkichi, Ogata Kamenosuke, and Hagiwara Kyōjirō). *Yuriika* (Eureka) 38, no. 11 (2006): 296–303.

———. *Taishō-ki shikō bijutsu undō no kenkyū* (Research into the rising arts movement of the Taishō period). Tokyo: Suakidoa, 1995.

Ono Kōji. *Warera wa Ranpo tanteidan* (Our Ranpo detective club). Benseisha, 1995.

Osaki Midori. "Dai-nana kankai hōkō" (Wandering in the seventh realm). In *Osaki Midori,* 82–215. Tokyo: Chikuma Shobō, 1991.

Ōtsuki Kenji. *Ren'ai seiyoku no shinri to sono bunseki shochi hō* (The psychology of love and sexual desire and methods of its analysis and management). Tokyo: Tōkyō Seishin Bunsekigaku Kenkyūjo Shuppanbu, 1936.

Ōuchi Shigeo. "Hamao Shirō no hito to sakuhin" (The life and works of Hamao Shirō). In *Hamao Shirō zenshū* (The complete works of Hamao Shirō), vol. 1, 525–38; vol. 2, 607–20. Tokyo: Tōgensha, 1971.

Ozaki Shirō. "Bishōnen no kenkyū" (Research on bishōnen). *Kaihō* (Liberation) 3, no. 4 (1921): 534–40.

Pater, Walter. *Bungei fūkō* [translation of *The Renaissance*]. Translated by Tanabe Jūji. Tokyo: Hokuseidō, 1915.

———. *The Renaissance: Studies in Art and Poetry (The 1893 Text)*. Edited by Donald L. Hill. Berkeley: University of California Press, 1980.

———. *Runesansu* [translation of *The Renaissance*]. Translated by Sakuma Masakazu. Tokyo: Shunshūsha, 1921.

Paton, W. R. "Strato's 'Musa Puerilis.'" In *The Greek Anthology*, 280–413. Cambridge, Mass.: Harvard University Press, 1918.

Pflugfelder, Gregory M. *Cartographies of Desire: Male–Male Sexuality in Japanese Discourse, 1600–1950*. Berkeley: University of California Press, 1999.

———. "'S' Is for Sister: Schoolgirl Intimacy and 'Same-Sex Love' in Early Twentieth-Century Japan." In *Gendering Modern Japanese History*, edited by Barbara Molony and Kathleen Uno, 133–77. Cambridge, Mass.: Harvard University Asia Center, 2005.

Reichert, Jim. "Deviance and Social Darwinism in Edogawa Ranpo's Erotic-Grotesque Thriller *Kotō no oni*." *Journal of Japanese Studies* 27, no. 1 (2001): 113–41.

———. "Disciplining the Erotic-Grotesque in Edogawa Ranpo's *Demon of the Lonely Isle*." In *The Culture of Japanese Fascism*, edited by Alan Tansman, 355–80. Durham: Duke University Press, 2009.

———. *In the Company of Men: Representations of Male–Male Sexuality in Meiji Literature*. Stanford: Stanford University Press, 2006.

———. "Representations of Male–Male Sexuality in Meiji-Period Literature." PhD dissertation, University of Michigan, 1998.

———. Review of *Cartographies of Desire: Male–Male Sexuality in Japanese Discourse, 1600–1950*, by Gregory M. Pflugfelder. *Journal of Asian Studies* 60, no. 1 (2001): 224–26.

Rimbaud, Arthur. *Collected Poems*. Translated by Oliver Bernard. Rev. ed. New York: Penguin Books, 1997.

Robertson, Jennifer. "Dying to Tell: Sexuality and Suicide in Imperial Japan." *Signs* 25, no. 1 (1999): 1–35.

———. *Takarazuka: Sexual Politics and Popular Culture in Modern Japan*. Berkeley: University of California Press, 1998.

Robinson, Paul. *Gay Lives: Homosexual Autobiography from John Addington Symonds to Paul Monette*. Chicago: University of Chicago Press, 1999.

Roden, Donald. *Schooldays in Imperial Japan: A Study in the Culture of a Student Elite*. Berkeley: University of California Press, 1980.

Ross, Alex. *The Rest Is Noise: Listening to the Twentieth Century*. New York: Farrar, Straus and Giroux, 2007.

Rubin, Jay. "From Wholesomeness to Decadence: The Censorship of Literature under the Allied Occupation." *Journal of Japanese Studies* 11, no. 1 (1985): 71–103.

———. *Injurious to Public Morals: Writers and the Meiji State*. Seattle: University of Washington Press, 1984.

Saeki Junko. "From *Iro* (Eros) to *Ai=Love:* The Case of Tsubouchi Shōyō." Translated by Indra Levy. *Review of Japanese Culture and Society* 20 (2008): 71–98.

———. *Ren'ai no kigen: Meiji no ai o yomitoku* (The origins of love: Analyzing love in Meiji). Tokyo: Nihon Keizai Shinbunsha, 2000.

Saitō Hikaru. "*Hentai seiyoku shinri* kaisetsu" (On *psychopathia sexualis*). In *Hentai seiyoku shinri* (The psychology of perverse psychology), edited by Saitō Hikaru, Kaisetsu section, 1–10. Tokyo: Yumani Shobō, 2006.

Sas, Miryam. "Subject, City, Machine." In *Histories of the Future,* edited by Daniel Rosenberg and Susan Harding, 203–23. Durham: Duke University Press, 2005.

Sasaki Teru. *Ennin Murayama Kaita* (Complete person Murayama Kaita). Tokyo: Maruzen Shuppan Sābisu Sentā, 2007.

Satō Akira. *Funsui shi kenkyū* (Research on the history of fountains). Tokyo: Intarakushon, 1999.

Satō Giryō, ed. *Gendai ryōki sentan zukan* (Pictorial of modernity, curiosity-hunting, and the trendsetting). Tokyo: Shinchōsha, 1931. Reprint, Tokyo: Yumani Shobō, 2005.

Satō Michiko. "Murayama Kaita 'Kosui to onna' o megutte" (On Murayama Kaita's "Lake and woman"). In *Kuroda Seiki, Kishida Ryūsei no jidai: Korekushon ni miru Meiji, Taishō no gakka-tachi* (The era of Kuroda Seiki and Kishida Ryūsei: Meiji and Taishō artists as seen in the collection), edited by Pōra Bijutsukan Gagkugeibu, 124–31. Ashigarashimo-gun: Pola Museum of Art, 2005.

Schalow, Paul Gordon. Introduction to *The Great Mirror of Male Love,* 1–46. Stanford: Stanford University Press, 1990.

Sedgwick, Eve Kosofsky. *Between Men: English Literature and Male Homosocial Desire.* New York: Columbia University Press, 1985.

———. *Epistemology of the Closet.* Berkeley: University of California Press, 1990.

Setagaya Torikku Kenkyūkai. "Kobayashi shōnen wa tensai gaka no e ga moderu" (The adolescent Kobayashi was modeled after a genius artist). In *Kindaichi shōnen no suiri misu* (Young Kindaichi's detective misses), 191–93. Tokyo: Uno Yoshitsugu, 1995.

Shamoon, Deborah. "Revolutionary Romance: *The Rose of Versailles* and the Transformation of Shojo Manga." In *Mechademia 2: Networks of Desire,* edited by Frenchy Lunning, 3–17. Minneapolis: University of Minnesota Press, 2007.

Sheppard, Richard. *Modernism—Dada—Postmodernism.* Evanston: Northwestern University Press, 2000.

Shibusawa Tatsuhiko. "Ranpo bungaku no honshitsu: Gangu aikō to yūtopia" (The true nature of Ranpo's literature: Toy love and utopia). In *Edogawa Ranpo zenshū* (The complete works of Edogawa Ranpo), vol. 2, 402–6. Tokyo: Kōdansha, 1969.

"Shini e to 'Shi no shima'" (Toward death and "the isle of death"). *Hōchi shinbun,* November 26, 1930, 6.

"Shin'ya no Asakusa ni runpen to kataru Edogawa Ranpo-shi" (Mr. Edogawa Ranpo talking to the workers in Asakusa in the middle of the night). *Yomiuri shinbun,* August 7, 1931.

Shokusanjin [Ōta Nanpo]. "Amayo monogatari" (Tales from a rainy night). In *Misonoya* (Thirty spokes), 411–32. Tokyo: Kokusho Kankōkai, 1917.

Silver, Mark. *Purloined Letters: Cultural Borrowing and Japanese Crime Literature, 1868–1937.* Honolulu: University of Hawai'i Press, 2008.

Silverberg, Miriam. "Constructing Japanese Cultural History." In *Japan in the World,* edited by Masao Miyoshi and Harry D. Harootunian, 115–43. Durham: Duke University Press, 1993.

———. *Erotic Grotesque Nonsense: The Mass Culture of Japanese Modern Times.* Berkeley: University of California Press, 2006.

Sunaga Asahiko. *Bishōnen Nihon shi* (A history of Japanese bishōnen). Tokyo: Kokusho Kankōkai, 2002.

———. "Ranpo no hisoka naru jōnetsu" (The secret passion of Ranpo). *Yuriika* (Eureka) 19, no. 5 (1987): 187–95.

———. "Shōnen" (Adolescent boys). In *Edogawa Ranpo,* 44–45. Tokyo: Heibonsha, 1998.

Suzuki, Michiko. "Writing Same-Sex Love: Sexology and Literary Representation in Yoshiya Nobuko's Early Fiction." *Journal of Asian Studies* 65, no. 3 (2006): 575–99.

Suzuki Sadami. "Eroticism, Grotesquerie, and Nonsense in Taishō Japan: Tanizaki's Response to Modern and Contemporary Culture." In *A Tanizaki Feast: The International Symposium in Venice,* edited by Adriana Boscaro and Anthony Hood Chambers, 41–53. Ann Arbor: Center for Japanese Studies, University of Michigan, 1998.

———. "Kaita no jidai" (Kaita's era). *Yuriika* (Eureka) 31, no. 7 (1999): 162–71.

———. *Modan toshi no hyōgen: Jiko, gensō, josei* (Expressions of the modern city: Self, illusion, and women). L'esprit nouveau series 7. Kyoto: Hakuchisha, 1992.

———. *Shōwa bungaku no tame ni* (For the sake of Shōwa literature). Tokyo: Shichōsha, 1989.

Suzuki Sadami and Matsuyama Iwao, eds. *Edogawa Ranpo.* Shinchō Nihon bungaku arubamu (Shinchō Japanese literature album) 41. Tokyo: Shinchōsha, 1993.

Symonds, John Addington. *In the Key of Blue, and Other Prose Essays.* New York: AMS Press, 1970.

———. *The Letters of John Addington Symonds.* Edited by Herbert M. Schueller and Robert L. Peters. 3 vols. Detroit: Wayne State University Press, 1967.

———. *The Life of Michelangelo Buonarotti.* New York: Modern Library, 1928.

———. *The Memoirs of John Addington Symonds: The Secret Homosexual Life of a Leading Nineteenth-Century Man of Letters.* Edited by Phyllis Grosskurth. Chicago: University of Chicago Press, 1986.

———. *A Problem in Greek Ethics: Being an Inquiry into the Phenomenon of Sexual Inversion.* London: n.p., 1901.

———. *A Problem in Modern Ethics: Being an Inquiry into the Phenomenon of Sexual Inversion.* London: n.p., 1896.

———. *Studies of the Greek Poets.* 3rd ed. London: A. and C. Black, 1920.

Symonds, John A., and Horatio F. Brown. *John Addington Symonds: A Biography.* New York: C. Scribner's Sons, 1895.

Tachibana Sotō. "Nanshoku monogatari" (Tales of male love). In *Tachibana Sotō wandārando: Yūmoa shōsetsu hen* (Tachibana Sotō wonderland: Humorous fiction), 6–88. Tokyo: Chūō Shoin, 1995.

Taguchi Ritsuo. "*Kotō no oni* ron" (On *The demon of the lonely isle*). *Kokubungaku: Kaishaku to kanshō* (Japanese literature: Interpretation and appreciation) 59, no. 12 (1994): 109–14.

*Takabatake Kashō: Bishōnen, bishōjo gen'ei* (Takabatake Kashō: Illusions of beautiful young men and women). Bessatsu Taiyō. Tokyo: Heibonsha, 1985.

Takahara Eri. *Muku no chikara: "Shōnen" hyōshō bungaku ron* (The power of spotlessness: On literary expressions of the "adolescent boy"). Tokyo: Kōdansha, 2003.

Takahashi Mutsuo. "Chi no teki mote: Murayama Kaita ni okeru shiga ryōsai" (With drops of blood: Murayama Kaita's talents in both poetry and art). *Geijutsu shinchō* (New tides in art) 48, no. 3 (1997): 70–73.

———. *Otoko no kaibōgaku* (Anatomy of the male). Tokyo: Kadokawa Shoten, 1978.

———. Personal communication, July 1, 2005.

———. *Seishun o yomu: Nihon no kindai shi ni-jū-shichi-nin* (Reading youth: 27 figures in modern Japanese poetry). Tokyo: Ozawa Shoten, 1992.

Takahashi Nobuyuki. "'Utsukushiki gakkō' o megutte" (On "the beautiful school"). *Yuriika* (Eureka) 38, no. 11 (2006): 8–22.

Takahashi Yasuo. "Kyōshū no genten" (The origin of longing). In *Inagaki Taruho*, 6–20. Tokyo: Kawade Shobō Shinsha, 1993.

Takayama Chogyū. "Tensai ron" (On genius). In *Chogyū zenshū* (The complete works of Chogyū), vol. 2, 218–27. Tokyo: Hakubunkan, 1905.

Takemiya Keiko. *Kaze to ki no uta* (The song of the wind and the trees). 10 vols. Tokyo: Hakusensha bunko, 1995.

———. "Tsuki" (The moon). In *Inagaki Taruho no sekai: Taruhosukōpu* (The world of Inagaki Taruho: Taruhoscope), edited by Korona Bukkusu Henshūbu, 32–33. Tokyo: Heibonsha, 2007.

Tamaki Tōru. *Shōwa tanka made: Sono seisei katei* (Until the tanka of the Shōwa period: The process of its formation). Tokyo: Tanka Shinbunsha, 1991.

Tamura Toshiko. "Akirame" (Giving up). In *Tamura Toshiko, Takebayashi Musōan, Ogawa Mimei, Tsubota Jōji shū* (Selected works of Tamura Toshiko, Takebayashi Musōan, Ogawa Mimei, and Tsubota Jōji), 5–64. Tokyo: Chikuma Shobō, 1957.

Tanaka Katsumi. *Haku Rakuten* (Bo Juyi). Kanshi taikei (Survey of Chinese poetry) 12. Tokyo: Shūeisha, 1964.

Tanizaki, Jun'ichirō. *The Children.* Translated by Anthony H. Chambers. In *The Gourmet Club: A Sextet,* 13–46. New York: Kodansha International, 2001.

———. "The Secret." Translated by Anthony H. Chambers. In *The Gourmet Club: A Sextet,* 47–68. New York: Kodansha International, 2001.

Tanizaki Jun'ichirō. *Tanizaki Jun'ichirō zenshū* (The complete works of Tanizaki Jun'ichirō). 28 vols. Tokyo: Chūō Kōronsha, 1966–70.

Terayama Shūji. "Shōnen tanteidan dōsōkai: Ranpo" (Reunion of the boys' detective club). In *Zoku Terayama Shūji shishū* (Second volume of the collected poetry of Terayama Shūji), 121–26. Tokyo: Shichōsha, 1992.

Toku, Masami. "Shojo Manga! Girls' Comics!: A Mirror of Girls' Dreams." In *Mechademia 2: Networks of Desire,* edited by Frenchy Lunning, 19–32. Minneapolis: University of Minnesota Press, 2007.

Tokugawa Musei. "Edogawa Ranpo-shi no shinkyō o kiku" (Listening to the psychology of Mr. Edogawa Ranpo). *Shin seinen* (New youth) 16, no. 1 (1935): 285–88.

Traubel, Horace. *With Walt Whitman in Camden.* Boston: Small, Maynard and Co., 1906.

Tsuikawa Kazuo. "Shōsetsu no naka no dōseiai: Edogawa Ranpo *Kotō no oni* to Mori Ōgai *Wita sekusuarisu*" (Same-sex love in fiction: Edogawa Ranpo's *The demon of the lonely isle* and Mori Ōgai's *Vita sexualis*). *Shōwa Yakka Daigaku kiyō* (Bulletin of Shōwa Pharmaceutical University) 28 (1994): 39–45.

Tsurumi Shunsuke. "Sono toki no ketsudan" (Decisions made at that time). In *Kaze to ki no uta* (The song of the wind and the trees), by Takemiya Keiko, 322–24. Tokyo: Hakusensha Bunko, 1995.

Turner, A. Richard. *Inventing Leonardo.* New York: Knopf, 1993.

Tyler, William J. "Making Sense of *Nansensu.*" *Japan Forum* 21, no. 1 (2009): 1–10.

———. Review of *In the Company of Men: Representations of Male–Male Sexuality in Meiji Literature,* by Jim Reichert. *Journal of Asian Studies* 66, no. 2 (2007): 557–60.

Ueda Bin. *Kaichōon* (The sound of the tide). In *Meiji Taishō yakushi shū* (Collection of translated verse from the Meiji and Taishō periods), 169–264. Tokyo: Kadokawa Shoten, 1971.

———. "Reonarudo da Winchi (Ge)" (Leonardo da Vinci [Conclusion]). *Nihon bijutsu* (Japanese art) 77 (1905): 16–21.

———. "Reonarudo da Winchi (Jo)" (Leonardo da Vinci [Beginning]). *Nihon bijutsu* (Japanese art) 76 (1905): 1–6.

Uno Kōji. "Aidoku suru ningen" (People whom I love to read). In *Inagaki Taruho,* 64–70. Tokyo: Kawade Shobō Shinsha, 1993.

Vasari, Giorgio. *The Lives of the Artists.* Translated by Julia Conaway Bondanella and Peter Bondanella. Oxford World's Classics. Oxford: Oxford University Press, 1998.

Vincent, Keith. "Hamaosociality: Narrative and Fascism in Hamao Shirō's 'The Devil's Disciple.'" In *The Culture of Japanese Fascism,* edited by Alan Tansman, 381–408. Durham: Duke University Press, 2009.

———. "A Japanese Electra and Her Queer Progeny." In *Mechademia 2: Networks of Desire,* edited by Frenchy Lunning, 64–79. Minneapolis: University of Minnesota Press, 2007.

Watanabe, Tsuneo, and Jun'ichi Iwata. *The Love of the Samurai: A Thousand Years of Japanese Homosexuality.* Translated by D.R. Roberts. London: GMP, 1989.

Welker, James. "Beautiful, Borrowed, and Bent: Boys' Love as Girls' Love in *Shōjo* Manga." *Signs: Journal of Women in Culture and Society* 31, no. 3 (2006): 841–70.

———. "Transfiguring the Female: Women and Girls Engaging the Transnational in Late Twentieth Century Japan." PhD diss., University of Illinois at Urbana-Champaign, 2010.

Whitman, Walt. *Selected Letters of Walt Whitman.* Edited by Edwin Haviland Miller. Iowa City: University of Iowa Press, 1990.

Yamamoto Jirō. "Kaita no hatsukoi" (Kaita's first love). In *Kaita no utaeru sono go oyobi Kaita no hanashi* (Songs of Kaita continued, plus remembrances of Kaita), by Murayama Kaita, 299–306. Tokyo: Ars, 1921.

———. "Kaita no shi" (Kaita's death). In *Kaita no utaeru sono go, oyobi Kaita no hanashi* (Songs of Kaita continued, plus remembrances of Kaita), by Murayama Kaita, 401–09. Tokyo: Ars, 1921.

Yamamoto Kanae. *Yamamoto Kanae no tegami* (Letters of Yamamoto Kanae). Edited by Yamakoshi Shūzō. Ueda: Ueda-shi Kyōiku Iinkai, 1971.

Yamamoto Sanzō. "Kaita to obasan" (Kaita and the middle-aged woman). In *Kaita no utaeru sono go oyobi Kaita no hanashi* (Songs of Kaita continued, plus remembrances of Kaita), by Murayama Kaita, 321–24. Tokyo: Ars, 1921.

Yamazaki Shōzō. "Saisho atta toki no Kaita" (Kaita when I first met him). In *Kaita no utaeru sono go oyobi Kaita no hanashi* (Songs of Kaita continued, plus remembrances of Kaita), by Murayama Kaita, 307–15. Tokyo: Ars, 1921.

Yamazaki Toshio. *Yamazaki Toshio sakuhin shū* (Collected works of Yamazaki Toshio). 3 vols. Kobe: Sabato Yakata, 1986.

Yanase Masamu. "Murayama Kaita-kun" (My buddy Murayama Kaita). In *Murayama Kaita no subete* (All about Murayama Kaita), edited by Kanagawa Kenritsu Kindai Bijutsukan, unpag. Kamakura: Kanagawa Kenritsu Kindai Bijutsukan, 1982.

Yosano, Akiko. *Tangled Hair: Selected Tanka from Midaregami.* Translated by Sanford Goldstein and Seishi Shinoda. New York: Cheng and Tsui, 2002.

Yosano Akiko. "Carmine-Purple: A Translation of 'Enji-Murasaki,' the First Ninety-Eight Poems of Yosano Akiko's *Midaregami.*" *Journal of the Association of Teachers of Japanese* 25, no. 1 (1991): 91–110.

Yosano Tekkan and Yosano Akiko. *Tekkan Akiko zenshū* (Complete works of [Yosano] Tekkan and [Yosano] Akiko). 25 vols. Tokyo: Bensei Shuppan, 2001–6.

Yoshida Ken'ichi. "Bundan kōgengaku: Sakka no shosai o miru" (Studies of the social phenomena of the literary establishment: Looking at the studies of authors). *Shinchō* (New tide) 31, no. 6 (1934): 142–47.

Yoshiya Nobuko. *Hana monogatari* (Flower tales). 3 vols. Tokyo: Kokusho Kankō Kai, 1995.

# Index

*Hentai seiyoku ron* (On perverse
   sexuality), 8–9, 100, 147, 162,
   251n11
*hentai shinri. See* perverse psychology
Hibiya Park, 117, 118, 260n28
Higashi Shunrō, 93–94
Hirano Ayu, 237; *Negachibu kotō no oni*
   (Negative demon of the lonely isle),
   237–40
Hirato Renkichi, 194, 268n6
Hirotsu Ryūrō, 168
Hirschfeld, Magnus, 150, 259n28,
   264n57
*Hōchi shinbun* (Hōchi newspaper), 229
homosexuality, 6–10, 23–27, 30–32,
   148; attitudes among contemporary
   young women, 240–41; criminaliza-
   tion of, 9–10, 147. *See also* male–male
   desire; queer history; same-sex love;
   spectrum of homosocial desire
homosociality, 12, 32–35, 112, 126, 133,
   137, 145, 167–68, 188, 208, 230, 241,
   267n102
Hori Tatsuo, 18, 252n34
hypnosis, 11, 96, 100–101

Ihara Saikaku, 158, 233
Ikeda Riyoko, 239
Inagaki Taruho, 12, 13, 15–20, 23, 24,
   28–32, 35, 78, 117, 192, 193–26, 229,
   230–33, 235; *A-kankaku to V-kankaku*
   (The A-sensibility and the V-
   sensibility), 29, 230; "Aru kōji no
   hanashi" (The story of a certain
   alleyway), 222; "Chokorēto"
   (Chocolate), 208; "Dōseiai no risō to
   genjitsu" (The ideals and reality of
   same-sex love), 31–32, 193–94, 229,
   230, 267n111; early career, 15–16, 23,
   194–98; "E-shi to no isseki: Dōseiai
   no risō to genjitsu o megutte" (One
   night with Mr. E: On the ideals and
   reality of same-sex love), 194;

"Fevaritto" (Favorite), 224; "Hana
   megane" (Pince-nez glasses), 197,
   203–8, 212, 216; *Hikō gahō* (Aviation
   pictorial), 197; influence on manga
   artists, 16, 74, 235, 237, 243–45; *Issen
   ichi-byō monogatari* (One Thousand
   and One-Second Stories), 78, 194, 196,
   268n7; "Kāru to shiroi dentō" (Karl
   and the white light), 216–18, 223,
   243–45; "Kokoa-yama kidan" (The
   strange tale of Mount Cocoa), 224;
   *Momoiro no hankachi* (The peach-
   colored handkerchief), 194; postwar
   works, 29, 224, 230–33; *Prostata-
   rectum kikaigaku* (A study of prostata-
   rectum mechanics), 29; publishing in
   women's journals, 16, 208–11;
   "R-chan to S no hanashi" ("The Tale
   of R-chan and S"), 203, 208–17, 220,
   221, 268n21, 269n27; "Shōnen
   tokuhon" (Youth reader), 117;
   *Shōnen'ai no bigaku* (The aesthetics
   of the love of boys), 29, 230–33;
   "Tsukehige" (The false mustache),
   218–21; *Tsuki no sanbun-shi* (A
   prose poem about the moon), 194,
   195; "Watashi no tanbishugi" (My
   aestheticism), 198–99, 201, 202, 218;
   "WC," 223
Inō Kiyoshi, 13, 48–52, 54, 56, 59, 62,
   65, 66, 69, 73, 79, 82, 104, 173, 175,
   255nn24 30
Inoue Shōichi, 117
Inoue Tetsujirō, 41
Inoue Yasushi, 230
interiority, and same-sex love, 7–8, 19,
   104, 198, 213–14, 221–22
interwar culture. *See* Shōwa period;
   Taishō period
*Ise monogatari* (Tales of Ise), 53
Ishida Minori, 235
Ishikawa Takuboku, 64, 256n46
Isoda Kōichi, 18, 48

JEFFREY ANGLES is associate professor of modern Japanese literature and translation studies at Western Michigan University. He is the award-winning translator of *Forest of Eyes* by Tada Chimako and *Killing Kanoko* by Itō Hiromi. He is coeditor of the short story collection *Japan: A Traveler's Literary Companion.*